SNUFF

Real Death and Screen Media

Edited by Neil Jackson, Shaun Kimber, Johnny Walker, and Thomas Joseph Watson

Bloomsbury Academic
An imprint of Bloomsbury Publishing Inc

B L O O M S B U R Y
NEW YORK • LONDON • OXFORD • NEW DELHI • SYDNEY

Bloomsbury Academic

An imprint of Bloomsbury Publishing Plc

1385 Broadway	50 Bedford Square
New York	London
NY 10018	WC1B 3DP
USA	UK

www.bloomsbury.com

BLOOMSBURY and the Diana logo are trademarks of Bloomsbury Publishing Plc

First published 2016

Library of Congress Cataloging-in-Publication Data
Kimber, Shaun, editor.
Snuff : real death and screen media / edited by Neil Jackson, Shaun Kimber,
Johnny Walker, and Thomas Joseph Watson.
pages cm
Includes bibliographical references and index.
ISBN 978-1-62892-112-0 (paperback) – ISBN 978-1-62892-114-4 (hardback)
1. Death in motion pictures. 2. Snuff films. 3. Death in mass media.
4. Mortality in motion pictures. 5. Motion pictures–United States–History and criticism.
I. Jackson, Neil, 1968- editor. II. Walker, Johnny, 1987- editor.
III. Watson, Thomas Joseph, 1987- editor.
PN1995.9.D37S68 2016
791.43'6548–dc23
2015025730

ISBN: HB: 978-1-6289-2114-4
PB: 978-1-6289-2112-0
ePub: 978-1-6289-2113-7
ePDF: 978-1-6289-2111-3

Typeset by Integra Software Services Pvt. Ltd.
Printed and bound in the United States of America

SNUFF

CONTENTS

PART TWO "SNUFF" ACROSS FILM AND TELEVISION 171

LIST OF FIGURES

FOREWORD

A CULTURE OF CHANGE

David Kerekes

Is this the place the killer Luka Magnotta was captured?

That was the first question. No need for an answer. The sign over the door had changed, but there was no mistaking that this was where it happened; through the corridor and out onto the Berlin streets the self-aggrandizing fugitive had been led in cuffs. The second question was equally moot: "Would you be willing to talk about it?" CCTV footage of the arrest showed the owner of the Internet café (Figure 1) slip out to make the call to police, shortly after Magnotta had entered

FIGURE 1 Inner-city locality of Berlin, where Luka Magnotta was captured (Photo: David Kerekes).

the building. I recognized the owner at the desk in front of me, inspired by my questions to slouch deeper into his chair and absently tap away on a computer keyboard. He mumbled something fast in German. There was nothing further to do or see and so I left.

Luka Magnotta played an important role in the update of *Killing for Culture*, the book I wrote with David Slater.[1] This was my reason for visiting the place of his capture and arrest; an urge to see one small piece of the puzzle, as if somehow all other pieces might then fall into place and the big picture be revealed. The craving for celebrity had pushed the Canadian model and small-time porn actor into increasingly heinous acts that he filmed and placed online. A clip showing the suffocation of two kittens was uploaded anonymously to YouTube (and quickly removed) in December 2010. More followed. Behind fake profiles and blog posts Magnotta sought to avoid detection, if not willing to abdicate responsibility entirely. The mythos he was fabricating culminated in the murder, desecration, and dismemberment of student Lin Jun. The clip, uploaded with the title *1 Lunatic 1 Ice Pick* in May 2012, was met with shock, disbelief, and bafflement. There were some who considered the grueling ten minutes the manifestation of the most enduring of urban legends, the snuff film. Others were not so sure. "I say fake," commented one viewer online:

> some of the cuts just look like rubber or … I dunno, just not real human flesh … would love to know one way or the other tho …

Snuff films: murder on camera for commercial gain. The world's first conference devoted to the mythology of snuff took place at the University of Bournemouth on a weekend in November 2012, a clear indication of how attitudes have changed in the last two decades: the organizers and a number of the delegates had arrived in academia on the back of fan interests. And also *Killing for Culture*, about which I was invited to talk.

Originally published in 1994 and updated shortly thereafter, *Killing for Culture* (Figure 2), a study of death on film, is considered ground-breaking for the most part. Neither of the early editions makes reference to the Internet, however, which is what sparked the 2015 revision. The Internet certainly existed in the mid-1990s, but the information superhighway was yet a humble backstreet. People watched videocassettes then, not YouTube.

Invited to explain how the book came about, I felt certain it could not have been written at any other point in time. Partly because as authors we were young and reckless, and partly because the door through which it appeared was not

---

[1]David Kerekes and David Slater, *Killing for Culture: An Illustrated History of Death on Film from Mondo to Snuff* (London: Annihilation Books/Creation Books, 1994). A second edition was published in 1995.

FIGURE 2 *Killing for Culture*, second edition, 1995.

accessible for long. Let me explain: Pop culture in the early 1990s was still defined by the printed word. It is the last era to be informed this way, the last revolution for the medium of print, when ideas circulated on paper rather than digitally online. *Killing for Culture* didn't appear in a vacuum; books and zines on outré topics were almost commonplace due to various small press and DIY publishers. Some made a concerted effort to explore the limits of free expression and/or question traditional values; others were simply content to shock. As one closely involved with the scene, J.R. Bruun observes

> there was a wave of so called "hate" zines in the late 1980s through early 1990s, as this was a time of a lot of true crime collecting by hipsters...and there was also a kinda pre-millennium, pre-apocalypse, nihilist feel to this whole mailbox/zine scene of killer groupies and Satanists...and Nazi chic.[2]

Adding to this a book about death on film was nothing haughty at all. It was absolutely logical at a time when transgression was a buzzword for the underground. As early as 1986, author Bob Black was considering the US publisher and book distributor Loompanics Unlimited in terms of societal shift. He drew a comparison with the hippies' *Whole Earth Catalog* from the late 1960s. But where that espoused Utopian ideals of self-sufficiency, innovative technology and personal growth, Loompanics was quite different: the *Whole Earth Catalog* as if edited by Friedrich Nietzsche. "Times are tough," wrote Black, "and nice guys finish last."[3]

Black's opinion that Loompanics is "visionary, almost mystical" carries weight. They took obstinate pride in supplying books not found in even the largest libraries. "We are the lunatic fringe of the libertarian movement," boasted their *1992 Main Catalog*,[4] where books on film and media sat with practical guides on how to kill. This was incendiary stuff and would keep Loompanics shy of the mainstream. They weren't alone.

Each generation is reactionary, be it punk in the 1970s, freaks in the 1960s, beatniks in the fifties. The 1980s and 1990s were no different in this respect, forging a counterculture as cynical as it was self-absorbed. Case in point: the quixotic status of Charles Manson and his hippy followers, brought to trial in 1970 for the Tate-LaBianca slayings. America considered them guilty, but the underground was torn. Guilty of murder or not, Manson had throttled the 1960s and with it the hippy ideal. Yet, for all his ills he was seen by some as symptomatic of the Vietnam War, himself a victim of the established order and hailed by

---

[2]JR Bruun email to the author, October 17, 2011.
[3]*Chaos* 4, edited by Joel Biroco (1986). Thanks to Stephen Sennitt for bringing this and other occultzines to my attention.
[4]The slogan very likely appears in earlier Loompanics catalogs, prior to 1992, but I no longer have them to hand.

factions of the underground press as the man of the year.[5] The dichotomy of the antihero was reawakened in the 1980s, visiting Manson anew in books such as *The Manson File*,[6] but also on more general terms through serial killers and mass murderers as some sort of noblesse oblige.

> When it all came, it came as a breath of fresh air. All that mass delirium, all those unrepentant necrophiles—where had this aesthetic terrorism been hiding all these years? Why had no one thought of bringing black messiahs and schizophrenic responses together before? It didn't matter, it was here now in *Apocalypse Culture*—a tome of all things "weird."[7]

Among the newly babbling brook of transgressive literature, *Apocalypse Culture* (1987) read like a psychotic *Reader's Digest*. The editor was Adam Parfrey, who, in 1984, created *EXIT* magazine with George Petros, a visual grab-bag of questionable intent giving an indication of what lay ahead. *Apocalypse Culture* seemed like a step waiting to be taken in the natural order of things. It was where "we" were coming from. The content itself wasn't the key, it was the package, which took subjects, irrespective of genre or convention, and quantified them. The culture was apocalyptic.

In the past, extreme books tended to be standalone artifacts, like *Covenant with Death* (1934) and *Violence in our Time* (1977), two volumes of disturbing photographic imagery decades apart. The mid-1980s were different in that they brought an increase of edgy arcana, polarizing the underground and helping to orchestrate attitudes.

Fan bases were evolving independent of one another. Points of contact between them gave the appearance of a cohesive underground movement,[8] when actually there was no conscious attempt at uniformity, much less direction. In Britain, magic was re-energized and thriving in the 1980s thanks to "occultzines" *Lamp of Thoth, Chaos International* and *Nox* among others, which focused on Chaos magick, a belief system more psychological than paranormal. On the other side of the tracks, film fandom was undergoing upheaval through black

---

[5]"MAN OF THE YEAR: CHARLES MANSON." This was the front page headline of Los Angeles underground tabloid *Tuesday's Child*, February 9, 1970, 1.

[6]*The Manson File*, edited by Nikolas Schreck (New York: Amok Press, 1988). This book is a revisionist take on Manson via unexpurgated letters, songs, art, testimony and other documents.

[7]David Kerekes, "Apocalypse Cultured," *Headpress* 1 (1991): 26–28. An illustration used in the article, taken from the Loompanics Unlimited *1990 Main Catalog*, was the reason *Headpress* had been rejected by at least one printer. The illustration was for the book *Home Workshop Explosives* by Uncle Fester. As many books in the Loompanics catalogs, it was "sold for informational purposes only."

[8]Points of contact may include interest in certain books, music, movies. A literal point of contact would be the Compendium bookshop (where I picked up my copy of *Apocalypse Culture* among others). No visit to London was complete without a detour to this oasis on Camden's high street, a worthy point when evaluating British counterculture.

economy and trade lists. The introduction of the Video Recordings Act 1984 inadvertently created a collector's market in movies no longer officially obtainable in the UK on videocassette. Predominantly these were "pre-certs," aka "video nasties," uncertified horror films whose gore content put them (and the people who collected them) in line for prosecution. The situation was one of unease, and inspired a glut of Brit zines, a subculture removed and at once similar to that of occultzines. The like of *Samhain, Imaginator, Shock Xpress* and many others featured reviews and interviews consumed by the issue of censorship, creating a united front among readers against a common enemy. In other words, a sense of us (the underground) and them (everyone else).

Horror fans in the USA were spared the "video nasties" and consequently the voice of its zines differed to that of Britain. Times Square, in particular 42nd Street, the sin and sleaze capital of the world, was eulogized. *Sleazoid Express* and *Gore Gazette* adopted a gonzo slant, with films an afterthought among writers who spoke of scoring bad movies in bad places. The abstraction was more acute in the 1990s. Among a new breed of zine, *Headpress* in the UK arrived with the bold cover proclamation: "BIZARRE CULTURE, DEVIANT CONCEPTIONS, CINEMATIC EXTREMES." *Headpress* was a platform for writing not necessarily related to film, although this was the background cofounders David Slater and I shared as pre-cert collectors, meeting for the first time to swap videocassettes beneath the Queen Victoria statue in Manchester's Piccadilly Gardens, downwind of the public lavatory like dodgy geezers.

From *Headpress* sprang *Killing for Culture*. Rather, it sprang from an idea to publish a special edition of *Headpress* devoted to mondo films. (*Psychotronic Video* had the same idea, with a two-part feature on the subject beating us to it.) The strain of commercial pseudo-documentary that emerged with *Mondo Cane* in 1962 had hit its stride in the late 1970s. But only now were these films coming into circulation via bootleg tapes. Earlier Mondo efforts that were beautifully shot and composed seemed twee and deflated in eyes fuelled by "video nasties"; the new mondo was much tougher than those before and more in tune with our trenchant sensibilities.[9] Key elements remained, such as death and the marketing of death. "We, the 1960s audiences," decreed J.G. Ballard of the original *Mondo Cane*, "needed the real and authentic (executions, flagellant's processions, autopsies etc.), and it didn't matter if they were faked."[10] Crafted by directors Antonio Climati, Mario Morra, brothers Castiglioni and others, this haunting parade—sometimes authentic, often not—rushed to the fore of the new mondo and intrigued us most.

---

[9]Mondo got a reboot with *Faces of Death* (John Alan Schwartz, 1978), which did receive a legitimate British release before falling foul of the Video Recording Act 1984 and becoming a bona fide "video nasty."
[10]J.G. Ballard, "An Exhibition of Atrocities: J.G. Ballard on Mondo Films," in *Sweet & Savage: The World Through the Shockumentary Film Lens*, edited by Mark Goodall (London: Headpress, 2006): 13–15.

The proposed special edition of *Headpress* never happened: *Killing for Culture* took its place, a book-length treatise on death as cinematic commerce and Mondo as harbinger of the snuff legend.

Academia didn't much like it. As late as 2002, in a review for *Postscript*, Ken Gelder wrote that the *raison d'être* of a book like *Killing for Culture* is "to excavate minor film genres that remain ignored by academics." In so doing it has to "pretend that [Mondo films] are both popular/influential and convoluted/complex."[11] Okay, the book baits the academy somewhat by acknowledging its ignorance. Truth is, when Gelder's words appeared in print, Mondo was not simply undervalued as a body of work spanning several decades but ignored absolutely. The popularity of these films, deduces Gelder, is doubtful. His lofty assumption is charged with irony. The book in your hands is evidence of how far opinion has since travelled.

As the twentieth century slowly peeled away, the end of the millennium fell onto the horizon like a gloomy fog, posing more of a threat the closer it got. One persistent rumor was that society might collapse at the new dawn; that computers could not handle the point at which 1999 became 2000, and technology would fail. Pamphlets appeared on remediation of the Year 2000 problem, much as they had in the days of civil defense when a kitchen table was protection against the Bomb. Needless to say, terrifying acts of insurrection suddenly seemed inevitable...

So, this was the world of the old *Killing for Culture*, a decade fidgeting in its last moments with deep-seated unease. The medieval mind-set of End Times prophecy had been realigned with ones and zeros, but media however was still based around print and television. New media began in a North London pub in 2011, when a friend of mine who calls himself Alex DeLarge confided he was involved in the Animal Beta Project. The purpose of the group, he said, was to locate and bring to justice one Luka Magnotta. The name meant nothing. But his videos had gained the attention of concerned citizens with various skillsets. Magnotta was killing animals in order to be famous, said DeLarge, who believed people would be next, possibly a snuff film.

The margins have become fudged. That's one reason the latest revision of *Killing for Culture* has taken so long to complete (perhaps available in shops by the time you read this). The likes of the Dnipropetrovsk maniacs, Islamic State and Magnotta were never a foreseeable part of the original "plan," goalposts change often in the new millennium. The visit to the Berlin Internet café, where Magnotta was apprehended, indicates the extent of these deviations, when the search for snuff films becomes a mad quest for clues deeper in meaning.

Apocalypse culture is now the Internet, its global authors prolific but lacking in imagination. They are not like Johnny Depp, who one day strolled into the

---

[11]Ken Gelder, "Review of *Killing for Culture*," *Postscript* 1, no. 3 (2002): 131–33.

publisher's London office and asked for a copy of *Killing for Culture*. This was prior to *The Brave* (1997), a movie about snuff he directed and starred in. He was wearing a cowboy hat.

FIGURE 3 David Kerekes, London, 2015 (Photo: Clare Butler).

ACKNOWLEDGMENTS

The editors would collectively like to thank Katie Gallof at Bloomsbury for having faith in our idea from the get go. It's been a genuine pleasure to work with her, and we hope to do so again. Bloomsbury's Mary Al-Sayed has been very friendly and accommodating, too. We'd also like to gratefully acknowledge Mark McKenna for designing the (excellent) book jacket; Bournemouth University's Centre for Excellence in Media Practice (CEMP) and the Narrative Research Group (NRG); Leon Hunt, for making a simple suggestion; and, finally, all of the contributors for their hard work over the last couple of years.

Neil would like to thank the following: my fellow editors, for their comradeship, enthusiasm and friendship; Sarah Barrow, Dave Boothroyd, Diane Charlesworth, Andrew Elliott, Louise Lawlor, Dean Lockwood, Mike Mason, Dave McCaig, Nigel Morris, Tom Nicholls, Antonella Palmieri, Tony Richards, and Adam Smith for professional support, encouragement, and advice; Martin Brooks, Marc Morris, Jonny Redman, Carter Stevens, and Paul Whittleton, for the crucial supply of research materials over the past few years; and finally, Phil Marson, Joanne, James, and Sophia for love, patience, and understanding—it must be difficult sometimes.

Shaun would like to thank: the coeditors of this collection (it has been great working with you since the "Realist Horror" panel at *Cine-Excess V* back in 2011); and Keri, for being so supportive of my research interests and accommodating of my choices in movies.

Johnny would like to thank: my coeditors for being a great bunch of colleagues and, most importantly, friends; Mark McKenna for his friendship and loyalty; Willis the dog for being an excellent research assistant; and Nikki for always being there (even when it gets really, really, grim).

Tom would like to thank: my fellow snuff warriors, Neil, Shaun and Johnny, with whom it has been a pleasure to work with over the course of this project. I would like to thank Steve Jones for his unwavering support, friendship and encouragement throughout the editorial process. Finally, I would like to thank Katherine Butler for listening to me talk about snuff movies and various other untoward topics, at length, many times over!

INTRODUCTION

SHOT, CUT, AND SLAUGHTERED: THE CULTURAL MYTHOLOGY OF SNUFF

Neil Jackson

It was kind of an interesting flick (!!)

ANONYMOUS[1]

If this snuff rumour goes on long enough,
eventually some asshole will do it for real.

AL GOLDSTEIN[2]

This book deals with a terrifying cultural phenomenon for which there is no proven starting point, merely speculation, conjecture, and confusion. Consequently, discussion of the so-called snuff movie is informed from the outset by the vexed question: do such things exist? While snuff has been present within popular and subcultural discourse, yet absent as a "proven" artifact, any study dealing seriously with the phenomenon is immediately obliged to stress the malleable nature of the debate. Therefore, the term "snuff" is applied liberally in the forthcoming pages in the discussion of fictional *and* documentary texts, a reflection of the manner in which the topic has seeped into general modes of discourse. Nevertheless, it seems important to stress that this book attempts neither to prove nor to disprove the disputed claims for snuff, a quest that is at once thankless and futile due to the ever-shifting comprehension of the term itself.

---

[1] Ed Sanders, *The Family* (Boston, MA: De Capo Press, 2002): 168.
[2] Quoted in Jay Lynch, "The Facts About the Snuff Film Rumors," *Oui*, July 1976, 118.

Rather, the aim of the book is to evaluate fictional and reality-based media narratives that have informed our understanding of the snuff phenomenon since its origins. Accordingly, the evolution of this particular folk devil is charted from a variety of perspectives, each providing an insight into real and imagined manifestations of the form. Although the methodologies are eclectic, there is a coherent discourse through which the issues might move forward sensibly and objectively, acknowledging historical manifestations in several media sites and observing the impact of new technologies upon modes of consumption.

Since its infiltration of popular cultural fears in the 1970s, a common assumption regarding snuff is that it combines explicit images of mutilation and defilement with hardcore sex. Discussion of snuff has often observed an unholy alliance of conventions from realist horror films and pornography, hybridizing disreputable generic modes emblematic of the lowest common cultural denominator. Several commentators have observed a shift from horror's gothic foundations since the 1960 release of *Psycho* (directed by Alfred Hitchcock) and *Peeping Tom* (directed by Michael Powell). Philip Brophy goes so far to define realism as "[the 1970s'] gulping, belching plughole"[3] that refined and diffused several genres simultaneously, while the visibility of a vaguely defined realist approach revealed a tension between what Andrew Tudor identifies as the "supernatural" and the "secular"[4] branches of the genre, with titles such as the *Last House on the Left* (Wes Craven, 1972), *The Texas Chain Saw Massacre* (Tobe Hooper, 1973), and *The Hills Have Eyes* (Wes Craven, 1976), foregrounding psychopaths, rapists, and cannibals rather than the threats embodied by supernatural or extraterrestrial entities.

Cynthia Freeland sees realist horror as a subgenre that "creates links between the dark side of male traits (violence, uncontrolled sexuality) and the heroic side (power, independence, etc.) … [it] legitimises patriarchal privileges through the stereotyped and naturalised representation of male violence against women,"[5] arguing that the emphasis upon male serial killers and sexual deviants is steeped in a (perhaps unconscious) legitimization of gender inequality, obfuscating wider issues of social deprivation, economic exploitation, political corruption, and institutionalized violence. She also sees an untapped potential for audiences to form a "critical awareness of its own interest in spectacle,"[6] and this emphasis upon the "spectacular" (particularly in relation to the affective mechanisms of sex

---

[3]Philip Brophy, "Horrality—The Textuality of Contemporary Horror Films," *Screen* 27, no. 1 (1986): 4
[4]Andrew Tudor, *Monsters and Mad Scientists* (Oxford: Blackwell, 1989): 8.
[5]Cynthia Freeland, "Realist Horror," in *Philosophy and Film*, edited by Cynthia Freeland and Thomas Wartenberg (New York and London: Routledge, 1995): 136.
[6]Ibid., 139. Several snuff-themed films, including *Peeping Tom, Cannibal Holocaust, Effects*, and *Special Effects* are focally concerned with the relationship between the creation and consumption of images of violence, actively encouraging the spectator to consider the limits of representation and moral responsibility.

and violence) stokes the fears of those who see the horror film as a dangerous sensory exciter that encourages imitative behavior. Consequently, the closer realist horror comes to its social referent, the more dangerous it is seen to become. This is particularly relevant in relation to early assumptions around snuff, wherein the murderous acts onscreen were seen to sate perverted or homicidal proclivities.

The sexual dimension of the realist horror film found a natural imaginary space within an emergent fictional snuff subgenre, its embodiment of deviant desire dislocating it from the notion of "art horror" (with its emphasis upon the supernatural and the *fantastique*) identified by Noel Carroll.[7] Consequently, Freeland argues that in order to construct any kind of critical or theoretical framework for realist horror, it is far more useful to consider it as a fictional adjunct to representations of death in news media, arguing that they can be "easily, commonly and quickly integrated into new feature film plots ... realist horror can present violent spectacles with an uncanny immediacy right before our eyes."[8]

This binds the debate amid particular stylistic conventions, including the use of the long take and its claim to veracity and authenticity. In this sense, snuff has become emblematic of the death-centered narrative as a "wild signifier," a term coined by Catherine Russell to illustrate her argument that death "remains feared, denied and hidden ... we should be prepared to understand this wildness as an opening up of representation."[9]

Russell's work is concerned with fictional film, but is very useful here in its identification of the limits to which the moving image can plausibly present an aesthetic of realistic violence. She argues that violent death constitutes "a special crisis in believability, a threshold of realism and its own critique"[10] and several snuff-themed films have negotiated this dilemma through foregrounding self-reflexive methods that seem at odds with realist aspirations. Tzvetan Todorov argued that there are *generic* and *social/cultural*[11] branches of verisimilitude, with frames of reference never necessarily being discrete, and just as conceptions of reality may be partially shaped through media, social and cultural objects are very often affected by basic truths. Therefore, within plausibly imagined snuff scenarios, foreknowledge of the dynamics of the corporeal is in constant tension with an understanding of cinematic conventions. Many films that have appropriated the snuff mythology both mediate and exploit discourses of death

---

[7]See Noel Carroll, *The Philosophy of Horror, or Paradoxes of the Heart* (London: Routledge, 1990): 179.
[8]Freeland, "Realist Horror," 134.
[9]Catherine Russell, *Narrative Mortality* (Minneapolis and London: University of Minnesota Press, 1995): 1.
[10]Ibid., 23.
[11]Quoted in Steve Neale, "Questions of Genre," in *Film Genre Reader II*, edited by Barry Keith Grant (Austin: University of Texas Press, 1986): 160.

imagery, accentuating the epistemological breakdown of the real and the fictional and problematizing Todorov's concepts of verisimilitude.

Despite its nominal basis in the depiction of mutually pleasurable sexual activity, hardcore pornography has often been characterized as harmful to social formations, with some radical feminists defining it as the cinematic expression of violent misogyny. Consequently, with its connotations of sexualized murder, the snuff film embodied pornography's most pernicious tendencies, the ultimate perversion of a morally and aesthetically impoverished form. Linda Williams sees the alleged existence of snuff as a corruption and betrayal of pornography's "knowledge-pleasure of sexuality"[12] and its (unfulfilled) potential to refute dominant patriarchal modes. Ideological assumptions regarding horror and pornography have been shaped by issues of objectification, abjection, terrorization, and control; combining those themes we soon arrive at the common denominator of male hegemony and its dominion over image manipulation, dissemination, and consumption. Even Williams, interested in identifying progressive possibilities within pornographic film, was frustrated by the arguments generated by *Snuff* (Michael and Roberta Findlay [uncredited], 1976). The visual rhetoric of that fictional, nonpornographic film's final sequence located it squarely within the adult film ghetto, "an utterly sadistic perversion of the pornographic genre's original desire for visual knowledge of pleasure."[13]

During its theatrical release, the appropriation of porn and horror tropes in *Snuff*'s advertising vividly brought together emotional and corporeal spectacle, elements central to what Williams dubbed "body genres" (pornography, horror, and melodrama).[14] Snuff becomes the ultimate corruption of the most exploitative elements of these "body genres," with Williams arguing that porn is "more often deemed excessive for its violence than for its sex, while horror films are excessive in their displacement of sex onto violence."[15] This should not be taken as a foundation upon which to build a critical vocabulary for the elusive, genuine porno snuff movie and, indeed, its existence would have manifold implications for her argument. However, it becomes very useful when we identify snuff thematics within fictional narratives. Some of the examples emergent from the international exploitation sector have become definitive statements of cinematic excess, displaying a complex interplay of voyeuristic, sadistic, and masochistic drives, charting gender iniquities inherent in processes of interpersonal power enabled by capitalism. This all points to a profound crisis in masculinity that paradoxically

---

[12]Linda Williams, *Hardcore: Power, Pleasure and the Frenzy of the Visible* (Berkeley: University of California Press, 1989): 3
[13]Ibid., 192.
[14]Linda Williams, "Film Bodies: Gender, Genre and Excess," *Film Quarterly* 44, no. 4 (1991): 2–13.
[15]Ibid., 2.

questions the dominance of the masculine cinematic gaze while giving it full rein in the most delirious way imaginable. Resultantly, the global appropriation of snuff's mythology brings all manner of sociocultural, socioeconomic, and sociosexual structures into sharp relief.

This porno–horror hybridization has influenced perceptions of what a real snuff movie might formally and narratively comprise, informing its representation in various fictional film genres (horror, melodrama, crime thriller, etc.). In fact, the assumed conventions of snuff have become sufficiently entrenched to the point where particular texts might be read as critiques of one another. Steve Jones[16] identifies the graphic representations of the notorious *August Underground* trilogy (Fred Vogel et al., 2001–2008) as unfettered reactions to the relatively discrete representations of snuff in mainstream Hollywood productions such as *8mm* (Joel Schumacher, 1999). This highlights the extent to which generic boundaries might be collapsed by the presence of snuff, and Jones encapsulates this very usefully when he argues that any imagined snuff scenario "hinges on the desire to know if snuff really does exist, what snuff depictions look like and fundamentally if there is truth in the myth."[17] Of course, snuff's status as a morally indefensible underground criminal practice moves it away from discussions of audio-visual real*ism*, into the tangible social dimensions of the *real*.

The etymology of the term "snuff movie" has its basis in common English slang, referring succinctly the act of "snuffing out" a human victim, providing a sense of a cruel and callous fate in which life is not merely taken, but casually extinguished like a candle flame. The linguistic association with "sniff" and its connotations of respiratory functions also evoke a victim's final, desperate breath. The designation "snuff movie" therefore provides a pithy encapsulation of its primary function: to exploit and record an act of homicide for the perverse edification of its maker and consumer. However, as a form of generic description, the term has been attributed to Ed Sanders in his 1971 book *The Family*, wherein it is claimed, without any form of substantiation, that members of the murderous Manson cult filmed some of their varied atrocities. Sanders states quite clearly that "I coined the term 'snuff film,'" but its origins lie in an interview he conducted with "a person who had been hanging around on the edges of the Family."[18] The revelations of this anonymous witness are couched in vagueness, typical of the lack of clarity which would inform the subsequent snuff mythology. However, they are significant for the tantalizing glimpses and fragments which would color the whole subsequent controversy

---

[16]Steve Jones, "Dying to be Seen: Snuff-Fiction's Problematic Fantasies of 'Reality,'" *Scope* 19 (2011), accessed July 15, 2015, http://nrl.northumbria.ac.uk/5145/1/Jones.pdf.
[17]Ibid., 10
[18]Sanders, *The Family*, 163.

and debate. Sanders' interviewee points to three different types of activity in the home movies shot by the Family: "(1) Family dancing and loving; (2) animal sacrifices; (3) human sacrifices."[19] The witness states "I only know about one snuff movie,"[20] describing sinister hooded figures violating the lifeless, headless corpse of an unidentifiable female victim. This textual detail is especially ironic in light of the ensuing focus upon the authenticity of the genuine snuff object: according to the individual providing the first anecdotal evidence, this supposed *urtext* does not actually provide a direct record of its victim's demise, but grisly images of its aftermath. Moreover, in its evocation of ritualistic slaying, the alleged film also draws upon the slightly hokey iconography of black magic, which had already infiltrated the mainstream of the horror genre by the late 1960s.[21]

The conflation of amateur pornography and quasi-occultist rites enacted upon animals and humans during "out-of-doors freak outs,"[22] locates this early manifestation of snuff within the growing disenchantment with flower-power idealism. Showcasing exploding cats, gutted dogs, and decapitated hippie chicks, the alleged films are useful signifiers for the derangement of 1960s free love ideals, charting a rapid degeneration into a new form of homicidal rebellion, overseen by a patriarchal overlord soon to become media monster. Small wonder that the snuff designation would be seized opportunistically by varied interest groups (both of a progressive and of a conservative political bent), seeing its potential as ideological ammunition against their variously identified foes.

Eithne Johnson and Eric Schaefer[23] have identified further rumors of snuff circulating as early as 1973 in the USA, initially through the actions of the Citizens for Decency group, and eventually reaching the pages of the *New York Post* and *Daily News* by 1975. Jay Lynch attributed the rapid spread of the rumors to a New York police detective, Joseph Horman, emphasizing the confusion caused by the common belief that snuff was imported from Mexico or Argentina. Despite the inconclusiveness of a Los Angeles police investigation—"the investigation found no evidence that such films exist" announced an LAPD spokesman[24]—Lynch also comments on the way in which these rumors found their way back to the USA, when the mutilated corpses of three prostitutes were discovered in Mendoza, Argentina, on October 6, 1975. Lynch comments "there was no evidence that

---

[19]Ibid., 165.
[20]Ibid., 167.
[21]See *The Devil Rides Out* (Terence Fisher, 1967), *The Curse of the Crimson Altar* (Vernon Sewell, 1968), and *Rosemary's Baby* (Roman Polanski, 1968). The irony here is the latter film's link to the Manson case—Sharon Tate, the pregnant wife of its director, Roman Polanski, was one of the victims.
[22]Sanders, *The Family*, 166.
[23]Eithne Johnson and Eric Schaefer, "Soft Core/Hard Gore: Snuff as a Crisis in Meaning," *Journal of Film and Video* 45, no. 2–3 (1993): 40–59.
[24]Lynch, "The Facts About the Snuff Film Rumors," 70.

these brutal murders had been *filmed*—only that there was rampant speculation in Argentina that this *might* have been the case."[25] Frustrated by the manner in which a moral panic on foreign soil had seeped into their own culture, Mendoza police officials speculated that filmed records of these homicides were possibly the work of ruthless pimps keen to warn wayward or disobedient whores in their charge.[26] It can only be speculated that these films *may* have found their way into the hands of enthusiasts for the outer reaches of pornographic experience.

Joseph W Slade has highlighted a rise in violent pornography in the period from the mid-1960s onward. Using a selection of 1,333 pre-1970s hardcore pornographic films and loops available at the Kinsey Institute, he points out that virtually every example "rejected violence almost entirely … [with rape] used as an enabling device 67 times (5% of the total)."[27] However, more aberrant behaviors such as "fetishism, scatology, bestiality, bondage, S & M and child molestation"[28] were a more pronounced and visible element of the range of material from the late 1960s onward. Aberrant pornography mobilized moral campaigners concerned with the spread of cultural liberalization in the early 1970s, and the media image of porno snuff was founded in reportage characterized by the panic-driven hyperbole of moral indignation. Julian Petley has addressed the ways in which newspapers, law enforcement agencies, and media outlets have often conspired (perhaps unwittingly) in a process of misinformation and misdirection. Analyzing reports of an underground ring of snuff video dealers in the UK in the early 1990s, Petley reveals that what was actually being sold was a selection of fictional exploitation or horror films, "mondo" documentaries and "shockumentaries"[29] of a diverse cultural pedigree, commenting "[w]hat is clearly happening … is that two completely different kinds of films are being conflated and confused with one another."[30]

Given that these words were published in the year 2000, it seems fair to add that it is no longer just *two* different types of film that are being utilized. Instead,

---

[25]Ibid.

[26]This finds its modern corollary in the videos uploaded to the Internet by Mexican drug cartels, gruesome records of the executions of enemies and expendable accomplices alike.

[27]Joseph W. Slade, "Violence in the Hardcore Pornographic Film: A Historical Survey," *Journal of Communication* 34, no. 3 (Summer 1984): 155.

[28]Ibid., 156

[29]Initiated in 1962 by *Mondo Cane* (Gualtiero Jacopetti, Franco Prosperi Paolo Cavara), the mondo film (and its generic offspring, the "shockumentary") mixed documentary and staged footage, presented as travelogues purporting to demonstrate the lifestyle conditions and peculiarities of cultures in a variety of international contexts. For a comprehensive overview, see David Kerekes and David Slater, *Killing for Culture* (London: Creation Books, 1993), Mark Goodall, *Sweet and Savage: The World Through the Shockumentary Film Lens* (London: Headpress, 2006), and Mikita Brottman, *Offensive Films* (Nashville, TN: Vanderbildt University Press, 2005).

[30]Julian Petley, " 'Snuffed Out': Nightmares in a Trading Standards Officer's Brain," in *Unruly Pleasures: The Cult Film and Its Critics*, edited by Xavier Mendik and Graham Harper (Guildford: FAB Press, 2000): 214.

snuff is characterized today by multiple visual documents, some of which cannot comfortably be classified as "films" at all, at least not in terms of established conventions of form, narrative, style, and characterization. The evolution of snuff now reveals a varied iconography, whose assumed basis in the corporeal veracity of pornography has moved significantly into other generic spaces that do not necessarily emphasize deviant human sexuality as a primary signifier. Nevertheless, sexualized murder was built into the definition of snuff developed by the US federal authorities investigating the phenomenon in its early stages. FBI special agent Ken Lanning explained:

> It has to be a visual depiction. It could be still pictures or moving images. On this visual image, someone was alive at the beginning and then dead at the end … this visual image is being put together for the sexual gratification of viewers and people look at this thing and get sexually aroused. Then, this visual depiction is commercially distributed.[31]

Lanning's comments betray assumptions regarding snuff's basis in the object/ subject dynamic of conventional pornography, incorporating elements of aesthetics, performance, consumption, pleasure, and economics. However, other commentators, whether for objective or partisan intentions, have provided a set of variations upon this basic guideline, clouding the waters in that it is alternately the generic roots of pornography, horror, and a more generalized documentary reality that are emphasized by individual authors. Jonathan Crane argues that snuff "represents the logical culmination of horror's descent,"[32] while Boaz Hagin alludes to production dynamics but de-emphasizes sexuality, describing "[a film] in which a real murder is committed in front of the camera to entertain and make a profit."[33] More politically charged is Catherine MacKinnon's definition, who is unequivocal in her use of the term "snuff pornography," in which "women or children are killed to make [a] film of a sexual murder [in which] doing the murder is sex for those who do it. The climax is the moment of death. The intended consumer has a sexual experience watching it."[34] Here, male creator and consumer join in a conspiracy of homicidal voyeurism, with extra emphasis upon the violation of children providing another level of deviance through which oppressive patriarchal rule might be understood and condemned.

---

[31]Lanning quoted in *Is Snuff Real*, UK Channel 4 documentary, broadcast 2006.
[32]Jonathan Crane, "Scraping Bottom," in *The Horror Film*, edited by Stephen Prince (New Brunswick, NJ: Rutgers University Press, 2004): 163.
[33]Boaz Hagin, "Killed Because of Lousy Ratings: The Hollywood History of Snuff," *Journal of Popular Film and Television* 38, no. 1 (2010): 45.
[34]Catherine Mackinnon, *Only Words* (Cambridge, MA: Harvard Press, 1993): 18.

In spite of such varied definitions, a tangible model remained undiscovered and inaccessible to the average individual and institutional authorities alike, and what is generally accepted is that no genuine snuff movie of this nature has ever been verified. As defined by the FBI, snuff involved the torture, murder, and mutilation of a female victim appended to a standard sexual scenario familiar from a multitude of 8mm sex loops, reputedly commissioned and distributed for the delectation of a shadowy group of sensation seekers. In the absence of the genuine article, a handful of fictional feature films *imagined* a snuff "aesthetic" as its salacious allure bled deeper into popular culture, with a striking level of stylistic recurrence *and* diversity on display. This has posed a key question to filmmakers: what, exactly, are the primary formal characteristics of this ill-defined phenomenon? In response, a *fictional* snuff aesthetic has developed from a variety of international production contexts.

It took an old-fashioned act of cinematic hucksterism to transform this furtive, whispered urban mythology into a sociocultural *bete noire*. When Alan Shackleton's Monarch Releasing Company unveiled *Snuff* to North American audiences, the one word title betrayed the company's intention to exploit and capitalize upon morbid curiosity. While promotional art claimed that the film was "made in South America … where life is cheap!," it was barely plausible that an established purveyor of lurid exploitation cinema had actually gone and done the unthinkable: promoted and released visual documentation of an actual sex-murder in pursuit of rapid, plentiful financial return. Indeed, there is a wry irony surrounding the film and its marketing campaign; while much of was made up of Michael and Roberta Findlay's cheap Charles Manson cash-in, *The Slaughter* (shot in Argentina in 1970 by the New York exploitation stalwarts), its inelegantly appended, climactic spectacle of supposedly real death was actually shot by the distributor in the apartment studio of established New York adult filmmaker, Carter Stevens. Life may have been cheap south of the US border, but it seems that production costs were cheaper still in the Big Apple's burgeoning porno subculture.

The ensuing controversy allowed *Snuff* to become emblematic of radical feminist concerns regarding violent pornography, despite the fact that it contained absolutely no hardcore content whatsoever,[35] and the publicity campaign had a somewhat detrimental effect once its implications took hold.

Particularly vocal and energetic in their condemnation were feminist activists and academics whose outright hostility to all pornography was fueled further

---

[35]For example, some pornographic feature films went to hitherto uncharted extremes in the depiction of rape and sexual torture: *Forced Entry* (Shaun Costello, 1972), *Sex Wish* (Tim McCoy, 1976), *Femmes De Sade* (Alex De Renzy, 1976), and *Waterpower* (Shaun Costello, 1977) all deal explicitly in hardcore visual representations of sexual dysfunction, rape, and antipleasure, seemingly designed to provoke liberals, conservative moralists, and radical feminist campaigners alike.

by the snuff phenomenon. As Johnson and Schaefer argue, "for feminists, the snuff film became the ultimate instance of backlash against women's liberation,"[36] defining it as a desperate, patriarchal counter-measure to the growing social, cultural, and political momentum of the women's movement. However, as Kerekes and Slater argue, "it didn't seem to matter, the absurdity of promoting a motion picture that purported to show actual on-screen murder,"[37] and despite the picketing and boycotting of theaters, *Snuff* was ultimately little more than a bad taste cinematic confidence trick, incorporating giveaway conventions of multiple camera angles, cutaways, and barely convincing prosthetics which betrayed the flimsy artifice underlying its central conceit.[38]

Through manipulation and manufacture, Monarch had deftly used the film's promotional tagline to deflect inevitable condemnation of American exploitation film practice into social anxiety over the perverse predilections of its geographical neighbors. The marketing allusion to South America capitalized upon rumors of imported snuff films, as well as the social indignities of military dictatorship in some countries south of the border where torture and political oppression was rife. This was underscored by the flippant, amoral attitude of Shackleton, who observed wryly that "if the murder was real, I'd be a damn fool to admit it. If it isn't real, I'd be a damn fool to admit it."[39] This induced a deft perceptual transference, from the linguistic connotations of torture and murder enacted by political supremacists, to the iconographic connotations of a stark female figure subjected to sexual victimization. This promotional invocation of foreign social peculiarities located snuff within discourses of trans-cultural exchange and contamination, sustained by several fictional narratives which presented snuff as a perverse practice imported from either the repressed underside of American popular culture, or from ideologically aberrant, sexually perverse nations beyond the shores of "civilised" western democracies.[40]

Despite this, the snuff phenomenon is very closely linked to cultural developments within the USA, and the early to mid-1970s saw a convergence of circumstances that allowed rumors of snuff to gestate. While abolition of

---

[36]Johnson and Schaefer, "Soft Core/Hard Gore," 42.

[37]Kerekes and Slater, *Killing for Culture*, 21.

[38]Carter Stevens commented "as for Shackleton's film, even the prosthetic shots weren't believable. I totally underestimated the gullibility of the average movie goer … Why would I worry about a silly special effects movie that wasn't even done very well?" (interview with author, June 26, 2012).

[39]Quoted in Brottman, *Offensive Films*, 94.

[40]For example, *Hardcore* (Paul Schrader, 1979) makes reference to snuff being produced in Mexico, while *A Serbian Film* (Srdjan Spasojevic, 2010) alludes to it being produced for foreign audiences, not domestic consumption. *Videodrome* (David Cronenberg, 1982) comments slyly on this tendency— while a sinister corporate organization plants the notion that snuff films were being broadcast via satellite from Malaysia, it is later revealed that they are part of a wider conspiracy of social control produced in Pittsburgh, USA.

the motion picture code in the 1960s accommodated an increased frankness in mainstream Hollywood, there had been wider distribution of sexually oriented exploitation films, such as "roughies,"[41] that dealt with rape and perversion. In tandem with this, television reportage of the Vietnam War, including images of dead soldiers and civilians, facilitated new audience perceptions of the human body's response or resistance to traumatic attack. Indeed, the 1960s produced two of the seminal (and wholly unplanned) documentary records of real violent death, each resonating on an unprecedented sociopolitical plain: Abraham Zapruder's 8mm film record of the death of John F Kennedy (filmed in Dallas on November 22, 1963) and NBC's footage of the summary execution of a suspected Vietcong prisoner in Saigon by police chief Nguyen Ngoc Loan (filmed February 1, 1968).[42] Therefore, death as media spectacle took root very publicly as part of an overarching discourse far removed from issues of pornographic representation, and both the JFK assassination and Saigon execution footage have achieved a cinematic ubiquity; their levels of physical detail (exploding body matter, spurting blood) gradually assimilated into the visual lexicon of violent death in fictional films.

The capture of these particular historical moments has engendered a sense of a fractured, incomplete *prehistory* of snuff, and Boaz Hagin has provided a useful yet problematic account of its emergence into mainstream consciousness, arguing that "the standard history of snuff is incomplete and needs to be augmented by additional historical accounts."[43] Hagin identifies a historical tendency, both within and beyond Hollywood films, in which lurid news coverage of death and disaster stokes the sensational interests of the audience, allowing for a critique of the relationship between the mass media and the often crass, exploitative approach to morbid spectacle. Initially, the citation of classic Hollywood texts such as *The Front Page* (Lewis Milestone, 1931), *His Girl Friday* (Howard Hawks, 1940), and *Ace in the Hole* (Billy Wilder, 1951) as important markers in the development of the snuff mythology seems somewhat incongruous. However, Hagin's incorporation of literary works such as Guillaume Apollinaire's 1907 short story, *A Good Film*,[44] and films such as *King Kong* (Merian C. Cooper, 1933) and *Medium Cool* (Haskell Wexler, 1968), both of which deal with filmmakers' manipulation and control of catastrophic or violent events through dubious documentary practice, places

---

[41]Intimations of wayward or violent sexuality were very often built into the titles of this subgenre (e.g., *The Sadist* (James Landis, 1963) *Scum of the Earth* (Herschell Gordon Lewis, 1963), *The Defilers* (David F. Friedman, 1965), and *Bad Girls Go to Hell* (Doris Wishman, 1965)). Jack Sargeant defines the roughies as "stories in which women—or 'girls'—are humiliated and generally abused by bad men."
[42]See Julian Petley's contribution to this volume.
[43]Hagin, "Killed Because of Lousy Ratings," 44.
[44]The story focuses upon a French film company that forces one of its unwitting actors to murder two young lovers. The film subsequently becomes a big success.

his argument within another distinct generic space: the mondo film. However, Hagin appears to make this observation unconsciously, at no point alluding to the significance of this pseudo-documentary form.

Perhaps more critically, Hagin never refers to two films that are crucial in charting a prehistorical evolution of the snuff phenomenon, each title emerging from beyond American shores: *Peeping Tom* and *The Wild Eye* (Paolo Cavara, 1967). As far as the initial parameters of the snuff debate were concerned, *Peeping Tom* serves as a virtual cultural prophecy, conflating the voyeuristic and homicidal impulses of a central character who records his perversions on film, forcing victims to see their own demise through a mirror mounted above the camera lens. These crimes are committed within the social confines of an underground sex industry where pornographic images are produced and circulated through nominally "respectable" business premises. This was before the term "snuff movie" had even been conceived, and *Peeping Tom* anticipated theoretical debates of the 1970s which focalized psychoanalytic and feminist positions on the dominant masculine cinematic gaze. The film effectively conceptualized snuff before its "official" inception in the 1970s, providing a sustained self-reflexive interrogation of the relationship between objectification, death, and visual pleasure that no other snuff-themed film has matched in terms of its unity and sophistication. *The Wild Eye* (given its scant distribution, the film is effectively the missing link between *Peeping Tom* and many later titles) has a much clearer relationship to *Cannibal Holocaust* (Ruggero Deodato, 1980), depicting a mondo filmmaker whose misanthropic, obsessive pursuit of human frailty and cruelty sees him exploiting opium addicts, bribing Buddhist monks, manipulating the execution of a Vietcong prisoner, and shooting an explosion in a bar without informing the staff or customers of the impending event about which he has been tipped-off. The self-reflexive tics of this Italian film address the moral obligations of the mondo subgenre that had achieved international success by appealing to prurient interest in the customs and lifestyles of foreign, often primitive cultures.

Perceptions of what snuff actually *is* transformed significantly in the wake of the 1976 *Snuff* debacle, and the subsequent evolution of realist horror tropes in a range of titles from both the Hollywood mainstream and the international exploitation market influenced the popular perception of what it might conceivably look like. Kerekes and Slater cite *Emanuelle in America* (Joe D'Amato, 1976), *Last House on Dead End Street* (Roger Watkins [as "Victor Janos"], 1977), *Hardcore* (Paul Schrader, 1979), *Cannibal Holocaust*, *Videodrome* (David Cronenberg, 1983), *Special Effects* (Larry Cohen, 1984), *Der Todesking* (Jorg Buttgereit, 1989), *Henry, Portrait of a Serial Killer* (John McNaughton, 1986), and *Man Bites Dog* (Remy Belvaux, Andre Bonzel, Benoit Poelvoorde, 1992), as fictional works central to the popular cultural construction of snuff, arguing that they "saw to it that snuff had form: it was hidden; was select; was one room and one camera; was black and white; was silent; was grainy; was colour with bad editing; was expensive. Was a commodity."[45] This list supports the sense of a subject ripe for exploration on the fringes of mainstream taste, and points to the rapidity with which other film cultures beyond the USA adopted the mythology of snuff before providing their own distinct interpretations. The list is also indicative of the way in which filmmakers had already begun to blur the contextual boundaries of snuff, seeing it as not only an extreme pornographic trope but also part of a serial killer's *modus operandi* and a feature of documentary authenticity.

Snuff-themed subplots also materialized in glossy, star-laden Hollywood thrillers, such as *Bloodline* (Terence Young, 1979) and *52 Pick-Up* (John Frankenheimer, 1986), based, respectively, on novels by Sidney Sheldon and Elmore Leonard[46] and snuff's potential as a pulp literary conceit attracted writers such as Jerry Bronson (in *Cut*, published in 1976) and Rex Miller (in *Frenzy*, published in 1988). Moreover, the snuff theme was seductive enough to attract the attention not only of now canonized filmmakers such as Paul Schrader and David Cronenberg, but also proved fertile territory for lesser feted figures (and sometimes porn directors) such as Aristide Massaccesi (using his "Joe D'Amato" pseudonym) and Roger Watkins.

As the fictional snuff subgenre has developed into the twenty-first century, the list of titles has grown considerably, expanding the generic parameters within which the debate might be carried out, including: *Strange Days* (Kathryn Bigelow, 1995), *8mm, Urban Legends: Final Cut* (John Ottman, 2000), *Feardotcom* (William Malone, 2002), *Vacancy* (Nimrod Antal, 2007), *Untraceable* (Gregory Hoblit, 2008), and *Sinister* (Scott Derrickson, 2012) from the Hollywood mainstream; *August Underground* and its sequels, *The Great American Snuff Film* (Sean Tretta, 2003), *Amateur Porn Star Killer* and its sequels (Shane Ryan, 2006–2009), *Live Feed* (Ryan Nicholson, 2006), *The Poughkeepsie Tapes* (John Erick Dowdle, 2007), *Penance* (Jake Kennedy, 2009) *Smash Cut* (Lee Demarbre, 2009), *Megan Is Missing* (Michael Goi, 2011), *The Slaughter Tapes* aka *Slaughter Creek* (Brian Skiba & Liam Owen, 2011), and *Pieces of Talent* (Joe Stauffer, 2014) from the US independent/exploitation

---

[45]Kerekes and Slater, *Killing for Culture*, 43.

[46]Sheldon's 1978 novel (described in Leonard Maltin's Film Guide as "one of those books read by California blondes when nobody wants to play volleyball") uses snuff in order to add one more layer to its villain's moral degeneracy. Sheldon revels in fetishistic details such as red ribbons adorning the female victims' necks and a male sex performer whose erection is like "a fucking watermelon." Known at this point in the novel as "the spectator," the description of his response to the death by strangulation is quite brazen, the excitable prose playing directly into the hands of antipornography feminists: "*Look at her eyes!* They were dilated with terror … she was still coming, and the deliciousness of her orgasm and the frantic shudder of her death throes were blending into one … the girl was dying, her eyes staring into the eyes of death. It was so beautiful … The girl had been punished. The spectator felt like God."

sector; *Killer Net* (Geoffrey Sax, 1999, made for TV), *My Little Eye* (Marc Evans, 2002), *The Last Horror Movie* (Julian Richards, 2003), *Snuff Movie* (Bernard Rose, 2005), *Resurrecting The Streetwalker* (Ozgur Uyanik, 2009), and *The Sleeping Room* (John Shackleton, 2015) from the UK; and from the rest of the international sector, *Benny's Video* (1992, Michael Haneke, Austria/Switzerland) *Tesis* (Alejandro Amenebar, 1996, Spain), *Snuff Trap* (Bruno Mattei, 2003, Italy), *Grimm Love* (Martin Weisz, 2006, Germany) *Snuff 102* (Mariano Peralta, 2007, Argentina), *Life and Death of a Porno Gang* (Mladen Djordjevic, 2009, Serbia) *Death Tube: Broadcast Murder Show* (Yohei Fukuda, 2010, Japan), *Closed Circuit Extreme* (Giorgio Amato, 2012, Italy), and *A Serbian Film* (Srđan Spasojević, 2010, Serbia).

This list is by no means exhaustive, but is wholly indicative of the manner in which snuff has infiltrated global popular culture as a recognizable and even commercially viable element, the value of direct linguistic association often built into the very title of the film itself. Moreover, the fact that the majority of these titles emerged from beyond the major studios of Hollywood, often playing to specialized arthouse or cult audiences, highlights the increasingly important role played by subcultural forms in the propagation of mainstream fears. If this range of titles might be loosely bound together as a nominal subgenre (regardless of their origins or aspirations as mainstream, exploitation, or arthouse objects), it has resulted in a set of recurring thematic and iconographic features crucial to any meaningful (sub) generic framework, defining snuff variously as:

> a perverse and murderous auteurist vision that privileges the terminal, and perhaps logical extension of the masculine cinematic gaze;
>
> the consequence of corporate, cultural, or political conspiracy, invoking gender and class-based levels of institutional and ideological disturbance;
>
> a violent, perverse, and pornographic sensory exciter and object of onanistic pleasure;
>
> a function of a deviant, serial murderer's sexuality;
>
> a catalyst for conservative recuperation, enacting a crisis for male hegemony.

This taxonomic approach goes some way to clarifying the thematic and structural function of snuff, and the stylistic apparatus that have come to define a snuff aesthetic have been absorbed into the broader developments of horror's audio-visual lexicon, often engendering a self-reflexive interrogation of the limit to which images of death can be incorporated into discourses of consumption, pleasure, violence, and sexuality. Furthermore, many so-called horror "mockumentaries" work within generic boundaries which are not confined by a realism linked to social verisimilitude, and the stylistic immediacy so often associated with the snuff text has been appropriated frequently by examples founded in nonrealist forms.

Consequently, the deployment of stylistic modes associated with realism provides scenarios steeped in the *fantastique* with an immediacy unachievable within classical constraints. Gary Rhodes cites *The Last Broadcast* (Lance Weiler & Stefan Avalos, 1998) and *The Blair Witch Project* (Daniel Myrick & Eduardo Sanchez, 1999) as films that "combine the real and the unreal into a collective narrative menagerie that proves difficult for audiences to know where the authentic ends and the fiction begins,"[47] and subsequent titles that achieved some level of mainstream success—for example, *Diary of the Dead* (George A Romero, 2007), *Paranormal Activity* (Oren Peli, 2007), *Rec* (Jaume Balaguero & Paco Plaza, 2007), *Cloverfield* (Matt Reeves, 2008), *The Last Exorcism* (Daniel Stamm, 2010), *Troll Hunter* (Andre Ovredal, 2010), and *The Devil Inside* (William Brent Bell, 2012)—indicate that there is now a level stylistic playing field for realist horror and "art horror" that, at least in formal terms, has allowed for a breakdown of intrageneric boundaries. The audio-visual signifiers of "location shooting, handheld cameras, imperfect or improvised compositions, camera settings, negative or print quality, degraded video imagery, lens phenomena, interview footage, use of telephoto and zoom lenses, direct camera address by the cast, print scratches, laboratory markings, and sound irregularities,"[48] are no longer the properties of films that seek exclusively to define diegetic space in direct relation to the socially and materially tangible.

For all of this focus upon the impact of the snuff mythology upon generic development, the rapid global infiltration by the Internet (and attendant impact upon the dissemination and experience of visual media) has shifted the debate further from the realms of the "purely" cinematic (and exclusively pornographic) to questions of the interactive audience engagement with images of real death online. This has allowed for the widespread distribution of, for example, the homicidal activities of sexual deviants, Eastern-European psychopaths, Mexican drug cartels, Islamic jihadists, and, most recently, militant extremists of the Islamic State. Examples of all of these activities have, one way or another, found their way into the public domain in the twenty-first century and, as if to underline their centrality to contemporary media debates, these noncommercial visual documents have often had titles bestowed upon them which make distinct their gruesome content (thus making them much more conducive to a rapid search engine result) and place them perversely within a tradition of lurid exploitation marketing strategies. However, unlike *Snuff*, these short films actually deliver upon the promise of unbearable horrors ingrained within the appended titles (*One Lunatic, One Ice Pick! Mexican Chainsaw Beheading! Three Guys, One Hammer!*). The very form of snuff has now been defined in relation to available audio-visual

---

[47]Gary Rhodes, "Mockumentaries and the Production of Realist Horror," *Postscript* 21, no. 3 (2002): 52.
[48]Neil Jackson, "*Cannibal Holocaust*: Realist Horror and Reflexivity," *Postscript* 21, no. 3 (2002): 36.

technologies, with the generic term "snuff movie" becoming "snuff video" and, in turn, "snuff website," a useful base point from which we can trace the development of snuff into the contemporary sphere.

The early emphasis upon snuff as a deranged extension of the standard porn film was enough to excite the interests of moral campaigners and radical feminist thinkers alike, the former seeking to condemn tasteless and outrageous movie marketing hyperbole, and the latter rejecting pornography for its reinforcement and affirmation of patriarchal structures dominant across all modes of thought. Today, even a billion dollar social-media enterprise such as Facebook finds itself embroiled in arguments over the legitimacy of death videos posted in the nominal interest of legitimate reportage.[49] Snuff, it seems, is no longer merely a process of exploitation in the pursuit of financial gain, but also an effective weapon in the contemporary dissemination of fear on several ideological platforms.

It is now no longer adequate to think of snuff as a cultural presence steeped exclusively in sexually violent imagery. Snuff fictions now run in parallel with documented images of actuality to the point where they are increasingly bound by a reflexive awareness of each other's properties, and while the whole phenomenon continues to draw sustenance from snuff's speculative roots, its status as a tool of economic and interpersonal power has now been refined and reinscribed. The traditionally defined pornographic snuff film is, at this moment, still a hypothetical model; its properties merely speculated upon and interpreted in various historical media spaces. Conversely, videos depicting the beheadings and mutilations of bound, helpless victims are a very real online phenomenon. What *has* remained constant is the narrative of victimization, in which sadistic desires are enacted and sated through a sparse, minimal visual process of total objectification. Whether the victim is a pornographic film performer, a hostage to ideological extremism, or an errant drug cartel operative, their gruesome onscreen demise exemplifies the limits to which human cruelty and abject corporeal spectacle might be exhibited and endured. This evolution, from porno emblem of patriarchal control to a tool of variously motivated interest groups, lies at the core of snuff's social, cultural, and political significance. The act of mere tease and titillation on a 42nd Street marquee has given way to a far more resonant and terrifying proposal, in which the potential of the death film has far-reaching consequences for the ways in which we might understand images of violence and murder.

---

[49]Such was the import attached to Facebook's policy on images of death and suffering, it not only prompted a response from the UK Prime Minister, it also expanded the snuff debate into areas encompassing the morality of corporate advertising, the provenance of the visual documents under consideration, and the limits and responsibilities of free expression. See Leo Kelion, "Facebook adds warnings to decapitations and other violence," *BBC News*, October 22, 2013, accessed June 10, 2015, http://www.bbc.co.uk/news/technology-24628909.

The present volume has been divided into two sections which deal, respectively, with the changing meanings and varied media manifestations of the whole snuff debate, but the issues which they address are never necessarily discrete, with a distinct level of crossover and interaction in terms of the range of material that is covered.

In the first chapter of Part One: The Changing Meanings of "Snuff," Julian Petley elaborates upon several perspectives sketched out in this introduction, contesting that online images of "real live death" have supplanted the fictional and documentary representations that concerned previous censors, regulators, and law enforcement officers. Providing a precise, detailed historical context, Petley offers a lucid account of the complexities and pitfalls of recent UK legislation which has potentially devastating consequences for personal liberties amid concerns over the reach and grasp of the "surveillance state."

Misha Kavka argues that cultural assumptions about snuff are confronted when we approach it as a "genre of affect," taking its form from the unknowability of the genuine article and a horrified titillation at the prospect of what will be seen, felt, and remembered. Kavka discusses snuff as a form that has reality only through its affective charge, with its forbidden thrill being generated by an "unrepresentable" moment.

Simon Hobbs highlights a previously marginalized, but keenly contested area of snuff mythology, addressing the ethical implications of real animal death imagery in films which are designed, conceived, and appreciated as either "art" or "exploitation." This raises questions regarding the place animals hold in the discussion of extreme imagery, and how their status as secondary species has been appropriated within particular production and reception contexts, expanding upon existing concepts of art and exploitation films.

Clarissa Smith argues that debates around pornographic simulations of violent sexual fantasy blur the distinctions to be made between retrograde, harmful depictions, and those which are founded in consensual S&M practices. Complementing the themes addressed by Petley, Smith suggests that this has had significant, potentially ruinous legal implications for those intent on exploring the outer extremes of sexual expression.

Xavier Mendik and Nicolò Gallio explore the promotion of the Italian cannibal subgenre as a transgressive form that courted censure and controversy. Considering differing release strategies of the subgenre, Mendik and Gallio offer a detailed study of the differing global reception of *Cannibal Holocaust*, demonstrating how fears it engendered melded with cultural connotations of realism and representation.

Mark McKenna offers a nationally specific account of the cultural fallout of *Snuff*'s 1976 release, arguing that this had a significant impact upon the film's early 1980s distribution and reception on home video in the UK. McKenna suggests that the varied travails of the UK release are mobilized in fans' disagreements over its history, collectability, and evaluation, as well as in the sociocultural positioning of the film's British video distributor.

Johnny Walker presents a critical overview of the infamous "shockumentary" video series *Traces of Death* (1993–2000), which emerged in the early 1990s, arguing that these films developed out of a confluence of attitudes derived from fan communities dedicated to extreme horror cinema and marginalized musical subcultures. Consequently, the series had a significant impact upon both the presentation and the consumption of death imagery on modern Internet shock sites.

Bringing Part One to a close, and following up strands developed in Walker's essay, Mark Astley provides a succinct and provocative account of the ways in which websites dedicated to the collation and dissemination of death and atrocity imagery have developed in parallel to a mainstream news media that has persistently shielded the public from extreme material readily available online. Placing specific emphasis upon the videos depicting the murder of both Western and Middle-Eastern hostages by Islamic extremists, Astley suggests that this archive of material not only reveals a record of ideologically motivated activity designed to instil terror and fear but also evinces an increasing audio visual sophistication, which draws sustenance from the sounds and images of violent horror cinema.

Part Two: "Snuff" Across Film and Television commences with Mark Jones and Gerry Carlin's consideration of how the living spectre of Charles Manson has continued to haunt cinematic snuff fictions. While rumor and anecdote prevail over evidence, they address the mediatization and the ongoing absence of the Family's alleged snuff activities, arguing that the mythic construction of the Manson snuff movies demands their existence, with cinematic representations of the Family sometimes interpreting these infamous artifacts through both diegetic elements and narrational modes.

Neil Jackson outlines the emergence of the snuff filmmaker as a key icon within American realist horror texts of the 1970s and 1980s. Set apart from the now common motif of sex murderer/serial killer who ritually shoots murder as part of their activities, Jackson argues that the representation of the snuff "auteur" allows for a reflexive interrogation of the extremes (and limitations) of the phallocentric tendencies of the horror film.

Xavier Aldana Reyes elaborates upon the significance of fictional "snuffumentaries," and how they foreground questions of voyeuristic spectacle. Reyes suggests that these films force audiences to escape their ordinary, extradiegetic role to become directly informed in the viewing process, providing an important twist upon the reflectionist logic of much contemporary horror.

Shaun Kimber provides a fascinating account of how a popular Hollywood horror film has utilized the iconography of snuff to construct a narrational mode steeped in the supernatural, very much distinct from the stylistic strategies essayed by Jackson and Reyes. Using both contextual industrial data and close textual analysis, Kimber addresses the manner in which *Sinister* has taken various tropes and motifs of transnational cinematic snuff fiction and adapted them into a palatable, commercially viable form that de-sexualizes its iconography in the pursuit of affective responses reliant upon scare tactics familiar to many contemporary popular horror film franchises.

Linda Badley's approach locates snuff's disputed mythology even more securely in both the horror genre's history and its global pantheon. Discussing cinema itself as a visual conduit for moments of living death, Badley contests that *Shadow of a Vampire* (E. Elias Merhige, 2000), a fanciful account of the making of F.W. Murnau's *Nosferatu* (1922), offers an elegy for both a cinema long past and one that is aware of its imminent extinction in the onset of the digital age. In this sense, the film not only seems cognizant of the deathly shadow of Murnau's masterpiece but also explores the relationship between art and mortality itself, a theme which lies at the center of snuff's cultural resonance.

Tina Kendall considers the privileged position that snuff has occupied within the paradigm of the "new extremism" of contemporary world cinema. This elaborates further upon material in Kavka's essay, arguing that the lure of snuff resides in its affective force, confronting audiences with a spectacle of death offered not just *to* the spectator, but *for* the spectator. Kendall argues that snuff embodies not merely a crisis of knowledge, but a crisis of response and, ultimately, responsibility, considering how these snuff fictions raise important questions about complicit witnessing and the affective and ethical dimensions of spectatorship today.

Bringing the collection to a close, Steve Jones interprets the narrative content of the *Amateur Porn Star Killer* films, examining what their form reveals about the self and consciousness. Jones contests that the films routinely disturb the seemingly absolute binary oppositions at the heart of self-conception, combining realism and violence with sustained first-person camerawork, exposing tipping points between victim/ killer, self/other, and life/death.

The essays in this collection are designed to enhance, illuminate, and develop all of the issues outlined in this introduction. Moreover, it is the aim of the editors to present the debate through an eclectic range of critical and theoretical approaches that provide the necessary tools with which to penetrate and clarify the ever mutating mythology of snuff.

PART ONE

THE CHANGING MEANINGS OF "SNUFF"

1 THE WAY TO DIGITAL DEATH

Julian Petley

Prologue: Flat Earth news

Thanks largely to the press, the myth of the "snuff movie" still refuses to lie down and die. Take, for example, this headline from the British newspaper the *Telegraph*, July 16, 2014: "Discovery Fined for Showing Torture and Dismemberment Before Watershed."[1] One had to read a full six paragraphs of the article before discovering, via a brief quote from Ofcom (the Office of Communications) that the programs in question contained "prolonged and disturbing *reconstructions* of torture, mutilation and murder."[2] The story appeared in other national papers too, although the *Star*, July 17, was the only one to cover the story and to fail to mention *at all* that the controversial scenes were in fact reconstructions. The story certainly had legs: Googling "Investigation Discovery," "Ofcom," and "female killers" produced 2,320 results, from national and local UK papers, as well as from the international press.

The original source of the story turned out to be an alert on July 16 from the Press Association which noted that the Investigation Discovery channel had been fined £100,000 for screening the series *Deadly Women* (2008–2014), which examined a number of real-life murder cases and contained "graphic depictions of extreme violence including torture, a child murder, and dismemberment of a corpse,"[3]

---

[1] Agencies, "Discovery Fined for Showing Torture and Dismemberment Before Watershed," *Telegraph*, July 16, 2014, accessed December 15, 2014, http://www.telegraph.co.uk/culture/tvandradio/10972185/Discovery-fined-for-showing-torture-and-dismemberment-before-watershed.html.
[2] Ofcom quoted in ibid. Emphasis added.
[3] http://www.medialawyer.press.net/article.jsp?id=9998419.

hours before the watershed. The alert also included, albeit not prominently, the quote from Ofcom about the series consisting of reconstructions.

Indeed, when Ofcom first reported on the series, in issue 246 of its *Broadcast Bulletin*,[4] on the very first page of the fourteen devoted to the series, the words "dramatic reconstructions" are used twice and the word "re-enacted" is used once, and the nature of the series remains abundantly clear throughout the following pages. The story was not picked up by the press. What gave rise to the Media Lawyer alert was Ofcom's announcement, on July 16, 2014, that it was imposing a sanction on Discovery for broadcasting the series at an inappropriate time.[5] But again, from the start of the seventeen-page Ofcom document, it is clear that the offending programs are reconstructions: the word itself is first used eight lines in from the early section explaining which particular rules of the *Ofcom Code*[6] had been breached. By contrast, in the alert[6] it occurs only once, about halfway through, and since—in a classic instance of what Nick Davies aptly calls "churnalism"[7]—most newspapers published the alert more or less verbatim, it would have been all too easy for the casual reader to have formed the impression that Investigation Discovery had been repeatedly broadcasting images of "real live death." Thus are myths and misconceptions propagated and sustained.

"A terrible fascination"

When the word "snuff" is used today, particularly in a condemnatory context, it is usually to denote precisely those images of "real live death" which now circulate in such profusion courtesy of the Internet, and which, unsurprisingly, given when they were published, feature in neither David Kerekes and David Slater's *Killing for Culture*,[8] nor my chapter on "snuff" in Graeme Harper and Xavier Mendik's collection *Unruly Pleasures: The Cult Film and its Critics*.[9] But there is nothing

---

[4]"Ofcom Broadcast Bulletin," no. 246, January 20, 2014, accessed December 15, 2014, http:// stakeholders.ofcom.org.uk/binaries/enforcement/broadcast-bulletins/246/obb246.pdf.

[5]Ofcom, "Sanction 95 (14) Discovery Communications Europe Limited," accessed December 15, 2014, http://stakeholders.ofcom.org.uk/binaries/enforcement/content-sanctions-adjudications/Discovery.pdf.

[6]I have been unable to find any press release relating to *Deadly Women* on the Ofcom website.

[7]Nick Davies, *Flat Earth News* (London: Chatto &Windus, 2009).

[8]David Kerekes and David Slater, *Killing for Culture: An Illustrated History of Death Film from Mondo to Snuff* (London: Creation Books, 1993). A second edition of this book was published in 1995 and a new edition is forthcoming, which will include discussion of images of death on the Internet.

[9]Julian Petley, "'Snuffed Out': Nightmares in a Trading Standards Officer's Brain," in *Unruly Pleasures: The Cult Film and Its Critics*, edited by Xavier Mendik and Graeme Harper (Guildford: FAB Press, 2000): 203–19.

essentially new about such images themselves, whether captured deliberately or by chance; although the coming of digital technology, along with changes to the broadcasting environment in many countries, has undoubtedly altered in significant respects the situation in which they are produced and circulated. What follows is in no sense a definitive list, merely a brief and selective indication of the long genealogy of photographic images of "real live death."

If we date the beginnings of camera photography to the 1820s, with the work of Nicéphore Niépce, then we can say that it was not long, by the standards of the time, before the camera was used to photograph dead people, since by the end of the 1830s, the first examples of photographic, as opposed to painted, postmortem portraiture had begun to appear.[10] But these peaceful memorabilia of loved ones were a far cry from the first really memorable photographic images of the dead, which were far from serene. These were depictions of the aftermaths of battles in the American Civil War (1860–1865), and are generally credited to Matthew Brady.[11] However, many of these were actually taken by his employees, particularly Alexander Gardner, in the early days of the war and before he left Brady's employ in 1862. It should be noted, however, that newspapers could not use these (or any other) photographs, for at this time they lacked the technique and equipment for making half-tone blocks. Brady and his teams would surely have filmed the battles themselves had the camera technology of the day enabled them to capture moving action, but, nonetheless, the images of the dead carry a powerful charge, and no more so than those showing the bloody aftermath of the Battle of Antietan in September 1862. As one historian has noted, the battle in question—which saw the death, wounding, or disappearance of over 22,000 people—"took a human toll never exceeded on any other single day in [America's] history", and so "intense and sustained was the violence, a man recalled, that for a moment in his mind's eye the very landscape around him turned red."[12] In October, the photographs of the battle that were taken by Gardner and his assistant were exhibited at Brady's New York gallery. An observation in the review of the exhibition, in *The New York Times*, October 20, 1862, is remarkably pertinent in the context of this chapter:

> Mr. Brady has done something to bring home to us the terrible reality and earnestness of war. If he has not brought bodies and laid them in our dooryards and along the streets, he has done something very like it. At the door of his gallery hangs a little placard, "The Dead of Antietam." Crowds are constantly

---

[10]Audrey Linkman, *Photography and Death* (London: Reaktion, 2011).
[11]Bray's photographs of the Civil War can be accessed freely via the U. S. National Archives' flickr page: https://www.flickr.com/photos/usnationalarchives/collections/72157622495226723/.
[12]Stephen W. Sears, *Landscape Turned Red: The Battle of Antietam* (New York: Mariner Books, 2003): xi.

going up the stairs; follow them, and you find them bending over photographic views of that fearful battle-field, taken immediately after the action. Of all objects of horror, one would think that the battlefield should stand preeminent, and that it should bear away the palm of repulsiveness. But, on the contrary, there is a terrible fascination about it that draws one near these pictures, and makes him loth to leave them. You will see hushed, reverend groups standing around these weird copies of carnage, bending down to look in the pale faces of the dead, chained by the strange spell that dwells in dead men's eyes.[13]

But equally pertinent is the fact that, on July 7, 1865, Gardner photographed the execution by hanging of four of the conspirators in the plot to kill Abraham Lincoln.[14]

Censorship and self-censorship

With the moving image came the possibility of capturing the actual instant of death on film in documentaries and newsreels. For example, on June 14, 1913, British Pathé newsreel cameras caught the moment when Emily Davison—a prominent women's activist (and key figure in the suffragette movement)—was fatally trampled at Epsom Derby when she stepped in front of King George V's horse (although the image is indistinct, and—contra the film's title card—she actually died four days later).[15] Much more dramatic and explicit (though not of course by present-day standards) was the Pathé footage of the fatal end of Frank Lockhart's attempt on the world land speed record at Daytona Beach, Florida, on April 25, 1928, in which Lockhart's body being thrown from his crashing car is clearly visible.[16] He died instantly.

Of course, what could actually be shown on public screens, particularly in the newsreels, was heavily mediated by the exercise of both official censorship and self-censorship. This was most certainly the case in the First World War, where both forms of censorship began on the battlefield and continued on the home front. In Britain, newsreels were not actually subject to inspection by the British Board of Film Censors (BBFC), but their contents were most certainly prone to self-censorship by those who produced them. The predominant attitude of the

---

[13]Anon., "BRADY'S PHOTOGRAPHS; Pictures of the Dead at Antietam," October 20, 1882, accessed December 15, 2014, http://www.nytimes.com/1862/10/20/news/brady-s-photographs-pictures-of-the-dead-at-antietam.html?smid=pl-share.
[14]Gardner's photographs can be accessed freely at the following website: http://murderpedia.org/male.H/h/herold-david-photos.htm.
[15]The newsreel can be found on YouTube: https://www.youtube.com/watch?v=wVrlLKAR1S0.
[16]The footage can be readily accessed via YouTube: https://www.youtube.com/watch?v=SzJ0dEXm6Nw.

newsreel companies to representing reality in general, and not simply warfare, was later neatly summed up by G.T. Cummins, the editor of Paramount, who in 1934 stated that: "The daily life of the whole civilized world is to be told in pictures, nothing must be omitted. But nothing must be included which the average man will not like."[17] Not upsetting the patrons clearly had a primarily economic motive, but it was also extremely important not to bring down the wrath of the local authorities on the cinemas within their jurisdiction, as they had the power to cut and ban films of all kinds. And certain local councils clearly had the newsreels within their sights. Thus, in 1938, after Hereford County Council had complained about newsreels containing footage of Japanese air attacks on Chinese cities during the Sino-Japanese War that had commenced the previous year, the Executive of the County Councils Association "formally requested the Home Secretary to make it an offence to display films depicting suffering or loss of life and to make all films showing events more than a week old subject to censorship."[18] The request was turned down, but within a year, Britain itself would be at war; as in all combatant countries, maintaining morale on the home front was paramount, and a huge amount of effort, both on the battlefield itself and back home, went into ensuring that graphic scenes of carnage were kept safely off the screen. Indeed, in the UK, newsreel footage shot during the liberation of the concentration camps in 1944 and 1945 was heavily sanitized before it was shown in cinemas—even though it served the useful purpose of reminding audiences of the horrors against which the country was still fighting. And over ten years after the end of the war, a documentary such as Alain Resnais' *Nuit et brouillard/Night and Fog* (France, 1955) found its horrific images of mass murder on an industrial scale toned down by censors in the UK, and a number of other countries too.[19]

Murders, suicides, and executions

Today, the images of "real live death" that cause the greatest concern are those of onscreen murders, suicides, and executions which circulate via the Internet and which are frequently denounced as a form of modern-day "snuff," but, again, there is nothing essentially new in such imagery.

---

[17]Cummins quoted in Nicholas Pronay, "British Newsreels in the 1930s: Their Policies and Impacts," in *Yesterday's News: The British Cinema Newsreel Reader*, edited by Luke McKernan (London: British Universities Film & Video Council, 2002): 149–50.
[18]Ibid., 151.
[19]See, for example, Ewout van der Knaap, ed., *Uncovering the Holocaust: The International Reception of Night and Fog* (London: Wallflower Press, 2006), and Sylvie Lindeperg, Nuit et Brouillard: *Un film dans l'histoire* (Paris: Odile Jacob, 2007).

Perhaps the best-known example of an onscreen execution is that of Nguyễn Văn Lém, a member of the National Liberation Front who, on February 1, 1968, during the Vietnam War (1955–1975), was summarily executed in a Saigon street by General Nguyễn Ngọc Loan, South Vietnam's Chief of National Police. The event was recorded as both still and moving images by Eddie Adams, an Associated Press photographer, and Vo Suu, an NBC cameraman.[20] Significantly, it is the still image that captures the moment of death most strikingly, only partly because in the moving image, the shot body of the prisoner is a blur, although the moving version does register the blood pouring from the victim's head as he lies on the ground.[21]

South Vietnam was also the arena for the well-known onscreen suicide of the Buddhist monk Thích Quảng Đức, who, in protesting the persecution of Buddhists by the government, publically set fire to himself at a road junction on June 11, 1963.[22] Photographs of the event were taken by a photographer for Associated Press, Malcolm Browne, and graced the front pages of many international newspapers. However, the filmed footage—as with that documenting the execution of Nguyễn Văn Lém—was more cautiously used by television networks and, in line with local broadcasting regulations, the degrees of graphicness differed from country to country.

The most famous example of an onscreen murder is surely that of President J.F. Kennedy at Dealey Plaza in Dallas on November 22, 1963. There were no television cameras at the location; however, the assassination was inadvertently captured on 8mm by an amateur photographer, Abraham Zapruder. Select images from Zapruder's footage would subsequently appear in *Life* magazine soon after the assassination,[23] but the footage itself wouldn't be shown publically until the trial of Clay Shaw—a New Orleans businessman who was acquitted of conspiring to assassinate Kennedy—in 1969. And, it wasn't until 1975 that the footage received its first network screening, on ABC's *Good Night America*, a late night show hosted by Geraldo Rivera. Oliver Stone incorporated the footage into his movie *JFK* (US, 1991), paying the Zapruder family approximately $85,000 for the film. It has been slowed down, blown up, and pored over ever since it was shot. Many of the films on YouTube explore the footage in close-up detail, frequently in

---

[20]An interesting discussion of the differences between the still and moving images of this event can be found on YouTube: http://www.youtube.com/watch?v=BGrsw6m9UOY.

[21]The footage can be accessed via the "shock site" site Best Gore (though viewers are warned that this site also contains fairly explicit adverts for hardcore pornography): http://www.bestgore.com/execution/saigon-execution-viet-cong-nguyen-van-lem-nguyen-ngoc-loan/.

[22]The footage of Thích Quảng Đức's death can also be accessed via YouTube: https://www.youtube.com/watch?v=VCEWSSVjrTw.

[23]Zapruder sold the footage to *Life* for a rumored $250,000. See Kerekes and Slater, *Killing for Culture*, 265–66.

order to try to prove conspiracy theories of one kind or another,[24] but even in its untreated form[25] it is horrific enough, particularly if one knows, from extratextual sources, what is actually going on.

With the coming of television, censoring images of "real live death" became more difficult. This was not because television lacked rules prohibiting the showing of certain kinds of images—it certainly didn't, although, as noted earlier, these, like the rules laying down the limits of the permissible on cinema screens, varied widely from country to country. But what made television much more difficult to regulate in this respect was its element of liveness, which brought with it the possibility of being caught unawares by violent death. Hence, for example, the murder on October 12, 1960 in Tokyo of Inejiro Asanuma, leader of the Japan Socialist Party, during a live debate on national television,[26] and the death, live (if indistinct) on NBC, of the murderer of President John F. Kennedy's alleged killer, Lee Harvey Oswald, by Jack Ruby on November 24, 1963.[27] But a very different, and much more revealing, example is provided by Yorkshire Television's live coverage[28] of the Valley Parade stadium disaster in Bradford, May 11, 1985, in which 56 people were killed and 265 injured when the main stand caught fire during a match between Bradford and Lincoln City. Although the event is still, of course, mediated, it is much less heavily mediated than the reports of the event on subsequent news broadcasts,[29] and the very liveness of the images of blazing people running or being dragged from the stand, coupled with the evident distress of the commentators, imbues them with a particularly disturbing quality.

As is clear from the above examples, the representation of "real live death" in the mainstream media has always been governed by various codes, rules, and regulations of one kind or another. And, stemming partly from the way in which these have been internalized by photojournalists and filmmakers, there are all sorts of mechanisms of self-censorship which operate in this area as well. But before we move on to examine such representations in the new media, it would be helpful to briefly examine how the "old" media have

---

[24]For example, the one by the prolific Robert Harris (not the novelist of the same name): https://www.youtube.com/watch?v=kq1PbgeBoQ4.

[25]Which can be accessed here: https://www.youtube.com/watch?v=w4L1CVX0FnA.

[26]Footage of the murder of Inejiro Asanuma can be found on Daily Motion: http://www.dailymotion.com/video/x66vpe_inejiro-asanuma-assassination-foota_news.

[27]The footage can be accessed via YouTube: https://www.youtube.com/watch?v=3n9VQ-dXrwQ.

[28]The live coverage can be accessed via YouTube: http://www.youtube.com/watch?v=svI7AgMFqJY.

[29]See, for example, the following YouTube video: https://www.youtube.com/watch?v=IrXmdtPO6LQ. This too contains some of the more distressing images seen in the live footage, but, in my view at least, their impact is somewhat lessened by the context in which they are placed. Nonetheless, one wonders if ITN (or the BBC) would show such images today on a mainstream news bulletin.

dealt with images of "real live death" via a résumé of part of Vivian Sobchak's seminal article on the subject.[30]

An ethical vision

Sobchak argues that whereas death is frequently displayed graphically in fictional cinema, "documentary film is marked by an excessive visual avoidance of death."[31] This is because when death is represented as real, "a visual taboo has been violated, and the representation must find various ways to justify the violation."[32]

Furthermore, the justification must be visible on screen, inscribed in the particular way in which the filmmaker has represented the dying or the dead. As Sobchak explains, the activity of filming death has become

> codified and used conventionally to visibly inscribe the text within the contours of what would normatively be considered an ethical vision of some kind. In its visibility, this activity of representing death thus constitutes a moral conduct: the conventionally agreed-upon manner and means by which a visually taboo, excessive, and essentially unrepresentable event can be viewed, contained, pointed to, and opened to a scrutiny that is, to varying degree, culturally sanctioned.[33]

The visual signs of the filmmaker's ethical stance are

> inscribed in and visibly represented by the camera's stability or movement in relation to the situation that it perceives, in the framing of the object of its vision, in the distance that separates it from the event, in the persistence or reluctance of its gaze in the face of a horrific, chaotic, unjust, or personally dangerous event.[34]

As I have argued elsewhere,[35] it was precisely *Cannibal Holocaust*'s (Italy, 1980) trampling on the carefully erected and culturally sanctioned distinctions between fictional and factual modes of representing death which made it so controversial— and indeed caused some to believe it to be a "snuff movie."

---

[30]Vivian Sobchak, "Inscribing Ethical Space: Ten Propositions on Death, Representation, and Documentary," in *Carnal Thoughts: Embodiment and Moving Image Culture*, edited by Vivian Sobchak (Berkeley, CA: University of California Press): 226–57.

[31]Ibid., 241–42.

[32]Ibid., 242.

[33]Ibid., 245.

[34]Ibid., 243.

[35]Julian Petley, "*Cannibal Holocaust* and the Pornography of Death," in *The Spectacle of the Real: From Hollywood to Reality TV and Beyond*, edited by Geoff King (Bristol: Intellect, 2005): 173–86.

Sobchak identifies five forms of ethical behavior in the documentary engagement with, and representation of, the event of actual death: the accidental gaze (where the event is caught seemingly unawares), the helpless gaze, the endangered gaze (which provides visible evidence of the personal risk taken to capture the images by the filmmaker), the interventional gaze, and the humane gaze. She also identifies the professional gaze, which is "more ethically ambiguous and suspect than the others, presenting problems of ethical judgement to both filmmaker and spectator alike."[36] This last gaze is

> marked by ethical ambiguity, by technical and *machinelike competence* in the face of an event that seems to call for further and more humane response … The concern for getting a clear and unobstructed image, and the belief that it is possible to strip the representation of human bias, perspective, and ethical investment, so that it is truly "objective," indelibly mark the inscriptions of the professional gaze with their own problematic ethical perspective in the face of both human mortality and the visual taboos surrounding it. (Emphasis in the original)[37]

As Sobchak points out, the visual "sign vehicles" which function to make the event of death "visible on the screen signify the manner in which the immediate viewer"[38] of the pro-filmic event—that is, the filmmaker with the camera—visibly mediates their own confrontation with death and charges it with an ethical meaning visible to others. But such "sign vehicles" are also the means whereby the viewer of the filmed images responds to them. To quote Sobchak:

> Before the nonfictional screen event of an unsimulated death, the very act of looking at the film is ethically charged, and this act itself is an object of ethical judgement. That is, the viewer is—and is held—ethically responsible for his or her visible visual response.[39]

Digital death

Sobchack's article was originally published in 1984 and was revised for republication in 2004. Since it first appeared, a very great deal has changed in the media landscape. First of all, the ever-increasing commercialization and hyper-competitiveness of the television marketplace have led to a proliferation of programs, and indeed of

---

[36]Sobchak, "Inscribing Ethical Space," 249.
[37]Ibid., 255.
[38]Ibid., 244.
[39]Ibid.

entire channels, dedicated to sensationalizing the "reality" which they claim to be representing, and death frequently looms large in such productions. Of course, the extent to which this has happened has depended on the different regulatory environments in which television finds itself in different countries, but it is surely significant that one of the first European countries in which *TV-realità*—or *TV-spazzatura* (TV-garbage), as it became known by its critics—was developed was in Italy, where it was a result of what has been called the "savage deregulation" of Italian television from the mid-1970s onward, the main driver and beneficiary of which was Silvio Berlusconi. Highly significantly in the present context, Ruggero Deodato has repeatedly claimed that his poisonous picture of voyeuristic television reporters and executives in *Cannibal Holocaust* was inspired by his revulsion at the sensational way in which Italian television news had reported the deaths and injuries caused by Red Brigade terrorist attacks in the 1970s.[40]

Second—and this is the much more significant change—since the mid-1990s, the Internet has been massively commercialized and popularized, and, within this process, there has occurred an eruption in blogs, social networking sites, and file sharing platforms. These phenomena used to be described collectively as Web 2.0, a phrase coined in 2005,[41] but are now generally referred to as "social media." The technologies that constitute them are not all new, but their widespread use dates from the early years of the new millennium.

Sobchak acknowledges that her article does not address "the conundrum of digital—or digitized—death,"[42] so it is to this that I now want to turn. However, before I do so, I want to note that the cornucopia of images of "real live death" that can be accessed on the Internet at the click of a mouse or the touch of a finger does have its antecedents in the huge number of movies which followed in the wake of Gualtiero Jacopetti, Paolo Cavara and Franco Prosperi's *Mondo Cane* (Italy, 1962) and which were given a new lease of life by the *Faces of Death* (Various, 1979–1996) franchise which kicked off in 1979.[43] That many of the mondo films were either cut or banned outright in the UK when they were first made, and then met the same fate again when they were released on video, demonstrates once again just how problematic images of "real live death" have proved to be for the authorities in Britain.

Given the absolute plethora of such images on the Internet, it would be almost impossible to construct a taxonomy of them. But it would certainly be safe to say

---

[40]See, for example, the director's remarks in Harvey Fenton, *Cannibal Holocaust and the Savage Cinema of Ruggero Deodato* (2nd Edition, Godalming: FAB Press, 2011): 19.
[41]Christian Fuchs, *Social Media* (London: Sage, 2014): 32.
[42]Sobchak, "Inscribing Ethical Space," 233.
[43]See Kerekes and Slater, *Killing for Culture*, 71–163; and Mark Goodall, *Sweet & Savage: The World Through the Shockumentary Film Lens* (London: Headpress, 2006).

that many of these in no way conform to any of Sobchak's ethical categories, and it is precisely their taboo-busting qualities which have made many of them so controversial, along with the fact that they are so widely and easily available to anyone online. Those which have caused the most outrage and brought forth calls for them to be banned in some way or other are those involving "executions" (usually beheadings), and other actions in which those behind the camera are clearly active participants in what is happening in front of it. Of the latter, the most disturbing is undoubtedly the video featuring the self-styled "Dnepropetrovsk maniacs,"[44] in which a man is brutally murdered by means of a hammer and screwdriver. He is, in fact, only one of twenty-one people whose murders were committed to film by the "maniacs" in the Ukraine in June and July 2007, although the prosecution failed to establish any reason for the murders. The film of the one killing which made its way onto the Internet is undoubtedly a "snuff movie" of sorts, although of course it is not in any way a "professional" or commercial product. This and other films were used in evidence in the trials of the three Ukrainians involved, two of whom received life sentences and one of whom was sentenced to nine years in prison—which neatly illustrates why it is highly unwise (quite apart from anything else) to make such films, and why so few appear to exist.

Another infamous death captured on film by its perpetrator involved the Rotenberg-based Armin Meiwes, who posted an advertisement on a (now defunct) underground website: The Cannibal Café. The advertisement explained how Meiwes was "looking for a well-built 18- to 30-year-old to be slaughtered and then consumed," and was answered by one Bernd Jürgen Armando Brandes. The two men would meet at Meiwes' home on March 9, 2001, where Meiwes cut off Brandes's penis, and both men attempted to eat it. Meiwes then placed Brandes in a bath for a number of hours, before moving him in to a purpose-built "Slaughter Room" where Meiwes slit his throat and proceeded to hang the body from a meat hook and devour parts of the flesh. The whole event was recorded on video. In 2004, he was sentenced to eight years in prison for manslaughter, but in 2006, after prosecutors appealed, he was given life imprisonment for murder. The video was used in the trial, which reinforces the point made above. A number of stills purporting to come from the video are available online, as is the archive of The Cannibal Café, which contains a number of Meiwes' postings.[45] The case has given rise to four of films: Rosa von Praunheim's *Dein Herz in meinem Hirn/Your Heart in My Head* (Germany, 2005), Martin Weisz's *Rohtenburg/Grimm Love* (Germany, 2006), Marian Dora's *Cannibal* (Germany, 2006), and Ulli Lommel's

---

[44]The video in question can be accessed, again, via the site Best Gore: http://www.bestgore.com/murder/dnepropetrovsk-maniacs-murder-guy-hammer-screwdriver-real-snuff-video/.
[45]These can be accessed here: http://lostmedia.wikia.com/wiki/The_Armin_Meiwes_Tape_(Recorded_in_2001).

Diary of a Cannibal (US, 2007). Of these, by far the most impressive is *Cannibal*, which, interestingly, is banned in Germany. The case is also the subject of "The Man Who Ate His Lover," an episode, shown on March 1, 2004, of the Channel 4 *Bodyshock* (2003–2006) series.

Of the videos showing beheadings, the most controversial include those of Daniel Pearl, a journalist with American and Israeli citizenship, in Pakistan in 2002,[46] and four which took place in Iraq in 2004: those of Mohammad Mutawalli,[47] an alleged Egyptian spy; Ken Bigley,[48] a British civil engineer; and Eugene Armstrong[49] and Jack Hensley,[50] both of whom were American civil engineers. Exactly paralleling the controversies generated by mondo movies of one kind or another, various execution videos have been accused of being fakes (although it should be stressed that there is no question that those depicted in them were murdered, the only question being whether they were actually murdered onscreen): these include Kim Sun-il who was captured and murdered in Iraq in 2004;[51] Nick Berg, an American businessman who met the same fate there in the same year;[52] and Paul Johnson, an American helicopter pilot who lived in Saudi Arabia and was killed there in 2004. It might also be added that there was rather less controversy about the circulation of images showing the hanging of Saddam Hussein on December 30, 2006.[53]

Is it legal? (1) Offensiveness

Images of "real live death" being so readily available on the Internet clearly raises ethical issues, but it also raises legal ones. Given that rumors about video collectors swapping "snuff movies" were regularly used by the police and Trading Standards Officers in Britain to justify raiding their homes and seizing their collections,[54]

---

[46]The footage of Pearl can be accessed via Youtube: https://www.youtube.com/watch?v=KghZhEd Auq8&bpctr=1405423292.

[47]The footage of Mutawalli's death can be accessed via Best Gore: http://www.bestgore.com/beheading/beheading-mohammed-mutawalli-egyptian-spy-iraq-video/.

[48]The footage of Ken Bigley's beheading can be accessed here: http://executions.justsickshit.com/2007/10/19/taliban-beheading-execution-of-ken-bigley/.

[49]The footage of Eugene Armstrong's beheading can be accessed here: http://www.bestgore.com/beheading/eugene-armstrong-beheading-death-video/.

[50]http://hardgore.prochan.com/hardgore/t/a4f_1352322390.

[51]See "Savage Beheading of South Korean Hostage Kim Sun-il," http://www.informationclearinghouse.info/article6369.htm.

[52]The footage of Nick Berg's beheading can be accessed here: http://www.bestgore.com/beheading/nick-berg-beheading-video-death-conspiracy/.

[53]The footage of Hussein's hanging can be accessed via Youtube: http://www.youtube.com/watch?v=eqwTvHIU43c.

[54]Petley, "'Snuffed Out'," 214–17.

the question inevitably arises of whether it is legal to distribute such material via the Internet. This is an extremely difficult question to answer, as I have been unable to locate any cases in which anyone has been prosecuted *specifically* for doing so. However, there are various British laws under which a prosecution could conceivably be brought, and these are worth exploring.

For example, section 127 of the Communications Act 2003 states that "a person is guilty of an offence if he sends by means of a public electronic communications network a message or other matter that is grossly offensive or of an indecent, obscene or menacing character."[55] The Malicious Communications Act 1988, which had its origins in legislation which made it an offence to send threatening letters, has now been extended to cover any "electronic communication or article of any description which conveys a message which is indecent or grossly offensive" if the purpose of sending it is to "cause distress or anxiety to the recipient or to any other person to whom he intends that it or its contents or nature should be communicated."[56] The problem here is the highly subjective nature of "grossly offensive." Furthermore, the distinction between what is merely offensive (and therefore legal) and grossly offensive remains unclear, which means that even someone who is aware of these laws may find it very difficult to judge whether the message which they wish to send is or is not likely to engage them.

In 2013, there were 3,363 cases heard in magistrates' courts involving messages which in one way or another engaged these two Acts. In several of these cases, the police and Crown Prosecution Service (CPS) were accused of overstepping the mark, and of conflating behavior that is unpleasant, stupid, or in bad taste with that which should rightly be considered criminal (such as inciting violence or conducting a campaign of harassment). As a consequence, in December 2013, the CPS issued new guidelines on prosecuting cases involving social media. These state that prosecutors should "exercise considerable caution" before bringing charges under these Acts,[57] and that

> there is a high threshold that must be met before the evidential stage in the Code for Crown Prosecutors will be met. Furthermore, even if the high evidential threshold is met, in many cases a prosecution is unlikely to be required in the public interest.[58]

---

[55]http://lawcommissionjustice.gov.uk.
[56]http://www.legislation.gov.uk/ukpga/1988/27/contents.
[57]Crown Prosecution Service, "Guidelines on Prosecuting Cases Involving Communications Sent via Social Media," accessed December 15, 2014, http://www.cps.gov.uk/legal/a_to_c/communications_sent_via_social_media/.
[58]Ibid.

The guidelines remind prosecutors that what these Acts criminalize is

> the sending of a communication that is *grossly* offensive. A communication
> sent has to be more than simply offensive to be contrary to the criminal law.
> Just because the content expressed in the communication is in bad taste,
> controversial, or unpopular, and may cause offence to individuals or a specific
> community, this is not in itself sufficient reason to engage the criminal law.[59]

Factors which will mitigate against prosecution include the fact that the "content
of the communication did not obviously go beyond what could conceivably be
tolerable or acceptable in an open and diverse society which upholds and respects
freedom of expression."[60] The guidelines also quote approvingly Lord Bingham's
remark that "there can be no yardstick of gross offensiveness otherwise than by
the application of reasonably enlightened, but not perfectionist, contemporary
standards to the particular message sent in its particular context. The test is
whether a message is couched in terms liable to cause gross offence to those to
whom it relates."[61]

All this may at first sight seem fairly reassuring, but as Adam Wagner asks:
"Do we really want police and prosecutors deciding what speech is tolerable
and acceptable? Do they have the experience, intelligence and social sensitivity
to do so? Will they be capable of leaving their own prejudices, including
political, religious and social views, at the door?"[62] And, as the Open Rights
Group noted:

> The very nature of some of the more controversial speech that may be posted
> online is that it will test boundaries of contemporary standards—even reasonably
> enlightened standards. The great majority of that speech should not attract
> prosecution. There is a danger that the appeal for "contemporary standards"
> to be applied to a particular message in its particular context may lead to a
> situation in which the expression of outrage or concern—by an individual or
> a group—may be considered sufficient to qualify a communication as "grossly
> offensive."[63]

---

[59]Ibid., emphasis in original.
[60]Ibid.
[61]Bingham quoted in Ibid.
[62]Adam Wagner, "New Prosecution Guidance on Offensive Speech Online: Sensible, but the Law Is
Still Out of Date," *UK Human Rights Blog*, December 19, 2012, accessed December 15, 2014, http://
ukhumanrightsblog.com/2012/12/19/new-prosecution-guidance-on-offensive-speech-online-
sensible-but-the-law-is-still-out-of-date/#more-16450.
[63]Open Rights Group, https://www.openrightsgroup.org/ourwork/reports/submission-to-dpp-
consultation-on-social-media-prosecutions.

Images of "real live death" circulated on the Internet by political groups as part of a campaign could be particularly vulnerable here. To take but two possible examples: groups drawing attention to the atrocities committed by government forces against the Tamil population during the civil war in Sri Lanka (1983–2009), or those protesting against the death and destruction visited on innocent civilians in the Gaza Strip by the Israelis in 2008–2009, 2012, and 2014—representation of which, along with representations of other conflicts, is habitually sanitized by the mainstream British media, thus making it all the more important, in the eyes of many, that these events are shown at least somewhere in all their true horror.

Is it Legal? (2) Terrorism legislation

Images of "real live death" could also fall foul of the Terrorism Act 2000 and the Terrorism Act 2006, which could be marshaled against not only those distributing certain kinds of material but also those possessing it. Here, images showing "real life death" in an explicitly political context could be vulnerable. Section 1 of the 2006 Act makes it an offense to publish a statement which is "likely to be understood by some or all of the members of the public to whom it is published as a direct or indirect encouragement or other inducement to them to the commission, preparation or instigation of acts of terrorism." Indirectly encouraging the commission or preparation of such acts includes any statement which (a) "glorifies the commission or preparation (whether in the past, in the future or generally) of such acts or offences; and (b) is a statement from which those members of the public could reasonably be expected to infer that what is being glorified is being glorified as conduct that should be emulated by them in existing circumstances." This section was originally introduced as a response to the so-called "preachers of hate," but could, in theory, be used to prosecute praise of any individual or group using political violence anywhere in the world (or indeed any individual or group that has done so in the past). "Indirect encouragement" and "inducement" are dangerously vague terms, and "glorification" could be understood to include expressions of support for, sympathy with or even understanding of terrorism. Meanwhile, Section 58 of the 2006 Act states that "a person commits an offence if (a) he collects or makes a record of information of a kind likely to be useful to a person committing or preparing an act of terrorism, or (b) he possesses a document or record containing information of that kind."[64] This section was originally introduced to make it possible to prosecute people for possessing bomb-making manuals and the like.

---

[64]http://www.legislation.gov.uk/ukpga/2006/11/contents.

What makes these clauses particularly disturbing is the controversially broad definition of terrorism contained in the 2000 Act. Section 1 of the Act defines terrorism as the use or threat of an action which "is designed to influence the government or an international governmental organisation or to intimidate the public or a section of the public, and the use or threat is made for the purpose of advancing a political, religious or ideological cause." [65] As David Anderson QC, the independent reviewer of terrorism legislation, has pointed out, Section 1 could be taken to mean that the writing of a book, an article, or a blog may amount to terrorism if its purpose is advancing a cause and influencing government. In his view, the word "influence" sets the bar much too low, and he recommended that "influence" be replaced with "compel, coerce or undermine," thus bringing the UK definition of terrorism more into line with that used by most other democratic countries and international organizations. [66]

That no actual charges have apparently been brought for the distribution or possession of images of "real live death" should not obscure the fact that there are those in the police who would very much like to be able to do so. This became abundantly clear from a significant number of responses by police officers to the consultation on "extreme pornography" which was launched by the Home Office in 2005, and which would lead to the possession of such material being criminalized by the Criminal Justice and Immigration Act 2008. [67] For example, Detective Sergeant Richard Sharpe of the Hi-Tech Crime Unit, Derbyshire Police, complained that:

There are people who will download material depicting beheading of kidnap victims such as those in Iraq. There are others that originate from Eastern bloc depicting executions of soldiers using knives in graphic display. There you have a problem in that scenes of these images will be displayed on certain television stations which make potential prosecutions almost impossible. I feel these are as abhorrent as any sexual content imagery.

Detective Inspector Colin Gibson of the Economic Crime Unit, Durham Constabulary, stated:

Whilst it is accepted that it is the intention to restrict any new offence to pornographic material many would argue that this is a conservative list and

---

[65] http://www.legislation.gov.uk/ukpga/2000/11/contents.
[66] Anderson quoted in Joshua Rozenburg, "How UK's Terrorism Law Targets Words, Not Just Guns and Bombs," *Guardian*, July 22, 2014, accessed December 15, 2014, http://www.theguardian.com/law/2014/jul/22/terrorism-law-targets-words-guns-bombs.
[67] These were originally available, with all the other responses to the consultation, on the Home Office website, but, as is usual in the case of completed consultations, they have been removed.

leaves room for development. Not all abhorrent images are produced for sexual gratification. Some are quite clearly just obscene and offensive and without a sexual connutation [sic] yet simple possession would still fall outside of current and proposed legislation. I use as an example the recent prosecution in Scotland where the offender circulated to others the decapitation of a hostage held in the Middle East. I am without doubt that this can be qualified as obscene and offensive yet due to the current state of legislation he could only be prosecuted for a breach of the peace.[68]

This is quite clearly factually incorrect. Detective Chief Inspector Rob Donagy, Cleveland Police, noted that:

Violent scenes without a sexual nature are specifically excluded from these proposals. While acknowledging the reason for this, the "Abhorrent to the Public" test would surely be met with these images. I consider that the basis for the current proposals (i.e., protection of vulnerable people involved and access to such material) would equally apply to extreme violent scenes without a sexual nature (e.g., snuff movies etc.).

It is, of course, very hard to gauge just how representative such views are of opinion within the police as a whole, but it is surely highly disturbing to find them expressed in a particularly extreme and ill-informed manner by the then General Secretary of the Police Federation of England and Wales, John Francis:

The circumstances in which the material is found is not, at the present time, considered when sentencing takes place, as only the image charged can be so considered. This applies when considering the sexual nature of an image. For example, so-called "snuff movies" whereby persons are actually killed on screen are currently not considered for a sexual motive. The circumstances in which the images are found should be considered. There is evidence of these movies being found with a great deal of pornography, which in itself is not illegal to possess. This also applies to mutilation images, scenes of crime images of murder victims, beheadings, etc. The question to be asked is why anyone would want these images in the first place. It is the circumstances in which they are found that implies a sexual motive. However, as legislation stands at present no account can be taken of them, as it is not illegal to possess these images.[69]

This issue raised its head much more publicly in the wake of the online video apparently showing the murder of the video of the American journalist James

---

[68]Unfortunately it has proved impossible to find a record of this case.
[69]The reasoning here is dubious in the extreme.

Foley in August 2014.[70] One says "apparently" because, although not exactly a fake, the video does not show what most of the mainstream media have claimed that it does. Reports in the *Guardian*,[71] *Telegraph*,[72] and *The Times* were the exception, pointing out that, at the start of the beheading, Foley remains strangely silent, and, while his neck is seen to be subject to at least six slashes, there is no evidence of blood. Moreover, the beheading itself is not shown: the process appears to start, then the video fades to black. As though to infer some time has lapsed, the video then fades back in, revealing Foley's decapitated head resting on his body. It is by no means clear that the person wielding the knife is the one speaking with the English accent on the soundtrack, since he is so heavily masked. The killing itself takes place off camera, and thus it remains equally unclear whether the man nicknamed by sections of the press as "Jihadi John" is the one who actually carried it out. Finally, the knife drawn across Foley's neck looks different from the one beside his dead body.

None of this, of course, is to deny for a moment that what happened to James Foley (and to his successors Steven Sotloff, David Haines, Alan Henning, and Abdul Rahman/Peter Kassig) is anything other than utterly barbaric and reprehensible. But, without wishing in any way to create a tasteless "gore score," it has to be pointed out that the video is not only far less graphic than many discussed in this chapter but also far less graphic than many Isis videos showing the killing of Iraqis and Syrians.[73] As in the case of the relative lack of concern shown in the west about the circulation of the video of the hanging of Saddam Hussein, and that of the last moments of Colonel Gaddafi,[74] there is quite clearly a double standard at work here. And one should also add that since "Jihadi John's" role in the Foley video has been used by Boris Johnson and others as propaganda for the idea that—entirely contrary to this country's international obligations—British citizens who fight on the "wrong" side in the Middle East should be stripped of their citizenship and rendered stateless, people should surely have the right and ability to be able to find out what the controversy is all about.

Within a very short time of the video's appearance, Scotland Yard issued a statement to the effect that "The MPS [Metropolitan Police Service]

---

[70]The video can be accessed at Best Gore: http://www.bestgore.com/beheading/islamic-state-executes-journalist-james-foley/.

[71]Nicholas Watt, Richard Norton-Taylor, and Josh Halliday, "Isis Beheading Video Brings Calls for Rethink of UK Domestic Terrorism Fight," *The Guardian*, August 21, 2014, accessed December 15, 2014, http://www.theguardian.com/politics/2014/aug/21/james-foley-isis-beheading-uk-counterterrorist-fight-in-crisis.

[72]Bill Gardner, "Foley Murder Video 'May Have Been Staged'," *The Telegraph*, August 25, 2014, accessed December 15, 2014, http://www.telegraph.co.uk/journalists/bill-gardner/11054488/Foley-murder-video-may-have-been-staged.html.

[73]To take but one possible example, see Best Gore: http://www.bestgore.com/execution/mass-execution-civilian-soldier-capture-mosul-isis-iraq/.

[74]See: http://gawker.com/5852485/heres-the-clearest-video-yet-of-gaddafis-capture.

counter-terrorism command (SO15) is investigating the contents of the video that was posted online in relation to the alleged murder of James Foley. We would like to remind the public that viewing, downloading or disseminating extremist material within the UK may constitute an offence under terrorism legislation."[75] This statement was reproduced entirely unquestioningly by most media outlets. Both Twitter and YouTube attempted to suppress the online circulation of the footage, with Twitter in some cases suspending accounts, and YouTube attempting to remove copies of the video that had successfully been uploaded. Only the lawyer David Allen Green challenged the police—and discovered that they were talking rubbish.

As Green revealed in the *Financial Times*,[76] he asked the MPS press office what was the specific criminal offense which covered the mere viewing of such a video. The general news desk could not help, and so it was arranged that a specialist antiterrorism press officer would call him. When she did so, she drew attention to the fact that the statement noted that viewing the video *may* constitute an offense, not that it necessarily will do so, and then mentioned vaguely sections 1 and 2 of the Terrorism Act 2006. However, as Green points out:

> Neither of those two complex and detailed provisions refer to "viewing" material. I pressed her on which actual wording in those sections supported the MPS's contention; and she replied it was a "matter of interpretation." But which particular wording was being interpreted, I asked, as even "matters of interpretation" need something to be interpreted. There was no answer. I said I would email so that the MPS could give me a considered response; and so I asked in writing if the MPS could please specify exactly under which law "viewing" the video "may" be an offence. One hour later came the simple reply: "The MPS statement stands," and no mention of any specific legislation.[77]

Thus, the MPS press office, which had produced and promoted the bold statement that "viewing" a video could itself be a criminal act under terrorism legislation, could not substantiate it when challenged—not by a journalist but by a lawyer. As Green concludes:

> People need reliable and accurate public information, and they have the right to expect it from the well-funded PR departments of UK police forces. If a

---

[75]http://www.theguardian.com/uk-news/2014/aug/20/police-warn-james-foley-video-crime-social-media.

[76]David Allen Green, "Is Viewing a Video a Criminal Offence Under Terrorism Law?," *The Financial Times*, August 21, 2014, accessed December 15, 2014, http://blogs.ft.com/david-allen-green/2014/08/21/is-viewing-a-video-a-criminal-offence-under-terrorism-law/.

[77]Ibid.

police force tells people something is against the law, then it should be able to instantly say on demand what that law is. The law should not be made up by press officers as they go along, especially in respect of matters such as terrorism where confidence in law enforcement agencies is crucial. It cannot be the role of any police force to publish alarmist and false statements about the criminal law.[78]

However, thanks to censorship by Google, Twitter, YouTube, and other corporate Internet giants, no doubt spurred on by the above-mentioned statement by the police, the video rapidly became more difficult to locate than any other mentioned in this chapter. And yet, just a couple of months later, on October 17, 2014, Britain's senior counter-terrorism officer, Scotland Yard assistant commissioner Mark Rowley, issued a statement in which he noted, among other things, that:

Leading the fight online is the Counter Terrorism Internet Referral Unit, a policing team that is currently assessing and, in partnership with the relevant Internet hosting company, is removing over 1,000 pieces of illegal content from the Internet each week. This includes videos of beheadings and other brutal murders, torture, and suicides. Over 80 percent of the material removed is Iraq and Syria related. In the last four years, the unit has ensured that 51,000 pieces of illegal and deeply damaging material have been removed.[79]

This was very widely reported in both the press and broadcast media, and yet, as far as I am aware, not a single journalist enquired which laws this material allegedly infringed or questioned the desirability of the police and ISPs effectively acting in concert as judge, jury, and executioner when it comes to the censorship of the Internet. Apparently, putting allegedly illegal material before a judge and jury and awaiting their verdict is a luxury which we can no longer afford—yet one more right which has been sacrificed in the interests of a nebulous, catch-all notion of "security."

Why watch?

There is undoubtedly a myriad of answers to the question of why so many people watch images of "real live death," including mere curiosity, a genuine desire to know more about the world, indulging in the "yuck" factor, bravado, and—it

---

[78]Ibid.
[79]http://content.met.police.uk/News/AC-Mark-Rowley-sets-out-counterterrorism-challenges-and-renews-public-appeal/1400027155128/1257246741786.

has to be admitted—seeking confirmation of their own beliefs, or trying to persuade others of their validity. But to argue that because certain people watch these videos for what others think of as the "wrong" reasons, it should be made impossible for anyone else to be able to see them is not only impractical, but it is also to endorse the kind of line habitually taken by the BBFC that just because certain "vulnerable" people may be "harmed" by certain images, and may then go on to "harm" society as a result, these images should be banned outright. This is not the place to rehearse the arguments against this kind of thinking, which are already well known, other than to say that the idea that the Foley video is liable to "turn" its viewers into jihadists is no more plausible than the idea that watching *Henry: Portrait of a Serial Killer* (US, John McNaughton, 1986) is liable to "make" its viewers into serial killers. Quite possibly it could be a factor in helping to confirm someone in their already deeply held views, but it is highly unlikely to be among the key factors, and it is quite impossible to conceive of it being the only one. This just is not how the media work—and especially media products which are so overtly propagandist in intent and form as the Foley video and its successors. Absolutely, no one is going to miss the all-too-clear message here, and viewers will accept it or—far more likely—reject it according to their already existing beliefs and values. Indeed, it could be argued that for most people, at least in the West, the video will perform an informative and broadly educational function by showing them what Isis is actually doing, and will almost certainly excite nothing but revulsion for their activities. Therefore, not only should it be able to be seen, but it ought to be seen. It should, of course, be borne in mind that videos such as this have long been used by far-right groups as part of what can only be called an anti-Islamic crusade. Take, for example, this posting by "Bulldog Editor" on Stormfront.org, one of many essentially white supremacist websites: "Our view at the Bulldog website is that we will stream ALL beheading videos to show the barbarism of these muslim [sic.] bastards. It is only by watching these videos and being shocked into reality that people can be made aware of the nature of the filth that the Anglo-Saxon community needs to oppose. It is no use protecting people from the truth." But again, it is surely important to know that such groups exist, and also to be exposed to their views, however shocking some may find them.

Such arguments are particularly relevant to the UK where, as I have argued elsewhere,[80] images of warfare are habitually sanitized by newspapers and broadcasters alike. As Martin Bell has concluded: "We have retreated too far, certainly in British television ... We should flinch less. We should sometimes be

---

[80]Julian Petley, "Let the Atrocious Images Haunt Us," *Tell Me Lies: Propaganda and Media Distortion in the Attack on Iraq*, edited by David Miller (London: Pluto): 164–75.

willing to shock and to disturb. We should show the world more nearly as we find it, without the anaesthetic of a good taste censorship."[81] And, I would add, particularly in cases of conflict for which we as a nation share responsibility, which most certainly includes the countries which are the sites of much of the atrocity footage discussed in this chapter, namely certain countries of the Middle East. Of course, this is not to argue that to see is to understand, let alone that to know about something terrible will necessarily serve as a spur to action. As Stanley Cohen (2001: 187) has argued, "the transubstantiation of one thing (images of brutality) into another (respect for human rights) can hardly be taken for granted,"[82] and how such images are perceived depends both on how they are presented by the media concerned and on what the viewer already knows about the context in which they are situated, as well as on their pre-existing attitude to that context. In this respect, Susan Sontag is quite correct to point out that "a photograph that brings news of some unsuspected zone of misery cannot make a dent in public opinion unless there is an appropriate context of feeling and attitude... Photographs cannot create a moral position, they can reinforce one—and can help build a nascent one."[83] In our image-saturated world, there is of course a danger that as images of atrocity become more and more visible, they also become less and less comprehended, or indeed comprehensible. Various critics have also warned about the dangers of image glut, desensitization, "compassion fatigue," and so on. However, this is not an argument for the diminution or suppression of images of atrocity, even if such things were possible. In 2003, in a significant revision of many of the positions taken in *On Photography*, Sontag argued that "it seems a good in itself to acknowledge, to have enlarged, one's sense of how much suffering caused by human wickedness there is in the world we share with others." In her view, those who are perennially surprised or incredulous

> when confronted with evidence of what humans are capable of inflicting in the way of gruesome, hand-on cruelties upon other humans, has not reached moral or psychological adulthood. No one after a certain age has the right to this kind of innocence, of superficiality, to this degree of ignorance or amnesia. There now exists a vast repository of images that make it harder to maintain this kind of moral defectiveness. Let the atrocious images haunt us. Even if they are only tokens, and cannot possibly encompass most of the reality to which they refer, they still perform a vital function. The

---

[81]Martin Bell, "TV News: How Far Should We Go?," *British Journalism Review* 8, no.1 (1997): 15.

[82]Stanley Cohen, *States of Denial: Knowing About Atrocities and Suffering* (Cambridge: Polity, 2001): 187.

[83]Susan Sontag, *On Photography* (New York: Delta Publishing, 1973): 17.

[84]Susan Sontag, *Regarding the Pain of Others* (London: Penguin, 2003): 102.

images say: This is what people are capable of doing—may volunteer to do, enthusiastically, self-righteously. Don't forget.[84]

Individuals are, of course, free to choose to look away or to forget. In a democracy, that is their right. But those in power in democracies, which now means corporate as much as state forces, should not be able to impose a form of mass ignorance and amnesia. That is not their right, and even to attempt to do so is to deny a fundamental right of their citizens.

Acknowledgements

I would like to thank Jane Fae, David Allen Green, Myles Jackman, Daithí Mac Sitígh, and Paul Moody for their help while I was researching the material for this chapter.

2 THE AFFECTIVE REALITY OF SNUFF

Misha Kavka

am a late-comer to snuff. That may sound like the start of a true-confessions memoir, but I mean it less as a personal revelation than a statement about the inherent temporality of the snuff film as a certain experience of extremist cinema. Indeed, I would argue that any viewer of snuff is a late-comer in the sense that the snuff film is always about a recursive temporality—experienced as anticipation, deferral, and retrospection. This temporality underpins the simultaneous promise and postponement of the real-life murderous event that defines the genre. Whether one's response is "when will I see it?" or "what have I just seen?," viewing snuff is characterized by a looking forward that constantly evokes a looking back. The appropriate grammatical tense for snuff's temporal tension, then, is the future perfect, or the present expectation of a future in which "I will have seen" something whose shocking, titillating, disgusting or disturbing impact may, in retrospect, turn out to have been transformative.[1] This shock that I anticipate having already experienced means that the compelling persistence of the snuff film, its refusal to fade away despite lack of any evidence for its actual existence, must be addressed in terms of the temporal cadences of its affective reality rather than simply its evidentiary basis. The mythology of snuff thus stretches beyond catalogs of disturbing realism to its promise of affective entry into a backward-looking future of the viewing subject: what will I be once I become the person who has seen "it"?

The "it" of snuff, of course, is the visual encounter with "real" death. On the one hand, this is the core impossibility of the snuff film. Scholars of

---

[1]The retrospectively recognized transformation associated with traumatic vision is currently best captured by the comedic but unsettling phrase, "You can't un-see this."

exploitation cinema insist on the mythic nature of this reality, since there has never been documented evidence of someone killed on camera for the purpose of commercial entertainment.[2] On the other hand, the myth of snuff remains powerful, feeding ongoing questions of what is real and encouraging the production of "faux" snuff, those films that purport to show actual death on camera. Unlike fiction films which take snuff as their theme, the marker of success in faux snuff, not to mention its degree of disturbance, is measured by the extent to which the death *could be* real.[3] The driver behind this continued fascination with snuff has been associated with the alluring spectacle of the real[4] as well as the appetite for transgression,[5] but we should be more precise: the fascination with snuff has to do with the possibility of seeing death—not as an outcome, but as a visually definable event in time. This is not just a fascination with the staging of death, which has become a common quotient in slasher and, more recently, "torture porn" film culture,[6] but specifically has to do with the visualization of *real* death. Vivian Sobchack, in her phenomenological investigation of documentary ethics, associates this enigmatic visualization with what she calls the "charge of the real," thereby connecting the apprehension of documentary events on screen with an embodied consciousness in the viewer.[7] Although the word "charge" indicates that the real, like death, carries affective weight, in most instances these charges run along different trajectories. It is precisely at the point where the charges of death and the real meet, however, that we find the affect of snuff, and where the rhythm of anticipation and retrospection begins to twist into the recursive temporality of the future perfect.

Eschewing questions of classification based on evidentiary reality, I will argue that the snuff film is not a genre, but rather an affect. Or, more accurately, the snuff film is a genre of affect, a kind of feeling that takes the form of a double temporality around a missing event. Inspired by Brian Massumi's work on the

---

[2]Julian Petley, "Snuffed Out: Nightmares in a Trading Standards Officers Brain," in *Unruly Pleasures: The Cult Film and Its Critics*, edited by Xavier Mendik and Graeme Harper (Guildford: FAB Press, 2000): 205–19.

[3]Steve Jones, "Dying to be Seen: Snuff Fiction's Problematic Fantasies of 'Reality,'" *Scope: An Online Journal of Film and Television Studies*, 19 (2011): 13, accessed July 10, 2014, http://nrl.northumbria.ac.uk/5145/1/Jones.pdf.

[4]Geoff King, ed., *The Spectacle of the Real: From Hollywood to Reality TV and Beyond* (Bristol and Portland, OR: Intellect, 2005).

[5]Martine Beugnet and Elizabeth Ezra, "Traces of the Modern: An Alternative History of French Cinema," *Studies in French Cinema* 10, no. 1 (2010): 11–38. DOI: 10.1386/sfc.10.1.11/1.

[6]See, for example, Steve Jones, *Torture Porn: Popular Horror After Saw* (London: Palgrave, 2013).

[7]Vivian Sobchack, "The Charge of the Real: Embodied Knowledge and Cinematic Consciousness," in *Carnal Thoughts: Embodiment and Moving Image Culture* (Berkeley, Los Angeles and London: University of California Press, 2004): 258–85.

"affective fact of fear,"[8] I aim to discuss the snuff film as a form that has reality only through its affective charge, which is bifurcated into "before" and "after." The most powerful element of this genre of affect is the feeling-to-come, a feeling of horrified titillation at the prospect of what will be seen: someone murdered on camera. The second element goes the other way, producing the revolted wariness of feeling-past and even feeling-passed-up, when it is not at all clear what one has just seen. The feeling-to-come is equal parts fear and excitement; the feeling-past is equal parts disgust and disappointment, for the event of actual killing on screen is both unwatchable and unseeable. This missing event is not the eruption of violence or the act of murder—both of which are highly visualizable and so culturally encoded as to have an ingrained legibility. Rather, the missing event is what cannot be represented or captured by the camera: the moment of death itself, projected from our unacknowledged desire for this moment. As I will show through an analysis of what I call "meta-snuff," the affective ambivalence of the snuff film, in its seemingly contradictory positive and negative dimensions, is generated by this unrepresentable moment, and the mythology of snuff is sustained by its perverse yet unfulfillable promise.

Sensation and the real: What is snuff?

It should be clear from the start that I am using the term "snuff" loosely, as a catch-all category for sexually arousing, murderous violence captured on camera, rather than as a designation for commercially distributed films in which someone is actually killed, often in a pornographic context (which is a more precise definition but also a far smaller, even an empty, category). To the limited extent that the snuff film has enjoyed scholarly attention, researchers have tended to focus on the question of its evidentiary reality, since this is what distinguishes the violence in snuff from the often far more graphic yet readily digestible violence of popular genre cinema, such as slasher films. Much has been written about the blurring of fictional and factual aesthetic conventions in the making and marketing of purported snuff films.[9] This parsing of blurred conventions goes far to explain why audiences may fall into the trap of believing in the "truth" of snuff or, more likely,

---

[8]Brian Massumi, "The Future Birth of the Affective Fact: The Political Ontology of Threat," in *The Affect Theory Reader*, edited by Melissa Gregg and Gregory J. Seigworth (Durham, NC and London: Duke University Press, 2010): 52–70.
[9]See for example, Petley, "Snuffed Out"; Julian Petley, "*Cannibal Holocaust* and the Pornography of Death," in *The Spectacle of the Real: From Hollywood to Reality TV and Beyond*, edited by Geoff King (Bristol and Portland, OR: Intellect, 2005): 173–85; and Vicente Rodriguez-Ortega, "'Snuffing' Hollywood: Transmedia Horror in *Tesis*," *Senses of Cinema*, Issue 36, July 2005, accessed July 10, 2014, http://sensesofcinema.com/2005/the-metaphysics-of-violence/tesis/.

be drawn into the puzzle of dissecting the real from the not-real. Nonetheless, analyses of the reality or fakery of onscreen killing tend to overlook an integral aspect of the culture of snuff. The snuff film, after all, is first and foremost about sensation, about making audiences *feel* something in response to the images shown on screen. Situated at the violent extreme of the "shockumentary" genre, the snuff film thrives on affect, that is, on the film's capacity to shock, horrify, terrify, or gross out the viewer at the same time as it promises a pleasurable, if not immediately comprehensible, surcharge to these negative feelings. Indeed, its promise of showing killing "for real" offers an affective pay-off that suggests the question of reality in snuff is about much more for audiences than a game with the filmmaker about who can outsmart whom.

The charge generated at the threshold between fact and fiction belongs to a larger cinematic context, one that has accompanied the moving image from its early history to the era of seamless digital manipulation. Vivian Sobchack has addressed this through a phenomenological lens by focusing on the "charge of the real" encapsulated by films that flirt with the boundary between fiction and documentary. Usefully for our purposes, she frames her discussion of this charge in terms of media ethics, specifically the ethics of using digital or cinematic technologies to "undermine the public's ability to differentiate fact from fiction, the real from the imaginary or 'irreal.' "[10] Drawing on two Robert Zemeckis films as examples—*Forrest Gump* (1994) and the lesser known *Contact* (1997)—Sobchack herself undermines the concern about the public's inability to differentiate documentary from fictional footage by noting that, of course, "in both instances, film viewers were hardly confused or fooled."[11] The fact that films which mix the real and "irreal" do *not* confuse viewers—even, we might argue, in a snuff film— goes to the heart of what Sobchack calls the paradox of such filmmaking: viewers can recognize the difference between fiction and fact on screen, despite the fact that these two "*different* logical types *as genres* are both reducible to the *same* logical type *as cinematic images*" (orig. emphasis).[12] This paradox can only be resolved by expanding the focus from images alone to "distinctive *subject relations* to a variety of cinematic objects" (orig. emphasis), which operate within the consciousness of a larger extra-textual world.[13] For Sobchack, then, viewers have the capacity to distinguish between fiction and documentary on the basis of an "experienced difference in our mode of consciousness,"[14] or what the phenomenological theorist of affect Sara Ahmed might call a differently embodied "orientation" toward the

---

[10]Sobchack, "The Charge of the Real," 258.
[11]Ibid., 259.
[12]Ibid., 260.
[13]Ibid., 261.
[14]Ibid.

object in question.[15] It is in this other mode of consciousness that Sobchack locates the charge of the real, where "the cinematic image may be 'charged' for us with an *embodied* and *subjective* sense of what counts as the *existential* and *objective* 'real.'"[16]

For Sobchack, this charge turns out to be, quite literally, a matter of life and death, for seeing a real death onscreen is the limit-case of the charge of the real. Her main example, so traumatically resonant that it appears in both "The Charge of the Real" and her earlier meditation on death in film, "Inscribing Ethical Space: Ten Propositions on Death, Representation and Documentary," is the death of a rabbit in Jean Renoir's film *Rules of the Game* (1939). Unlike faux-snuff films of a much later era—for instance, *Cannibal Holocaust* (Ruggero Deodato, 1980), which also includes the real death of animals—Renoir's film does not purport to be a documentary, however fictionalized. On the contrary, it is clearly a fiction film, except for one documentary moment: the death of a rabbit in a hunting sequence. For Sobchack, this rabbit is far more than a metaphor for genre-crossing; rather, its death is that which punctures the film's fictional membrane with an existential finality that cannot be rescinded. The rabbit may have appeared for the sake of the fiction, but it dies "in the space of the real, where death counts because it is irreversible."[17] As such we *feel* its death differently from the climactic death of the fictional character André Jurieu, which "does not elicit the same level of subjective and physical shiver we feel as our very bodies 'know' the existential difference between the character's and the rabbit's ... death."[18] The rabbit's onscreen demise is charged by the "extracinematic and extratextual" knowledge,[19] experienced in our very bodies, that in this instance there is no lapine actor—unlike the human—that will walk away from the shoot unharmed.

Julian Petley has made the connection between the death of the rabbit in *Rules of the Game* and the animal deaths in *Cannibal Holocaust*, arguing with Sobchack that both function to transform narrative space into documentary space.[20] In *Cannibal Holocaust*, the purpose is quite clear. As Neil Jackson has noted,[21] the stylistic equivalence in this film between documentary footage of animal killing and fictionalized footage of human mutilation and death is intended to erase generic differences and disrupt the viewers' extracinematic knowledge, thereby creating

---

[15]Sara Ahmed, *Queer Phenomenology: Orientations, Objects, Others* (Durham, NC and London: Duke University Press, 2006).

[16]Sobchack, "The Charge of the Real," 268. Emphasis in original.

[17]Ibid., 270.

[18]Ibid., 271.

[19]Ibid.

[20]Petley, "*Cannibal Holocaust* and the Pornography of Death," 180.

[21]Neil Jackson, "*Cannibal Holocaust*, Realist Horror, and Reflexivity," *Post Script: Essays in Film and the Humanities* 21, no. 3 (2002): 42.

a documentary contagion that makes all of the extreme acts in the film equally charged with the real. This directorial tactic is a trick of sorts, an introduction of epistemological ambiguity to the fissure between documentary and fiction that, according to Sobchack, viewers otherwise know fully well through their bodies how to distinguish. Interestingly, Sobchack herself allows for "relatively rare" instances of epistemological ambiguity, an admission that gives rise to her one mention of the snuff film, whose "undecidable status as documentary or fiction" generates the "titillation, ethical outrage, and moral charge" that lie at the heart of snuff mythology.[22] I do not disagree with this assessment, but—with Steve Jones—I am more inclined to argue that the truth-effect (and affect) of snuff is less about confusing viewers with formal trickery than about the appeal of a certain *fantasy* of "really" seeing death. As Jones found in his analysis of online reviews of faux snuff films, "knowledge of [their] fictional construction 'didn't matter' in comparison with the emotional effects and the apparent reality of the action."[23] In other words, to treat viewers as potentially duped by the technical blurring of fact and fiction underestimates the "charge" of real death because it does not allow us to address why and to what extent viewers would *want* to see nonfictional, onscreen death in the first place. "Titillation" begins to get at the link between death, sensationalism, and the real, but it threatens to set aside as perversion what I suspect to be a more common curiosity to know what death looks like—and *feels* like.

The surcharge of the real

To explore this curiosity, let us leave aside the "twitch of the death nerve" of *Cannibal Holocaust*'s disemboweled turtle[24] and take a human instance of real death, one that less graphically testifies to the powerful but ethically uncomfortable urge to see dying captured on camera. I am referring to the death of British reality star Jade Goody from cervical cancer in March 2009, in the midst of a stormy national debate about the ethics and ontology of mediating real death. The immediate cause of the debate appeared to be Goody's refusal to withdraw from public view even when it was confirmed that she was dying. Indeed, her terminal diagnosis was delivered on screen as part of a reality TV show about her illness, culminating in her valedictory wedding to boyfriend Jack Tweed. Yet for all of the insistence, even in the obituaries, that Goody "died just as she chose to live, full-on in the glare of the limelight,"[25] the closing weeks of her life in fact constituted a media

---

[22]Sobchack, "Charge of the Real," 265.
[23]Steve Jones, "Dying to be Seen," 13.
[24]Petley, "*Cannibal Holocaust* and the Pornography of Death," 179.
[25]Jade Goody obituary, *Sunday Mirror*, March 22, 2009.

withdrawal for Goody. Over and over, however, commentators "misremembered" that she had died in the media spotlight, despite there being no footage of her time at home prior to her death, no shots of her dying moments, no stills of Goody lying in rest, nor even funeral footage from inside the chapel. The extent to which the myth continued to circulate that Jade Goody had died on camera is testament to the power of the fantasy that she would do so, that we could trust the classless Jade to go that far. Even sympathetic responses to Goody revealed how much the public wanted to imagine that they *had* seen "the once bright and funny young woman bec[oming] increasingly penned in by ambulances, gurneys, scanners and scalpels—all the machinery of death."[26] This, as it turned out, was a fantasy *mise-en-scène*, its props borrowed from a plethora of fiction films and TV programs that have set up the visual terms in which we understand and *desire* onscreen death as affective reality.

While Jade Goody's death was far from being a snuff film, there are nonetheless similarities to be drawn. Numerous critics at the time were appalled by her willing exposure to the flaying effects of the camera and equally appalled by the public's morbidly insatiable curiosity and complicity in watching her die. Among the ethical debates that raged there were not a few commentators who contended that Jade had sold herself to death by TV for the entertainment of the media public.[27] Although Goody was well remunerated for her relationship with the media, even as a dying woman, the public interest in seeing her die on screen evokes similarities with a far more brutal, nonconsensual form of deathly "entertainment," namely execution videos. Popularized by the leaked amateur video of Saddam Hussein's hanging in 2006, execution videos of hostages have recently multiplied as a macabre tool in the political arsenal of the Islamic State.[28] Of course, neither mediated celebrity deaths nor execution videos are snuff as such—not least because the reality of the death is not in question—but there is nonetheless a central shared element between these moments of dying on camera and the mythology of snuff. Both appeal to, and indeed generate, a desire to see the moment of passing, to have it captured and recorded on camera, so that we, too, might be able to visualize our unknowable but inevitable future. This will to see death is the first kind of charged real that we must take into account.

---

[26]Phil Gladwin, "Reality Bites: Writers Get Clever," *Script Magazine*, May/June 2009, 36.
[27]See for example, A.N. Wilson, "Parkinson is Right, Jade Represents a Paltry and Wretched Britain—But the Real Villain is Reality TV," *MailOnline*, April 8, 2009, accessed May 15, 2009, http://www.dailymail.co.uk/debate/article-1168395/A-N-WILSON-Parkinson-right-Jade-represents-paltry-wretched-Britain–real-villain-reality-TV.html; and Carol Midgely, "Jade Goody: Why Resent the Brutal Reality Show That Her Dying Has Become?," *The Times*, February 19, 2009, accessed May 15, 2009, http://www.timesonline.co.uk/tol/comment/columnists/carol_midgeley.
[28]See Julian Petley and Mark Astley's respective chapters in this collection.

The problem, as with Jade Goody and any life snuffed out on screen—even that of a rabbit—is that the passage from life to death is an unseeable moment. The indexical signs of death or dying in documentary leave us with a representational deficit. As opposed to the obsessive, even hysterical ardor with which death can come to the screen in symbolic fictions, documentary is confronted with the unrepresentability of death. No one, after all, can say what it has been like to die; no filmmaker can stage the "truth" of the event for the camera; and no camera can capture dying except *en avance* as a lived process, or *en arrière* as a corpse. This very unvisualizability compels the viewer to circle around what is not there, to anticipate and double back, and ultimately to imagine that one has, just perhaps, achieved this vision. The circling in turn generates an affective intensity that is doubly charged by loss, by the missing moment which is figurable only in and as fantasy. On the one hand, death is that which we desire to see but can never grasp, and on the other it is that which we fear to see, turning our gaze away precisely at the point when the fantasy might be exposed as such.

The "charge of the real" in snuff may well be constituted by the "unsettling epistemological ambiguity" between fiction and documentary, as Sobchack argues and Petley neatly lays out with reference to *Cannibal Holocaust*. Importantly, however, there is also what we might call a surcharge of the real, generated by the imbrication of sensation and fantasy with the witnessing of real death onscreen, especially if that death is staged for the camera and framed as such. This surcharge goes beyond epistemological ambiguity, defined in terms of evidentiary reality, to the realm of *affective* ambiguity. The pertinent question is less "did someone really get killed?" than "do I really want to see someone get killed?," which is answered by "no"…and "yes." The appeal of snuff is thus constituted by the blurring of positive and negative affects, by the anticipatory thrill of what might appear on screen underscored by the retrospective horror of having-seen. Equal parts fear and excitement, disgust and disappointment, the vaunted but missing moment of encounter with death generates both a charge *and* the need to discharge the sensation of this palpably horrific real.

Rather than being a subset of the mockumentary genre, as Sobchack frames it in "The Charge of the Real," or even a subset of the shockumentary, as scholars of extreme cinema posit, the snuff film thus mobilizes a disturbing ambiguity of affect, a conglomeration of feeling that circles around a missing event. It is for this reason that, under the heading of snuff, we so often find not actual or even faux snuff, but films that could be called *meta-snuff*. These films are not about parsing the difference between the real and the irreal, since we know them to be fictional, but are rather about encompassing the "real" of snuff within an envelope that amplifies, but also protects us from, the affective surcharge of the real.

The prophylaxis of meta-snuff: *8mm*

The negotiation of extreme "carnal resonance," Susanna Paasonen's neat phrase for the bodily affects of Internet pornography,[29] is both the theme and the charge of the subgenre of meta-snuff, namely films that are reflexively *about* snuff rather than *doing* snuff. In part an efflorescence of the apocalyptic appetite that developed in the lead-up to the new millennium (and which, it must be said, has never receded), meta-snuff films tie spectatorial identification to a character who is discovering a snuff film rather than to the snuff killer/filmmaker himself. The striking feature of meta-snuff is thus the emphasis on *watching someone watching*, an activity that has recently blossomed in the Internet phenomenon of "reaction videos," where people film themselves during their initial viewing of pornographic and/or violent viral videos.[30] From the thriller genre[31] to extremist horror[32] to the online videos where the camera is aimed at the face of the viewer rather than the filmed content, the thrill of meta-snuff has to do with the projective visualization of death mapped as sensations of seeing on someone else's face and body. Meta-snuff footage thus registers a fascination with the affective response—that "subjective and physical shiver we feel,"[33] according to Sobchack—more so than with the onscreen murder itself. In effect, meta-snuff *protects* us as viewers from the transformative shock of seeing through the operations of a double deferral: the diegetic deferral of climactic violence (a key aspect in the films *Tesis* and *Gut*) and the extra-diegetic displacement of our own watching onto a stand-in spectator.

The film *8mm*, despite being considered a critical and commercial failure (perhaps due to its uneasy positioning between underground cinema and the Hollywood mainstream), is an excellent site for an investigation of the affective deferrals that sustain meta-snuff. The premise of the film is that a private investigator, Tom Welles (Nicolas Cage), is hired by the exorbitantly wealthy and recently widowed Mrs. Christian (Myra Carter) to probe the authenticity of a disturbing 8mm film found in the late Mr. Christian's private safe. The reality of the diegetic film, "where a girl appears to be murdered," according to Mrs. Christian, is initially dismissed by Tom with breezy professional confidence: "What you seem to be talking about is called a snuff film. And from what I know, snuff films are a kind of urban myth—sex industry folklore. There's no such

---

[29]Susanna Paasonen, *Carnal Resonance: Affect and Online Pornography* (Boston, MA: MIT Press, 2011).
[30]See, for example, the numerous YouTube clips of first-time viewers of extremist videos that use the numbering meme, from the pornographic "2 Guys 1 Horse" (2005) and "2 Girls 1 Cup" (2007) to the recent necrophilic "1 Lunatic 1 Ice Pick" (2012).
[31]For example, *Tesis* (Alejandro Amenábar, 1996) and *8mm* (Joel Schumacher, 1999).
[32]For example, from *Videodrome* (David Cronenberg, 1983) to *Gut* (Elias, 2012).
[33]Sobchack, "The Charge of the Real," 271.

thing." Of course, Tom finds out how wrong he is when he is made to watch the 8mm film, but the key to *8mm* as meta-snuff is that this early viewing scene is staged in such a way that makes our watching of snuff about *his* watching. Technically, *8mm* repeats some of the cinematic conventions for showing a character watching something that spectators are not meant to see, such as over-the-shoulder or behind-the-head shots in extreme shallow focus. And, indeed, the first draft of Andrew Kevin Walker's screenplay calls for a standard shot/reverse shot alternation between the diegetic screen and an increasingly uncomfortable Tom Welles, with the murder itself occurring offscreen but reflected in Tom's reactions (Figure 2.1).

What ended up in the final cut of the film, however, is both more radical and more instructive. The snuff-viewing sequence begins *in medias*, with over-exposed grainy footage, backed only by the sound of a clattering projector, showing a scantily dressed girl with greasy hair blinking into the light of the diegetic camera, eyes drugged and baleful. Meanwhile, the extra-diegetic camera tracks back and to the left, slowly revealing Tom in a deep-focus long shot at the left side of frame, watching the film with the projector light casting rays into the darkness beside him. At this point we realize that we have been watching the film from the *back* of the diegetic screen, with Tom visually serving as the stand-in for our front-on watching as well as the affective measure of the disturbing footage that is now out of focus on the right, in a split-screen effect. Tom's grimacing face and tense body convulsively buckle and flinch in involuntary response to the actions that he continues to watch on our behalf. When the diegetic screen shows a man in a leather face-mask and vest held together by chains selecting a Bowie knife from a laden tray, there is a cut to a medium close-up of Tom closing his eyes and touching his brow with his fingers; he then forces his eyes open but retains the hand on his

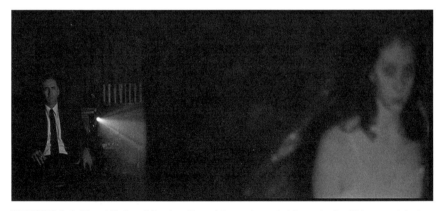

FIGURE 2.1 Tom Welles (Nicolas Cage) tensely watching what will turn out to be a snuff film in *8mm*, dir. Joel Schumacher (Columbia Pictures, 1999).

forehead, so that he is watching the film through his fingers, just as we might if Tom were not there to do it for us. As the diegetic screen erupts in an out-of-focus, extreme close-up of the Bowie knife in stabbing motions, the camera once again tracks left and the field of vision expands to include Tom, taking the paraphysical body blows for us and cycling through ever more breathless viewing reactions until the film spools off the projector.

Throughout this sequence, we viewers of meta-snuff have been engaging in a temporal and spatial logic of prophylactic displacement. Encouraging our affective ambivalence, *8mm* allows us to embrace the promise of snuff but spares us having to face the "right" side of the screen, instead refracting the murderous event through the face and body of the stand-in who sees. Our fearful anticipation of horrific events is cushioned by Tom's bodily response, as he flinches, grimaces, wipes his brow, covers his eyes, and generally exhibits all the affective signs of reluctant but captivated viewing. Whereas I noted earlier that the first kind of charged real is our desire to see the moment of death so as to visualize our inevitable future, *8mm* offers a painful glimpse of the second register of the charged real: our desire to see not simply the moment of death, but to engage visually in a moment of *killing*.[34] By channeling this unspeakable urge through Tom, we have, in effect, just had our cake and eaten it, too.

Appropriately, *8mm* ends with an unmasking, but one that refuses viewers any comfortable position because it threatens to take snuff out of the extreme and locate it firmly in the grid of ordinary desire. After exhaustively violent narrative episodes in which Tom dispatches first the perverse pornographer who arranged the shoot, then the smug lawyer who bankrolled the snuff film (at Mr. Christian's behest) and finally the sleazy porn scout who procured the girl and held the camera, he faces one lone survivor: Machine (Chris Bauer), the man in the mask and vest who butchered the girl on camera. In a desperate effort to understand the driver behind snuff, Tom forces the unmasking of Machine to get at the "truth," only to find the worst possible revelation: Machine is actually a bespectacled, pudgy guy called George, who says of his motivation, "I don't have any answers to give … I do it because I like it. Because I want to." Our shockingly ordinary desire to be visually complicit with killing is both captured and refuted at this moment: the monster is George (not us), but the monster is also everyman. Through Tom, our heroic stand-in, the meta-snuff film inserts a requisite minimal distance between us and the monster, between our sense of self and the unspeakable desire that drives our watching.

---

[34]This second kind of charged real might go some way to explaining the morbid appeal of ISIS execution videos, which in the West tend to be officially blocked as soon as they are posted—not, presumably, for ethical reasons but rather because of fears that they might, through the affective ambivalence of visual complicity with killing, incite future jihadists to join ISIS.

Affect and temporality

In what way, though, might this desire operate beyond the meta-snuff film, in examples of faux snuff and, more disturbingly, of extremist violence circulating on gore sites or in execution videos that do not offer the viewer a stand-in? In these instances, the affective ambiguity of snuff is no doubt intensified by the viewers' willingness to believe that the onscreen deaths are real, but I have been arguing that the terms of the debate about the factuality of the killing must be shifted. Most discussions of the reality of snuff, as we have seen, end up in a cul-de-sac of epistemological ambiguity, where the lack of any empirical evidence for the existence of snuff films fails to explain the persistence of the collective belief that snuff *could be* real. Rather, the longevity and persistence of the myth of snuff suggests that the question of factuality is the wrong one to pose. The conditional tense of the "*could be* real" offers a clue about how to shift the terms of the debate: rather than this being a matter of evidence-based reality, we should be thinking in terms of the temporality of the real, which may turn out to be a much more elastic matter.

Without losing sight of my earlier insistence on sensation, I would suggest that the stubborn presence of the snuff mythology can best be understood in terms of what Brian Massumi calls "the logic of affectively legitimated fact."[35] This logic refracts the stark question of the reality of death performed for the camera through two other terms, affect and temporality, thereby producing a diagrammatic triangulation where all three terms operate in relation to one another. This approach also shifts the analysis of the snuff film from production to reception, from the question of what special effects or formal elements make a snuff film compelling to the question of what compels audiences to seek out "real" death on screen. By shifting the question of the reality of snuff to this triangulation of interrelated terms, we are able to discuss the snuff film as a form that has reality for audiences in and through the double temporality of its affective charge: fearful anticipation and self-confirming, if nauseated, retrospection.

Drawing a distinction between the event as actual fact and as affective fact, Massumi is interested in the relationship between affect and threat as a way of grasping the curious effectivity of the nonevent that threatens to happen but never materializes as "a clear and present danger." Characterizing the first decade of our century in terms of a series of threat-events which never materialized, from Saddam Hussein's putative possession of weapons of mass destruction to various pandemics, Massumi pointedly asks, "How could the nonexistence of what has not happened be *more* real than what is now observably over and

---

[35]Brian Massumi, "The Future Birth of the Affective Fact," 54.

done with?"[36] The answer, laid out in a series of propositions, has to do with the affective potential of threat to *feel* real because the future event cannot, in fact, be disproven: "Threat is not real in spite of its nonexistence. It is superlatively real, because of it."[37] As a prime example, Saddam Hussein's possession of WMD, albeit fictional, took on a reality as discursive threat that has since had far-reaching geopolitical consequences. Add to this the power of fear, which is the specific affect of threat, and we are left with a reality that occupies our present but arrives with affective force from the future: "Fear is the anticipatory reality in the present of a threatening future. It is the felt reality of the nonexistence, loomingly present as the *affective fear* of the matter" (orig. emphasis).[38] That which is not (yet) real, in other words, has the capacity to be made to *feel real* through affective anticipation: "What is not actually real can be felt into being."[39]

Anticipation, however, is both a feeling and a temporality. The affective fact defined by anticipation of threat thus occupies a dual time zone, in a relay between present and future that is grammatically expressed as the conditional. The threat *could* materialize at any moment; it is both open-ended and ongoing, capable of affective contagion[40] precisely because it can neither be disproven nor closed off in the past as a completed event. The threat is always before us, fulfillable according to the preemptive temporal logic of the double conditional. In the case of Hussein and WMD, Bush's militaristic apologia for the war in Iraq insisted that *if* Hussein *could have* had WMD, then he *would have*, at which point it became a criminal irresponsibility of the State not to act to protect its people.[41] In the case of the persistent power of snuff, the same temporal logic applies: if it *could have* been real, we feel in retrospect, then it *would have*. The only difference between the national security version and the snuff version of this logic is that in snuff the temporality between "could have" and "would have" must remain as the minimal distance of epistemological ambivalence, for otherwise we would lose that slim line of protection, offered for instance by meta-snuff, between our sense of self and the desire that drives us to *watch*.

In order to bridge the gap between Massumi's concern with political events and our concern with snuff events, I wish to rephrase his claims about the political function of fear into claims about its filmic function by replacing the word "threat" with "death." Usefully for our purposes, Massumi opens the door to such a sleight of hand by wryly observing that nonevents have the power to command media

---

[36]Ibid., 52.
[37]Ibid., 53.
[38]Ibid., 54.
[39]Ibid.
[40]Ibid., 58.
[41]Ibid., 53.

attention: "We live in times when what has not happened [e.g. the threat of an avian flu pandemic] qualifies as front-page news."[42] In terms of our replacement approach, this is equivalent to asking how the nonevent, the putative but fictional event of death in the snuff film, can be real—can indeed be "more real" on the media screen than what is observably true. Let us try the death-for-threat replacement experiment with four particular claims made by Massumi as observations:

- Threat is from the future. It is what might come next.
- Threat does have an actual mode of existence: fear, as foreshadowing. Threat has an impending reality in the present. The actual reality is affective.
- *Observation*: If we feel a threat, there was a threat. Threat is affectively self-causing.
- *Corollary*: If we feel a threat, such that there was a threat, then there always will have been a threat. Threat is once and for all, in the nonlinear time of its own causing.[43]

This is what comes of the observations if we replace "threat" with the word "death":

- *Death* is from the future. It is what must come next.
- *Death* does have an actual mode of existence: fear, as foreshadowing.
- *Death* has an impending reality in the present. The actual reality is affective.
- The ontology of death: "*Death* is not real in spite of its nonexistence. It is superlatively real, because of it."

Q.E.D.: the nonevent of death in snuff film has affective reality: "Death is once and for all, in the nonlinear time of its own causing."

Whether sliding out of frame, as in *8mm*, or delivered in jarringly out-of-focus close-ups and quick edits, as in *The Great American Snuff Film* (Sean Tretta, 2003), or aestheticized into blooms of cut skin and rivulets of blood, as in *Flower of Flesh and Blood* (Hideshi Hino, 1985), the death-event is missing onscreen except as that which is always about to come or has just passed. The snuff death is thus not "really" there, but is nonetheless so charged as to be affectively real. It is missing in at least three senses: it is not real death; even if it were real, death itself is unfilmable; and to the extent that it does appear, we engage in strategies of deferral and displacement, jumping over the terrifying gap in anticipation of a

---

[42]Ibid., 52.
[43]Ibid., 53, 54.

future perfect moment when we will already *have seen*. Watching snuff films thus involves a temporal toggle between present, future, and past, consisting of fearful anticipation of a future moment in which we will already have seen something whose queasy affect confirms in retrospect that it *could have* been real. Add to this the unspeakable factor of our desire to watch snuff in the first place, and we have to conclude that the threat of this "affectively legitimated fact"[44] has but one object: this thing that I cannot know, that threatens me from the future, is my own desire to watch and be complicit in snuff killing. It is this threat that I must protect myself against, shading my eyes in an effort to (not) see, but it is also through this affective ambivalence that death in snuff functions as real. As Massumi points out, that which threatens from the future cannot be disproven. No snuff film can prove its reality, but then again no snuff film has to. Ultimately, it does not matter whether snuff films exist or not, can be located or not, since the affect is what is real. The feeling shall make it so.

---

[44]Ibid., 54.

3 ANIMAL SNUFF

Simon Hobbs

This chapter reflects upon the use of actual violent death in fictional films, defining an alternative area of critical study that consolidates and elaborates upon the broader scholarship of genuine cinematic violence. That alternative area is henceforth, and for lack of a more evocative term, referred to as "animal snuff." After an exploration of the cultural parameters of this subgeneric category, it will be determined how these images of actual animal slaughter have been understood within the critical sphere, the impact this has upon the cultural conceptualization of screened animal killings, and how they affect judgments of the films in which they appear. Finally, in order to map critical commentary as important elements within the wider understanding of the films under consideration, a paratextual methodology will be deployed, utilizing *Weekend* (Jean-Luc Godard, 1967) and *Cannibal Holocaust* (Ruggero Deodato, 1980) as examples of films which circulate amid distinct reception discourses, eliciting varied responses for their use of real animal death in the pursuit of both textual metaphor and spectatorial provocation.

As a cinematic concept, snuff originally referred to the illegal recording of a premediated, unsimulated murder created for the purposes of both scopophilic pleasure and economic gain. Boaz Hagin notes that snuff films have haunted the popular imagination for decades,[1] and while its actual existence is debatable, it has entered into the horror film lexicon, where images of pseudosnuff in narrative feature films seek to replicate the proposed existence of real death films.[2] Although clearly illusory, these fictional representations of murder both influence and confirm the expectations audiences retain regarding the aesthetics of genuine snuff images, further advancing the legend surrounding the phenomena while

---

[1]Boaz Hagin, "Killed Because of Lousy Ratings: The Hollywood History of Snuff," *Journal of Popular Film and Television* 38, no. 1 (2010): 44.

[2]See Steve Jones, "Dying to be Seen: Snuff-Fiction's Problematic Fantasies of 'Reality,'" *Scope* 19, (2011), accessed July 10, 2014. http://nrl.northumbria.ac.uk/5145/1/Jones.pdf.

giving it a tangible visual register. Primarily, the fictionalized sequences imitate certain amateurisms, with handheld cameras, poor quality film stock, and subpar video reproduction reflecting the illegitimate and prohibited nature of the action. As a result, pseudosnuff relies largely upon a realist mode, immediately evoking a pre-established sense of authenticity through a duplication of the visual motifs associated with documentary filmmaking. Additionally, these simulated acts are often loaded with sexual overtones, the cheap porno loop aesthetics merging with the ocular register of simulated murder, and intimations of sadomasochistic desire.

Whereas pseudosnuff proliferates within fictional narratives, a *type* of snuff film circulates on Internet "shock sites." In an age saturated with theoretical notions of reality—a cultural climate that Steve Jones argues is changing the way audiences engage with pseudosnuff[3]—these websites (of which Bestgore.com remains a chief example) host and collate various video clips and pictures designed to disgust and repulse the visitor, accommodating videos which serve as an effective index of all manner of accidental, premeditated, and legally sanctioned real death. The footage that proliferates on these sites circulates as perhaps the most accessible and authentic form of snuff available for consumption in the present climate.

Yet, it must be recognized that much of the footage present on these sites was not created or intended for commercial distribution and has often been disseminated and consumed prior to their categorization on such websites. Consequently, while some material has been collected and reframed in an arrangement which encourages scopophilic (as opposed to onanistic) identification, it did not originate within a traditional commercial setting and subsequently inhabits a separate category of the snuff phenomena. In relation to this, Julian Petley argues that snuff has been largely defined by popular media mythmaking, generated by the underground distribution of controversial imagery seen within the horror genre, and has been used to aid the stricter censorship of fictional cinematic violence in the UK.[4] Here, the inconsistent and slippery nature of snuff is exposed, a characteristic which helps to further define the conceptualization of actual animal slaughter within nominally fictional settings.

Animal snuff, due to its focus upon nonhuman living creatures, occurs independently from the questions surrounding authenticity which plague traditional snuff discourses. American films such as *The Hunting Party* (Don Medford, 1971), *Pink Flamingos* (John Waters, 1972), *Apocalypse Now* (Francis Ford Coppola, 1979), *Southern Comfort* (Walter Hill, 1981), and *Vampire's Kiss* (Robert Bierman, 1988) have provided some of the rare instances of real death

---

[3]Ibid., 2.
[4]Julian Petley, "Snuffed Out: Nightmares in a Trading Standards Officer's Brain," in *Unruly Pleasures: the Cult Film and Its Critics*, edited by Xavier Mendik and Graeme Harper (Guildford: FAB Press, 2000).

available within commercial cinema, capitalizing upon the unsimulated spectacle of the premeditated death of a living organism within the narrative's fictional space.

As Akira Mizuta Lippet argues, the actualization of animal snuff is inextricable from its cultural reading due to the ethical implications and societal anxiety surrounding the slaughter of animals for spectacle.[5] Additionally, the term "animal" (as used in the familiar Hollywood end credits disclaimer "no animals were harmed in the making of this film") only includes a part of the broader natural world, most often encompassing nonhuman mammals, birds, and reptiles.[6] Therefore, there remains certain flexibility into what can be classed as "animal" within cinematic discourses. Furthermore, notions of cinematic realism and the division of fictional and documentary modes heavily impact upon the reading of onscreen slaughter, as either a mode of entertainment or a factual chronicling of events created for educational purposes. Moreover, the treatment of animals shifts considerably in both historical and geographical terms, as contrasting attitudes and cultural rituals define how filmmakers and audiences engage with the representation of nonhuman beings. It is these fluctuating attitudes, which to an extent reflect the unstable definitions of traditional snuff, which must be further explored in order to appropriately define the strictures of the animal snuff category.

Therefore, from the outset, the vexed question of what constitutes an "animal" must be considered. In the first instance, it is crucial to specify here that "animal" refers to nonhuman creatures as the term itself is selective. It proves useful to refer to the work of Peter Beatson, who states that "humans forge a large part of the destiny of many other species. Animals' life experiences and their very identities are to a very large extent determined by how humans think and feel about them."[7] Beatson's idea of animal lives being shaped by human thoughts and emotions allows us to more readily navigate how they become defined and treated within the cinematic realm. Consequently, this level of influence in attempting to shape and control the animal world has produced a hierarchy that dictates both the legal status and the levels of sympathy, shock, and "worth" afforded particular species within film narratives. At the top of this structure rests the mammal, due mainly to humans' evolutionary status within the category, followed by birds and, to a slightly lesser extent, reptiles. Fish, the last of the vertebrates, live in a diametrically opposed space to humans and are therefore generally thought of as things rather than living beings.[8] As a result, they inhabit a zone lower on the hierarchical

---

[5]See Akira Mizuta Lippit, "Death of an Animal," *Film Quarterly* 56, no. 1 (2002): 11.
[6]Ibid., 9.
[7]Peter Beatson, "Mapping Human Animal Relations," in *Theorizing Animals: Re-thinking Humanimal Relations*, edited by Tania Signal and Nik Taylor (Boston, MA: Brill, 2011): 23.
[8]See Andrew Linzey, *Project Muse. The Global Guide to Animal Protection* (Urbana: University of Illinois Press, 2013): 47.

ladder and are thus afforded less protection both culturally (in regards to over-fishing and ocean pollution) and cinematically. Finally, insects, cephalopods, and crustaceans, due mostly to the oft-repeated assertion that they are incapable of feeling pain and suffering,[9] occupy a sector which offers them minimal care and compassion. This basic breakdown, which itself contains a certain instability (dolphins are both mammals and sea dwellers, yet are considered "worthy" due to their heightened intelligence), impacts the limitations and boundaries of animal snuff in a variety of ways.

Firstly, it raises questions regarding what can indeed be considered as animal snuff. It is perhaps clear that the violent onscreen death of a large mammal, like the ox in *Apocalypse Now*, fits the criteria of animal snuff due to the social and cultural positioning of the animal. However, what about the killing of insects, or sequences of fishing in which real fish are caught? It is clear that further delineation is needed to construct a robust category which accounts for these subjective and emotive readings of animal life.

Objectification is central to any debate concerning the human treatment of animals, and is vital to a definition of animal snuff. Dawne McCance argues that animals have been "turned into stone" by human interaction, positioning them as useful and disposable products within the urbane economy.[10] As focal elements in socio-cultural activity as varied as food production, industrial labor and pet ownership, animals live as subservient to humans, inscribing the latter's power and superiority in any level of interaction or exchange. This position is born from the power relations that inform language, and more importantly, the lack of "language" (comprehendible to humans) present within the animal kingdom. Through the desire and the ability of the human race to theorize the animal world, categories and concepts have been created and agreed upon which socially justify certain human/animal behaviors and conducts.[11] Animals cannot contest these categorizations and treatments and are further cast as subservient to human life and culture.[12] This concept of language as a source of power over the animal "other" is fundamental to not only the power dimensions which motivate animal snuff as a cinematic tool, but those that allow its circulation within the cinematic sphere, rationalizing what Beatson calls the process of "fatal contact."[13]

---

[9]Ibid., 40.
[10]Dawne McCance, *Critical Animal Studies: An Introduction* (Albany: State University of New York, 2013).
[11]Lisa Kemmerer, "Theorising 'Others,'" in *Theorizing Animals: Re-thinking Humanimal Relations*, edited by Tania Signal and Nik Taylor (Boston, MA: Brill, 2011): 69.
[12]Arran Stibbe, *Animals Erased: Discourse, Ecology, and Reconnection with the Natural World* (Middletown, CT: Wesleyan University Press, 2012): 19.
[13]Beatson, "Mapping Human Animal Relations," 26.

Paul Sheehan agrees that the screen manifestation of animals rests at the core of understanding otherness,[14] while Randy Malamud concentrates further upon notions of supremacy by asserting that most onscreen human–animal encounters see an expression of harm via pathways of power.[15] Immediately, Malamud's framing of harm and power becomes applicable to the conceptualization of animal snuff, with the act of slaughter dependent on the exertion of human omnipotence—most often in the form of a lethal strike with a weapon. Consequently, the function of the human is centralized, meaning a filmed act of animal on animal violence, such as those commonly featured on nature programs, is not animal snuff due to the lack of human interaction (although arguably, the results of such material could provoke similar levels of shock and sympathy).

Accordingly, irrespective of any animal's position within this subjectively motivated hierarchal structure, the application of force leading to death is fundamental to the rendition of animal snuff. Thus, the killing of an ox (*Apocalypse Now*) or a cockroach (*Vampire's Kiss*), when presented as a constituent narrative event or spectacle, is by definition a sequence of animal snuff. Nevertheless, it is important to be mindful of the subjective and emotive dialogs that inform discussions of ethics and return to the earlier discussion of the animal hierarchy. In order to navigate the categorical boundaries of animal snuff, it is imperative to note that due to the subjective opinions that motivate the consideration of nonhuman beings across societal sectors, different instances of screened animal slaughter carry different levels of shock, compassion, and horror. Consequently, certain sequences circulate as more obvious and blatant examples of the act.

In animal snuff, human supremacy is enabled due to both the physical activity of inflicting damage upon the creature's body and the manipulation inherent within the practice of creating a visual record of the act. Home video and, in turn, digital technology has ensured that sounds and images of slaughter and pain can be paused and replayed by a human consumer within the private sphere. In line with Lippet's suggestion that, through the act of recording animal death the creature is given a second life,[16] the process of consumption further exposes the power relations that rest at the center of animal snuff. Through the act of visual consumption, especially prevalent in the age of advanced home technologies, the audience can control the event, killing and bringing life to the animal at will. Here, both the onscreen perpetrator and the spectator agree (explicitly or implicitly) with the exertion of power over the animal figure.[17] Therefore, animal snuff is defined

---

[14]Paul Sheehan, "Against the Image: Herzog and the Troubling Politics of the Screen Animal," *Substance: A Review of Theory & Literary Criticism* 37, no. 3 (2008): 122.
[15]Randy Malamud, "Animals on Film: The Ethics of the Human Gaze," *Spring* 83 (2010): 2.
[16]Lippit, "Death of an Animal," 13.
[17]Stibbe, *Animals Erased*, 20.

as a phenomenon which reinforces humankind's drive toward violent dominion over the animal body, enacting physical harm and recording its effects, allowing the human consumer to command, maneuver, and manipulate the electronic reproduction of the living being, thus accentuating this grim narrative spectacle of the real.

The two channels of power must run adjacently, meaning that the act must be both an originally choreographed, unsimulated turn of violence undertaken against a living organism, and a sequence placed within a commercially viable, fictional cinematic product. This taxonomy eliminates the instances of accidental animal death which occur during the production process of numerous narratives and never actually appear (or at least draw attention to themselves) onscreen. Hence, the reported deaths of various livestock during the production of *The Hobbit: An Unexpected Journey* (Peter Jackson, 2012) does not constitute animal snuff as the creatures perished offscreen and their demise was not part of the film's narrative framework. Similarly, the animal deaths which enabled historically the production and economic progression of the film industry fall outside of the parameters of the category. While Erik van Ooijen notes that a large number of films show the yields of slaughter, through either food or props,[18] the lack of actual recorded killings denies the viewer the modes of consumption and titillation intrinsic to discourses surrounding snuff footage.

By collapsing the barriers between reality and fantasy, Donald Anderson argues that unsimulated death breaks the promise cinema has with its audience that the events witnessed are a fabricated enactment.[19] For this reason, premeditated animal death on film is a paradoxical cinematic entity, a document of the real which is framed within an imaginary fictional realm, actualizing the relationship between documentary and fiction inherent in the mythology underpinning the urban legends of snuff. However, this argument is further convoluted by the presence of real death within many documentaries. Brutal scenes of animal slaughter are present within documentary texts such as *Sharkwater* (Rob Stewart, 2006) and *The Cove* (Louie Psihoyos, 2009), and although the sequences are as violent, shocking, and emotive as many examples of animal snuff in fictional films, they are not classified as such due to their reliance upon what van Ooijen usefully terms "the journalistic rule of simply registering rather than provoking the violence."[20] It is this strict adherence to anominal actuality within the documentary realm which is essential to its distinction from the animal snuff category. In short, the

---

[18]Erik Van Ooijen, "Cinematic Shots and Cuts: On the Ethics and Semiotics of Real Violence in Film Fiction," *Journal of Aesthetics & Culture* 3 (2011): 10.
[19]Donald Anderson, "How the Horror Film Broke Its Promise: Hyperreal Horror and Ruggero Deodato's *Cannibal Holocaust*," *Horror Studies* 4, no. 1 (2013): 111.
[20]Van Ooijen, "Cinematic Shots and Cuts," 12.

distinction is defined through the stark fact that these instances of abuse would be happening independent of the camera's presence and are not organized for, or motivated by the purposes of a fictional narrative.

In this sense, the animals that appear within these documentaries are not "performers" but subjects. As Gregory Szarycz work on the animal actor highlights, the history of animals in film has been beset by uncertainties about how far image makers can go in setting up events for the camera, and the level of assistance needed to get the animals to "perform."[21] Although Schung Cauflield suggests that animals are anti-performers—unrestricted by the constraints of traditional "acting" and therefore capable of a certain freedom and spontaneity not afforded human actors[22]—the role of humans as instigators of violence during animal snuff removes the ability of animals to circumvent performance, and forces it to conform to the enactment of human will. Thus, the animal must "act" accordingly and "perform" its role through to the instance of its death. Hence, within the processes of animal snuff, the creature is provided with the maximum human assistance in the "performance" of its duties, a human/animal relationship absent in the documentary mode.

Nevertheless, pseudodocumentary phenomena such as the Italian mondo cycle, most notably in the form of *Mondo Cane* (Gualtiero Jacopetti, Franco Prosperi and Paolo Cavara, 1962) and *Africa Addio* (Gualtiero Jacopetti and Franco Prosperi, 1966), further problematized images of both animal and human suffering, relishing in their taboo material and often featuring sequences of ritualized violence, sexual explicitness, and animal slaughter. Often set within the "untouched," but politically unstable environments of Africa and South America, the mondo cycle traded off the promise of forbidden spectacle, combining straight documentary reportage, staged or recreated events and pre-existing footage to create a hybrid mode which drifts between a rendition of actuality and a rigorously, often opportunistically preplanned manipulation of the events occurring onscreen. This combination, as Mark Goodall notes, has made the mondo cycle difficult to analyze as it does not fit comfortably into traditional cinematic histories or categories.[23]

Significantly, this manipulation of reality affects audience perceptions of the multiple acts of animal slaughter that litter mondo narratives. As much of the footage deployed within Mondo cinema circulated prior to its encasement within

---

[21]Gregory Szarycz, "The Representation of Animal Actors: Theorizing Performance and Performativity in the Animal Kingdom," *Theorizing Animals: Re-thinking Humanimal Relations*, edited by Tania Signal and Nik Taylor (Boston, MA: Brill, 2011): 167.

[22]Schung Caufield, "The Plight of the Screen Animal: Animal Disappearance and Death on Film," *Film Matters* 2, no. 2 (2011): 21.

[23]Mark Goodall, "Shockumentary Evidence: The Perverse Politics of the Mondo Film," in *Remapping World Cinema: Identity, Culture and Politics in Film*, edited by Stepanie Dennison and Song Hwee Lim (London: Wallflower Press, 2006): 118–25.

the pseudodocumentary format, it is perhaps useful to suggest that it falls into the documentary category. However, in the case of the mondo film, the way these sequences are appropriated and reframed within the narrative affects the manner in which they are consumed. The structure of the mondo films relied upon loosely related sequences that, through western eyes, cataloged acts of cultural peculiarity and excess, objectifying a racially encoded, colonial "other." It seemed quite appropriate then, that this generic reduction of human figures to objects of bestial curiosity would also accommodate quite comfortably a morbid curiosity regarding the exterior and interior form of the animal body within these narratives. As Goodall states, Mondo films' actively engage with the cinema of attractions,[24] enticing the audience through hyperbole and sensation. The eschewing of the educational base of documentary film recodes the images of animal death and mutilation within the furnishings of exploitation, with the body and its destruction spectacularized while harboring the voyeuristic gaze common within both fictional pseudosnuff images and those that proliferate on "shock" websites. Therefore, the classification of animal snuff is dependent, especially within the consideration of mondo cinema, on the way the audience are asked to gaze at images of death and how the film seeks to influence the spectator's consumption and comprehension of the act. In mondo cinema, through a framework which incorporates elements of travelog and exoticism, underpinned by a persistent and fearful racism, the spectator is invited to indulge in the corporeal spectacle of both human and animal mortalities.

Unlike the mondo cycle, "straight" nonfictional renditions of animal death (as seen in countless wildlife documentaries) have allowed filmmakers to circumvent accusations of prurience and exploitation. However, several notable films, in a process similar to that which prevails within mondo cinema, use sequences of slaughter within a fictional composition. In addition to those American examples cited earlier, European films such as Sergei Eisenstein's *Strike* (1925), Georges Franju's *Le Sang des bêtes* (1949), Rainer Werner Fassbinder's *In a Year of Thirteen Moons* (1978), Gaspar Noé's *Carne* (1991), and Michael Haneke's *Benny's Video* (1992) feature instances of industrialised or agricultural slaughter. Yet, these documented acts, recorded but not conventionally directed by the director, are rehoused within fictional narratives, assuming the varied status of symbol, allegory, or metaphor and are appreciated today as legitimate techniques amid the staples of art cinema practice. This process raises questions regarding the "snuff-like" qualities of the sequences, created within a documentary mode yet given significance within the scripted narrative and collapsing the barriers between fiction and reality. However, even though the practice of repositioning the real

---

[24]Ibid., 119.

within fictional constructs remains, the prevailing discourse of exploitation that informed audience engagement with mondo narratives is removed. Within these principally fictional narratives, the audience is not forced to consume the acts as a series of taboo spectacles, but rather to engage with the images in a state strongly diluted by the overarching engagement with a fictional construct. In this sense, these scenes, despite sharing the linage of mondo cinema, would have happened irrespective of the camera's presence, mediating the association with a cinema of attractions and ultimately allowing them to exist on the peripheries of the animal snuff category.

In this context, the lines separating fiction and reality for animal snuff are often indistinct, altering both the narrative significance and ethical implications of the events witnessed. However, what often resonates is a sense of the animal body as a tool of human supremacy within a wider sensationalist lexicon. Yet, attitudes regarding the treatment of animals shifts significantly on a trans-global basis, meaning opinions regarding exploitation and abuse are deeply ingrained within specific cultural traditions that are rarely stable. Exposed neatly within the differing dietary codes of particular religious practices, and mapped extensively in *The Global Guide to Animal Protection*, animals are given a mutable significance depending on their geographic location and cultural surroundings. This—like the earlier discussion of animal hierarchies—impacts the classifications implicit within animal snuff and its borders, as the screened death of any animal stimulates different reactions in specific cultural circumstances.

A key instance of this is present within Park Chan-wook's *Oldboy* (2003), a South Korean film that achieved global success and recognition, as well as inspiring a Hollywood remake in 2013. The film achieved a certain notoriety partly due to the sequence in which Dae-su Oh (Min-sik Choi), after being released from a mysterious incarceration, consumes a live octopus in a restaurant. The visualization of this event is a clear expression of power over the animal being, providing the sequence with a perceptual and emotional frisson that runs as a parallel construction to the film's narrative momentum. Although the act encompasses the chief determinants of animal snuff, the ingestion of a live octopus carries a differing cultural reading within the context of its domestic exhibition and consumption. Despite the fact that western audiences might view the sequence with revulsion due to its sheer unfamiliarity and removal from accepted norms of social behavior and culinary decorum, the consumption of live octopus, called Sannakji, is an accepted convention of Korean cuisine. This normalizes the action within its regional discourse, removing the shock inherent in the cinematic and cultural comprehension of animal snuff.

Therefore, the categorization of such a sequence as animal snuff is dependent upon the viewer's cultural background. This shifting discourse, which opens up the interpretation of animal snuff to cultural and geographic subjectivity, is vital in framing what is meant by such a generic category and the type of sequences it can be applied to. The example of *Oldboy* exposes western ideological assumptions which motivate definitions of animal snuff, drawing attention to the limitations of a globally inclusive category. Therefore, it is perhaps useful to suggest that animal snuff must retain a flexibility, allowing for not only the inherently emotive subject matter, but also a level of cultural subjectivity that points to the innately slippery nature of snuff in general. The vast international discrepancies in the cultural treatment of animals mean that animal snuff must be recognized as a malleable cinematic form shaped and defined by the cultural needs of the author(s) and the national cinema in which they are active.

Significantly, while open to debate along cultural and geographical lines, animal snuff assumes other layers of contention and debate within the critical sphere. This has been given further resonance through the penetration of real animal slaughter in both "high" and "low" cultural environs, and can be usefully mapped out when considering the distinctions drawn between Jean Luc Godard's *Weekend* and Ruggero Deodato's *Cannibal Holocaust*. Although encased within the differing cinematic environs of art and exploitation cinema, these films feature comparable sequences of animal slaughter which portray the death of living creatures in line with the taxonomy outlined above. Addressing these narratives and their critical identities allows for an exploration of how animal snuff's cultural status is also influenced by critical assumptions regarding "quality" and value, its varied usage navigating the intersections of, and barriers between "high" and "low" culture.

Cannibal Holocaust is the *ne plus ultra* of the Italian cannibal movie, a subgenre which reared its head sporadically for the best part of a decade and was characterized by other titles such as *Deep River Savages* (Umberto Lenzi, 1972), *Last Cannibal World* (Ruggero Deodato, 1977), *Mountain of the Cannibal God* (Sergio Martino, 1978), *Eaten Alive!* (Umberto Lenzi, 1980), and *Cannibal Ferox* (Umberto Lenzi, 1981). These titles attained notoriety for their incorporation of real animal death imagery (sequences that were often recycled across different films, a practice that in itself points to the importance producers and distributors placed upon the shock value inherent in such practices), often orchestrated specifically by the filmmakers themselves and amplifying body horror elements already present through the conventional utilization of special make-up and prosthetics in the simulation of human death and evisceration. *Cannibal Holocaust* is easily read as a response to the mondo cycle itself, constructing a (self) conscious, condemnatory discourse against the contemptuous, destructive and, ultimately, homicidal acts of a group of American documentary filmmakers shooting a documentary entitled *The Green Inferno*. This element of the film develops in parallel to its own prurient and exploitative approach to its most sensational aspects, frequently in the form of sequences depicting rape and sexual mutilation, but perhaps most disturbingly through the genuine animal killings performed by cast members within the nominally fictional realm. As Neil Jackson[25] has argued, although primarily driven by narrative considerations, the film is replete with self-reflexive deviations from conventional classical style. The film depicts the deaths of six animals (a coati, a turtle, a spider, a monkey, a snake, and a pig), and although each instance is important to the broader discourses of animal snuff, Jackson notes that the slaughter of the turtle is the most explicit and prolonged example of animal mutilation to occur over the course of the narrative.[26] This scene, as Julian Petley points out,[27] is shot in a mock documentary style, further exposing the shifting borders of animal snuff, which in turn plays upon the claims to veracity evinced in the film's opening title proclamation that "for the sake of authenticity, some sequences have been retained in their entirety."

The sequence sees the characters haul the turtle out of a shallow river, whereupon it is swiftly beheaded via a single machete blow. Although this can be assumed to have resulted in an instantaneous death, Petley notes that the portrayal of the act in such vivid, unflinching and detailed close-up makes the audience aware that both the event itself and the creature whose demise the camera has observed were incontrovertibly real.[28] The events that take place thereafter, such as the removal of the shell and organs, are undertaken against a lifeless (but noticeably twitching) cadaver, with the corpse being disembowelled and amputated while members of the *Green Inferno* crew mockingly hold up removed body parts to the camera, anticipating revulsion and abhorrence on the part of any potential audience member. The manner in which the characters interact with the deceased corpse furthers the sequence's relationship to traditions of snuff, as both the tactile manipulation and visual presentation of the carcass is crucial to the comprehension of the scene. Importantly, within the prolonged duration of the sequence, the shot selection deliberately lingers on severed limbs and disembowelled organs in order to stress the corporeality of the act.

In contrast, *Weekend* is embedded securely within the framework of European art cinema of the 1960s, a status accorded through its place within a particularly politically engaged phase of the career of Jean Luc Godard. The film's narrative, such as it is, is articulated through a nonclassical form, encompassing direct camera address, unconventional structural elements (such as intertitles), nonsequential editing and prolonged image duration, all underpinned by a strong engagement with, and interrogation of aesthetics and their ideological underpinning in the 1960s and beyond. Furthermore, while the cultural image of Deodato is steeped

---

[25]See Neil Jackson, "*Cannibal Holocaust*, Realist Horror, and Reflexivity," *Post Script* 21, no. 3 (2002): 32–45.

[26]Ibid.

[27]Julian Petley, "*Cannibal Holocaust* and the Pornography of Death," in *Spectacle of the Real: From Hollywood to Reality TV & Beyond*, edited by Geoff King (Bristol: Intellect Books, 2005): 178

[28]Ibid., 180.

in the stigma of cinematic controversy due to the status of *Cannibal Holocaust* and *House on the Edge of the Park* (1980) as seminal Euro-exploitation films, Godard's critical image is ingrained within the general understanding of political counter-cinema and auteur filmmaking. This notion is evident within David Nicholls' argument that "Godardinism"[29] became an aesthetic style that could be copied by other filmmakers. This evaluation of Godard positions him at the forefront of cinematic innovation and advancement, and thus grants his cinema a "high" cultural capital denied to the work of filmmakers like Deodato.

Weekend's presentation of animal death occurs as Roland and Corinne Durand (played by Jean Yanne and Mireille Darc) are captured during a country drive by a group of leftist revolutionaries. Here, a static camera films the slaying of a pig and bird in two unedited sequences. The pig's head is struck with a large sledgehammer, and as it twitches from the impact, it has its throat stabbed twice and finally slit. Following that, the fowl is swiftly decapitated, leaving the effect of a lethal blow visible while the process of death is depicted in full. Although the scene is shorter than its equivalent within *Cannibal Holocaust*, featuring none of the extended mutilation of the carcass seen in Deodato's film, it still utilizes the anticipation of an emotional frisson implicit within the anticipated response to images of genuine death, forcing the audience to consume the same transgressive spectacle of human control and animal objectification.

Significantly, the animal snuff in *Weekend* is preceded by title cards that read "The September Massacres," a historical allusion that refers the spectator to events of the French Revolution in 1792 that resulted in the death of many imprisoned counter-revolutionaries. The proximity of this formal strategy to the animal snuff sequences amplify the film's engagement with the socio-political ramifications of French history, allowing the sequence of real death to function within a metaphorical framework. This is a marked contrast to the layers of social and cultural commentary embedded within *Cannibal Holocaust's* use of animal death, in which the appropriation of mondo aesthetics supports an interrogation of the limits of film and television culture as conduits of a fragile, mediated "truth."

Gerard Genette notes that critical practice, whether in the form of short reviews or long-form articles, can be approached as paratextual items and examined as artifacts that maintain the ability to characterize, define, and change the meaning of a film. Identifying such critical writings as "epitexts,"[30] these ultimately influence what John Ellis calls the "narrative image"[31] and are crucial in forming

---

[29]David Nicholls, "Godard's *Weekend*: Totem, Taboo and the Fifth Republic," *Sight and Sound* 49, no. 1 (1979): 22.

[30]Gerard Genette, *Paratexts: Thresholds of Interpretation* (Cambridge: Cambridge University Press, 1997): 344.

[31]John Ellis, *Visible Fictions: Cinema, Television, Video* (London: Routledge, 1992): 31.

its predominant identity and ultimate sense of cultural worth, often prior to the actual experience of the film by general audience members.

In evaluating the use of animal death imagery in *Weekend* and *Cannibal Holocaust*, it is useful to reflect upon David Bordwell's notion of "conceptual fields"[32] and Xavier Mendik's and Ernest Mathijs' idea of the "high white" tradition.[33] Bordwell argues that films are given meaning through interactions with critically selected schemas,[34] and that "the critic constructs meaning through a complex process of assumption, testing, projection, inferential trial and error, and comparable activities."[35] These frameworks are informed by external factors, and Bordwell argues that readings can be tailored to suit certain impulses. Mendik and Mathijs's work builds on this, arguing that European film criticism is motivated by certain pre-established frameworks which seek to cater exclusively for highbrow tastes.[36] Due to the influence these conceptual frameworks and hierarchal taste structures retain over the shaping of a film's cultural identity, we can begin to understand how critical interpretations respond to animal snuff, grafting additional meanings to its onscreen manifestation.

The conceptual fields used to frame *Weekend* and *Cannibal Holocaust* are oppositional, and it can be claimed that this difference is embedded within the discourses of taste discussed by Mendik and Mathijs. While it is clear that these two films occupy a place in the long history of "high" and "low" taste slippage mapped by several film scholars (including Mark Betz,[37] Joan Hawkins,[38] and Jeffery Sconce[39]), and although a shared set of thematic preoccupations can be found within the portrayal of two societies (one nominally civilized, the other characterized by notions of primitive savagery) damaged by the failures of capitalism and European bourgeois cultures of consumption, much of the scholarship contributes (deliberately or inadvertently) to the longstanding critical hierarchy which sees a validation of art cinema over exploitation industries. An assessment of various reviews of *Weekend* provides evidence of this, as it becomes

---

[32]David Bordwell, "Film Interpretation Revisited," *Film Criticism* 27, no. 3 (1993): 93–119.

[33]Ernest Mathijs and Xavier Mendik, "Introduction: Making Sense of Extreme Confusion: European Exploitation and Underground Cinema," in *Alternative Europe: Eurotrash and Exploitation Cinema since 1945*, edited by Ernest Mathijs and Xavier Mendik (London: Wallflower Press, 2004): 1–18.

[34]Bordwell, "Film Interpretation Revisited," 102.

[35]Ibid., 103.

[36]Mathijs and Mendik, "Introduction," 3.

[37]Mark Betz, "Art, Exploitation, Underground," in *Defining Cult Movies: The Cultural Politics of Oppositional Taste*, edited by Mark Jancovich, Antonio Lazaro Reboll, Julian Stringer, and Andy Willis (Manchester: Manchester University Press, 2003): 202–22.

[38]Joan Hawkins, *Cutting Edge: Art Horror and the Horrific Avant Garde* (Minneapolis: University of Minnesota Press, 2000).

[39]Jeffrey Sconce, " 'Trashing' the Academy: Taste, Excess and an Emerging Politics of Cinematic Style," *Screen* 36, no. 4 (1995): 371–93.

clear that the precirculating auteur status of Godard clearly initiates a critical framework which seeks to consolidate and affirm his canonization.

Instances are present within the work of John Westbrook,[40] who explores Godard's film through appropriation of Georges Bataille's work on expenditure, applying a schema based within reoccurring concepts of intellectual thought,[41] and Peter Whitehead, who emphasizes *Weekend's* social and political value through an in-depth discussion of Third World poverty.[42] Further evidence appears within Jan Dawson's examination of *Weekend*, in which she contests that:

> We are more distressed by the sight of the skinned rabbit than by all the carnage on the highway. And it is here that Godard makes his strongest attack on "civilised" society. [...] Because we are used to averting our eyes from what goes on in the slaughter-house and the farmyard.[43]

Here, the act of snuff is judged on an artistic plane, an approach that is also adopted by James Macbean:

> Only up to a certain point are we still safe and secure in our knowledge that the dead bodies on the screen are not really dead [...] But when we see one of the hippie band slaughter a live pig and a goose, the props are knocked out from under us. Suddenly we don't know where we stand.[44]

Thus, the images of animal slaughter in *Weekend* are read through its representational modes, a style of film interpretation familiar within the assessment of culturally validated artifacts and one which allegorizes the act of snuff.

It is important to note that, since the late 1990s, scholars have cast *Cannibal Holocaust's* use of animal killings within a similar metaphorical framework, rescuing the film from the condemnatory discourse that plagued its initial reception as an exploitation *bête noire*. Andrew DeVos argues that the animal mutilation is used to shock the audience into reflection,[45] while Petley

---

[40]John Westbrook, "Digesting Godard Filming Bataille: Expenditure in Week-End," *Contemporary French and Francophone Studies* 9, no. 4 (2005): 345–52.

[41]Ibid., 351.

[42]Peter Whitehead, "Week-End," *Films and Filming* 15, no. 5 (1969): 34.

[43]Jan Dawson, "Week-end," *Sight and Sound* 37, no. 3 (1968): 152.

[44]James Macbean, "Godard's *Weekend*, or the Self Critical Cinema of Cruelty," *Film Quarterly* 22, no. 2 (1968–1969): 41.

[45]Andrew DeVos, "The More You Rape Their Senses, the Happier They Are: A History of *Cannibal Holocaust*," in *Cinema Inferno: Celluloid Explosions from the Cultural Margins*, edited by Robert Weiner and John Cline (Lanham, MD: Scarecrow Press Inc., 2010): 77.

highlights the film's critique of mercenary media voyeurism.[46] Furthermore, Carolina Jauregui argues for the film to be recognized as a metafiction,[47] while Ed Morgan goes so far to contest that the film's adoption of faux mondo conventions serve as a prism through which we can discuss law and the truth in contemporary Middle Eastern conflicts.[48] Accompanying these partly recuperative critical strategies is the process of embedding the acts of animal snuff within critical interrogations of the limits of realist narrative. This is clear within Jackson's approach, who argues that the film integrates the style and form of the gloatingly presented animal death sequences with the mimetic aspects of the human deaths, blurring the distinction between real and fictional violence and seeking to convince the viewer that the human slayings are as genuine as the animal deaths.[49] Understood through these critical insights, the instinctual, dismissive, and morally outraged response to animal snuff is converted into a field in which death imagery might in some way enhance a level of aesthetic appreciation of formerly despised cultural objects, something increasingly common within the academic film study of marginal or neglected exploitation cinema, but virtually always present within the "high" minded critical engagements afforded Godard.

Though these critical approaches engage with *Cannibal Holocaust's* different layers of meaning, its history has both affected, and been affected by the reception cultures that surround it, meaning that the film's cultural status has often eclipsed or frustrated its claim to depth and complexity. Petley's work neatly articulates this concept, which is vital to the overall legitimization of Deodato's film, but acts as one of many examples foregrounding its relationship to controversy.[50] Morgan also unintentionally partakes in this process, endeavoring to reposition Deodato's film within a broader cultural discourse, but isolating and advertising the secular violence and brutality of the narrative by claiming that "Deodato has exploited violence, the journalistic obsession with violence, and the viewers' obsession with journalistic violence all at once."[51] This recalls the common accusation that, while at times confronting the audience directly in its consumption of violence, the film still revels in its explicit articulation, a feature ignored within the critical elaborations upon *Weekend*, however, appropriate

---

[46]Petley, "*Cannibal Holocaust* and the Pornography of Death," 177.
[47]Carolina Jauregui, "'Eat It Alive and Swallow It Whole!': Resavoring Cannibal Holocaust as a Mockumentary," *Invisible Culture* 7 (2004): 7.
[48]Ed Morgan, "*Cannibal Holocaust*: Digesting and Re-Digesting Law and Film," *S. Cal. Interdisc* 16 (2006): 555–70.
[49]Jackson, "*Cannibal Holocaust*, Realist Horror, and Reflexivity," 41.
[50]Petley, "*Cannibal Holocaust* and the Pornography of Death," 175.
[51]Morgan, "Digesting and Re-Digesting Law and Film," 557.

and justified such an observation might prove to be. Steve Rose adopts a more condemnatory position, stating:

> the get-out is that the film-makers in *Cannibal Holocaust* are the real savages. They are shown goading, raping and even killing to get sensational footage for the media back home. In real life, though, Deodato was doing something suspiciously similar.[52]

Wheeler Winston Dixon dismisses the film entirely, arguing that "*Cannibal Holocaust* and its ilk are depressing, degrading documents, inherently inhumane and senselessly cruel."[53] These latter statements are typical of a common critical tendency that has dismissed the film, one that has developed in parallel to the attempts of those earlier commentators that strove to place the animal slaughter within established scholarly methods. Either way, it has become a model of contentious critical discourse, the critical dialogue securing its place within broader issues of cinematic controversy in which death imagery might somehow be legitimated within the conceptual framework of both narrative and art-film conventions.

Fundamental to the controversy surrounding *Cannibal Holocaust* is the manner in which the cast itself becomes implicated in the act of animal slaughter, a participatory element that dislocates the actors from any mere appreciation of "performance." Indeed, the performative gestures of the cast (mocking laughter, faux "gross out" facial contortions, the deliberate, manual placement of severed bodily parts in front of the camera lens), particularly during the turtle decapitation and evisceration, are very conscious of the potential revulsion that will be inspired through their actions. This is crucial to a fuller comprehension of the prevailing conceptual field in which the film operates, and this is clearest within Jackson's argument. He highlights the manner in which the audience witnesses at once both a fictional character *and* the actor playing that role in the process of killing and mutilating the animal, lending an additionally provocative layer to the film's thematic exploration of environmental and creative exploitation.[54] Petley elaborates upon this argument, restating the limits of the film's moral pontifications, proclaiming that "the fact that the scenes of animal killing in *Cannibal Holocaust* serve to make the scenes of human death and injury more convincing does not, of course, serve to justify their staging."[55] Indeed, these authors are correct to

---

[52]Steve Rose, "Cannibal Holocaust: 'Keep Filming! Kill More People!,'" accessed January 13, 2014, http://www.theguardian.com/film/2011/sep/15/cannibal-holocaust.

[53]Wheeler W. Dixon, *A History of Horror* (New Brunswick, NJ: Rutgers University Press, 2010): 138.

[54]Jackson, "*Cannibal Holocaust*, Realist Horror, and Reflexivity," 41.

[55]Petley, "*Cannibal Holocaust* and the Pornography of Death," 180.

emphasize the recklessness and cruelty of the film's use of animals in the pursuit of sensory manipulation, the participation of the cast (and, of course, the director himself) restricting the film's acceptance as a "legitimate" exploration of violence in entertainment media. Ultimately, this condemns the film to the exploitation ghetto, and contains it within a critical discourse mired in discourses of reclamation and defensiveness. More significantly, this refusal to grant an absolute moral or ethical pardon is not apparent amid the critical consensus which allows *Weekend* to retain its status as an art house landmark, an auteurist intervention in the politically charged cinema of the 1960s. Rather, Godard and his crew are largely freed from accusations of venality and social or environmental irresponsibility, allowing commentators such as Macbean to commend their role in making visible the latent symbolic resonance in the visualization of slaughtered swine and fowl: "getting angry at Godard and blaming him for this death is only bad faith ... All Godard has done, after all, is to film an act which we, in our society, have others commit for us thousands of times each day."[56]

The refusal to implicate Godard and his crew in an unethical process of animal slaughter has a large bearing on the way *Weekend* is framed within the wider discourse of animal snuff, allowing it to inhabit the fringes of the concept. In contrast, the continued critical attention paid to the treatment of animals within *Cannibal Holocaust* highlights the problems inherent in any scholarly attention afforded the film. Petley, Morgan, and Jackson all seek to defend *Cannibal Holocaust* up to a point, their analyses of the animal death and mutilation drawing further attention to the film's utilization of those sequences within a broader, often intelligent engagement with violence as a theme, while acknowledging its place within the "low" cultural category of exploitation cinema. Ironically, this might tend to lend weight to the shock-horror, tabloid level hyperbole which has greeted the film over the years. Indeed, the academy's acceptance and engagement with texts that have inspired widespread revilement and revulsion might ultimately serve as inadvertent promotion, leading to questions regarding responsibilities and obligations in the scholarly study of taboo imagery. In arguing for the possible legitimacy of morally contentious acts of artistic expression, wherein living creatures are terminated and torn asunder in the service of visual spectacle and visceral response, such criticism itself functions as a further provocation which in some cases, regardless of the author's stated intentions, might be read as endorsement or justification.

Animal snuff has become a textual loci for broader discussions regarding the deeply problematic relationship between humans and the animal world, a constituent element of what Arran Stibbe has termed the "destructive discourse."[57]

---

[56]Macbean, "Self Critical Cinema of Cruelty," 41–42.
[57]Stibbe, *Animals Erased*, 6.

Weekend escaped moral scrutiny through acceptance of its cultural importance, thus enabling the animal killings to function as a legitimate artistic choice rather than an act of cruelty. Conversely, *Cannibal Holocaust* became defined by its part in the exploitative processes involved in the filmed killing of animals, and has become characterized as an example of aberrant cinematic practices in a disreputable cultural space. However, focus upon Deodato's film allows for a more balanced view of the cultural processes which inform any discussion of animal snuff, drawing upon examples from differing taste economies. Animal snuff is a malleable cinematic category, one that is affected and partly defined by specific cultural backgrounds, emotive registers, and taste hierarchies. However, it is also determined by certain presiding factors that remain consistent across geographical borders, not least of which is premeditation and authorial provocation within a nominally fictional realm. Regardless of the authorial intent or any eventual critical reclamation and acceptance of films which have consciously foregrounded real death imagery, animal snuff is forever marked by its potential for titillation and corporeal spectacle, factors which inevitably affect any assessment of consumption and, ultimately, comprehension. Indeed, the shifting, slippery definition of animal snuff, shaped by the broader subjective discourses which envelop animal–human relations, allows it to fit neatly alongside the highly contested discourse of "traditional" snuff, providing both an actualization of its main concerns while remaining vulnerable to its inherent inconsistencies.

4 BREATHING NEW LIFE INTO OLD FEARS: EXTREME PORNOGRAPHY AND THE WIDER POLITICS OF SNUFF

Clarissa Smith

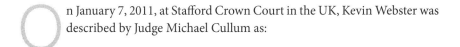

n January 7, 2011, at Stafford Crown Court in the UK, Kevin Webster was described by Judge Michael Cullum as:

> of previously good character. As a man of good character he is entitled to suggest he is less likely to be guilty as he has not offended before. He is not young. He has not come to police attention before or since. He has the choice to remain silent.[1]

Some hours later, having seen the menu for lunch, the jury came to the unanimous verdict of "Not Guilty" on all charges. Arrested in August 2009, Webster has the dubious honor of being the first person to go to jury trial for the possession of "extreme pornography," a charge made possible by the introduction of provisions in Part 5 of the Criminal Justice and Immigration Act 2009 (CJIA).[2]

---

[1]Backlash, "A Judge's Summing Up," accessed December 2, 2014, http://www.backlash-uk.org.uk/the-law/monitoring-prosecutions/a-test-of-realistic/a-judges-summing-up/.

[2]I acted in this case as an expert witness for the Defence (as did Feona Attwood, then at Sheffield Hallam University) and presented testimony exploring the textual formation and history of the images charged, their production and reception. Such testimony is not presented as a *defence* of pornography but as a means of guiding members of the Court towards an understanding of the specificities of particular texts as *representations* and how and why they might fail to meet the provisions of the legislation, particularly around questions of *realism* and *likelihood* rather than *risk* of serious injury.

Also known as "The Dangerous Pictures Act," the CJIA has been on the statute in England and Wales for almost six years and, as I write this, is currently being augmented by further provisions to outlaw images of rape to bring legislation into line with regulations in Scotland.[3] This legislation, and its "refiguring of 'obscenity' from 'an extreme explicitness of representation' into 'perverse' representation"[4] as well as its shifting of responsibility from production/distribution to possession, illustrates the continuing spectral presence of the "snuff movie" in discussions of pornography and its impacts. Indeed, as I will discuss, the UK government's moves to outlaw "extreme" pornography seemed partly driven by a conviction that the snuff movie is not merely a chimera but, facilitated by the accessibility and anonymity of the web, a viable, if disgusting, commercial commodity. In this chapter, I examine elements of the legislation, the argumentation, and the research used to justify its provisions—the claims of the growth and the widespread availability of pornography glorying in sexual violence and assertions of its possible effects. Alongside that discussion, I explore some of the images prosecuted in R v Webster and how the trial illustrates a "crisis over the meanings of pornography" wherein "the identification of 'extreme' pornography has given voice to a range of anxieties about media spectacularization of the body"[5] which have their antecedents in older concerns about the commercial possibilities of the snuff movie.

The legislation

Part 5 of the Criminal Justice and Immigration Act specifically outlaws the possession of any image if it is both "extreme" and "pornographic" and if it:

---

[3]Proponents of the provisions have suggested that harmonisation is entirely practical, but have yet to indicate why adopting the Scottish model is necessary (see Clare McGlynn and Erika Rackley, "Why Criminalise the Possession of Rape Pornography," in *Durham Law School Briefing Document* [Durham: Durham University, 2014]). The Scottish statute has been in operation since 2011 and yet proponents of the changes to English law did not, during the consultation process, make any reference at all to successful prosecutions in Scotland, or to any (however small) changes in the status of women, reduction in violence towards women or to the prevention of sexual assault as a result of those prosecutions. The necessity for the changes to the law in England and Wales has not so far been evidenced but, as I finish this final draft, the legislation has received Royal Assent—discussion and debate of the additional provisions was miniscule. See Clarissa Smith, "The War on Porn: Questions of Representation, Realism and Research" (keynote presentation presented at *1984: Freedom and Censorship in the Media – Where Are We Now?* University of Sunderland, London Campus, April, 2014).
[4]Linda Williams, "Porn Studies: Proliferating Pornographies On/Scene: An Introduction," in *Porn Studies*, edited by Linda Williams (Durham and London: Duke University Press, 2004): 1–6.
[5]Feona Attwood and Clarissa Smith, "Extreme Concern: Regulating 'Dangerous Pictures' in the United Kingdom," *Journal of Law and Society* 37, no. 1 (2010): 171.

portrays, in an explicit and realistic way, any of the following—

(a) an act which threatens a person's life,

(b) an act which results, or is likely to result, in serious injury to a person's anus, breasts, or genitals,

(c) an act which involves sexual interference with a human corpse, or

(d) a person performing an act of intercourse or oral sex with an animal (whether dead or alive), and a reasonable person looking at the image would think that any such person or animal was real.[6]

These provisions were, in part, a response to Graham Coutts' murder of Jane Longhurst in 2003. During his trial, it was argued that "Coutts had been downloading pictures of dead women, strangulation, rape and murder as he had done for eight years"[7] and, following the trial, the victim's mother gathered a petition of 50,000 signatures calling for a ban on websites such as Necrobabes,[8] which Coutts had visited. Support for the Longhurst campaign came from various British newspapers and two Ministers of Parliament who argued that even if the images on those websites had not caused Coutts to murder Jane Longhurst, they had "normalized" his perverse sexual interests. Snuff movies were referenced during Labour MP Martin Salter's contributions to the second reading of the CJIA as examples of violent pornography. Home Office Minister Vernon Coaker argued in support of the new provisions suggesting that "The vast majority of people find these forms of violent and extreme pornography deeply abhorrent."[9]

Campaigners also argued that the UK's primary piece of legislation governing pornography—the Obscene Publications Act 1959—was no longer fit for purpose in the internet age when every conceivable sexual taste is catered to. As the *Daily Mail* thundered,

… it [Longhurst's murder] could have happened only in this high-tech age, committed by someone whose murderous fantasies were fuelled by appalling images freely available on the Internet.[10]

---

[6]"Criminal Justice and Immigration Act 2008 (c4) Part 5," accessed March 13, 2009, http://www.opsi.gov.uk/acts/acts2008/ukpga_20080004_en_9.

[7]*Brighton Argus*, February 5, 2004, accessed June 8, 2015, http://www.theargus.co.uk/archive/2004/02/05/5097827.Jane_Longhurst___The_verdict/?ref=arc.

[8]This site is hosted in the United States.

[9]Coaker quoted in *Daily Mail*, "Victory for Victim's Mum in Crackdown on Web Sex Violence," August 30, 2006, accessed June 8, 2015, http://www.dailymail.co.uk/news/article-402874/Victory-victims-mum-crackdown-web-sex-violence.html.

[10]Daily Mail, "My Sister was Murdered by a Man Obsessed with Violent Internet Porn. So Why Won't Anyone Help Me to Close These Websites Down?," September 30, 2004, repeated in the House of Lords by Baroness Buscombe, reported in Hansard, October 13, 2004, Column 366, accessed June 8, 2015, http://www.publications.parliament.uk/pa/ld200304/ldhansrd/vo041013/text/41013-31.htm.

Interestingly, advocates of the provisions did not suggest that the acts depicted on Necrobabes and other websites of concern were actually *real*. Instead, particular emphasis was being placed upon the possibilities of "harm" being caused to viewers and the rest of society by the "normalizing" of practices of asphyxiation, bondage, domination, and submission. Tellingly, argumentation in favor of the provisions drew on narratives used in other campaigns against "problem media": for example, assertions that "extreme pornography" was a *new* problem, that its images were more graphic, more violent, more real than ever seen before and that the technology exacerbated these problems, are all accusations leveled at media forms as various as the "horror comics," the "video nasties" and video games.[11] As with these other "horrible" media, extreme pornography was regarded as a phenomenon produced outside the UK, utilizing new technologies to breach the boundaries of the island state and operating largely invisibly to the authorities. National newspapers reported Coaker as saying,

> Such material has no place in our society, but the advent of the internet has meant that this material is more easily available and means existing controls are being by-passed. We must move to tackle this.[12]

With additional space, it would be possible to show how the campaign for the legislation was a textbook example of what Bill Thompson described two

---

This argument is strategic rather than factual. As Carline has argued, "To demonstrate the need for censorship Jane Longhurst's death was presented as unusual. Yet the law has, for many years, excused men who kill their partners—some walking out of court with a suspended sentence after successfully pleading provocation (see McColgan, 2000). Femicide is far from uncommon and unusual, with statistics demonstrating that on average two women a week are killed by a partner or ex-partner (Povey, 2009: 21). Moreover asphyxiation or strangulation is the second most common method of killing women (Povey, 2009: 11). Thus to construct this murder, as tragic as it is, as an unusual event caused by the impact of extreme pornography is problematic, and its supposed remedy—censoring extreme pornography—will do little to prevent the deaths of women in domestic settings." See Anna Carline, "Criminal Justice, Extreme Pornography and Prostitution: Protecting Women or Promoting Morality?," *Sexualities* 14, no. 3 (2011): 318.

[11]See for example Martin Barker, *A Haunt of Fears: The Strange History of the British Horror Comics Campaign* (London: Pluto, 1984); *The Video Nasties: Freedom and Censorship in the Media*, edited by Martin Barker (London: Pluto, 1984); Martin Barker and Kate Brooks, *Knowing Audiences: Judge Dredd, Its Friends, Fans, and Foes* (Luton: University of Luton Press, 1998); Martin Barker, Jane Arthurs, and Ramaswami Harindranat, *The Crash Controversy: Censorship Campaigns and Film Reception* (London: Wallflower Press, 2001); *Ill Effects: The Media/Violence Debate*, edited by Martin Barker and Julian Petley (London: Routledge, 2002); and Henry Jenkins, "The War Between Effects and Meaning: Rethinking the Video Game Violence Debate," in *Digital Generations*, edited by David Buckingham, et al. (London: Routledge, 2006): 19–31.

[12]Tania Branigan, "Violent Porn Ban 'A Memorial to My Daughter': Bereaved Mother Welcomes New Law," *Guardian*, August 31, 2006, accessed December 2, 2014, http://www.theguardian.com/politics/2006/aug/31/humanrights.ukcrime.

decades ago as the "Hezekial" impulse, wherein campaigners feel a necessity to "blow the trumpet of doom" to ensure that no one is unaware of the threat about to befall society.[13] Suffice to say that campaigners made extensive use of hyperbole in their claims about the nature and content of the material, bringing the hideous object into view through forms of *description*; as the dread of such imagery operates best if the majority have not and cannot see it, campaigners worked to render extreme pornography *unseeable*.[14] This is a connected but perhaps more complex set of actions than the "contradictory gesture" which Linda Williams has described as "the very quintessence of on/scenity" whereby campaigners bring to attention material they define as obscenity to keep it off scene.[15]

This sleight of hand was apparent in the government's Rapid Evidence Assessment (REA), which claimed that pornographic imagery is so problematic to even describe individual images was likely to render the work of the commissioned academic researchers "unscientific," hence:

> Direct quotes of … explicit descriptions [from the studies included] have not been repeated in this report because the nature of the material was "too extreme." Instead, it has been described in more neutral terms. This has been done to avoid the risk that these descriptions would function as extreme pornographic material for the reader, producing sexual arousal and orgasm to material that depicts or enacts serious sexual violence, explicit serious violence in a sexual context, or explicit intercourse or oral sex with an animal (bestiality).[16]

In the official documentation then, pornography (of all kinds) was supposedly so "powerful" that even legislators, researchers, and other interested readers must be protected from themselves. Such framing re-energized the widespread suggestion that to even *engage on any level* with material designated as "extreme" by MPs, campaigners, and news media outlets was to lay oneself open to the possibility of

---

[13]Bill Thompson, *Soft Core: Moral Crusades Against Pornography in Britain and America* (London: Continuum, 1994).

[14]See Steve Jones, "Dying to be Seen: Snuff-Fiction's Problematic Fantasises of 'Reality'," *Scope* 19 (2011). See also Misha Kavka's contribution to this volume.

[15]Linda Williams, *Hard Core: Power, Pleasure, and the "Frenzy of the Visible"* (Berkeley: University of California Press, 1999): 288.

[16]Catherine Itzin, Ann R. Taket, and Liz Kelly, *The Evidence of Harm to Adults Relating to Exposure to Extreme Pornographic Material: A Rapid Evidence Assessment* (London: Ministry of Justice, 2007): 4. The very notion of a rapid evidence assessment is strange—actually, rapidity is the last thing needed right now; rather, some self-critical thinking about the state and status of evidence and understanding is essential. Specific problems with the REA are explored in Attwood and Smith, "Extreme Concern."

copy-cat behaviors or, for those such as Conservative Peer Lord Hunt who spoke for the provisions, the likelihood of becoming very ill:

> I actually felt very sick [seeing the images], because they were pretty disgusting images, and I frankly find it horrific that they are available and that people can see them. I am sorry, but I do not take this very liberal approach of "if it does no harm to the people taking part, why should we worry about it?" I do worry about it, and about the access that people have to that kind of disgusting material.[17]

According to proponents of the law, "extreme" material was, in itself, so powerful that it was too risky to allow the *sight* of fantasy scenarios:

> …we should err on the side of caution. The stakes are too high: violent sexual crime committed against a person leaves serious harm and widespread distribution of extreme pornography creates a real risk (even though impossible to quantify) of such harm.[18]

At the same time, the British public was invited to respond as "ordinary people" to the horrors of this material—to recognize its inherent dreadfulness and to trust in its categorizations by the "experts" in favor of legislation. Writing in the academic *Journal of Information, Law and Technology*, Julia Hornle had no qualms in admitting her understanding of extreme pornography was based on assumption and trust:

> Most ordinary people (including the author!) regard extreme pornography as disgusting and extremely offensive. Although *I have not conducted empirical research into this area, I assume that* many examples of extreme pornography depict violence by men against women in a sexual setting and if the new provisions contribute to preventing the social acceptability of such material, this *seems* an important step to protect the bodily integrity and dignity of women (or indeed other subjects of extreme pornography).[19]

---

[17]Lord Hunt of Kings Heath in House of Lords, reported in Hansard (HL Deb, April 21, 2008, c1357).
[18]Julia Hornle, "Countering the Dangers of Online Pornography-Shrewd Regulation of Lewd Content?" *European Journal of Law and Technology* 2, no. 1 (2011): 10.
[19]Ibid., 8, emphasis added. The significance of this studied ignorance is amplified when one realises that Hornle is also a member of the board of ATVOD, the body given delegated powers from OfCom to govern video on demand services in the UK and which has been given powers, introduced in the Audiovisual Media Services Regulations 2014, to prohibit content that is refused a classification by the British Board of Film Classification (BBFC) on UK VOD services.

Such approving commentary seems to suggest that the legislation was intended to ensure that those appearing in pornographic imagery were not harmed in the production of it. In fact, such protection was *not* a primary issue for members of parliament or the upper house—as Lord Hunt clarified during the debate in the House of Lords:

> We are targeting that material not on account of offences which may or may not have been committed in the production of the material, but because the material itself, which depicts extreme violence and often appears to be nonconsensual, is to be deplored.[20]

As often happens when legislation arises out of emotive events and media outcry, considered contemplation of the evidence was jettisoned in favor of an insistence on consensus. Dissent was characterized as the selfish protection of personal interests: highly individual interests pitted against the harms being perpetrated on women as a class, and with the potential to cause further damage to the nation's children. The climate of consensus was made possible by commentators doing their utmost to condemn any interest in "this extremely nasty pornography that in no circumstances could be counted as art"[21] as sick, pathological, dangerous, and the material itself as without ambiguity, straightforwardly expressing an interest in committing murder or violence against women. When such claims were met with counter-argument (about recognizing individual privacy, pornography as representation and not "acts of violence," and the likelihood of consensual activities being caught under the purview of the law), proponents returned to "common sense." In the last moments of the debate, Lord Hunt played his trump card: "it is plain common sense that when people continuously use some of these revolting images it has an impact on their behaviour."[22]

Extremity

The legacy of snuff is visible in these debates because, as Downing suggests, it "marks the nexus of a set of cultural fears and fascinations that cluster around fantasies about extremity, the exceeding of limits, and the exercise of violent power in the service of eroticism."[23] Much has been written on the burgeoning

---

[20]Lord Hunt of Kings Heath in House of Lords reported in Hansard (HL Deb, April 21, 2008, c1358).
[21]Hunt, Hansard (HL Deb, April 21, 2008, c1358).
[22]Hunt, Hansard (HL Deb, April 21, 2008, c1361).
[23]Lisa Downing, "Stuff and Nonsense: The Discursive Life of a Phantasmatic Archive," in *Porn Archives*, edited by Tim Dean, Steven Ruszczycky, and David Squires (Durham, NC: Duke University Press, 2015): 249.

of "extreme" texts in recent years and their rearticulation of the divide between obscene and on/scene. Images and practices previously associated with porn and obscenity have become recategorized as chic, cool (or indeed as unremarkable), while others are relegated to the realm of the taboo. The complaints about the Obscene Publications Act and its lack of fitness for the twenty-first century have some purchase when we note that "extreme explicitness of representation"[24] is no longer the measure of obscenity; instead, perversity is the particular issue. Linda Williams has argued that in the US, the prosecution of sex crimes has "moved away from the notion of explicit sex and towards the targeting of scapegoat-able 'deviants', "[25] and that sexual representations and villainous others "take their place as convenient objects of blame" for a variety of social ills.[26] We can understand this culture of blame through the concept of the "sex panic," a scholarly paradigm for the extreme emotional reactions accompanying incidents involving sex. It builds on the notion that reactions such as "fear, anxiety, anger, hatred, and disgust" over sex have considerable force because they are conventional in a particular time and place.[27] Sex panics participate in a wider "politics of fear," as they draw from and impact other areas of social life that are infused by fear.[28] We can see this in the UK where "child pornography" has come to stand in for the material abuse of children and concerns about violence are displaced onto consensual sex practices such as BDSM, onto the figure of "a homosexual sadomasochist stalking defenceless children,"[29] and onto extreme porn. As Lancaster has argued sex panics "give rise to bloated imaginings of risk, inflated conceptions of harm, and loose definitions of sex."[30]

Elements of these "bloated imaginings" can be seen in the responses to contemporary European art-house cinema, whose images of sex and violence are both graphic and seemingly intentionally confrontational,[31] to the subgenre of torture porn and its spectacles of pain and terror[32] and to the "shock" videos, which circulate on the internet as forms of twenty-first century *Grand Guignol*

---

[24]Linda Williams, "Pornographies On/Scene, or Diff'rent Strokes for Diff'rent Folks," in *Sex Exposed: Sexuality and the Pornography Debate*, edited by Lynn Segal and Mary McIntosh (New York: Rutgers University Press, 1992): 233.

[25]Linda Williams, "Second Thoughts on *Hard Core*: American Obscenity Law and the Scapegoating of Deviance," in *More Dirty Looks: Gender, Pornography and Power*, edited by Pamela Church Gibson (London: BFI, 2004): 166.

[26]Ibid., 170.

[27]Janice M. Irvine, "Transient Feelings: Sex Panics and the Politics of Emotions," *GLQ: A Journal of Lesbian and Gay Studies* 14, no. 1 (2008): 1–40.

[28]Roger N. Lancaster, *Sex Panic and the Punitive State* (Berkeley: University of California Press, 2011).

[29]Williams, "Second Thoughts on *Hard Core*," 170.

[30]Lancaster, *Sex Panic and the Punitive State*, 2.

[31]*The New Extremism in Cinema: From France to Europe*, edited by Tanya Horeck and Tina Kendall (Edinburgh: Edinburgh University Press, 2011).

[32]Steve Jones, *Torture Porn: Popular Horror After Saw* (Basingstoke: Palgrave Macmillan, 2013).

"self-scaring."[33] As Feona Attwood notes, institutional responses to such imagery have expressed worries that culture is increasingly "*cruel … a set of concerns which draw on familiar notions of media effects and the obscene [in which] media [are] immersive and contagious.*"[34]

In the drama of extreme porn, there is a collapse of anxieties about the growing sexualization and mediatization of society, exhibiting fears of a broader "turn to the extreme" across a range of cultural forms and about an appetite for graphic spectacles of the body.[35] This turn to the extreme is apparent, not only in porn, horror, or reality TV, but in scenes of "opening up" the body in television drama and documentary, and the portrayal of torture and terror in both fictional and factual media.[36] Such images are linked through their interest in extreme states—sexual or otherwise—and the strong reactions they evoke. In both instances, the body's unruliness or its vulnerability are key. As Dean Lockwood notes, what the kinds of concern around extreme media highlight is the work of horror and porn as "body genres,"[37] presenting and provoking sensation and affect. In the current climate, both register as extreme and unruly.

The problem of course is that all pornography raises the problematic relation between representation and practice, performance and life, seen and concealed, fake and authentic, documentary and fiction, fantasy and reality. As long as the fantasies represented are "acceptable" and fit within the sanctioned boundaries of human sexual practice, pornography can be tolerated. As always, the problem lies with the fantasies that are more ambivalent, those which bring to the fore embodied performances, which bring the questions: How can those people do *that*? How can people *like* that? What on earth might these interests mean?

The Prosecution: R v Webster

The original indictment included more than 1,000 still images—a collection of around 80 photosets each comprising between 20 and 90 individual images telling a variety of stories with titles such as *Slave in a Cave, The Breathless Jogger, Going All The Way*, and *Security Breach*. The entire set was most probably purchased together from an online

---

[33]Julia Kennedy and Clarissa Smith, "His Soul Shatters at About 0: 23: Spankwire, Self-Scaring and Hyberbolic Shock," in *Controversial Images: Media Representations on the Edge*, edited by Feona Attwood, Vincent Campbell, I.Q. Hunter, and Sharon Lockyear (Basingstoke: Palgrave Macmillan, 2013): 239.

[34]Feona Attwood, "Immersion: 'Extreme' Texts, Animated Bodies and the Media," *Media, Culture & Society* 36, no. 8 (2014): 1187.

[35]Dean Lockwood, "All Stripped Down: The Spectacle of 'Torture Porn'," *Popular Communication* 7, no. 1 (2009): 40–48.

[36]Steve Jones and Sharif Mowlabocus, "Hard Times and Rough Rides: The Legal and Ethical Impossibilities of Researching 'Shock' Pornographies," *Sexualities* 12, no. 5 (2009): 613–28.

[37]Linda Williams, "Film Bodies: Gender, Genre, and Excess," *Film Quarterly* 44, no. 4 (1991): 2–13.

repository called the Progressive Art Project for a total of $39.95;[38] at the time of the prosecution, individual photosets were also available from a number of websites located in the states including Sleepyrealm.com and some of its subsidiary sites such as Battlingbabes.com and Hypnobabes.com. All of the photosets on the indictment were credited to Drop Dead Gorgeous (DDG), a company which has specialized in highly stylized representations of women in various states of peril, often termed "dead-skirts," "necro-porn," or less pejoratively as "damsel in distress." The Progressive Art Project's collections of photosets were advertised as "photo-plays" alongside a disclaimer that the materials depicted fantasies, employed models conforming to USC2557 provisions,[39] and that no one was harmed in their production.

In the prosecution case, individual images were isolated from their "published" groups (as I have had to do to illustrate this chapter): the prosecution's motive in singling out images reflects the tendency in academic and other discussions of porn to suggest that "the meanings of pornography" can be deduced from a single image, or indeed, from no image at all![40] The images in R v Webster were not offered for sale as single "pin-ups" but in individual sets constructing narratives, with the protagonists being shown from different angles, often with a focus on the face, on the hands, and on the sexual organs. Thus, although they are still photographs, in *sets*, they offer storied movement and pace. Indeed, most of the images on the indictment could only be read as pornographic if they were seen as a set—on their own, many of the images are simply of women posing in nondescript rooms, or close-ups of a woman appearing to scream. Taken together as sets, there is an eroticised narrative but equally, taken together as sets, the artifice of the *mise-en-scène* and performance is clear, thus undermining the contention that the photos *realistically* depict injury.

Indeed, DDG favored a particular style of presentation and aesthetic sensibilities: highly colored, highly styled, and high camp.[41] The majority of the photosets in the case featured Nikki Steele; Lissa Noble also featured in three of the sets and was credited as the main photographer for DDG.[42] Noble's work and DDG's output are

---

[38]DDG's images had all been available on Necrobabes where they were available to purchase as individual sets, when that site was closed, the images were hosted at the Progressive Art Project and made available in lots of three or four sets or as the entire collection.

[39]In the United States Code of Regulations, under title Title 18, Section 2257, no performers under the age of 18 can be employed by adult industry production companies. As part of the enforcement of the age restriction, all adult industry production companies are required to have a Custodian of Records that documents and holds records of the ages of all performers and must post a statement on all publications to the effect that their performers are all of age.

[40]See discussion in Chuck Kleinhans, "Introduction: Prior Constraints," *Cinema Journal* 46, no. 4 (2007): 96–101.

[41]Information gleaned from numerous websources—many of them members-only sites, I am not including the names of these sites in order to preserve the anonymity of individual posters.

[42]Female performers are named in the blurb for the photosets. In the majority of cases males are not, except by first names—which may or may not be their actual or stage names.

described as "a throwback to porn past" on websites discussing different kinds of fetish material—specifically, the company offers an old-fashioned aesthetic which eschews "realism" and goes for an excessive and expressive artifice, even frivolous, play-acting. The particular pleasures of the images are partly dependent upon their parody of mainstream pornography alongside their depiction of the "damsel in distress" as a melodramatic character-type.

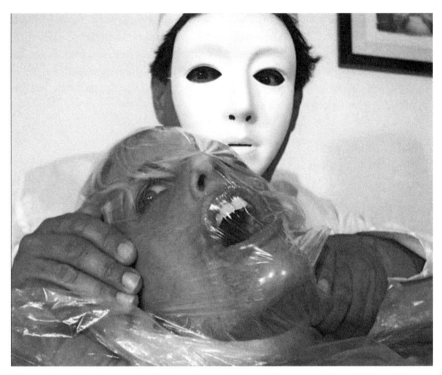

FIGURES 4.1–4.2 Bagging a Nurse (Drop Dead Gorgeous).

For example, in one set entitled *Bagging a Nurse*, Nikki Steele is photographed entering a room dressed in satin-look nurse's uniform. Sitting on a sofa, Nikki takes up a book and begins to read: the scenario is established as a nurse's workday break. As she reads, a man wearing a white mask pops up from behind the sofa. Nikki does not see him. The man then suffocates her with a plastic bag and through the following sixty or so images pulls the bag over her head, moves her around the room, onto a coffee table and onto the floor. She appears to die.

In this photoset, the scene is connected to mainstream pornography through the choice of vertiginous high heels, exaggerated make-up, and the satin nurses outfit which might be considered as trashily "sexy." All of these elements can be considered iconic of pornography but they have no place in a "realistic" portrayal of a nurse's staffroom break. The stereotypically saucy clothing combines with the elements of melodrama in the original "damsel in distress" narrative, to effectively parody both genres; if the "victim" is supposed to be sweet and innocent, why is she wearing such overtly sexualized clothing?[43] The scene also

---

[43]To avoid any confusion, I am referencing the generic conventions of damsel in distress narratives, *not* victim blaming.

plays with the conventions of the horror film, with the male model dressed as the serial killer Michael Myers from the long-running and widely popular *Halloween* franchise (1978–2009). Both outfits would be recognizable to any viewer with even a passing familiarity with popular culture and are clearly cheap and cheerful joke shop purchases. Again, it is possible to read this as an ironic reference to the low production values and tawdry cliché of much mainstream porn production.

Interestingly, none of the 1000-plus images featured any actual sexual congress, no penises in orifices (in fact, no penises in sight at all), or any overtly or specifically sexual moves (where body parts were revealed this can be read as resulting from the photographed "struggle"). If we agree that most pornography inevitably features sexual congress as its main narrative element then the narrative progression here, where murder is the goal rather than sex, creates an ironic juxtaposition of cheeky sexiness and grotesque horror. I am not suggesting that the primary response to these images is to see them as a joke but that, coupled with the other parodic elements, the images have a playful intention. That humorous intent is reinforced by the fact that the nurse is reading a book by Iyanla Vanzant entitled *Don't Give It Away!*; if the double entendre is not clear, the book's subtitle—*A Workbook of Self-Awareness and Self Affirmations for Young Women*—is clearly being sent up as the young woman reading it is totally unaware of the man emerging from behind the sofa to attack her.[44]

Furthermore, the images are saturated in exaggeration—the poses, the facial expressions, the moves are all given excessive emphasis in ways reminiscent of mainstream porn's expressions of pleasure but also of camp-styles of horror acting and excess. As Attwood commented in her evidence to the Court, the images are very similar to stills from high camp "Hammer Horror" films a la *The Vampire Lovers* (1970, UK, dir. Roy Ward Baker) and *Lust for a Vampire* (1971, UK, dir. Jimmy Sangster).[45] While the female body *is* displayed for maximum visibility (so there is an appeal to sexual interest), the facial expressions are also significant for their appeal to a melodramatic sensibility. Taken together—the posing and the expressions—these conventions actually emphasize the pretense at the heart of the images. As was argued in court, these are important stylistic conventions which are part of DDG's "damsel in distress" narrative and which contribute to the constant fracturing of any stable notion of the ontological *real* in these images. Hence, these are not images of "the real," or of a "real death," or a "real murder."

---

[44]Iyanla Vanzant, *Don't Give It Away!: A Workbook of Self-Awareness and Self-Affirmations for Young Women* (New York: Simon and Schuster, 1999).
[45]See, for instance, Peter Hutchings, *Hammer and Beyond: The British Horror Film* (Manchester: Manchester University Press, 1993).

The photo-story *Bagging a Nurse* entails viewers recognizing and perhaps assessing Nikki Steele's ability to represent and perform feeling, physical and emotional effort, fear and humiliation, horror and surprise. Surprise and hyperbolic horror do seem to be a significant factor in these images. In Set 5, *Security Breach*, the almost identical *mise-en-scène* and posing is repeated again and again as Steele is shown being stabbed in the stomach by the man: the knife is pushed into her stomach up to the hilt, while Steele mugs her way through various poses, presenting her body as she stumbles back onto the furniture, slumps down the wardrobe, slides to the floor. Her wide-eyed expressions and grimaces convey none of the realistic pain and terror one might expect from a professional actress but that seems to be precisely the appeal: there is exaggeration and excessive demonstration of the same horrible moment over and over again. At the same time I think it is important to recognize that these images have none of the stylizing of "cruelty" others have explored in torture porn or extreme cinema[46]—in their brightness and their absolute stageyness, they draw attention to a particular kind of pro-am production.[47]

DDG is a recognized brand in this field of porn production (albeit a small niche market), yet the production values in these images are fairly basic. For more than twenty years, it has been possible to produce professional-looking images and film on not much more than a domestic camera. Indeed, domestic digital video cameras have even enabled the development of particular forms of vérité film-making, notably in genres such as horror (as other essays in this volume attest). Thus, it is rather remarkable that these images do not attempt any verisimilitude; the lighting is bright (almost clinical in the instance of the *Bath Toy* set), suggesting that *visibility* is key here rather than attempting to make the images appear as contemporaneous records or documents of an actual murder.

The make-up and blood are amusingly amateurish, and obviously so. For example, in image 10,044 (part of *The Park Bench Ripper* set), the camera focuses on Nikki's face and neck showing the "wound" after her throat has been cut. The "special effect" consists of a straight line clearly marked in purple with some red paint around it. No attempt has been made to render torn flesh or a gaping wound, in spite of the wide availability of such make-up on the high street. I was intrigued to find on a fan-site that it is precisely this amateurism that is prized by fans of

---

[46]See Jones, *Torture Porn*. See also William Brown, "Violence in Extreme Cinema and the Ethics of Spectatorship," *Projections* 7, no.1 (2013): 25–42.

[47]For a discussion of the various conventions of amateur and pro/am pornographies see Federico Zecca, "Porn Sweet Home: A Survey of Amateur Pornography," in *Porn After Porn: Contemporary Alternative Pornographies (Cinema Mapping Pornographies)*, edited by Enrico Biasin, Giovanna Maina, and Federico Zecca (Udine: Mimesis Press, 2014).

these productions. Fan commentary on these sites draw attention to an original etymology of "amateur" as someone who does something for the love of it and was posted in reference to Lissa Noble. Here then, amateurism is a marker of belonging

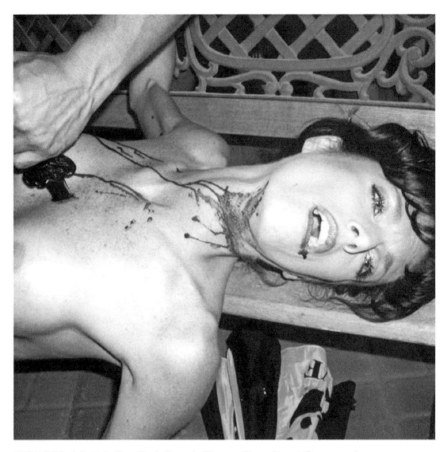

FIGURES 4.3–4.4 The Park Bench Ripper (Drop Dead Gorgeous).

to a community of sexually like-minded individuals in which productions are collaborative[48] and authentic.[49]

Given that this *is* a professional production, I am not suggesting that these images are simply badly made. On the contrary, there are clearly aesthetic choices being made here and they demonstrate that there is a high level of ironic knowingness in the production of these images and the parodic elements of each of the undercut photosets, both the representation of the murder and the sexualized form of it. Therefore, the "amateurism" and its associated lack of realism is a key

[48]DDG productions were often bespoke—made in response to a request (and payment) from a community insider.
[49]On alt pornographies see Clarissa Smith, "It's Important That You Don't Smell a Suit on It: Aesthetics of Alt Porn," in *Porn After Porn: Contemporary Alternative Pornographies (Cinema Mapping Pornographies)*, edited by Enrico Biasin, Giovanna Maina, and Federico Zecca (Udine: Mimesis Press, 2014).

component of the aesthetic conventions and pleasures for knowledgeable viewers of these images.

Furthermore, none of the easily achieved bodily "special effects" such as beads of sweat, or tears are used—throughout the various attacks the models' make-up remains in place, hair hardly mussed up, clothes awry but not torn, extremely long fingernails remain intact and the "murderer" shows very little sign of effort on his part, apart from the theatrically gritted teeth. Thus, all the scenes stress their construction as precisely role-play, refusing documentary, or even more basic styles of indexical realism.

Of course, many feminist writers have argued that the point is the symbolic violence done to women in this kind of imagery, that it is not important whether or not the images are in themselves *realistic*, but that they conform to a particular way of thinking about the female body as inviting violence, an idea suggested by Jane Caputi in *Age of the Sex Crime*:

> Amidst the incomprehensibility of the horror itself is yet another incomprehensible factor. There seems to be no sure way to discern on film what is a faked murder and what is a real one, which is a "symbolic annihilation" and which is an actual one. Here, the characteristic messages of the unreality of sexual violence and the insignificance/unreality of women fuse purely with the properties of the medium, as the camera itself works to confound the eye. This truly is phallic glamour.[50]

Such a description of the camera's power to confound the eye suggests a remarkably pessimistic understanding of media literacies. So too, the invocation of the "unreality" of sexual violence toward women and women's "insignificance" refuses to acknowledge the very complex relations between fantasy and reality at work in media, including pornographic, representations.

Playing dead

Media studies' research into audiences has demonstrated the fallacy of the "average viewer," but if such a group did exist, I suggest they would be unlikely to interpret the images in the photoset *Mistress Blade* as a document of an actual murder. In this set of photographs, Paige Sommers is stabbed in the right breast by Lissa Noble, who chokes Sommers with her left hand. Sommers' mouth is open as if screaming and Noble gives a sideways look to the camera. The image is extremely

---

[50]Jane Caputi, *The Age of Sex Crime* (Bowling Green, OH: Bowling Green State University Popular Press, 1987): 168–69.

camp: Noble is dressed in what can only be described as a dominatrix uniform of leather bustier, cap and long black gloves. Her glance to camera (complete with quirked eyebrow) is exaggerated and pantomimeish betraying that the scene is posed. Again, as with all the images in the indictment, there was no attempt to make the images in this set appear real: the knife is clearly a stage property; there are no signs of actual exertion on the part of either model and no indication of involuntary physical reactions to being stabbed or strangled.

Commentaries on the fan site, Femme Fatalities (Bluestone's erotic death fetish community website) suggest that Nikki Steele's reputation is secured as someone who is "great at *playing* dead" which would imply that those in the know absolutely understand that she has not been murdered to make a set of images. Added to this, the fact that Steele's output is cataloged on websites under her name, therefore, she clearly cannot be being killed in every one of the twenty or so photosets she stars in. From my own viewing and from research I conducted on various fan-sites and discussion boards, the fantasy on offer is not simply the murder *per se* but the process of loss of control on the part of the victim. Hence, the establishing shots of the victim being taken-unawares (*Bagging A Nurse*); the false sense of security of the victim: she thinks she is consenting to the SM scene (*Mistress Blade*) or she's enjoying a drink with a man (*Going All The Way*) but then the mood changes. The ensuing pictures illustrate the female protagonist's awareness of the fact of being duped, and then of the utter powerlessness of her situation. This seems to be an important pleasure for fans posting on fan-sites. The photosets need to appear "credible" but not "real": so her facial expressions need to express her horror and fear but no suffering. As one poster to a fan-site put it, "the woman being raped has to look credibly helpless ... but I have no interest in seeing scenes where someone might actually be suffering." And another, "There's a huge difference between movies that are made with the intention to appeal to those of us who like rape and torture, and movies that are made to show us how bad that is in real life."[51]

Indeed, if it looks "real" then it precisely fails in its eroticism. What this seems to suggest is that for those who are interested in these rape fantasies, or these necro sites, there is an understanding of the differences in modalities and representations of rape and/or torture which the legislation is ill-equipped to comprehend. It is important to recognize that the meanings of representations of death or murder have multiple valances, which the legislation also refused to acknowledge. In that refusal of the diverse and possible attractions of viewing death, the legislation (and proponents of it) also elides the historical antecedents of "death fetish" imagery. As Elizabeth Bronfen has demonstrated, eighteenth century romantic approaches to death in literature and art, posed death as "a moment of beauty ... a

---

[51]Citations are not given here, to protect the anonymity of posters to the site.

transformation…to be yearned for with an erotic ache, and, in this sense, to be understood as the beginning or continuation of a narrative."[52] The eroticization of the death bed is a considerable symbolic pleasure in gothic, romantic, and sensation fictions,[53] however, modernizing and civilizing impulses during the Victorian era saw the eclipse but not complete disappearance, of such "gothic relish" for death, and it is still very visible in horror narratives and other forms of contemporary popular media. Thus, despite the steer for consensus around the exceptionality and "vileness" of "extreme pornography" outlined in earlier sections of this chapter, interests in eroticized images of "death" are neither new, nor without complexity.

"Disturbances of genre and category"[54]

As was reported to MPs and Lords at the time of the Act's passing through both Houses of Parliament, the original clause on realistic portrayals was confusing, badly conceived, and seemingly ignorant of the vast array of audience research into viewers' complex negotiations and sense making of the relationships between fantasy and reality in, among other media forms, reality television, television drama, documentary, novels, children's cartoons, action films, fantasy films, historical event films, and pornography.[55] Despite the many criticisms of the wording relating to "realism" and "appears to be real," the amended form of words that made it into the Act was also drafted without any due regard to the research into modalities of reality.

For legislators and other commentators on the legislation, all this was lost in their disapproval for the fantasy of sexualized murder. Indeed, it is that linkage of sex and death that was particularly disturbing as if the breach of generic boundaries was a new phenomenon. The emotive mode used by prolegislation campaigners and by prosecutors draws on an established discourse in which "pornography" has been used, not to describe a media genre, but is employed as a figure of speech for texts which enact violence against women, showing them "…tied up, stretched, hanged, fucked, gang-banged, whipped, beaten and begging for more."[56] A view expressed in the Rapid Evidence Assessment is that pornography

[52]Deborah Lutz, "The Dead Still Among Us: Victorian Secular Relics, Hair Jewelry, and Death Culture," *Victorian Literature and Culture* 39, no. 1 (2011): 130.

[53]Elisabeth Bronfen, *Over Her Dead Body: Death, Femininity and the Aesthetic* (Manchester: Manchester University Press, 1992).

[54]Attwood, "Immersion," 1192.

[55]Clarissa Smith et al., "Memorandum Submitted by Dr Clarissa Smith et al (CJ&I 341)," 2006, accessed June 8, 2015, http://www.publications.parliament.uk/pa/cm200607/cmpublic/criminal/memos/ucm 34102.html.

[56]Andrea Dworkin, *Pornography: Men Possessing Women* (London: Women's Press, 1979/1999): 201.

"corrupts … desire" by fusing arousal and orgasm with violence, objectification, and degradation.[57] The impulse to separate off forms of amusement and to maintain strict boundaries between types of representation is not actually new. That kind of delineation began to occur in the late nineteenth century as part of regulation of leisure sites into particular kinds of licensed spaces, and the general disparagement of "uncivilized" entertainments. Contemporary classificatory agencies such as the British Board of Film Classification perform their duties with regard to possible "effects" on likely viewers, seeming most worried by materials that blur generic boundaries. For example, material that is "likely to encourage an interest in sexually abusive activity" is singled out for cuts to receive a certificate.[58] The guidelines also seek to classify harm as "includ[ing] not just any harm that may result from the behaviour of potential viewers, but also any moral harm that may be caused by, for example, desensitising a potential viewer to the effects of violence and reinforcing unhealthy fantasies."[59] Other statements from the BBFC have indicated worries about "'graphic rape or torture,' 'sadistic violence or terrorization' and 'sex accompanied by non-consensual pain, injury or humiliation'"—these may appear entirely reasonable given that the discursive construction of extreme porn, in Parliament and associated press reports, rendered any possibility of being aroused by this stuff abnormal and that all "right-thinking" viewers would recognise that fantasies of rape were surely unhealthy. But as has been argued in relation to the controversy over David Cronenberg's *Crash* (1996), "very often the 'meanings' discovered are not those experienced (enjoyed, absorbed) by the analyst, but are ones attributed as possible 'effects' on others."[60] Moreover, the refusal to recognize the common heritage behind many kinds of popular entertainment, and not just in their capacities to "move the body,"[61] is part and parcel of worrying about "illicit" pleasures dating back to the *Grand Guignol* and earlier. Such worrying is intensely political, as Johnson notes:

> In arguing for the criminalization of individual possession on the basis of claims about the protection of social morality, section 63 places the law firmly in the difficult terrain of regulating the private sexual life of individuals in relation to ideas about a common or shared morality.[62]

[57]Itzin et al., *The Evidence of Harm to Adults*, 37.
[58]British Board of Film Classification, *BBFC Guidelines: Age Ratings You Trust* (2014): 24, accessed June 8, 2015, http://www.bbfc.co.uk/sites/default/files/attachments/BBFC%20Classification%20Guidelines%202014_5.pdf.
[59]Ibid., 3.
[60]Barker et al., *The Crash Controversy*, 150.
[61]Williams, "Film Bodies."
[62]Paul Johnson, "Law, Morality and Disgust: The Regulation of 'Extreme Pornography' in England and Wales," *Social & Legal Studies* 19, no. 2 (2010): 151.

The Court in Stafford required that expert evidence explore the textual formations of the images charged under the Act and allowed space for examination which moved beyond literal or ideological readings. Although the Court was interested in facts, there was space to introduce the possibilities for understanding the indicted material, and pornography in general, as material and embodied, producing affect, intensities of experience, bodily sensations, and sensory responses. In cross-examination, it was possible to suggest that the specific aesthetics, acts, and performances had particular resonances, which could not simply be read off the surface of the images as either positive or negative.[63]

Even so, in the R v Webster trial, prosecuting counsel Darron Whitehead was not willing to let go of the possibility that the images are harmful. In his closing speech, Whitehead said:

> We know the images were fake, we know it isn't a knife in someone's breast. The question is whether it is realistic or portrayed in that way. You have to be satisfied the people in those images are real. Plainly they are. The intentions of the persons within those images, the actors and actresses, are irrelevant. It is what is depicted in those images which is material.
>
> Why is there a need for this new legislation? There is a need to regulate images portraying sexual violence, to safeguard the decency of society, and to protect women.[64]

For all the talk about "realism" in these images, what really haunts legislation, prosecutions, and popular discourse alike is the idea of arousal, the pleasure, and the horror of being *aroused* by death, of having sexual fantasies about death. Even those who would want to reject the normative critique of regulation find themselves in difficult waters when genres are conflated. In his exploration of the BBFC's refusal in 2008 to give a classification to Rob Rotten's *The Texas Vibrator Massacre* (thereby rendering its distribution in the UK illegal), Thomas Joseph Watson concludes that "the film offers very little in the way of comic respite"[65] as if

---

[63]Some might suggest that it is perfectly reasonable to test these issues in the Courts however in practice this means that an accused can be subjected to the considerable stress of a lengthy prosecution process—up to a year awaiting trial, considerable expense, the loss of employment, estrangement from family and friends—only to be acquitted because their specifically *sexual* interests in the images were not proven. There are significant costs to the public purse in prosecutions but more than that are the costs to individuals, as I write, one former defendant, Andrew Holland has launched a human rights challenge to the CJIA's Extreme Porn provisions. For details, see http://obscenitylawyer.blogspot. it/2014_10_01_archive.html (accessed June 8, 2015).
[64]Quoted in Staffordshire Newsletter, "Man, 47, Denies 'Fake Images' Porn Charges," January 6, 2011, accessed December 2, 2014, http://www.staffordshirenewsletter.co.uk/Man-47-deniesfake-images-porn-charges/story-20152291-detail/story.html.
[65]Thomas Joseph Watson, "There's Something Rotten in the State of Texas: Genre, Adaptation and *The Texas Vibrator Massacre*," *Journal of Adaptation in Film and Performance* 6, no. 3 (2013): 397.

humor could rescue the film, or would remove the ambiguities of its conflation of genres, and its potentials for horrific and sexual affect. While Watson's argument referenced the BBFC's justification of its rejection of *The Texas Vibrator Massacre* on the basis of the film's "tone," it succumbs to what I see as the (understandable, but too often cowardly) reluctance of media scholars to grasp the nettle of problematic audience pleasures except where those pleasures can be accommodated through recourse to claims of artistic intent, irony, or humor.

Conclusion

In this chapter, I have considered the legislative and judicial contexts in which so-called "extreme porn" has been discussed in the UK, with a specific focus on those instances where sexual violence is depicted and in which linkages are made between sex and death, and where "death" itself is eroticized. At the time of writing, the "extreme porn" provisions have been augmented by legislation outlawing possession of rape imagery in the UK. These new regulations, written into the Criminal Justice and Courts Act, came into force in 2015. Rape and "sexual violence" constitute a significant part of the phenomenon of "mainstream extreme cinema" and understanding audience engagements with and pleasures in these is a fraught and risky business. As is evidenced in the BBFC guidelines, the very idea of viewing sexual violence carries with it a host of perceived worries, in particular, that depictions of rape or "sexual murder" may cause sexual arousal—any depiction judged likely to arouse viewers, and especially male ones, is regarded as *per se* dangerous. There is, however, a powerful discourse of "redemption" for risky sexual representations (especially in "art house" cinema), whereby critics and regulatory bodies, such as the BBFC, redefine unusual, and/or dangerous images as "unerotic" to make them "safe," as in films such as *Baise Moi* (dir. Virginie Despentes, Coralie, 2000) or *Irreversible* (dir. Gaspar Noe, 2002). To admit that such films featuring violence *are also* sexually arousing is to attach a strong trace of danger to them, because within much public discourse arousal is seen as basic, compulsive, overriding, and therefore, likely to give rise to antisocial/copy-cat behaviors. While such films are the subject of much controversy, they ultimately circulate in a context of "art cinema," whereby assertions of serious (creative and/or political) intent recuperate their shocking and problematic depictions of rape and sexual violence.

Such redemptive readings are rarely accorded to avowedly pornographic materials—certainly not to the kinds of productions discussed here. The all-too-ready dismissal of pornography as a "functional" media means that its "purposes" are always already suspect and hence tend inexorably to "harm and deprave," contributing to (if not, in some accounts, causing) the "eroticization of violence" against women in the wider culture. Often the problem lies not in individual instances of pornographic production themselves but in the conception of the "uses" to which porn might be put by particular groups. Martin Barker has suggested that institutionally funded research, at least in the UK, has played a significant role "in the construction of what I have come to call 'figures of the audience,' and that others have called 'audience myths,' or 'audience presumptions.' These are, in brief, culturally produced and -circulating claims about the nature of 'dangerous social groups'."[66]

The model of pornography (always a singular entity), which underpinned the introduction of the "extreme porn" provisions and the forthcoming "rape porn" provisions, is a relic of the inchoate, but nevertheless influential, characterizations of snuff as the nadir of modern media. The repeated claims in the calls for legislation—that explicit sexual scenes containing any element of "violence" necessarily endorse or encourage violence against women—work with a formulation of explicit scenes as "unnecessary" elements in any representation. That construction can only work if coupled with a formulation of audiences as always and already "dangerous" by dint of their potential interests in the explicit, as Martin Salter MP suggested:

No-one is stopping people doing weird stuff to each other but they would be strongly advised not to put it on the internet. At the end of the day it is all too easy for this stuff to trigger an unbalanced mind. These snuff movies and other stuff are seriously disturbing. Many police officers who have to view it as part of their job have to undergo psychological counseling.[67]

In this, I think it is imperative that media researchers must take a hard look at some of their own assumptions—the refusal of senior media academics to protest against the proposals in 2007 and again in 2013/2014 demonstrates a failure to stand by the evidence of a vast research tradition that rejects the putative figures of the "vulnerable audience." The legislation against "dangerous" desires and fantasies is not equipped to understand the very representations it seeks to criminalize. As I hope I have demonstrated here, representations of "sexual violence" have their own generic specificities—well-recognized by those who engage with them—their eroticized "violence" is more complex than simple endorsement of "rape" or "strangulation." And yet…

It is relatively simple to point out the stupidities of the legislation on a case by case basis—given access to some of the images prosecuted in the Webster trial,

---

[66]Martin Barker, "'Knowledge-U-Like': The BBFC and Its Research," in *Controversies: Histories and Debates in Film Controversy*, edited by Julian Petley and Stevie Simkin (Basingstoke: BFI/Palgrave Macmillan, forthcoming).

[67]Salter quoted in Chris Summers, "'Extreme' Porn Proposals Spark Row," *BBC News*, July 4, 2007, accessed June 20, 2009, available at http://news.bbc.co.uk/1/hi/uk/6237226.stm.

most readers of this chapter will congratulate themselves that they too would see the idiocy of the prosecution, indeed, may laugh at the ridiculousness of the images and exclaim how could these have been taken to Court? And yet ... I have to ask the questions, where were you when the legislation was being proposed, when the call went out for signatories to contribute alternative positions to the consultation process? Where are you when the cases are reported in the press? How often do you dismiss such things as *just* another moral panic?[68] ... But good for you if you see the stupidity in *this* case!

The usual oppositions of "real" versus "fantasy" prove themselves useless in understanding the meanings, the appeals, and the modalities of response to imagery like *Bagging a Nurse*, or indeed any of the media forms which have been likened, over the last forty years, to snuff. Media scholars have yet to formulate an alternative language for talking about "dangerous" narratives which absolutely do not fall back on that simple division. I have one place of agreement with would-be censors—that it is not good enough for *any* media scholar to suggest that what is on-screen (TV, cinema, or computer) or on the page "is *only* fantasy!" As if that simple statement explained anything! This book is about the cultural legacies of snuff. How amazing might it be if we went beyond noting the resilience of campaigns for prohibition to begin the difficult work of presenting an alternative, evidenced and robust position, to their cultural illiteracies?

Acknowledgments

Research and writing are always improved by collaborations and especially so in a highly emotive area such as this. I have been lucky enough to be surrounded by kind and inspiring colleagues—too many to mention here—but I would like to express my sincere gratitude to Feona Attwood, Martin Barker, Mark McKenna, and John Mercer for their conversations and support in helping me knock this essay into shape. I would also like to thank the editors of this collection for putting it together in the first place, and for their patience. Kudos also to the law specialist in sexual freedoms, Myles Jackman (http://mylesjackman.com), for his indefatigable work on the Webster case and on behalf of others who have fallen foul of the CJIA. The campaign group, Backlash (http://www.backlash-uk.org.uk), also deserve recognition for their continuing challenge to the "dirty pictures act"— keep up the struggle!

---

[68]Of course, it is much more than that for those individuals whose lives are turned upside down by a prosecution. See reportage following the Simon Walsh (R v Walsh, 2012) trial for detail, but bear in mind that he was a man with powerful friends and a professional career he could resume. Others have not been so fortunate.

5 FROM SNUFF TO THE SOUTH: THE GLOBAL RECEPTION OF *CANNIBAL HOLOCAUST*

Nicolò Gallio and Xavier Mendik

Introduction: Theatrical Ambiguity and the Snuff Canon

Beautiful, yet brutal. Repulsive and arguably racist. Avant-garde but ultimately objectionable. Much has been written about Ruggero Deodato's *Cannibal Holocaust* (1980) and its status as one of the most extreme films ever made. Yet, decades after its controversial release, the infamous flick is still here, challenging taboos and confusing realist categories. Filmed in Colombia in 1979, Deodato used his former neorealist training as Roberto Rossellini's assistant to powerful effect, creating a nihilistic narrative fiction whose documentary-*like* techniques were to revolutionize the nature of realist horror cinema. With its complex narrative composition and innovative fusion of dramatized and realist techniques, *Cannibal Holocaust* initiated a trail-blazing trend of "found footage horror" that continues to influence contemporary filmmakers.[1]

However, the film's stylishness was overshadowed by its savage scenes of real-life animal cruelty and staged sexual suffering, which led to the movie being banned in many territories. *Cannibal Holocaust* ignited controversies wherever it

---

[1] For an introduction to found footage see Alexandra Heller-Nicholas, *Found Footage Horror Films. Fear and the Appearance of Reality* (Jefferson, NC: McFarland, 2014).

was released as part of wider condemnations of horror trends that were literally "too" real. The film was initially seized in Deodato's native Italy when it briefly hit the screens at the beginning of the 1980s, leading the director to have to engage in a lengthy and high-profile court case in defense of his creation. As reviewers of the Italian trial noted, the prosecutor considered the film detrimental to human dignity for sixteen sequences, where he observed an insistence in bluntly representing gory details of sadism and violence toward people, animals, and things.[2]

When *Cannibal Holocaust* later appeared on video in the UK in 1982, it was regularly under the spotlight during the video nasties media frenzy as a key title linked to the potential desensitization and moral corruption of the teenage British populous. Controversy and confusion continued to surround the film following its release, with many critics believing that *Cannibal Holocaust* constituted a "death film," in which actors, as well as the aforementioned animals, were knowingly killed in its making. In this respect, the film constitutes an example of supposed "snuff" cinema whose status is bound up with what Alexandra Heller-Nicholas recently defined as "a hyperactive theatricality of ambiguity, rumour and moral panic."[3]

This "hyperactive theatrical ambiguity" was premised on a set of audio–visual anchors that closely allied the appearance of annihilation to actuality footage: handheld and often unfocused camera work, direct and intermittent sound, a fusion of real-life protagonists with staged performers, the quasi-pornographic depiction of rape, and an unnerving "realist" representation of a castration. Referring to the film *Snuff* (Michael and Roberta Findlay [uncredited], 1976) from which the contemporary death film phenomenon takes its name, Heller-Nicholas recalls the legendary tale of how exploitation producer Alan Shackleton famously employed these profilmic tendencies to commercialize the previously unreleased Manson clan dramatization, *The Slaughter*, directed in 1971 by Michael and Roberta Findlay. As indicated in other chapters in this volume, not only did Shackleton omit opening and closing credits for the production to enhance its *vérité* feel, but he also added the now notorious epilogue, in which an actress appears to be violated onscreen in murderous finale to the production. As Heller-Nicholas notes, these controversial diegetic and extra-diegetic features were

---

[2]ORIG. "[…] il pubblico ministero aveva ritenuto il film lesivo della dignità umana per sedici sequenze, in cui si era rilevata una compiaciuta insistenza nel rappresentare crudamente particolari raccapriccianti di sadismo e violenza (sessuale) e non, verso persone, animali e cose." Anon., "Seicondanne a Milano per *Cannibal Holocaust*," *Cinecritica* no. 6 (1980): 26. Unless otherwise noted, Italian and French reviews were translated by Nicolò Gallio.

[3]http://cinephile.ca/archives/volume-5-no-2-the-scene/snuff-boxing-revisiting-the-snuff-coda/, accessed September 12, 2014.

complimented by an additional level of hyperactive theatrical ambiguity, which employed sensationalist advertising further used to enhance the myth of death unwinding on the screen. These tactics, along with the anonymized and ominous tagline of "The film that could only be made in South America … where life is CHEAP!," ensured that by "the time the hoax was exposed, it was too late: *Snuff* had captured the interest of the public, and an urban legend was born."[4]

Arguably, it was a similar use of hyperactive theatrical ambiguity that marked the structuring and release of *Cannibal Holocaust*. Not only does the film begin with an intertitle claiming that "For the sake of authenticity, some sequences have been retained for their entirety," it also ends with an epilogue purporting that suppressed atrocity footage shown in the film details was released to the public, resulting in a projectionist receiving a "two month suspended sentence and fined $10,000 for illegal appropriation of film material." These attempts to create what Heller-Nicholas has defined as the "snuff coda" extended beyond these two ambivalent segments to include contracts distributed to key performers in the film requiring them to drop out of sight for a set period of time, to reinforce the myth that they had perished during the production of *Cannibal Holocaust*.

As a result of these stylistic and marketing strategies, David Kerekes and David Slater argue in favor of an international "snuff" reception of *Cannibal Holocaust* from 1981 onward, with critics and commentators frequently presuming that the controversial scenes of actual animal slaughter extended to the demise of performers within the fiction. The authors here cite a variety of sources across a broad ten-year timeframe, such as the magazines *Photo* (from January, 1981) and *Fantasy Film Memory No 1* (from 1990) and national newspapers such as *The Independent* (from April 6, 1993) to consider how these snuff allegations spanned distinct cultures and differing decades:

> In France, following an article in the magazine *Photo*, news began to spread that *Cannibal Holocaust* "was the [film] in which men were really dismembered, beheaded, castrated and *mangiati vivi*!" This completely erroneous fact continues to be trotted out by the ill-informed and by lazy journalists. In Britain, in April 1993, a raid on a comic mart in Birmingham (emotively referred to as "children's fair" by the press) was reported as having resulted in "the first known seizure in the city of a snuff video"—in reality, a copy of *Cannibal Holocaust*.[5]

---

[4]Ibid., 3.
[5]David Kerekes and David Slater, *See No Evil: Banned Films and Video Controversy* (Manchester: Headpress Critical Vision, 2000): 112.

Readers were reportedly so shocked that they started to write to film magazines asking for detailed information. In June 1993, after the raid in Birmingham, the British film magazine *Empire* received a letter from Luton, Bedfordshire:

> Dear Empire,
> I read a story in The Daily Mail about "snuff" movies which were seized in Birmingham. Among the films mentioned were *Cannibal Holocaust, Cannibal Ferox* and *Driller Killer*. What exactly *is* a snuff movie, are those actually snuff movies and if not, do snuff movies really exist?
> Peter Johnson.[6]

Clearly, while film critics had already exposed the hoax the word-of-mouth around these alleged snuff films refused to die. Actually, it was fuelled from time to time by Deodato himself. Indeed, regarding the snuff allegations, he has often provided contradictory answers. Once he stated: "I needed unknown actors that by contract could "disappear" for one year. I wanted the viewers to think that the film was a snuff movie."[7] While at some other time, when asked "What do you think of snuff movies?," he replied: "They're illegal movies that no professional director would even think to shoot. I've never seen one but unfortunately I know that they exist. They're part of the vilest market of pornography and I don't want to be linked with that trash at all."[8]

By threatening cultural and visual boundaries because of its distinctive director and unique visual style, *Cannibal Holocaust* remains then a fluctuating cultural artifact that warrants further investigation. To explore this in more detail, this chapter considers the international reception of *Cannibal Holocaust*, identifying both the shared features of condemnation across the differing regions, as well as very nationalistic modes of interpreting Deodato's film during the early 1980s. By isolating potential similarities of critical discourse around *Cannibal Holocaust*'s "realistic" features and wider politics, we also hope to open up a space to begin to discuss the "snuff" movie phenomenon within recent debates around "primitiveness" within a Southern Italian context.

---

[6]"Q&A," *Empire* no. 48, June 1993, 34.

[7]ORIG. "Avevo bisogno di attori sconosciuti che per contratto potessero 'sparire' per un anno. Volevo che il pubblico pensasse di aver visto uno *snuff movie*," *Nocturno Dossier* no. 73, "Monsieur Cannibal. Il cinema di Ruggero Deodato," August 2008, 35.

[8]ORIG. "Sono film clandestini che nessun regista professionista si sognerebbe di realizzare. Io non ne ho mai visti ma purtroppo so che esistono. Fanno parte del più vile mercato pornografico e non voglio assolutamente essere associato a certe porcherie." Gordiano Lupi, *Cannibal! Il cinema selvaggio di Ruggero Deodato* (Roma: Edizioni Profondo Rosso, 2003): 93.

An "Illegal Appropriation of Film Material": Deodato's Dark Jungle Docu-Drama

With its narrative emphasis on the quest to recover lost documentary footage from a film crew who appear to have violently perished on assignment in the Amazon, *Cannibal Holocaust* sits easily within wider, controversial debates around death cinema, by actively seeking to confound the boundaries between actuality and fiction. The film begins with a televised news report introducing the four intrepid documentary filmmakers who have vanished in the South American wilderness, while attempting to document cannibalistic tribes who continue to exist in primitive conditions there. This opening reportage identifies the group as headed by the maverick movie-maker Alan Yates (Gabriel Yorke), and his girlfriend Faye Daniels (Francesca Ciardi), whose previous documentary projects have achieved notoriety for their extreme exposes of postcolonial suffering in emergent African states. The news report then uses a montage sequence to introduce noted NYU anthropologist Harold Monroe (played by American porn veteran Robert Kerman), while confirming that he has been sent on an expedition funded by an American news corporation to recover the film crew.

The extended reportage opening to *Cannibal Holocaust* immediately establishes a realist frame for the initial jungle expedition that follows, while also confirming this locale as the basis of both primitive sexual relations and random acts of savagery. Here, Monroe's journey takes him into the heart of the infamous "Green Inferno," the Amazonian wilderness dominated by three warring tribes that have previously encountered Yates and the film crew with fatal results. During this expedition, he functions as a horrified and concealed observer to the ritual punishment of a local female adulterer with a murderous phallic shaped weapon, before being forced to adopt a series of crude practices to win the trust of local tribes who have retained the film crew's final and fatal footage.

Writing in the article "*Cannibal Holocaust*, Realist Horror and Reflexivity,"[9] Neil Jackson argues that the film is composed of two distinct strands: by dividing the narrative between Monroe's quest and the subsequent screening of the film crew's lost footage in New York. In so doing, *Cannibal Holocaust* uses a series of realist film techniques to implicate its audience in the acts of brutality unfolding. As we discover when the found footage is screened by TV executives in New York, the demise of Alan Yates and his film crew is prefigured by the extreme acts of savagery they enact upon the Amazonian landscape and its inhabitants, to secure the ultimate in sensationalist documentaries. Some of the atrocities perpetrated by the crew include the massacre of an entire village of women and elderly natives,

---

[9]Neil Jackson, "*Cannibal Holocaust*, Realist Horror, and Reflexivity," *Post Script* (Summer 2002) (online version pp. 1–13).

who are herded into a large tent before the building is set on fire. The cameraman's gleeful comment of "Just like Cambodia" as he records the villagers suffering functions to enforce the realist veracity of what is being recorded, via reference to wider war crime reporting that was in circulation at the time of the film's release. Indeed, the relationship of sadistic reportage, recorded potency, and realism are even more marked in the sexual crimes committed by the explorers. In a grisly key encounter, the group capture and then gang rape a young Indio girl, with the male crew members taking turns to hold the camera in between participating in the sexual assault. As the lone Western female filmmaker in the group, Faye Daniels is the only crew member to object to the rape, but her reasons remain ambivalent here, as she critiques her crew members for wasting precious film stock on what she defines as a porno insert. This sequence is itself complemented by the later scene, where the crew returns to film the rape victim, who as a consequence of being violated by the outsiders is found suspended on a lethal wooden pole that runs from the victim's vagina to her mouth. Linking these two scenes together, Jackson argues that "Murderous phallic penetration thus becomes a central motif of the film, providing a linkage to the potentially fatal function of the movie camera ... "[10]

These comments reinforce the opening TV narration's account of Alan Yates "armed with cameras, microphones and curiosity" indicating the extent to which *Cannibal Holocaust* equates the documentary camera to acts of enforced violation. As well as being closely associated with violent defilement, the documentary lens of *Cannibal Holocaust* also functions as a vehicle of visual deception, by masking or obscuring its fictionalized scenes of human suffering to draw them closer to the unpalatable sequences of actual animal slaughter. For Jackson, the use of *vérité* features such as visual flares, abrupt wipes, or whip pans function not only to disguise the special effects required to show the evisceration of Indio victims (and eventually Yates and his crew when the villagers rebel in the film's closing scene) but also collapses the distinction between the staged suffering and the unsimulated scenes of animal cruelty in the film (most infamously in the scene of a giant live turtle being disembowelled alive by the filmmakers in real time).

These realist inserts effectively represent "deceptive montages,"[11] the impact of which is further reproduced in a documentary excerpt screened for Monroe in New York, which gives the protagonist further evidence of Yates' filmic oeuvre. Entitled *The Last Road to Hell*, the short film is a record of genocide occurring in African and East Asian cultures and splices together scenes of mass exodus with tribal conflicts and civilian executions before a firing squad. This documentary insert, in which acts of violence increase rapidly, ends with the scene of a young boy being executed by a Cambodian military squad. Described by the assembled

---

[10]Ibid.,7.
[11]Ibid., 10.

news corporation representatives as "pretty powerful stuff," the sequence not only confirms the use of realist motifs within *Cannibal Holocaust*'s wider narrative frame but functions to further confuse the boundaries of fact and fiction, when it is revealed to Monroe that the whole excerpt was staged by Yates and his crew for dramatic impact. However, as Jackson notes, *The Last Road to Hell* footage is derived from actual atrocity news reporting, which Deodato assembled for *Cannibal Holocaust*, and, therefore, "The implications of this are crucial—a series of real documentary fragments are presented as manipulated, orchestrated, and unreal, within a film which, while fictional, makes bogus claims to authenticity."[12]

These circulating layers of realist ambiguity further complicate the distinction between factual and the fictional within *Cannibal Holocaust*, thus adding to its supposed snuff mystique. This is confirmed by the last segment of found footage that Monroe and the television executives assess. According to Jackson, "The final sequences of the found footage once more refer to the 'authenticity' of its violence and the potentially gruelling experience it presents to the audience."[13] Here, Yates and the film crew become entrapped by the once peaceful tribe they have abused, who then mutilate them through a range of violent acts that include castration, beheading, and (in the case of Faye), a group sexual assault that mirrors the film crew's previous attack on the female Indio victim. Befitting the most sustained and extreme simulated encounter in the film, Jackson here notes the frenetic nature of the camera work, which is dominated by a range of semi-concealed long shots and frantic zoom functions, reiterating its realist effect in these final visceral moments. The final image from the found footage of the main filmmaker and master sadist Alan Yates being dismembered before the camera, while his lifeless eyes directly address the camera lens (and that of the viewing spectator beyond) seems a controversially fitting close to the disputed status that real life death holds within *Cannibal Holocaust*, and which similarly dominated its international reception.

From Theatrical Ambiguity to Realist Reception

As indicated earlier, *Cannibal Holocaust* is challenging precisely because it breaks the safety shelter of traditional works of art, merging staged and real deaths. What emerges in the international reception of the film are a series of very specific interpretations of the film's transgressions (both in terms of violence *and* realism), which also seem to differ across distinct geographical territories. When we look at the Italian reviews from the time the film was released, it becomes clear

[12]Ibid., 4.
[13]Ibid., 9.

that critics blame the director for creating a realist canvas "of brutal butchery, sex and violence"[14] that audiences are forced to endure. These comments represent a very personal attack on Deodato, who was accused of being responsible of conceiving an accumulation of repulsive scenes that exceed the extremes of porn cinema.[15] The film is frequently framed as an entry to "the 'slash-and-eat' subgenre,"[16] and can therefore be dismissed as a catalog of sadism that aimed at stimulating the vilest reactions in the viewers. Recurring words largely referred to bodily reactions, something that nowadays is commonly related to so-called "body horror,"[17] such as "gory,"[18] "appalling,"[19] and "gruesome."[20]

French reviews from the early 1980s provide some similarity to the Italian reviews outlined earlier, by also focusing on the viewer's physiological responses to the film. However, these comments are supplemented with a more pointed political mode of critique, with frequent use of adjectives and terms such as "racist and fascist,"[21] "misogyny,"[22] "ignominy,"[23] and "bloodiest sensationalism"[24] being

---

[14]ORIG. "[…] una interminabile accozzaglia di efferatezze di bassa macelleria, sesso e violenza." l. p., *L'Unità*, February 12, 1980. Italian reviews originally published in daily newspapers, although missing some data, were collected in *Film guida—Rassegna della critica cinematografica italiana*, edited by E. Ottonello, F. Pagano and L. Rainusso.

[15]ORIG. "[…] un accumulo di scene ributtanti, da bassa macelleria, di stupri e violenze d'ogni genere, al cui confronto i corrivi pornofilm figurano come campioni di decoro." L. A., *Corriere della sera*, February 16, 1980.

[16]ORIG. "*Cannibal Holocaust, Cannibal Ferox*, sono solo alcuni titoli del filone squarta-e-mangia." a. ma., "Quando il cinema si fa antropofago," *La rivista del cinematografo* no. 7 (1981): 328.

[17]See *Screen* 27 no. 1 (1986).

[18]ORIG. "[…] il pubblico ministero aveva ritenuto il film lesivo della dignità umana per sedici sequenze, in cui si era rilevata una compiaciuta insistenza nel rappresentare crudamente particolari raccapriccianti di sadismo e violenza […] verso persone, animali e cose." Anon., "Sei condanne a Milano per Cannibal Holocaust."

[19]ORIG. "[…] un allucinante catalogo di compiacimenti mortuari […] un film ripugnante […] questo tipo di film punta sugli effetti peggiori, su stimoli bassamente emozionali." M. C. B., *Il Secolo XIX*, March 1, 1980.

[20]ORIG. "Il film […] è una galleria di raccapriccianti scene dall'inizio alla fine." Anon., "Cannibal Holocaust," *Segnocinema* no. 14 (1984): 45.

[21]ORIG. "Non seulement artistiquement on est plus bas que le dernier des nanars mais, et je pèse mes mots, *Cannibal Holocaust* est un film raciste et fasciste qui a été conçu comme tel pour faire du fric sur tout ce qu'il y a de dégradant." Jean Roy, "Cannibal Holocaust," *Cinéma* no. 81, June 1981, 126.

[22]ORIG. "Produit de la surenchère dans le domaine de l'horreur, *Cannibal Holocaust* ne mériterait qu'un silence méprisant sans la tartuferie énorme de ses auteurs […] une misogynie agressive […] clichés racists." A. G., "Cannibal Holocaust," *Positif* no. 243, June 1981, 65.

[23]ORIG. "Curieux film atrocement paroxystique qui se situe à la croisée de plusieurs courants propres au cinéma italien de grande consommation. Le film d'aventures exotiques […] la seconde filiation: celle du cinéma 'vomitif.' Lequel s'exerce alternativement dans la fiction débridée et le pseudo documentaire. Sur ce registre. *Cannibal Holocaust* bat tous les records de l'ignominie." J.Z., "Cannibal Holocaust," *La revue du cinema* (1981): 50.

[24]ORIG. "Revoici nos écrans envahis par ces détestable pseudo documentaires construits sur la recherche du sensationnalisme le plus sanguinaire et véhiculant un solid fond de racisme!" Anon., "Cannibal Holocaust," *Amis du film* no. 299 (1981): 20.

used to describe it. As a result, these interpretations become increasingly sarcastic, comparing Deodato to Mussolini.[25] Making jokes with the film's closing statement, they charge the director and the screenwriter of being the real cannibals of the piece.[26] More recently, French reviewers dealing with reissues or DVD releases of *Cannibal Holocaust* focus instead on its legacy, so that the general tone is less scathing. Writers give credit to the fact that the film, which sits at the crossroad of snuff and mondo,[27] is one of the last avatars of far-right politics that spread the "Golden Age" of the commercial transalpine production, [28] has a very loyal fan base, and decades later, has acquired the status of a "cult" movie with the ability for its most notorious messages to be re-read.

In contrast to the above receptions, reviews from Anglo-Saxon countries focus less on physiology and politics, but seem more interested in speculating on the film's aesthetics. UK reviews from mid-1990s onward underline *Cannibal Holocaust*'s "paradoxical nature": "brutal and extreme" but "intelligent."[29] They also remind us the public reaction to the movie: "While some see a powerful visionary work [...] others see only cruel exploitation."[30] Framing the film as the first mockumentary/found footage fiction, later reviews reflect on the way it engages the viewers, acknowledges Deodato's craftsmanship, and praises its clever construction, the technical details and the debate fake/real ensued.[31] Reviews from the United States do not buy "the film's 'liberal' message on civilized man's cruelty to primitive people" because it "is old hat and rendered ludicrous by Deodato's inclusion of much extraneous gore effects and nudity, as well as the genre's usual (and disgusting) killing of animals on camera."[32] In more recent reviews too, Deodato has not been forgiven for those killings: "Deodato is a

---

[25]ORIG. "De Ruggero Deodato, on peut dire, comme, en 1940, les Anglais de Mussolini: 'si vous rencontrez cet homme, changez de trottoir.'" F. G., "Cannibal Holocaust," *Cahiers du Cinéma* no. 326, July 1981,63.

[26]ORIG. "'Qui sont les vrais cannibales?' Réponse gagnante: 'Ruggero Deodato et Gianfranco Clerici.'" Raymond Lefèvre, "Cannibal Holocaust," *Image et Son* no. 361, May 1981, 42.

[27]ORIG. "Monument de mauvais goût pour certains, petite merveille d'hyperréalisme et d'audace pour d'autres, le mythique *Cannibal Holocaust* [...] À la frontière du snuff movie [...] et du *Mondo Cane*." Patrice Doré, "Cannibal Holocaust," *Séquences* no. 241, January/February 2006, 30.

[28]ORIG. "[...] il est aussi l'un des derniers avatars d'une veine d'extrême droite qui a traversé cet âge d'or de la production commerciale transalpine." Vincent Malausa, "Contre Cannibal Holocaust!," *Cahiers du Cinéma* no. 671, October 2011, 55.

[29]See *Eaten Alive! Italian Cannibal and Zombie Movies*, edited by Jay Slater (London: Plexus, 2002). "Fascinating *because* of its paradoxical nature and its refusal to acknowledge its contradictions" (Mark Savage, 107); "one of the most brutal and extreme films ever screened [...] an intelligent, if heavy-handed, jibe at mondo exploitation." (Jay Slater, 108–09).

[30]Julian Grainger, Harvey Fenton, and Gian Luca Castoldi, *Cannibal Holocaust and the Savage Cinema of Ruggero Deodato* (London: FAB Press, 1999): 63.

[31]J. B., "Cannibal Holocaust," *Sight and Sound*, January 2012, 85.

[32]Lor., "Cannibal Holocaust," *Variety*, June 19, 1985, 26.

monster, mercilessly exploiting the natives, butchering virtually every animal in his path (on film), and rubbing our noses in entrails ... "[33]

According to Kerekes and Slater, there is little doubt that some of the human killings are real: the stock footage used in *The Last Road to Hell* sequence showing fire squads executing people is indeed probably taken from newsreels shot in Nigeria and Southeast Asia.[34] Although it is widely known that Deodato purposely set up a promotional campaign involving the disappearance of the actors, he also played with the frightening idea of real deaths providing different answers when asked for explanations. Sometimes he admitted that the executions were real and that he acquired the stock footage from a British company;[35] on other occasions, he stated that he shot the firing squad inserts in Rome, at De Paolis Studios: "Although people believe that the sequence portrays real human killings—he stated to Italian magazine *Nocturno*—I reenacted it in the style of Jacopetti."[36]

Deodato's comments about adapting the techniques developed by Italian documentary filmmaker Gualtiero Jacopetti prove significant for not only the creation of *Cannibal Holocaust* but also its subsequent reception. As one of the key figures behind the Italian "mondo" movie craze of the 1960s, Jacopetti popularized the use of sensationalist documentary techniques to chart the changing and confrontational cultural practices around the world. As evidenced by titles such as *Mondo Cane* (1962) and *Africa addio* (1966), Jacopetti's "mondo" productions became controversial for stitching documentary footage and staged atrocities together, to connect traditional rituals with the changing values of the industrialized world.[37] While the mondo film's overreliance on abstract stock footage elevated the genre to the realms of cult collage, the cycle's emphasis on scenes of animal slaughter as a cruel site of exotic spectacle clearly connect them to Ruggero Deodato's later work.

For Jackson, part of the confusion around *Cannibal Holocaust*'s snuff status revolves around its utilization of two cinematic subgenres, which function across the fictional and factual divide. In terms of its fictional elements, the film draws

---

[33]Michael Atkinson, "Cannibal Holocaust," *The Village Voice* 51, no. 1, January 4–10, 2006, 66.

[34]David Kerekes and David Slater, *Killing for Culture. An Illustrated History of Death Film from Mondo to Snuff* (London and San Francisco, CA: Creation Books, 1994): 48.

[35]Lupi, *Cannibal! Il cinema selvaggio di Ruggero Deodato*, cited: 92.

[36]ORIG. "Alcune delle [scene] più raccapriccianti sono state fatte a Roma, alla De Paolis. Per esempio, la scena della fucilazione a cui assistiamo durante il filmato promozionale, realizzato dai quattro giornalisti, l'ho girata sotto le mura di Roma. Quel filmato credono sia stato fatto con spezzoni di immagini vere, invece alcune le ho ricostruite io, alla Jacopetti," *Nocturno Dossier* no. 73, cited: 35. On cannibal movies see also *Nocturno Dossier* no. 12, "Bon appetit! Guida al cinema cannibalico," June 2003.

[37]See Mark Goodall, *Sweet & Savage: The World Through the Shockumentary Film Lens* (London: Headpress, 2006).

on the 1970s' Italian cannibal film cycle, which charted the violent collision between European explorers and ritualistic tribes who retain a ritualistic coda. As illustrated by titles such as *Deep River Savages* (Umberto Lenzi, 1972), *Emanuelle and the Last Cannibals* (Joe D'Amato, 1975), *Mountain of the Cannibal God* (Sergio Martino, 1978), and *Eaten Alive!* (Umberto Lenzi, 1980), this cycle often made reference to external realism via the inclusion of either still photography or a "discovered" documentary insert purporting to expose a ritual culture's customs. *Cannibal Holocaust* provides the most sustained attempt to fuse a level of realism into its fictional narration, which Jackson sees as evidencing the mondo tradition of fusing "mixed documentary and staged footage"[38] to reproduce an exotically realist imagery. As he notes:

> *Cannibal Holocaust* adopts the travelogue aspect in several sequences, with numerous cutaways to images of local wildlife, helicopter shots of the jungle landscape, and the use of genuine native extras. However, the film owes most of its significant debt to the mondo film through the incorporation of unsimulated footage in which animals are killed. This does not consist of inserted stock footage but original material in which cast members are seen committing the acts in question. This achieves a momentary sense of extraction from the fictional world … [39]

If Deodato's debt to the mondo film can be signaled via a realist confusion occurring at the visual axis, then it is further signaled by his use of veteran composer Riz Ortolani, who also scored some the most melancholic melodies for Jacopetti's most significant titles.

Echoing Jackson's comments about the duel influences from which *Cannibal Holocaust* derives, it is noticeable that its wider international reception under the "fictional" category of "cannibal/horror" is far from assured. Indeed, reviews spanning from Italy to the UK, from France to Canada and United States, which constitutes part of the current international reception of the movie, suggest that the film and its director were more closely received via links to the sensationalist mondo documentary and snuff references, and this was the basis on which the film was condemned, marginalized, and blamed. As Mikita Brottman notes, "*Cannibal Holocaust* was the first 'Cannibal mondo' film, standing at the crossroads of the cannibal cycle of the late 1970s and early 1980s and that other celebrated Italian cinematic tradition, the mondo movie."[40] This spurious affiliation has been underlined more than once: while Harvey Fenton refers to

---

[38]Jackson, "*Cannibal Holocaust*, Realist Horror, and Reflexivity," 3.
[39]Ibid.
[40]Mikita Brottman, *Offensive Films* (Nashville, TN: Vanderbilt University Press, 2005): 113.

Deodato's work as "the Bastard son of the mondo genre,"[41] which in turn is "a genre that is a close cinematic relative of the horror mockumentary,"[42] Carolina Gabriela Jauregui defines *Cannibal Holocaust* as "a hybrid trans-genre film,"[43] and for some reviewers, it unarguably falls into the mondo category.[44] Its modular structure is a critical point when focusing on the film-within-the-film sequences discussed earlier. As Julian Petley further recognizes, after showing the slaughter of animals, a process of association and osmosis regulates "the verisimilitude of the scenes in which humans are apparently mutilated and killed," thus confirming its murderous mondo conceit.[45] Related issues of voyeurism, racism, and abomination that have been highlighted by reviewers are thus also projected onto the director. Deodato then seems to be one of the most hated filmmakers after Gualtiero Jacopetti, the so-called "Godfather" of the mondo film, who was defined by journalists and film critics no less than a "gravedigger-filmmaker" suffering from a "congenital morbid sadomasochistic mysticism."[46]

Snuffing up the South

While Jacopetti's 1960s' mondo productions are comparable to the later cannibal fictions of Deodato, both in terms of the shared "realist" features and the race-based controversy that they generated, their mutual depiction of "primitive" landscapes and its inhabitants are also of interest here. While the international reception of both *Cannibal Holocaust* and the mondo's images of sexuality, race, and region give these narratives a pseudo-global feel, it is also possible to argue that these films reflect far more local concerns that emerged within Italian society during the 1960s and 1970s.

This period heralded rapid social development, alongside changing images of Italian womanhood, which the mondo movie often mimicked (such as Jacopetti's 1963 production *Women Around the World*, which compared the traditional and contemporary renditions and distortions of female desire). Although the

---

[41]Julian Grainger, Harvey Fenton, and Gian Luca Castoldi, *Cannibal Holocaust*, 64.

[42]Gary D. Rhodes, "Mockumentaries and the Production of Realist Horror," *Post Script* 21, no. 3 (Summer 2002): 52.

[43]Carolina Gabriela Jauregui, "'Eat It Alive and Swallow It Whole!': Resavoring *Cannibal Holocaust* as a Mockumentary," *(In)visible Culture* 7, March 2006.

[44]"Perhaps the most extreme tissue sample of the dare-you-to-look 'mondo' genre that emerged in the '60s." Atkinson, "*Cannibal Holocaust*," 66.

[45]Julian Petley, "*Cannibal Holocaust* and the Pornography of Death," in *The Spectacle of the Real: From Hollywood to "Reality" TV and Beyond*, ed. Geoff King (Bristol and Portland: Intellect Books, 2005): 179.

[46]ORIG. "[…] necroforo-cineasta" affetto da un "congenito morboso misticismo sadomasochistico." Anon., "Jacopetti," *Cinema 60* (1967): 16.

mondo myth promoted an image of social and sexual emancipation, Italy's new manufacturing wealth remained largely concentrated in its northern and central regions. This unequal distribution of opportunity promoted policies of mass migration, which themselves exposed long-standing tensions between an industrial Italy and its more primitive, rural South. With its troubling proximity to the Middle East, wild untamed landscapes and even more untamed inhabitants, Italy's rural region conveyed a duel status of fascination and fear within the national psyche, embodied by the term *Mezzogiorno*, or "Southern problem."

To this extent, Italian cultural theorists such as John Dickie have argued that Italian representations of the "primitive" are less racial, and more regional in exposing the internal contradictions between the differing geographical spheres of the culture that has produced them. While these discourses remain essentially contradictory and irreducibly ethnocentric, they also ensure "that vague geographical definition"[47] becomes a structuring trope for the southern region and its inhabitants. As Dickie notes:

> […] the diversities within both North and South are as great as those between them. The South, moreover, is at different times taken to mean "South and islands" and "mainland South." It sometimes includes Rome and sometimes stops below it.[48]

If the Italian South remains an ambivalent sphere that becomes irreducible and interchangeable with other African and "Oriental" zones of otherness, it explains the importance of the differing "scientific" policy and cultural practices which have been employed to theorize this disputed Italian sphere. As indicated in Dickie's important study "Stereotypes of the Italian South," this began with Alfredo Niceforo's volume *L'Italia Barbara Contemporanea* (aka *Contemporary Barbarian Italy*, 1898) and later included Edward Banfield's 1957 study *The Moral Basis of a Backward Society*, which reveals the extent to which criminological, sociological, and even cranial data have been used as a template of regionalized distinction that continues to seep into popular culture *and* consciousness. Indeed, defining Niceforo's original study as "almost an inventory of stereotypes of the South in the late nineteenth century,"[49] Dickie notes that this influential Italian publication confirms:

> The South was one of Italy's most important banks of Otherness. The barbarous, the primitive, the violent, the irrational, the feminine, the African … these

---

[47] John Dickie, "Stereotypes of the Italian South," in *The New History of the Italian South: The Mezzogiorno Revisited*, edited by Robert Lumley and Jonathan Morris (Exeter: University of Exeter Press, 1997): 116.
[48] Ibid.
[49] Ibid., 118.

and other values, negatively connoted, were repeatedly located in the *Mezzogiorno* as foils to definitions of Italy.[50]

While Dickie finds an obsession to aestheticize and anaesthetize the southern landscape in the nineteenth-century journals, such as *L'Illustrazione Italiana*, such publications with their emphasis on the rustic rural landscape harboring dangerous clans and an untamed environment draw parity with some of the controversial imagery later replicated in the cinema of Jacopetti and Deodato. Indeed, from the 1800s onward, the theme of northern intellectuals and explorers "going down south" to document, study, and expose rural depravity became a common trope that passed from eugenic study, to ethnographic expose before finally becoming popularized in the 1960s mondo movies, and the 1970s' Italian cannibal films which replaced them.

Since the beginning of the mondo cycle in 1962, with the now seminal *Mondo cane* (Gualtiero Jacopetti, Paolo Cavara and Franco Prosperi), Central and Southern Italian regions were filmed as places where strange and bizarre traditional rituals took place. To this extent, *Mondo cane* provides an insert around the cult of Rodolfo Valentino in the city of Castellaneta, which finds its place alongside the cargo cult in New Guinea. Further southern/uncivilized inferences abide in the film, with one sequence shot in Cocullo, in the region of Abruzzo, where the statue of Saint Dominick is carried through a procession and believers follow it with hands full of snakes. The speaker then reminds us that Nocera Tirinese, in the region of Calabria, is known for the bloody rites of the "battienti," that exalts the Christ's flagellation and "whose origins are obscure." Finally, in the Roman cemetery of the Capuchins "death has been assigned a decorative task," while on Isola Tiberina, the "Red Sacks" brotherhood looks after human remains "protecting the bones from the ravages of times."

As with the subsequent cinema of Deodato, it is not just the southern emphasis of Jacopetti's films, but also their style, structure, and content that created different tones, and sometimes even seen as conflicting aspects: *Mondo cane* was an "Impressive, hard-hitting documentary feature [...] brash and provocative [...] Yet the total effect is grimly stimulating from the visual standpoint, depressing in the conclusions drawn."[51] Even though reviewers generally praised its technical aspects, from Antonio Climati's camera work to Riz Ortolani's score and "a cruel editing" capable of drawing the limits of a civilization with a certain ruthlessness;[52]

---

[50]Ibid., 119.

[51]Hawk., "Mondo Cane," *Variety*, May 16, 1962.

[52]ORIG. "[...] un montaggio crudele [...] che riesce a tracciare, con una certa spregiudicatezza, i limiti di una civiltà." Gregorio Napoli, "Mondo cane di Gualtiero Jacopetti," *Film Selezione* 3 no. 12 (July–August 1962): 52.

despite its "tremendous exploitation possibilities,"[53] the film was seen as a "catalogue of horrors,"[54] whose strength lied in those scenes was sadism, displayed to stimulate the vilest reactions in the viewers.[55]

Although Jacopetti proved himself "[…] a filmmaker of outstanding ability and force,"[56] he was generally considered nothing more than a "cinematographic garbage man"[57] whose merit was "having discovered and spread—claiming to be a realistic document—the sado-masochistic taste for bloodshed, the brutality, the violence, the morbidity and every bloody situation."[58] Therefore, *Mondo cane* was labelled as "[…] one of the most depressing, revolting motion pictures ever made […] a movie peep show, a sickening, sadistic film, equivalent to and of dubious appeal only to those who are intrigued by two-headed babies in bottles or other mutations of the human mind and body."[59]

Given these premises, it is not surprising that when Jacopetti was involved in the shooting of *Africa addio* (Gualtiero Jacopetti and Franco Prosperi, 1966), his interest for the south of the world was seen as a mere chance to provide new themes to a career based on exploitation. In this film, the theme of the south is expanded to the African continent, shifting from weirdness toward an exotic postcolonial gaze, which soon prompted allegations of racism, sadism, and lack of historical dimension. Like the Amazons for Deodato years later, Africa was a land where mystery, magic, and death originated a compelling mix, a primitive force able to attract "a filmmaker equipped with a camera and a good dose of wit and power of observation."[60] Surrounded by allegations of executions staged for the camera and speculations on the re-enactment of historical tragedies,[61] *Africa*

---

[53]Anon., "Mondo Canc," *Kinematograph Weekly*, November 15, 1962, 30.

[54]J. G., "Mondo Cane," *Monthly Film Bulletin* 30 no. 348 (January 1963): 3.

[55]ORIG. "I punti di forza spettacolari del film, in sostanza, sono quelli in cui più si dispiega il sadismo, il che non è né fare satira né documentare, ma solo puntare sulla sensazione di bassa lega." Ernesto G. Laura, "Mondo cane," *Bianco e Nero* 23 no. 5, May 1962, 67.

[56]Mandel Herbstmann, "Mondo Cane," *The Film Daily*, March 26, 1963, 8.

[57]ORIG. "[…] Il netturbino cinematografico Gualtiero Jacopetti." Lino Miccichè, *Cinema italiano degli anni '70* (Venezia: Marsilio, 1979): 121.

[58]ORIG. "Un grande successo hanno i film di Gualtiero Jacopetti […], a cui si deve riconoscere il merito di aver scoperto e contribuito a diffondere, spacciandolo per documento realistico, il gusto sadomasochista per lo spargimento di sangue, la brutalità, la violenza, la morbosità e ogni situazione cruenta." Gian Piero Brunetta, *Storia del cinema italiano. Dal 1945 aglianni Ottanta* (Roma: Editori Riuniti, 1982): 791.

[59]James Powers, "Italian Picture A Sadistic Orgy," *The Hollywood Reporter*, February 20, 1963, 3.

[60]ORIG. "[…] un cineaste dotato, oltre che della macchina da presa, di una buona dose di sagacia e di spirito di osservazione." (a.a.), "Mondo cane," *Intermezzo* 17, no. 7–8 (April 30, 1962): 67.

[61]"Did Jacopetti and Prosperi just happen to be in the right place at the right moment, or were the killings staged expressly for their benefit? *Africa Addio* prompts questions like this at every turn." Anon., "Africa addio," *Monthly Film Bulletin* 34, no. 405 (October 1967): 159.

addio was praised in the US[62] but dismissed by the Italian press as a fabricated and gratuitously violent documentary, lacking any historical dimension and using "sadistic tricks"[63] to hit the viewer. Exploiting the slaughter of African animals and tribal feuds for the sake of bloodshed, the film was labeled as "despicably racist,"[64] "paternalistic and antidemocratic."[65]

Conclusion

By emphasizing themes of a European explorer or thrill-seeker abducted by savages during a remote expedition, the Italian cannibal films expanded the exotic content of the mondo movies by adding an important fictional drive to stock scenes of lush landscape and local wildlife. These later movies were often set in a variety of international locations beyond the normal Italian realm. However, the cycle remained an intrinsic example of what we could term as "mezzogiornosploitation," for domestic audiences familiar with myths surrounding the barbaric, flesh-eating tendencies of their southern countrymen. It was a theme that Deodato himself explored in *Last Cannibal World*, which once again used documentary reportage to present an air of realism to its grisly jungle proceedings. With the later *Cannibal Holocaust*, Deodato added the innovative twist of changing his western explorers from scientists to documentary filmmakers, resulting in the snuff effect that this chapter has explored. By launching this trend of found footage violence, *Cannibal Holocaust* has left an indelible and bloody imprint on the realist film landscape that continues to influence international horror productions well into the twenty-first century.

---

[62]An overview of the reviews from the Unites States include: "fearlessly filmed at personal danger [...] edited with skill and honesty"; "A bold, no-holds-barred documentary look at Africa [...] as eruptive as a thunderstorm"; "magnificently photographed and shrewdly edited, but not for the squeamish"; "A shattering, unforgettable documentary." Respectively quoted in: Charles S. Aaronson, "Africa Addio," *Motion Picture Herald* 237, no. 5 (February 1, 1967): 654; Mandel Herbstman, "Africa Addio," *The Film Daily*, January 13, 1967, 6; Margaret Hinxman, "Africa Addio," *The Daily Cinema*, June 9, 1967, 5; Hawk., "Africa, Addio!," *Variety*, March 9, 1966.

[63]ORIG. "[...] il ricorso a espedienti sadici, la continua sottolineatura necrofila dei particolari filmati, gli accorgimenti impiegati per colpire lo spettatore, facendo prevalentemente leva su meccanismi inconsci, denotano una dannosa tendenza alla sopraffazione." A. Galante Garrone, "Nella possibilità di mentire il pericolo maggiore del cinema," *Cinema Nuovo* no. 180 (1966): 86.

[64]ORIG. "Africa addio è un ignobile film razzista che, tuttavia, merita di essere analizzato e discusso per il grado di pericolosità sociale contenuto nella sua ideologia, nel suo successo commerciale e nei suoi procedimenti mistificatori." Redazione, "Anatomia di una mistificazione. Africa addio un film di propaganda razzista," *Cinema 60*, no. 57 (1966): 33.

[65]ORIG. "[...] prima di essere razzista, *Africa addio* è un film paternalistico e antidemocratico." Sandro Zambetti, "Africa addio! Una tecnica utilizzata per un basso e ignobile servizio," *Cineforum* no. 53, March 1966, 239.

6 A MURDER MYSTERY IN BLACK AND BLUE: THE MARKETING, DISTRIBUTION, AND CULT MYTHOLOGY OF *SNUFF* IN THE UK

Mark McKenna

n the USA, in 1976, theatrical screenings of Michael and Roberta Findlay's *Snuff* triggered a month-long FBI investigation into whether or not the film depicted an actual murder in its final scene.[1] It was therefore almost inevitable that the film's eventual release in the more conservative British market would be problematic.

Some six years before it was scheduled for a release on UK home video in 1982, a US investigation had ruled that the murder depicted in the film was quite clearly simulated.[2] However, *Snuff* entered into an increasingly censorious climate in the UK following concerns over the advertising used to promote home video releases of horror and exploitation films, which, because of a loophole in the law, were not legally required to be submitted to the British Board of Film Censors for certification. The release of uncensored films such as *SS Experiment Camp* (Sergio Garrone, 1976), *I Spit on Your Grave* (Meir Zarchi, 1978), and *The Driller Killer* (Abel Ferrera, 1979) would prompt an influential article in *The Sunday Times* in which journalist Peter Chippendale warned of the "video nasties": graphic horror videos that he alleged were "far removed from the traditional horror film … dwell[ing] on murder, multiple rape, butchery, sado-masochism, mutilation of women and Nazi

---

[1] See David Kerekes and David Slater, *Killing for Culture: An Illustrated History of Death Film from Mondo to Snuff* (London: Creation Books, 1995).
[2] Ibid.; Mikita Brottman, *Offensive Films* (Westport: Vanderbilt University Press, 2005): 79–95.

atrocities."[3] These are the criteria which would soon come to define the "video nasties," and of which *Snuff* would be emblematic.[4]

This chapter examines the cult mythology that has developed around *Snuff* in the UK, paying particular attention to the role of its distributor, Astra Video, and the role of horror film fan communities in furthering and shaping that mythology. The chapter is ultimately concerned with the nationally specific context in which *Snuff* was first distributed in Britain, and more specifically, how the film's UK video release has become the subject of heated and, at times, vituperative argument, among fans and collectors of the video nasties.

Snuff's murky UK distribution history is littered with inconsistencies and discrepancies, so as a means of being as clear as possible, what follows is divided into two sections, both of which investigate the distribution of *Snuff* in the UK and its subsequent legacy as a collector's item among video-nasty fans. First, drawing on contemporaneous reports that featured in the video consumer press, the video trade press and national newspapers in the 1980s, it constructs a chronological history of *Snuff* in the UK. From there, in the second section, discussion will move to consider those parts of *Snuff*'s British distribution narrative that have proven most contentious and speculative in video collecting communities, and will address the gaps in the formerly outlined history that have prompted debate and furthered the mythology surrounding the film. The chapter will conclude by considering the importance of the contested British history of *Snuff* within and beyond collector culture. Indeed, while the mythology surrounding snuff films is typically positioned as being cross-cultural, and most frequently relates back to the question of whether or not they exist,[5] there is also a nationally specific mythology surrounding the distribution of *Snuff* in the UK. This chapter aims to examine certain elements of that mythology.

Made in Croydon…where life is cheap! A chronological history

The release of *Snuff* in Britain has been discussed at some length by Julian Petley in his contribution to *Unruly Pleasures: The Cult Film and Its Critics*: " 'Snuffed out':

---

[3]Peter Chippendale, "How High Street Horror Is Invading the Home," *The Sunday Times*, May 23, 1982.
[4]The cultural history and legacy of the video nasties has been widely discussed in academic research. See, for example, *The Video Nasties: Freedom and Censorship in the Media*, edited by Martin Barker (London: Pluto Press, 1984); Kate Egan, *Trash or Treasure? Censorship and the Changing Meanings of the Video Nasties* (Manchester: Manchester University Press, 2007); and Julian Petley, *Film and Video Censorship in Modern Britain* (Edinburgh: Edinburgh University Press, 2011).
[5]Julian Petley, " 'Snuffed Out': Nightmares in a Trading Standards Officer's Brain," in *Unruly Pleasures: The Cult Film and Its Critics*, edited by Graeme Harper and Xavier Mendik (Guilford: FAB Press, 2000).

Nightmares in a trading standards officer's brain."[6] However, the film's distribution history has rarely been acknowledged within the academy[7] and most discussion of its troubled dissemination has been restricted to either coffee table volumes or has appeared in online discussions on video collector forums such as Pre-Cert Video.[8] In this material, there is much debate around whether or not the film was indeed *ever* "officially" released by a named distributor onto the UK market. So conflicting are the arguments that the film's "true" distribution history remains in doubt.[9]

One of the arguments put forward is that Croydon-based Astra Video—a company known in the trade for its horror videos[10] (including some subsequently banned as video nasties) and which had originally promoted *Snuff* as one of its forthcoming titles in 1982—in actuality, never released it, and that the film only ever circulated in Britain as a pirated cassette. This is an argument evinced in the book *See No Evil: Banned Films and Video Controversy*, which was cowritten by prolific fanzine publisher David Kerekes, as well as in *Shock! Horror!: Astounding Artwork from the Video Nasty Era* and *The Art of the Nasty*, in addition to the DVD box set *Video Nasties: The Definitive Guide*(Jake West, 2010); the latter of which were all produced under the purview of recognized cultural intermediaries on the video-nasty era and moderators of the Pre-Cert forum, Marc Morris, and Francis Brewster.[11] These works collectively purport that while Astra had initially planned to release the film, exhibiting the tape at a video trade show in 1982, the company

---

[6]Ibid., 210–19.

[7]Petley touches very lightly on these issues, but his article is mostly concerned with the birth of the snuff mythology, and the way that the mythology has been framed in British newspapers. Ibid., 211.

[8]The moniker "pre-cert" explicitly refers to video-cassettes released in Britain prior to 1984, before the introduction of the Video Recordings Act (VRA), and thus before it was a legal requirement for all films released on video to be "*cert*ified"—deemed "suitable" for audiences—by the British Board of Film Censors. These videos have become increasingly sought after and the Pre-Cert Forum has become an important hub for collectors of these cassettes and related ephemera.

[9]At the time of writing, a simple search for "Snuff" on the Pre Cert Forum returns 478 threads containing thousands of posts, with many of these threads dedicated entirely to the debates that persist around it.

[10]One of Astra's notable early releases, *The Best of Sex and Violence* (Various, 1981)—which was a compilation of salacious clips from a range of exploitation titles—set the bar for what was to follow.

[11]David Kerekes and David Slater, *See No Evil: Banned Films and Video Controversy* (Manchester: Headpress, 2000); Marc Morris, Harvey Fenton, and Francis Brewster, *Shock! Horror!: Astounding Artwork from the Video Nasty Era* (Guilford: FAB Press, 2005); Nigel Wingrove and Marc Morris, *The Art of the Nasty* (Surrey: FAB Press/Salvation, 2nd edition, 2009). Marc Morris is perhaps the most notable name of all here. He is one of the founders of the Pre-Cert forum (along with Francis Brewster), is known in the fan community for his extensive early video collection, and was the producer of *Video Nasties: The Definitive Guide* and *Video Nasties: The Definitive Guide Part 2* (which he also distributed through Nucleus Films: a company he co-owns with film director, Jakes West). Significantly, Morris' collection is frequent seen the background of the talking heads segments of the *Video Nasties* documentaries.

withdrew the release in response to the mounting pressure that was being levied against the video industry, following advice from their legal representation.[12] However, seeing as though copies of *Snuff* did circulate, albeit without Astra's branding (or any company logo for that matter), some commentators and collectors have debated that Astra may well have been responsible for the release after all, but had "taken the copies already prepared and released them... without distributor information on them (to make cash and avoid the law)."[13] In light of these debates, this section scrutinizes trade and consumer press of the 1980s to trace this contested distribution history of *Snuff*, and to shed light onto areas of conflicting discourse that have contributed to the shaping of *Snuff*'s mythology in British collector circles.

Some aspects of the history put forward in *See No Evil, Shock Horror, Art of the Nasty*, and *Video Nasties: The Definitive Guide* can be verified via the examination of contemporaneous press reportage. An article published in *Television and Video Retailer* confirms both the presence of *Snuff* at the trade show alluded to above and Astra's involvement in its release, reporting that the film was showcased by Astra at Manchester's Northern Software Show (NSS) on May 23 and 25, 1982, and that "trade appeared to be booming."[14] Indeed, the film was apparently so popular that Astra's CEO, Mike Behr, claimed that the company had already taken orders for 2,500 units by the end of the first day,[15] while the *Daily Express*, reporting on May 28, confirmed the anticipated widespread distribution of the film: "A new commodity will be available on your high street next week—a film called 'Snuff' which anyone will be able to buy over the counter at some of the 12,000 video shops throughout Britain."[16]

From these reports, it would appear that Astra had all intentions of releasing *Snuff*. Moreover, given the film's notoriety, the reports of the film's popularity would also appear credible, seeing as though Astra's other horror and exploitation titles (many of which, as with *Snuff*, were licensed from the US distributor Wizard Video) were performing similarly well at trade shows throughout the country.[17] However,

---

[12]Kerekes and Slater, *See No Evil*, 48, 254; Marc Morris et al., *Shock Horror!* 239; Wingrove and Morris, *The Art of the Nasty*, 29; Kim Newman upholds this argument in his contribution to *Video Nasties: The Definitive Guide*.

[13]Bigandy, "The Evolution of Astra's SNUFF," June 7, 2010, accessed June 8, 2014, http://pre-cert.co.uk/forum/showthread.php?t=16401&highlight=blue+snuff. See also Kerekes and Slater, *See No Evil*, 254.

[14]Anon., "Snuff Snuffs It," *Television and Video Retailer*, June 1982, 24.

[15]Anon., "Protests Expected over Astra Release of US 'Snuff' Movie," *Video Business* 2, no. 8, June (1982): 6.

[16]Tony Dawe, "This Poison being Peddled as Home Entertainment," *The Daily Express*, May 28, 1982, 7.

[17]*Television and Video Retailer* ran a feature on the London Heathrow Software Show, which took place earlier in the year, and reported that "Mike Behr, Astra's managing director, says that over 1,000 units of *I Spit on Your Grave* were sold and that *Schlock*, 'a monster comedy about an ape-man who goes bananas' [...] saw around 900 sales." See Anon., "The Wizard from LA," *Television and Video Retailer*, June 1982, 52.

as momentum against the video nasties escalated from the press,[18] releasing a film such as *Snuff*, which purported to feature a genuine murder, could have mobilized the kinds of legal action that Behr, in an earlier interview, had scoffed at: "There's no censorship laws on video at all. What can they [the authorities] do about it?"[19] Following the aforementioned article in the *Daily Express* which drew on *Snuff*'s apparent "scenes of rape and mutilation and murder so realistic that the cover asks: 'are the killings in the film for Real?'"[20] Astra was forced to backtrack on any previous claims about *Snuff*'s supposed veracity: a factor that Behr tried to hype at the NSS, by "refusing to preview [scenes from] the film" to potential clients.[21] Obviously feeling the turning tide, and in response to the negative publicity, Behr felt it necessary to clarify his position with the industry magazine *Video Business* the week after the NSS, explaining that "of course [*Snuff* is] not a real snuff movie ... It's a publicity stunt." He continued, explaining that, because of the rising video-nasty controversy he could see "[the] release of the film lead[ing] to [legal] problems" and, for that reason, his company would "only be keeping the film on the market for about a month."[22]

What should be clear is that, by June 1982, Behr was at least appearing to exercise a certain degree of caution regarding the release of *Snuff*. By opting for a limited release, it is arguable that he was at once recognizing the profits that could be amassed from stocking a controversial film with wide media exposure, but by the same token restricting its release to try to circumvent any future legal consequences. Behr's trepidation certainly demonstrates a restraint at odds with how he had originally intended to promote the film.

In the very same issue of *Video Business*, Astra had taken out a full-page advertisement which promoted its release of *Snuff* alongside another visceral horror film, and future video nasty, *Blood Feast* (Figure 6.1). The ad, which was based on material that had been used to promote the films' US video releases, was highly sensational: with grisly painted artworks for each film—a man holding a meat clever over the bloodied corpse of young woman for *Blood Feast*, and a crazed psychopath wielding an axe over the image of a woman's bloodied hands for *Snuff*—were positioned side-by-side under the deliberately provocative banner: "WALL-TO-WALL GORE—Two powerful releases from ASTRA." In a style reminiscent of a grind house double-bill, the advert emphasized both films' graphic and visceral qualities and, significantly, their

---

[18]Petley, *Film and Video Censorship in Modern Britain*, 23–43.
[19]Behr cited in Chippendale, "How High Street Horror Is Invading the Home." See also John Martin, *Seduction of the Gullible: The Truth Behind the Video Nasty Scandal* (Liskeard: Stray Cat Publishing, 2007): 14.
[20]Dawe, "This Poison Being Peddled as Home Entertainment," 7.
[21]Anon., "Snuff Snuffs It," 24.
[22]Anon., "Protests Expected over Astra Release of US 'Snuff' Movie," 6.

FIGURE 6.1 "Wall-to-Wall Gore"—Astra Video promotes *Snuff* alongside *Blood Feast*.

"power" to affect the viewer,[23] working to contradict whatever cautiousness Behr was trying to exercise elsewhere.

However, for all that this particular advert seemed to delight in provocation, by the following issue of *Video Business*, the magazine reported that Astra had withdrawn the film.[24] Listed simply under the headline "SNUFF," the company stated that, in response to "attacks by the British press," and as a company "[p] roud of its reputation for integrity and honesty," Astra wanted to avoid any confusion that had arisen regarding *Snuff*'s supposed scenes of real live death. While the company believed that the film did not show "any unacceptable scenes

---

[23]As Julian Petley has argued, the video nasties were often portrayed by the media as "potential or actual causes of violence." Julian Petley, "'Are We Insane?': The 'Video Nasty' Moral Panic," *Recherches sociologiques et anthropologiques* (2012) http://rsa.revues.org/839. For more information about the media effects debate surrounding video nasties see, for instance: Martin Barker, *The Video Nasties*; Guy Cumberbatch, "Legislating Mythology: Video Violence and Children," *Journal of Mental Health* 3, no. 4 (1994): 485–94; Kenneth Thompson, *Moral Panics* (London: Routledge, 1998): 90–91; and James Kendrick, "A Nasty Situation: Social Panics, Transnationalism and the Video Nasty," in *Horror Film: Creating and Marketing Fear*, edited by Steffen Hantke (Jackson: University Press of Mississippi, 2004): 153–72.

[24]Anon., "DPP Ponders the Case Against 'Horror' Videos," *Video Business* 2, no. 9, mid-June (1982): 1.

of violence," it felt that the film had "been sensationalised [by the press] into something that it is not."[25]

At this stage, a public announcement recognizing the film's fictional content would seem to have functioned as a restorative measure, and by mid-1982, it would seem that Astra had attempted to sever all ties with the film. However, by September 12, *The Sunday Times* reported that *Snuff* had indeed made its way onto market. In the article, Behr, in defense of himself and his company, claimed that the film the *Sunday Times* purported to be *Snuff* simply *could not have* been *Snuff*, because the master copy had reportedly been returned to the US before any copies of film had actually been made for UK distribution. Behr also claimed, somewhat tenuously, that the film that the *Sunday Times* purported to be *Snuff* was "not *Snuff* at all," but rather "a compilation of various *cuts* under the snuff label."[26]

However, in spite of Behr's insistence, the film had in fact made its way on to UK market, and irrespective of his claims, to the contrary, the content had remained unchanged. As noted previously, however, neither the packaging of the cassette (which reworked the same image Astra had used to promote the film in *Video Business*) or, indeed, the label on the cassette itself, made any reference to Astra at all. These factors have contributed to the assumption that this was an unofficial, bootlegged, release of the film; a position reinforced by Behr in his retrospective interview for *Shock Horror* in 2005.[27] Ironically, by February 1983, the consumer magazine, *Video Viewer*, reported that the Department of Public Prosecutions (DPP) was considering prosecuting Astra for allowing copies of Snuff to be leaked onto the market, which has worked to continue those debates concerning Astra's apparent distance from the release of *Snuff*, namely, because Astra was targeted by the DPP despite there being no conclusive evidence about the company's involvement in the distribution.[28]

All these factors have featured prominently in discussions among video collectors concerning the distribution of *Snuff* in Britain. In fan communities, questions are repeatedly asked about Astra's involvement in the circulation of the film. This had led to the repeated examination of the minutia of detail surrounding the film: from the video's contentious historical timeline, to the cassette and its packaging. All of these factors have been scrutinized in an attempt to secure the provenance of *Snuff*. In light of this, the next section will examine the major debates that have taken place.

---

[25] Astra press release, "SNUFF," *Video Business* 2, no. 9, Mid-June (1982): 4.
[26] *The Sunday Times*, September 12, 1982.
[27] Morris et al. *Shock Horror!*, 239.
[28] Anon., "Tougher Times on the Way for Video Nasty Distributors," *Video Viewer* 2, no. 8 (1983): 8.

Snuff or "F" for "fake"?: Key debates, speculation, and cultures of collecting

According to much discussion in books and online, the release of *Snuff* that Astra intended to market to the public prior to withdrawing it, had different artwork to the version that eventually found its way onto the high street. It is worth unpicking these differences, for they have proven important factors within video collecting culture.

In both Astra's intended original release (hereby referred to as the "official" version) and in the assumed pirated release (hereby, "unofficial"), the central imagery on the front of both tape covers remains the same: a maniacal figure is depicted wielding an axe over a pair of female hands that are bound in rope and bleeding from the wrists. The background of the image shows a screaming face between two sets of studio lights, indicating the iconography of the film set that would become central to the film's mythological status.[29] The film's title is positioned beneath these images, capitalized in 3-D lettering, with a bloodied slash running across the middle. The artwork from the official release frames these images in a pale-blue border, which has led to the nickname "blue-sleeve *Snuff*" among collectors. On this version, the legend "the original legendary atrocity shot and banned in New York" is emblazoned in red typeface at the top of the cover, and Astra's "AV" insignia, along with the words "Cult Video," are displayed prominently on the front, spine, and rear of the cover.

The "Cult Video" label is particularly significant, for it indicates that the artwork of the blue-sleeved version is a replication of that used on the US release of the film by Wizard Video, the company from which Astra had licensed it. In fact, a similar styling is present across two other releases that Astra acquired from Wizard, including *Blood Feast* (which has a red border) and *I Spit on Your Grave* (which has yellow border) (Figure 6.2). The front cover of the blue-sleeved *Snuff* clearly identifies "Cult Video distributed exclusively in the UK by Astra Video" and provides company credits alluding to Monarch Films, the company responsible for the film's theatrical distribution in the US. The rear of the cover depicts a scaled-down copy of the central cover image above a synopsis detailing the controversial nature of the film's subject matter. Tellingly, the synopsis ends with the rhetoric "are the killings in this film real? You be the judge!" The rear also displays a copyright prosecution notice that verifies the legitimacy attached to this particular release: namely, that it was a genuine Astra product.

---

[29]The background image was reused a number of times by different companies in different contexts. The chief example is Media's release of the Mexican horror film, *Demonoid* (Alfredo Zacarías, 1979), which positions the blue screaming face behind an image of a sword-wielding demon standing tall, with two scantily-clad women at its feet.

FIGURE 6.2 The respective Astra Video covers for *Blood Feast, I Spit on Your Grave* and "blue-sleeve" *Snuff*.

Comparatively, the "unofficial" release lacks any form of insignia other than a vertical strip on the video spine to indicate that it is a "VHS" cassette. The cover imagery lacks the blue border of the "official" release and is rendered primarily in black; hence, video collectors designating it "black-sleeve *Snuff*" (Figure 6.3). The artwork for this version comprises the entire front of the cassette and the capitalized legends "the original legendary atrocity shot and banned in New York" and "the actors and actresses who dedicated their lives to making this film were never seen or heard from again" are emblazoned in yellow typeset at the top and bottom of the video cover (the latter is also present on the blue-sleeved version, although is less pronounced). The synopsis on the rear of the packaging is replicated from the blue-sleeved version verbatim, albeit with the title *Snuff* capitalized in red. The black-sleeved version of the tape therefore contains far less information than its "official" counterpart; a factor which, without question, served to heighten the mystique surrounding its release into the UK marketplace.

The presence of these two different versions of the same film has retrospectively led video-nasty collectors to assume that Astra *did* in fact release the film, albeit as a "bootleg," and in spite of several protestations from Behr, who has claimed that he had nothing to do with it, and, contrarily, that the film was distributed by a "well-known video piracy gang."[30] Certainly, it is the noted differences between the blue-sleeve and black-sleeve versions that have become the basis for most debate. Such arguments are typical of video-nasty collectors who continuously discuss the authenticity of tapes released, the companies that released them, and

---

[30]Behr quoted in Morris et al., *Shock Horror!*, 239.

FIGURE 6.3 The "unofficial," minimalist, "black-sleeve" version of *Snuff*.

the circulation of pirates and duplications.[31] The sustained analysis of such debates allows for a nuanced exploration of the British chapter in *Snuff*'s legacy, and how the video release(s) of the film, and the enduring appeal of the tape(s) among horror fans, have meaningfully contributed to the wider mythology of the snuff movie.

Kate Egan, drawing on the work of Kerekes and Slater, has argued that, at one time, collectors of video nasties prioritized seeking out uncut copies of contentious films: what Egan calls the "most *politically authentic* version of a banned title." However, given the further proliferation of many of the video nasties on DVD and Blu-Ray, collectors nowadays tend to "focus on the *historically authentic* value of such videos." That is to say, in contemporary collecting culture, less of an emphasis is placed on the *films*, with more of an emphasis being placed on owning original, authentic cassettes—including artwork and shell cases—from the early 1980s. Egan argues that this underscores recognition of "the marked importance of the original videos' cultural history and their re-constituted status as 'origin objects' within British horror video collecting culture."[32] However, because there is so much confusion surrounding the release of *Snuff*, and whether or not the version that initially made it onto the market was a bootleg, this surely begs the question: which, out of the blue-sleeved and black-sleeved versions, constitutes the "origin object"? Indeed, if, as David Blight (summarizing the work of Charles Lindholm) has suggested, "authenticity is generally regarded as an absolute value— the authentic is consistently superior to the inauthentic,"[33] then no such "absolute value" can be applied to the UK release(s) of *Snuff*.

For some fans, the blue-sleeved version is the more dubious of the two. This is because, although an image of the blue-sleeve artwork (replete with Astra insignia) did appear in an issue of the consumer magazine *Video Viewer* in early 1983 (Figure 6.4)—leading many to speculate that some promotional copies that were never intended for general distribution made it onto the market—none of the collectors I have contacted recall having seen physical copies of the tape in rental shops during the video-nasty era. In fact, according to a lengthy discussion thread on the Pre-Cert Video forum, physical copies of the blue-sleeved variant did not begin to emerge until the early 1990s, with the rise of fanzines (and their classifieds sections, where video tapes could be openly bought, sold, or

---

[31]For detailed insights into the practices of video nasty collectors, see Egan, *Trash or Treasure?*, 154–81; and Kerekes and Slater, *See No Evil*, 287–313.

[32]Egan, *Trash or Treasure?*, 158.

[33]David Blight, *Niche Publications and Subcultural Authenticity: The case of Stealth magazine*, unpublished thesis, the University of Sydney, 2008, accessed March 31, 2014, http://ses.library.usyd.edu.au//bitstream/2123/3930/1/davidblight_08_honsthesis.pdf.

Tougher times on the way for Nasty distributors

Prepare yourself for the ultimate experience. This video cassette will change your attitude to life.

THE ORIGINAL LEGENDARY ATROCITY SHOT AND BANNED IN NEW YORK

ASTRA VIDEO

The recent seizure of two video cassettes described by the police as "unbelievably horrible" has raised the already loud outcry against the video 'nasties' to fever pitch.

Copies of **Faces of Death**, which includes amongst other scenes footage of a monkey being clubbed to death, have been seized from a video shop in London and handed over to the Director of Public Prosecutions.

Also under examination are copies of **Snuff**, a tape which purports to show genuine killings and was withdrawn by its distributors before release in this country. Some copies, however, have found their way into rental shops, and the DPP is now considering prosecuting

the distributors under Section 2 of the Obscene Publications Act which carries a maximum penalty of three years' imprisonment.

Until now, tapes have been prosecuted under Section 3 of the Act, which merely entails forfeiture under a magistrate's warrant. The relative lightness of this penalty has angered Mrs. Mary Whitehouse, who claims that fines and forfeiture orders together with the delay involved in bringing such cases to court is letting distributors off too easily. In reply, the DPP has promised that next time they consider a video obscene they will prosecute under Section 2 of the Act.

Further confusing the issue is the recent introduction of a classification scheme for video-tapes. The scheme is based on the new British Board of Film Censors' categories for cinema films which include a special 'Club' rating for those films which at present would be denied a certificate and restricted to screenings in private clubs. This movie is seen as an indication that the BBFC's role is changing from that of censorship to classification.

In the case of videotapes, however, the submission of tapes for rating will be at the discretion of the distributors concerned, although it is hoped that video shops will stock only those tapes which carry a rating.

The scheme is the brainchild

of the Video Working Party which, under the chairmanship of James Ferman, secretary of the BBFC, has been debating whether to treat video in the same way as publishing (i.e. something you look at in the privacy of your own home) or to legislate for it like the cinema.

The fact that the classification scheme for video is only a voluntary restriction seems to indicate that the debate is not yet settled. Certainly the distributors themselves seem confused and wary when it comes to the legality or otherwise of their tapes.

Thorn-EMI recently requested dealers to return all copies of **The Burning**, after it

was discovered that the master tape from which the duplications were made was an uncensored version of the original cinema release. When the film first came before the BBFC, fifteen seconds were cut before an 'X' certificate was granted.

And in a recent raid by police on a Manchester video shop, several copies of **Endless Love** were confiscated even though the film was granted an 'AA' certificate when it was released in cinemas. The film is in fact a fairly innocuous teenage romance story but, according to the shop's owner, all the police were interested in was the slogan "She was 15" on the cassette's cover.

She is 15. He is 17. The love every parent fears.

FIGURE 6.4 An article in *Video Viewer* features an image of "blue-sleeve" *Snuff*.

traded) and film memorabilia fairs (where video nasties were often sold "under the counter").[34] Because of this, forum members have gone to great lengths to

---

[34]As Marc Morris argued on the forum: "All known blue sleeve variants were not known to any collectors prior to the early 90s," September 5, 2011, accessed March 31, 2014, http://pre-cert.co.uk/forum/showthread.php?t=26047&highlight=blue+snuff. This is a position supported by a number of forums members, and even Behr himself, who has suggested that, "Charles Band, the rights owner, probably shipped them [the blue sleeves] to Belgium [in the 1980s], and that further illicit copies entered the UK from there" (Behr quoted in Wingrove and Morris, *The Art of the Nasty*, 239). On British horror film fanzines in which video nasties were sold and/or traded, see Kerekes and Slater, *See No Evil*, 287–313 and Egan, *Trash or Treasure?*, 106–27; on film fairs and video nasties see *Video Nasties 2: Draconian Days*.

examine each other's copies of blue-sleeved *Snuff*, to determine any factors that may either expose their tapes as "dodgy" fakes,[35] or to confirm their authenticity.

The main area of scrutiny relates to printing inconsistencies, including typeface and punctuation irregularities, color variation, pixelation, and other deficiencies (such as the appearance of crinkles and white marks), which infer that the blue-sleeved covers may have been produced in a later period, from a damaged or reproduced master copy.[36] Such debates, because of their prevalence, have raised enough of a question mark over the provenance of the blue-sleeved version to lead to a ban being imposed by Pre-Cert moderators on all sales until further information arises that can legitimize its release. A result of this is that the black-sleeved version, which has continued to circulate among collectors over thirty years, which definitely *was* available to rent in the 1980s, and yet which was thought *at the time* to be a bootleg, has paradoxically become regarded, by some, as the original—and thus "authentic"—release. It has been imbued with a sense of authenticity precisely because it "came first" chronologically. This is irrespective of whether or not Astra was involved with the release. Yet, while the "bootleg" may ironically have been granted an aura of legitimacy in some corners of video-nasty fandom, the fact that its origins remain unknown, complicates the application of an "absolute value."

In November 2013, it appeared as though fans' questions were about to be answered. An eBay auction advertised an "original" poster for the UK video release of *Snuff*,[37] which the seller claimed to have purchased from a video shop in Birmingham in 1983.[38] The poster utilized all the elements of the black-sleeved artwork—the same image, the same 3-D title, the same tagline—though crucially incorporated two important new additions: the logos for both Astra and Wizard. Collectors on the Pre-Cert forum steered clear of the auction, due partly to the worn condition of the poster and high reserve price of £200.00, but mostly because of speculation from some forum members that it simply *could not* be genuine, because, to their mind, Astra never officially released the film in the first place.[39] As one Pre-Cert member suggested, he would have expected the poster

---

[35] As one forum member has it, following the first alleged appearance of blue-sleeved Snuff in the 90s, "more appear[ed] via eBay and trade lists" in the period after, including, "a number of known dodgy copies, in the 2000s." See "SNUFF Blue Sleeve," June 14, 2010, accessed February 7, 2014, http://www.pre-cert.co.uk/forum/showthread.php?t=16562.

[36] See the following threads for lengthy discussions: "Black Snuff: Snide or Pride?" July 7, 2011, http://pre-cert.co.uk/forum/showthread.php?t=24511&highlight=blue+snuff&page=2; "SNUFF or F for Fake!," June 10, 2010, http://pre-cert.co.uk/forum/showthread.php?t=16454&highlight=blue+snuff, and "SNUFF Blue Sleeve." All accessed May 5, 2014.

[37] http://www.ebay.co.uk/itm/151154244637?clk_rvr_id=827275770339&rmvSB=true.

[38] Graham Foley.e-mail exchange with author, November 17, 2013.

[39] "Lastmarine," "Now Then, Now Then, Now Then: SNUFF Astra Video Poster!" October 30, 2013, accessed January 12, 2014, http://www.pre-cert.co.uk/forum/showthread.php?t=40761.

found on eBay "to have been publicising a BLUE sleeved *Snuff*,"[40] because that was the version which was known to have had originally carried the logos and other company information. The fact that the poster bore more similarity to the "unofficial" release, encouraged some to consider the emergence of the poster proof "that Astra were [sic.] behind the black sleeve release" after all.[41]

It is perhaps precisely due to the fact that no one is able to verify whether or not the blue-sleeve version circulated in the early 1980s, nor whether Astra were indeed behind the black-sleeve release, that the mythology surrounding *Snuff* has been compounded. These ongoing debates demonstrate that, as Belk has observed, collecting is "a shared passion that transcends utilitarian concerns,"[42] indicating an investment beyond the simple acquisition of a desired object. As shown in this section, video-nasty collectors debate information within their shared community, which is then analyzed in terms of its validity in relation to the known/unknown parts of an object's history. From the individual desire to solve the "mystery" of *Snuff*'s British release, to the sharing of knowledge within the community, or even the less altruistic motivation of simply maintaining the monetary value of particular versions,[43] there is continued investment from collectors into the mystery of this notorious enigma from British history.

Of artifacts and artifice: Conclusion

George Plasketes, writing about vinyl record collecting, has claimed that:

> the passage of cultural icons [...] and their accompanying artefacts and products, can often result in the emergence-or submergence-of a subculture, made up of those who [...] determinedly cling to the artefact, collecting or preserving a part of it because of the meaning and experience contained within.[44]

Such a process of subcultural preservation would appear to resonate with the discourse surrounding the video-nasty collectors discussed in this chapter. As Egan has observed, the meanings attached to the nasties have changed over time; with the term itself having being used to describe, "a set of film titles, a specific

---

[40]"Bigandy," "Now Then, Now Then, Now Then".
[41]"Hellochas," "Now Then, Now Then, Now Then".
[42]Russell Belk, *Collecting in a Consumer Society* (London: Routledge, 2001): 35.
[43]See, for example, "Scorpio," "SNUFF (BLUE ASTRA)," September 23, 2010, accessed May 11, 2014, http://pre-cert.co.uk/forum/showthread.php?t=18497&highlight=blue+snuff.
[44]George Plasketes, "Romancing the Record: The Vinyl De-Evolution and Subcultural Evolution," *Journal of Popular Culture* 26, no. 1 (1992): 109–22.

set of video versions, a set of historical events and a personal consumption experience."[45] In a recent interview, Jake West, the director responsible for the aforementioned *Video Nasties* documentaries, spoke nostalgically of the early 1980s, stating that, "as much as [I am] opposed to censorship, it gave [my] generation of film viewers a thrilling sense of the forbidden."[46] West here acknowledges the retrospective, generational, creation of a community in direct opposition to the legislative frameworks governing home-viewing in the UK. This is a view reiterated by Mark Meakin in a recent online poll charting the decline in the censorship of horror films in the UK. Meakin attributes the relaxation of the censors largely to the development of the Internet, stating that "nothing is hard to get but it takes the fun out of trying to get hold of stuff like the good old (well, bad) days."[47]

The "personal consumption experience" of the video-nasties collector demonstrated by both West and Meakin is irrevocably linked with a sense of the illicit and the "forbidden" opportunities provided by the "video nasties." However, as we have seen, the search for the "historical authenticity" of the video nasties is also a primary factor for many video-nasty fans: not least, in the highly contentious case of *Snuff*. Indeed, as Desmond Coke suggested in 1928, in his book *Confessions of an Incurable Collector*:

> It must not be thought, though it too often is, that the collector's only joy is in the actual buying. When he [sic] has got his purchase … the real fun is only just the beginning. There is the closer inspection than was possible; the showing to a fellow expert (spare your other friends); the choice—and making—of a place to put it.[48]

For collectors of the video nasties, the "real fun" is in the learning and transmitting of knowledge related to the origins and legacy of certain video releases. These kinds of readings hold considerable weight in the collecting community. In the case of *Snuff*, debates transcend the simple acquisition of an object, moving into arenas where collectors can interpret a history that is in a continual state of renegotiation. The ongoing discussions around *Snuff*, therefore, afford collectors an opportunity to scrutinise the most contested parts of that history, while in the

---

[45]Egan, *Trash or Treasure?*, 5.

[46]Laurence Phelan, "Film Censorship: How Moral Panic Led to a Mass Ban of 'Video Nasties,'" *The Independent*, July 13, 2014, accessed July 14, 2014, http://www.independent.co.uk/arts-entertainment/films/features/film-censorship-how-moral-panic-led-to-a-mass-ban-of-video-nasties-9600998.html.

[47]Dracucarr, "POLL HELP: Video Nasties and Censorship," *Cult Movie Forums*, accessed July 20, 2014, available at: http://www.cultmovieforums.com/forum/threads/poll-help-video-nasties-and-censorship.11300/page-5.

[48]Demond Coke, *Confessions of an Incurable Collector* (London: The Whitefriars Press, Ltd., 1928): 16.

process, contributing to its ongoing examination, redefining themselves not only as archivists and custodians but as historians, too.[49]

Early publicity material promoting *Snuff* asked us to question "Are the killings in this film real?" This is the question which loomed over the film's release in America, and, as this chapter has shown, prevented the pinning down of an official, traceable history of its release in the UK. It was also a question that, as Julian Petley notes, was a primary concern for the British press throughout the 1990s, namely, when hyperbolic reports first began to come in about the video-nasty black market and those horror fans participating in it.[50] Yet, this is not the question that has prompted the most intrigue from British video collectors. Rather than being concerned about the film's supposed veracity, instead, collectors have debated at length the film's distribution history in the UK. And while, for the broader public, such information may seem trivial when confronted with a film purporting to show the genuine death of a human, the questions posed by *Snuff*'s shady presence on the UK video market has added a new, and decidedly national, dimension to cultural mythology of the snuff movie.

---

[49]Egan, *Trash or Treasure?*, 175.
[50]"The story of 'snuff' in Britain clearly demonstrates how the constant peddling of a myth has succeeded not only in legitimating excessive censorship but also in criminalising those who collect horror videos and even tarnishing them with the taint of paedophilia." Petley, "Snuffed Out," 219.

7 TRACES OF SNUFF: BLACK MARKETS, FAN SUBCULTURES, AND UNDERGROUND HORROR IN THE 1990s

Johnny Walker

This chapter seeks to explore the centrality, and significance, of underground horror films to fan cultures in the 1990s, demonstrating how a swelling interest in gory paracinema[1] coincided with the emergence of an array of contemporary, direct-to-video "death films" which collated sequences of genuine human tragedy and atrocity for the purposes of entertainment. Drawing specifically on the little-acknowledged *Traces of Death* (Various, 1993–2000) series and its producer, Dead Alive Productions, I will show how, at a time when fans went to great lengths to obtain explicit and gory exports of uncensored horror and death films, Dead Alive sought to align itself with a new breed of horror film fan, producing a series of videos that, in various ways, chimed with discourses that surrounded fan subcultures. Additionally, the chapter will briefly reflect on how the series was positioned to appeal beyond the arena of horror film fandom, reaching out to niche music subcultures, before concluding with a discussion of the legacy of the *Traces of Death* series in the twenty-first century.

---

[1] Jeffrey Sconce, "'Trashing' the Academy: Taste, Excess and an Emerging Politics of Cinematic Style," *Screen* 36, no. 4 (1995).

The elusive snuff movie had been a sporadic feature of press discourse on both sides of the Atlantic since the mid-1970s,[2] but concern over its actual existence in the UK appeared to reach its apex in the early 1990s. British newspapers reported that genuine snuff films were being traded at horror video collectors' fairs, circulated in school playgrounds and, worse still, traded in pedophile rings.[3] In the US, fears of snuff were also generating mainstream media coverage. In 1991, actor Charlie Sheen reportedly called the FBI after having watched a film in which a young woman was, Sheen believed, dismembered *for real*.[4]

However, it soon transpired that neither the British press nor Sheen was correct in their assumption. Assessing the British press reaction, Julian Petley demonstrated that the press had rather foolishly mistaken pirated versions of "video nasties"[5] bought from film fairs for something far more sinister, resulting in a situation whereby the ongoing institutional reticence toward wholly fictional horror and violent entertainment being consumed in the domestic sphere "[was] being spiced with references to the entirely mythical 'snuff' movie."[6] As for the "snuff movie" Sheen claimed to have seen: it was soon established that this was *Flower of Flesh and Blood* (Hideshi Hino, 1985), the second entry in the technically accomplished, but resolutely fictional Japanese video series, *Guinea Pig* (1985–1988).[7]

Nevertheless, for all these high-profile, frenzied misjudgments, the fact that fictional horror films were being confused with genuine snuff is a significant point. Such confusion would appear to suggest that media coverage had equated the alleged underground practice of snuff production and distribution with both the makers and dedicated fan consumers of trashy, disreputable horror films. The reasons for this are clear, if ultimately ridiculous. The advent of home video in the late 1970s meant that, through to the 1990s, doors were opened for the production and transnational circulation of violent films that were unlikely to

---

[2]See the introduction to this collection.

[3]Julian Petley, "Snuffed Out: Nightmares in a Trading Standards Officer's Brain," in *Unruly Pleasures: The Cult Film and Its Critics*, edited by Xavier Mendik and Graeme Harper (Guildford: FAB Press, 2000).

[4]David Kerekes and David Slater, *Killing for Culture: An Illustrated History of Death Film from Mondo to Snuff* (London: Creation Books, 1995): 173.

[5]"Video nasties" is a moniker given to thirty-nine videos that were banned in Britain before the passing of the Video Recordings Act 1984: a law which dictated that all videos needed to be certified by the British Board of Film Classification prior to release. On the "video nasties" moral panic, see Julian Petley, "'Are We Insane?' The Video Nasty Moral Panic," 2013, http://rsa.revues.org/839. See also Mark McKenna's contribution to this collection.

[6]Petley, "Snuffed Out," 214.

[7]Kerekes and Slater, *Killing for Culture*, 173. See also Anon., "Snuff Video Shook Star," *The Daily Record*, August 13, 1994, 13.

get any sort of "formal" release.[8] Horror film fans swiftly began duplicating and swapping cassettes of what, at the time, were often exotic rarities from a whole range of territories. These included older, controversial films that were being sought out because of their banned status, such as the infamous Italian "mondo" films of the 1960s,[9] "shockumentaries" or "death films" such as *Faces of Death* (John Alan Schwartz, 1978), graphically violent, realist horror fictions such as *Cannibal Holocaust* (Ruggero Deodato, 1980), and cult gore films of directors such as Herschell Gordon Lewis.[10] Also, highly desirable were more recent films such as the *Guinea Pig* series and a number of other gruesome films from East Asia (primarily Japan) that had been shot solely for the horror video market. The infamy of this new strain of eastern extreme cinema derived chiefly from their unflinching and direct corporeality, a feature that was compounded in the eyes of western audiences, because so little was known about their production context.[11] While these films were definitely not "snuff,"[12] they certainly fell within the parameters of "schlock,"[13] and their exotic qualities and gory content, along with their informal international distribution channels, ensured that they remained intriguing to genre connoisseurs who embraced video as a means of acquiring films that were deemed out of step with mainstream (and often heavily censored) horror production. The video black market allowed for the circulation of uncut and unregulated films, with the audience often acquiring unofficial, pirate copies from underground networks of distribution, film fairs similar to those Petley

---

[8]"Formal" is used to signify mainstream distribution that is legal and above board. "Informal," by comparison, refers to things like piracy, and other "shadow economies of cinema." See Ramon Labato, *Shadow Economies of Cinema: Mapping Informal Film Distribution* (London: BFI, 2012). On underground horror, see Steve Jones, *Torture Porn: Popular Horror after Saw* (Basingstoke: Palgrave Macmillan, 2013), 171.

[9]For an in-depth history of the original mondo cycle, see Mark Goodall, *Sweet & Savage: The World Through the Shockumentary Film Lens* (Manchester: Headpress, 2006).

[10]See Randy Palmer, *Herschell Gordon Lewis, the Godfather of Gore: The Films* (Jefferson, NC: McFarland, 2006).

[11]Little academic attention has been paid to this series. However, for a lucid overview of the films and their distributor Japan Shock Video, see Jay Slayer, "Flowers of the Flesh," *The Dark Side* no. 87 (2000): 40–43.

[12]While *Cannibal Holocaust* and *Faces of Death* both used sequences of genuine animal slaughter, "snuff," in the context of this essay, is employed only in relation to the expiration of human life.

[13]"Schlock" is term often used to invoke gory, and often cheap, horror and exploitation cinema. See, for example, Sconce, "'Trashing' the Academy," 6. See also Kay Dickinson, "Troubling Synthesis: The Horrific Sights and Incompatible Sounds of Video Nasties," in *Sleaze Artists: Cinema and the Margins of Taste, Style, and Politics*, edited by Jeffrey Sconce (Durham, NC: Duke University Press, 2007): 167. It should be noted, however, that some films once dismissed on these grounds, have now been reappraised. This is certainly true of *Cannibal Holocaust*. See Simon Hobbs, as well as Xavier Mendik and Nicolo Gallio's, respective contributions to this volume. See also Simon Hobbs, "*Cannibal Holocaust*: The Paratextual (Re)Construction of History," in *Popular Media Cultures*, edited by Lincoln Geraghty (Basingstoke: Palgrave Macmillan, 2015).

discusses, or from mail-order adverts in the pages of horror-themed magazines. Indeed, it was through the indirect contact with the editor of one such American magazine, *Deep Red*, that Sheen's copy of *Flower of Flesh and Blood* was acquired.[14]

As far as the British press was concerned then, it appeared that the market for horror-video collectors was the same as that for genuine snuff. Horror fans, just like the elusive snuff producers, were unknown quantities, and appeared to operate in society's darkest corners. In the US, the production and distribution of the amateur publication, *Deep Red*, was similarly peripheral and little understood beyond its hardcore readership: a factor which no doubt compounded Sheen's belief that what he was watching was a genuine snuff movie from the lower reaches of a pernicious underground. It was the anonymity of both the films and their audiences that abetted the films' veracious, and thus illicit, potential.

Some of the notable death films to be released on the US home video in the late 1980s and the early 1990s include *Death Scenes* (Nick Bougas, 1989), *Death Scenes 2* (Nick Bougas 1992), and *Faces of Death IV* (1990), *V* (1995) and *VI* (1996). However, while these examples attempted, with varying degrees of success, to target the niche market for underground horror cinema,[15] it was the *Traces of Death* series that spoke more outwardly to horror film fan communities. Comprising five films produced and released between 1993 and 2000, *Traces of Death* was the flagship production of Dead Alive, a low-end distributor which would go on to be a central force in the low-to-no-budget, direct-to-video (DTV) horror market throughout the 1990s.[16] In showcasing scenes of arbitrarily linked real live death, body modification and atrocity for shock value (including shots of corpses in a morgue, autopsy footage and untelevised news footage in which people are shot or blown up), the first *Traces of Death* anticipated the imminent boom in Internet "shock sites,"[17] and shared the affective aspirations (if not the tone) of contemporaneous reality television shows such as *America's Funniest Home Videos* (1989–present), due to its "repetition and [...] very limited palette of formal variations."[18] However, Dead Alive was also riding a much more marginal wave of horror interest: devising *Traces of Death* to tap into a demand for horror

[14] See Kerekes and Slater, *Killing for Culture*, 173.

[15] Kerekes and Slater, *Killing for Culture*, 152–59.

[16] Dead Alive's first release was a violent Hong Kong/Chinese film, *Men Behind the Sun* (Tun Fei Mou, 1988), which depicts in graphic detail the Japanese torturing Chinese prisoners during World War II. The company's second release was an amateur "shot on video" film of German origin: *Violent Shit* (Andreas Schnaas, 1989).

[17] See Julian Petley and Mark Astley's respective contributions to this volume.

[18] Jason Middleton, *Documentary's Awkward Turn: Cringe Comedy and Media Spectatorship* (London: Routledge, 2014): 123. On the confluences between reality television and "death film" see Randy Squalor, "Postcard from Colonel Kurtz: RealiTV [sic] and the Death Film," in *Flesh and Blood... Compendium!* (Guilford: FAB Press, 2004): 340–47.

film product that was, in one respect, fresh, challenging and beyond the taste dictates of mainstream horror (and thus in keeping with the fearsome reputation of films such as the *Guinea Pig* series) while, in another respect, building upon a legacy of films such as *Faces of Death*, using its cult aura to give visibility and credibility to its new, and frankly amateurish, product.

Yet, it was precisely the film's amateur, "do it yourself" qualities and its associations with the obscure interests of horror film fans that were paramount to Dead Alive's efforts in successfully presenting the film as a worthy investment to its prospective audience. The video black market was, by its very nature, an underground affair, driven by and designed to appeal to a cadre of videophiles set on valorizing "all manner of cultural detritus."[19] In the classified ads of mainstream horror magazines, such as *Fangoria*, genre enthusiasts passionately marketed such films to like-minded readers, mindful of the fact that they were unlikely to get any coverage in the main body of the magazine. The ways that such products were advertized did much to underscore how unusual and at odds with mainstream culture these films were, reaffirming the subcultural credentials of both the sellers and their consumers. Due to issues of cost, the ads were typically very modest affairs, often made up of merely a few lines of text or, at most, a small image. In an effort to make their product appear distinctive, they utilized short and sharp hyperbole akin to the "noisy, vulgar spiel"[20] of ballyhoo typical of exploitation film distributors of the past. Examples included low-end video bootlegging firms, such as Threat Theatre, which sought to entice *Fangoria*'s readership with the question: "DO YOU LIKE SADISTIC SEX, VIOLENCE AND TORTURE?"[21] (Of course, the question would appear to be wholly rhetorical, working under the assumption that the inevitable response of the magazine's readership would be: "Yes, we do!"). Similarly, other advertisements offered "INDEPENDENT VIDEOS" of the "amateur, semi-pro & schlock" variety,[22] as well as "SHOCKUMENTARIES AND CULT HORROR CLASSIC VIDEOS," including "FACES OF DEATH—DEATH SCENES—SHOCKING ASIA—MONDO CANE—ASSASSINATIONS OF THE 20TH CENTURY AND OTHER CULT HORROR AND SCI-FI,"[23] and "GORY, VIOLENT, UNCUT HORROR, MONDO, SLEAZE AND EXPLOITATION VIDEOS,"[24] as well as "horror obscurities" and "taboo subjects" from "THE MACABRE VIDEO UNDERGROUND"[25] (Figure 7.1). Even companies that

---

[19]Sconce, "'Trashing' the Academy," 372.
[20]Eric Schaefer, "*Bold! Daring! Shocking! True!*": *A History of Exploitation Films 1919–1959* (Durham, NC: Duke University Press, 1999): 103.
[21]Advertisement for Threat Theatre, "Classified Ad Vault," *Fangoria* no. 121 (1993): 78.
[22]Advertisement, "Classified Ad Vault," *Fangoria* no. 120 (1993): 64.
[23]Advertisement, "Classified Ad Vault," *Fangoria* no. 127 (1993): 82.
[24]Advertisement, "Classified Ad Vault," *Fangoria* no. 133 (1993): 76.
[25]Advertisement, "Classified Ad Vault," *Fangoria* no. 134 (1993): 88

FIGURE 7.1 "Shockumentaries and Cult Horror Classic Videos": A classified ad from a 1993 issue of *Fangoria*.

were not selling videos, but merchandise such as T-shirts, were capitalizing on the booming interest in extreme horror, selling garments featuring "mass murders [...] all *very graphically depicted.*"[26] The *Traces of Death* films were evidently cultivated to ride this wave of interest in the visceral, the real and the taboo. Through the reappropriation of real-life atrocity footage, the films were responding a niche sector of the horror fan community which, as the aforementioned ads suggest, were less interested in mainstream product than marginal and independent fare beyond Hollywood's approach to the genre, which would inevitably impinge upon the range of titles available in "your sterile video-chain."[27]

It would therefore be reasonable to propose that the *Traces of Death* series constituted a hybrid moving-image extension of American horror fanzines

---

[26]Advertisement for Underground Screen Prints, "Classified Ad Vault," *Fangoria* no. 122 (1993): 78. Emphasis added.

[27]Advertisement for Video Wasteland, "Classified Ads Vault," *Fangoria* no. 127 (1993): 82.

that facilitated niche tastes in the 1980s and 1990s, being informed by a similar DIY sensibility. These were typically "independent, non-commercial, amateur publications"[28] that were "different"[29] to—and, more often than not, reacting against[30]—the "commercially orientated" *Fangoria*, and its tendency to focus on glossy, mainstream films.[31] The *Traces of Death* series, in a way comparable to underground zines such as the aforementioned *Deep Red* and others such as *The Splatter Times, Subhuman, Gore Gazette,* and *Blackest Heart*, boasted an enthusiasm for the marginal and the abject, advocating a zealous resistance to the mainstream that the likes of *Fangoria* were seen to endorse.[32] Dead Alive was, as with the fanzine publishers, very much an amateur start-up company with limited resources and, in the early days at least, relied upon selling copies of its films through mail-order catalogs advertised in magazines. In collating "actual scenes of human destruction,"[33] and then releasing them as feature-length videos, the company seemed to embody, as per the zines, a carefree "interest in putatively indefensible outrage for outrage's sake."[34] Similar to the game-changing exploitation films of the past that the fanzines celebrated, such as *Blood Feast* (Herschell Gordon Lewis, 1963), which had pioneered "special-effects scenes of torture and dismemberment in graphic color,"[35] Dead Alive prided itself on providing horror fans with a product that was promoted as being more outrageous than anything extant in contemporary horror cinema. Consequently, conveying a sense of subcultural distinction akin to that possessed by underground horror fans became a key element of the company's brand image.

The films' narrator, Brain Damage (voiced by Damon Fox for parts *I* and *II*, and then by Darrin Ramage from parts *III* to *V*), was particularly significant to the series' fan-friendly tenor. Direct, tasteless, and blackly humorous, Damage's irreverent tone mimicked the "fuck you" attitude of revered zine editors such as Shawn Smith of *Blackest Heart*, and was central in reinforcing the film's DIY aura.[36] As David Sanjek once suggested of such editors, Damage's "juvenile fascination with grue and gore" was a key component of the series, as was his "insist[ence] upon the pleasures to be found in the consumption of [...] raw, undiluted imagery."[37] And

---

[28]David Sanjek, "Fans' Notes: The Horror Film Fanzine," *Literature/Film Quarterly* 18, no.3 (1990): 151.
[29]John Szpunar, *Xerox Ferox: The Wild World of the Horror Film Fanzine* (Manchester: Headpress, 2013): 10.
[30]Sanjek, "Fans' Notes," 151–52.
[31]Kate Egan, *Trash or Treasure? Censorship and the Changing Meanings of the Video Nasties* (Manchester: Manchester University Press, 2007): 107.
[32]Ibid., 106–08.
[33]Voice-over, *Traces of Death*.
[34]Sanjek, "Fans' Notes," 151.
[35]Schaefer, *"Bold! Daring! Shocking! True!,"* 289.
[36]See Szpunar, *Xerox Ferox*, 672–89.
[37]Sanjek, "Fans' Notes,"152.

just as "fanzine editors feel obliged to no one, save their subscribers,"[38] Damage exudes a similar sense of exclusivity and identifies his audience from the outset: we are his "disciples of death" and are encouraged to "revel [together] in the terrors of the tormented." This posits that "we," as assumed fans of niche horror, are part of a community who, through sharing and understanding such bizarre interests, are also in possession of the exclusive credibility Damage represents as a gatekeeper of marginal tastes.

Key to the tone of many fanzines was the destabilization of notions of good taste and an aspiration to be as objectionable as possible. As such, a number of publications employed a provocative, misanthropic tone that was tempered through a knowing irony and playfulness. For instance, issue number three of *Blackest Heart* carried the tagline "EXTREME HATRED"[39] and, in its promotion, claimed hyperbolically to be the "most dangerous, perverted, degrading, angry, cruel, hateful, sexist, underground-horror-exploitation mag in the whole damn world!"[40] This kind of assaultive hyperbole is evident in the *Traces of Death* films. By offering sardonic and seemingly amoral commentary over filmed instances of human tragedy, Brain Damage shares the "nihilistic manner" of the zine editors.[41] His running commentary, for instance, is often accompanied by booming, cruel, laughter, and he speaks of the most gruesome images with the most ardent enthusiasm. Indeed, just as it was typical of fanzine editors—in echo of classic exploitation distributors—to promise an "uncensored" and "powerful" insight into the "THE UNDERGROUND WORLD OF HORROR,"[42] Damage fervently offers up "the most graphic and ghastly images ever brought forth on any screen!"[43] In *Traces of Death IV: Resurrected* (Darrin Ramage, 1996), he boasts of how "proud" he is to showcase "the most heinous collection of birth defects," before cutting to a sequence of grisly illustrations. In *Traces of Death II: It Just Got Deader* (Darrin Ramage, 1994) he, over footage of a tightrope performer struggling to maintain balance on a windy day, proclaims: "the last remnants of brain in his head now will surely be glistening on the pavement soon!" Following the performer's inevitable fall to death, Damage continues with macabre glee: "His screams must have been devastating; though he had wonderful form!" And, in the series' third entry, *Dead and Buried* (Darrin Ramage, 1995), Damage boasts: "*Traces of Death III* is proud to bring to you the exclusive footage of the El Salvador Death Squad at their *best*." The film then proceeds to show amateur video footage of the Salvadorian Civil War, in which a group of armed men set fire to woodland as they pursue a civilian. They

---

[38]Ibid.
[39]*Blackest Heart* (3) 1994, 1.
[40]Advertisement for *Blackest Heart* issue 3, "Classified Ads Vault," *Fangoria* no. 131 (1994): 78.
[41]Sanjek, "Fans' Notes," 151.
[42]Advertisement for *Blackest Heart* issue 1, "Classified Ads Vault," *Fangoria* no. 121, (1993): 78.
[43]Voice over, *Traces of Death II*.

then pin him to the ground, castrate him, cut his tongue out, scalp, and then behead, him; all the while laughing and joking to the camera. Damage ignores the tragedy at the core of these sequences, and, perhaps most troublingly, encourages the audience to laugh along. The redeployment of these sequences as entertainment, for shock value, directly mimics the jocular and the distasteful fanzines and their readership which, as titles like *Blackest Heart* would suggest, were knowingly positioned as being at odds with good taste, political correctness, and morality.

In the original mondo films of the 1960s—which, it must be remembered, were originally produced for mainstream audiences—the kinds of sequences that the *Traces of Death* films showcase would typically have been afforded some degree of critical commentary. As Eric Schaefer notes, exploitation films dealing in taboo subjects would typically be preceded by a "square up," a statement at the beginning of a film which, as a means of justifying the film's lurid, provocative content, would (insincerely) "apologize for the necessity of bringing an unsavory subject to light" or "claim the producer's earnest hope that such exposure will put an end to an evil or bring about a greater understanding."[44] Mondo films also had square-ups of sorts, and, as with the kinds of films Schaefer discusses, were mostly framed as educational and informative, rather than as prurient and salacious.[45] The *Traces of Death* films, by way of comparison, are explicitly *unapologetic* and *openly exploitative*, and discard the square-up trope altogether: a choice that bolsters the series' oppositional tone. As the British Board of Film Classification reported in 2005, when the first *Traces of Death* was rejected a certificate, and thus prohibited a video release, the film:

[could not] accurately be described as "documentary" as [it] failed to present any journalistic, education or other justifying context for the images shown. Rather the [work] presented a barrage of sensationalist clips, the purpose of which appeared to be prurient entertainment. The trivialization of human and animal suffering was exacerbated by the loud music soundtrack and the tasteless inclusion of occasional "comic" […] voiceover.[46]

Put differently, the makers seek to reject faux claims to sincerity that would have potentially made their film more palatable for a wider audience. They make it explicit how such films are designed to cater, as Damage asserts in *Traces of Death III*, to a new cult of "gorehounds" and not, as the opening title card for all of

---

[44]Schaefer, *"Bold! Daring! Shocking! True!,"* 71.

[45]*Faces of Death* also adopted such an approach. Hosted by a (fictional) University Professor, Frances B. Gröss, the film plays out as though it were a documentary of academic intrigue and not as the "freak show exploitation" film it truly is. See Kerekes and Slater, *Killing for Culture*, 136–41.

[46]*British Board of Film Classification Annual Report* (London: BBFC, 2005): 75, accessed April 5, 2015, http://www.bbfc.co.uk/sites/default/files/attachments/BBFC_AnnualReport_2005.pdf.

the sequels asserts, "CHILDREN or the SQUEAMISH of any kind." Thus, similar to the oppositional "frat-boy sensibility" typical of fanzine editors, the *Traces of Death* films revel in the "evil" that a conventional square-up would try to cloak, infantalize or emasculate those who cannot stomach it, and, in the process, fortify the series' nonconformist credentials.[47]

For all that the *Traces of Death* series was riding a wave of contemporary interest, its effect also partly hinged on an explicit acknowledgment of the past. That is to say, whereas Dead Alive was trying to orientate the series as being *different* to most other contemporary horror films (just as the fanzine editors were presenting their publications as different to mainstream horror magazines), the company was also keen to present the series as remaining firmly within the parameters of the horror genre. Indeed, horror fans were the series' target demographic (and remain so to this day).[48] Resultantly, the series tipped its hat to horror films which were either deemed to be indisputable classics, or which had gained recent interest due to the video black market. Horror fanzines, as a means of setting themselves apart from the likes of *Fangoria*, would often set out to celebrate older horror films that were long forgotten by the mainstream media. Kate Egan, writing about the 1990s British horror magazine *The Dark Side*, has shown how the likes of *Fangoria* were often dismissed by *The Dark Side*'s readership for focusing on the "new and vacuous" rather than older material which was imbued with a sense of history and, by extension, subcultural authenticity. *Fangoria*, because of its tendency to review, promote and endorse new, mainstream product, was thus rendered "inauthentic" among hardcore horror fans.[49] This is a binary that Mark Jancovich has also explored in relation to what he sees as a distinction drawn by fans between "authentic" and "inauthentic" types of horror. The former, Jancovich argues, is constituted by gory marginal works and the "secret and/or illegal" lengths fans go to acquire them (i.e., the horror video black market supported by underground zines), while the latter is constituted by "mainstream" horror production (i.e., those films given most coverage in issues of *Fangoria*).[50] This is a method of distinction that extends, of course, to the fans themselves. The *Traces of Death* series, as we have seen, expresses an allegiance to the underground, its fans and, by extension, the subcultural authenticity that surrounds them. As such, on several occasions, the

---

[47]Sanjek, "Fans' Notes," 154.

[48]As Darrin Ramage, former co-founder of Dead Alive, recently stated to *Gorezone* magazine: "I call this [the 'shockumentary'] a sub-genre of horror, if you will, because it is horrific." See John Torrani, "Assault Yourself: An Oral History of Death Tapes," *Gorezone* no. 33 (2015): 7.

[49]Egan, *Trash or Treasure?*, 106–08.

[50]Mark Jancovich, "'A Real Shocker': Authenticity, Genre and the Struggle for Distinction," *Continuum: Journal of Media and Cultural Studies* 14, no.1 (2000): 25–26. See also Mark Jancovich, "Cult Fictions: Cult Movies, Subcultural Capital and the Struggle for Distinction," *Cultural Studies* 16, no. 2 (2000): 306–22.

films intertextually hark back to "authentic" horrors of years gone by, as a means of acknowledging the subcultural capital its makers share with its desired audience.

The opening shot of *Traces of Death Part IV* shows a graveyard, replete with ornate gothic headstones. The scene is black and white and appears to have been shot on low-end film stock (likely 8mm) and depicts Brain Damage walking slowly among the tombstones, zombie-like. Considered in light of the film's subtitle, this sequence is most obviously paying homage to the opening scene of genre cornerstone *Night of the Living Dead* (George A. Romero, 1968), when Barbara (Judith O'Dea) attempts to escape the clutches of the shuffling corpse that just killed her brother. Indeed, the low-angle shots, and the shaky camera work succeeds in evoking the low production values of the original film, while also helping to situate *Traces of Death IV* as part of a tradition in credible, DIY, horror cinema. Taken in the context of the late 1980s/early 1990s, the scene resonates with horror fan's continued interest in directors such as George A. Romero, as well as Italian filmmakers such as Lucio Fulci and Umberto Lenzi, whose zombie and cannibal films were frequently discussed in the pages of zines such as *Deep Red*,[51] *The Dark Side*, and others.[52] Such references worked to reaffirm the series makers' subcultural capital, displaying an implicit awareness of horror cinema's past, at a time when the genre struggled to remain untarnished by all that contemporary developments had come to signify. Such allusions are apparent throughout the series and, in other instances, are even more overt than in the example just given. In the first film, Damages goes so far to directly namecheck controversial Italian horror films of a kind similar to those celebrated by contemporary fans of underground horror:

> We are proud to offer you this very rare footage of the actual skin and face collections of Ilse Koch; the *real* Ilse, immortalized in numerous movies...

The films to which Damage is referring are *Ilsa, She Wolf of the SS* (Don Edmonds, 1975) and its sequels, films based on the exploits of the wife of a Nazi general who, during the Second World War, reputedly "order[ed] lampshades made from the

---

[51] This fanzine took its name, incidentally, from Dario Argento's classic gialli *Profondo Rosso* (1975). Raiford Guin's explores the significance of this film (and other classic Italian horror films) in relation to US horror video culture in "Blood and Black Gloves on Shiny Discs: New Media, Old Tastes, and the Remediation of the Italian Horror Film in the United States," in *Horror International*, edited by Steven Jay Schneider and Tony Williams (Detroit, MI: Wayne State University Press, 2005): 15–32.

[52] *The Dark Side* sits comfortably in between "fanzine" and "prozine." It is, and has always been, a glossy affair that is circulated throughout the UK and abroad, but has nowhere near as wide a readership as *Fangoria*. Through the 1990s *The Dark Side* would often run features on gory Italian horror films of the 1970s and 1980s, largely because of such films' centrality to the "video nasties" panic in Britain. On the video nasties panic and horror fandom see David Kerekes and David Slater, *See No Evil: Banned Films and Video Controversy* (Manchester: Headpress, 2000), and Egan, *Trash or Treasure?*

skin of tattooed prisoners and [had] ditch diggers beaten for looking at her after she paraded above them in a short skirt without underwear."[53] As Alicia Kozma has it, the first film in the cycle "has become the representative example" of the "Nazisploitation" cycle of the 1960s and 1970s.[54]Nazisploitation films—produced in response to the global popularity of "women in prison" and "sexploitation" movies[55]—were, through their unsavory blending of historical trauma, violence and eroticism, just one of the kinds of exotic horror films both reported on and sold in underground fanzines. They were also films that, due to their grounding in historical actuality, resonated with the other kinds of realist-inflected horror product that was so readily sought after by videophiles. Invoking films that distastefully (albeit deliberately) juxtaposed sexually violent titillation with the atrocities of the Holocaust, as well as the cult legacy that surrounds them, *Traces of Death IV* resonated with the outwardly offensive tone integral to the horror fan's (and, by extension, fanzine's) maintenance of an outsider status. In the minds of its makers, these invocations work to concretize the *Traces of Death* films as a series that understands, and is itself a part of, the exclusive arena of underground horror.

We have seen how conveying an awareness of the horror genre's past and present was crucial to the projected subcultural authenticity of the *Traces of Death* films. However, besides the horror film and its dedicated fan community, the series also alludes to a subcultural category of music which became a key component in its stylistic strategies: from *It Just Got Deader* onward, the footage of real-life horrors is played out against a raucous metal music soundtrack. Steve Jones has acknowledged this musical subgenre's relationship to several notable underground horror films, particularly in what he calls the "hardcore horror" independent cinema that emerged in the wake of the so-called "torture porn" phenomenon of the 2000s. Jones notes that *August Underground's Mordum* (Jerami Cruise, Killjoy, Michael Todd Schneider, Fred Vogel, Cristie Whiles, 2003) features scenes shot at niche metal gigs and even features a role played by vocalist of the cult group, Necrophagia. Jones contests that these "musical associations" are a means to "evince the filmmakers' subcultural credibility" because underground metal, in a manner reminiscent of politicized punk and hardcore of the 1980s, exists outside of the cultural mainstream.[56] There were also notable confluences between the underground horror fan community and the underground (or "extreme") metal scene in the 1990s, which are worth

---

[53]Daniel H. Magilow, "Introduction: The Nazi Image in Low-Brow Cinema and Culture," in *Naziploitation! The Nazi Image in Low-Brow Cinema and Culture*, edited by Daniel H. Magilow, Elizabeth Bridges, and Kristin T. Vander Lugt (London and New York: Continuum, 2012): 2.

[54]Alicia Kozma, "Ilsa and Elsa: Nazisploitation, Mainstream Film and Cinematic Transference," in *Naziploitation!*, 55.

[55]Julian Petley, "Nazi Horrors: History, Myth, Sexploitation," in *Horror Zone*, edited by Ian Conrich (London: I. B. Tauris, 2009): 213.

[56]Jones, *Torture Porn*, 172.

unpacking in light of the *Traces of Death* series. These confluences are particularly significant because both extreme metal and the modes of underground horror under discussion here were born of the same historical moment.

Keith Kahn-Harris dates the emergence of extreme metal, along with subgenres such as "death metal" (encompassing bands that write and perform songs addressing themes of violence, sexual depravity, and human expiration), to the mid-1980s. Central to his definition are noted differences between extreme metal bands whose reputations have historically relied on word-of-mouth (such as pivotal late 1980s/early 1990s death metal acts Cannibal Corpse and Obituary) and those more commercially oriented heavy metal bands that have achieved a broader reach and mainstream success (such as Iron Maiden and Mötley Crüe). Indeed, clear comparisons can be made between Kahn-Harris' definition of this musical movement to the oppositional politics of underground horror film fandom and the *Traces of Death* series:

> In contrast to heavy metal's mainstream commercial reach, extreme metal is disseminated through small-scale "underground" institutions that extend across the globe. The differences between extreme metal and most other forms of popular music are so pronounced that those who are not fans may not see its considerable internal differences. Extreme metal music frequently teeters on the edge of formless noise. Whereas heavy metal was at least intelligible to its detractors as "music," extreme metal may not appear to be music at all and its attendant practices may appear terrifying and bizarre. On the edge of music, on the edge of the music industry, extreme metal thrives.[57]

Traces of Death, as we have seen, stands in opposition to conventional narrative cinema (and, for that matter, documentary cinema) in a way that is not dissimilar to how extreme metal rejects the formal properties of most other popular forms of music. Likewise, the audience that *Traces of Death* was produced for, as with extreme metal fans, relied on small trading "networks," and had, on these grounds, been rendered similarly "terrifying and bizarre" by the mainstream media.

However, there is yet another way in which the series aligns itself explicitly with death metal culture. In the introductory framing sequence of *Traces of Death III*, Brain Damage is presented as a death metal fan, framed in a dark, candlelit room, dressed in heavy metal regalia, including a T-shirt identifying the specialist label, Relapse Records, and a baseball cap which carries the logo of the extreme metal band, Core (Figure 7.2). Dressed in this way, Damage conveys a sense of authenticity, and his apparent knowledge of a band and a label likely unfamiliar to a significant proportion of dedicated music enthusiasts, let alone general audiences,

---

[57]Keith Kahn-Harris, *Extreme Metal: Music and Culture on the Edge* (Oxford: Berg, 2007): 5.

FIGURE 7.2 Death metal fan: Brain Damage in *Traces of Death III* (Dead Alive Productions/Brain Damage Films, 1995).

would imply that he is himself a part of the extreme metal scene. Having explained in grisly detail what kinds of visceral imagery awaits the audience, he proceeds to introduce "some of the hottest talent in the metal industry... Messhugga, Core, Deceased, Hypocrisy, Dead World, Mortician and Gorefest, just to name a few." His voice is emphatic and gruff, echoing the "growled vocals" of extreme metal bands,[58] while his identification of the likes of Deceased, Dead World, and Gorefest appropriately typifies the content of the film. The same is also true of the songs which feature on the soundtrack by these and other artists: "Traces of Death" by Mortician, "Blood Everywhere" by Dead World, "Slaughtered" by Hypocrisy, "Sadistic Intent" by Sinister, "Violent Generation" by Brutality, "Bodily Dismemberment" by Repulsion and "Into the Bizarre" by Deceased. These kinds of song titles and band names were typical of extreme metal bands of the 1980s and 1990s, resonating with the abject preoccupations of contemporaneous underground horror cinema. As with the *Guinea Pig* series and, indeed, the *Traces of Death* films, the lyrical content of death metal bands would center on themes of "human weakness, mortality" and, perhaps most crucially "gore."[59] These were all

---

[58]Ibid., 3

factors that resulted in some bands having material banned in several countries in the early 1990s.[60] Therefore, the pairing of *death* metal music with *death* imagery in the *Traces of Death* films can be seen as an apposite means of emphasizing Dead Alive's penchant for contravening moral (and, it is implied, legal) codes of conduct. Furthermore, the controversy surrounding niche death metal was almost literally a dissonant musical echo of the concern the UK and US news media's concerns had expressed about snuff and horror film communities and collectors. Ultimately, the practice of conflating horror with extreme metal music distinguished Dead Alive's product from the prevalent mainstream horror films of the period, which often had heavy metal soundtracks produced by the kinds of wide-reaching bands mentioned earlier.[61] Moreover, in light of Matt Hills argument that "fans of trash horror other and devalue" horror orthodoxy on account of their being "overly commercial and non-underground,"[62] Dead Alive, through doing the opposite of its Hollywood contemporaries, heightened *Traces of Death*'s dissentient aura.

The foregoing analysis of fan cultures, horror fanzines, and briefly, niche musical interests, has shown the ways that "real live death" was appropriated by Dead Alive in its *Traces of Death* series, indicating its subcultural authenticity among underground horror fans. Furthermore, it is evident how Dead Alive operated amid a range of historical circumstances, while responding distinctively to its historical moment, using lo-fi technology to create a series of films that were at odds with mainstream horror culture of the time. From a historical perspective, the influence of the *Traces of Death* series is clear, with Internet sites such as Rotten.com and Bestgore.com having provided similarly affective content for the digital age. In accumulating random images of death and atrocity footage, they convey the same kind of formal arbitrariness as *Traces of Death*, while adopting a familiar sardonic tone: Rotten.com's slogan, e.g., is "Pure Evil since 1996."[63]

---

[59]Keith Kahn-Harris, "Death Metal and the Limits of Musical Expression," in *Policing Pop*, edited by Martin Cloonan and Reebee Garofalo (Philadelphia, PA: Temple University Press, 2000):84.

[60]As Kahn-Harris explains, in relation to the band Cannibal Corpse: "in Germany, government censors banned the first three albums [*Eaten Back to Life* (1990), *Butchered at Birth* (1991), *Tomb of the Mutilated* (1992)] because of their covers and lyrics. There have been similar problems in Australia, New Zealand, Canada, Taiwan, and South Korea." See Kahn-Harris, "Death Metal and the Limits of Musical Expression," 87.

[61]For example, rock legend Alice Cooper provided the soundtrack to *Friday the 13th Part VI: Jason Lives* (Tom McLoughlin, 1986) and the mainstream metal band Dokken provided the title song for *A Nightmare on Elm Street 3: Dream Warriors* (Chuck Russell, 1987). Similarly, Gene Simmons, the bass player of the iconic "shock rock" band, KISS, along with former Black Sabbath front man, Ozzy Osbourne, appeared in the rock music-themed *Trick or Treat* (Charles Martin Smith, 1986).

[62]Matt Hills, "Para-Paracinema: The *Friday the 13th* Films as Other to Trash and Legitimate Film Cultures," in *Sleaze Artists: Cinema at the Margins of Taste, Style, and Politics*, edited by Jeffrey Sconce (Durham, NC: Duke University Press, 2007): 224.

[63]Rotten.com, accessed May 1, 2015, http://rotten.com.

In 2006, the creators of Rotten.com would go on to establish Shockumentary.com, a website dedicated exclusively to the sale of death films, from which the *Traces of Death* series (according to the site, "Probably the best shock series available") is obtainable.[64] The existence of this site demonstrates not only how *Traces of Death* has influenced the form and tone of contemporary shock sites but also, and perhaps most crucially, the cult status that the series has amassed since its humble beginnings. Indeed, in a way similar to horror fanzines of the 1990s, *Traces of Death* has been sewn into the tapestry of historically authentic horror cinema. By the same token, it is also a series that has come full circle. No longer strictly on the periphery, it is now celebrated in niche circles as being iconic. Brain Damage Films,[65] the company that now boasts ownership, derives its name from the series narrator, his face featuring prominently in the company logo. Once obscure and anonymous, this would suggest Brain Damage is now a recognizable commodity (indeed, he now makes special guest appearances at horror film conventions).[66] Moreover, in 2015, the series was featured alongside both *Faces of Death* and *Death Scenes* in a "death tapes" retrospective in the pages of the prozine, *Gorezone*: an offshoot publication of *Fangoria*, no less.[67]

Emerging from a marginalized and little-known subcultural space, *Traces of Death* was once a film that was shockingly transgressive, taking inspiration from an underground shadow economy. However, these factors would suggest that the series has now entered, and has been at least partially validated by, the mainstream voice of the horror genre. The availability of a collector's edition DVD box set from Amazon.com suggests that the films can no longer be successfully imbued with their original sense of danger or, indeed, the subcultural kudos of the underground from which they stem. Rather, they are now easily contained and, by proxy, understood. *Traces of Death*, having achieved canonical status, is now at odds with both its amateur origins and the underground aura its producers originally strived to achieve and maintain.

Acknowledgments

I would like to thank Neil Jackson, Steve Jones, and Tom Watson for providing helpful and insightful comments on an earlier draft of this chapter.

---

[64]Shockumentary.com, accessed May 1, 2015, http://shockumentary.com.
[65]Brain Damage Films was established when Darrin Ramage, one of the co-founders of Dead Alive, left the company, to establish his own. Alongside the now historically authentic *Traces of Death* films ("the oldest and best!"), he sells a host of other death films, including the *Shock-X-Treme* (Various, 1997–2006) and *Facez* [sic.] *of Death 2000* (Various, 2000-unknown) series' and *Executions II* (Unknown, 1995).
[66]Darrin Ramage, email interview with author, May 13, 2015.
[67]Torrani, "Assault Yourself," 7.

8 SNUFF 2.0: REAL DEATH GOES HD READY

Mark Astley

Since the kidnap and filmed murder of the *Wall Street Journal* reporter, Daniel Pearl, in February 2002, the urban myth of the "snuff video," where the death of a human being is staged primarily for the benefit of the unblinking eye of the camera, has been transformed into an easily accessible and quotidian reality. In light of the historically and culturally varied interpretations of the term, what we mean here by "snuff" is simply a premeditated human death that would not exist without the intention of pointing a camera and capturing the event for a variety of sexual, political, and financial purposes. The dissemination of execution videos, as radical Islamist propaganda and macabre entertainment at the turn of the millennium, established a pattern of transmission and reception that endures to the present.

In one sense, the song remains the same, with the 2014 decapitation and 2015 burning alive of hostages staged, as media events by Islamic State of Iraq and the Levant (IS)—now referred to simply as Islamic State (IS)—in Syria and Iraq following the template laid down by its forerunner Al Qaeda in Iraq in 2003.[1] Yet, snuff has fundamentally changed over the past decade. Early high profile execution videos of western hostages, like those of Nick Berg and Ken Bigley, were characterized by a grainy, chaotic aesthetic redolent of the manner in which snuff has manifested in the fictional cinematic realm. In contrast, the majority of recent IS atrocities are glossy, professional, and technically accomplished. The release by IS of the execution video of the kidnapped American journalist, James

---

[1] Steve Rose, "The Isis Propaganda War: A Hi-tech Media Jihad," *Guardian*, October 7, 2014, accessed October 20, 2014, http://www.theguardian.com/world/2014/oct/07/isis-media-machine-propaganda-war.

Foley, in mid-August 2014 (which did not depict the beheading itself but rather its grim preamble and his mutilated body instead), saw the emergence of Snuff 2.0, with IS producing and distributing a sequence of visually sleek representations of body horror and death that heralded in a new professionalism in the use of the tormented and ruined body as propaganda.[2] If the iconography of the IS videos was consistent with their Al Qaeda forebears, with captives in orange jumpsuits and executioners swathed in black or wearing military apparel, the technical limitations and disorganization that marked the emergence of snuff had acceded to a slickly choreographed and skilfully edited new media product.

What was interesting about the coverage in the UK tabloid press was that newspapers such as the *Sun* and *Daily Mail* offered textual readings of the videos that highlighted their deliberate stylization and technical accomplishment. The *Mail* labeled the Foley video "a gruesomely slick production" and compared it to the Berg video, commenting on the film's makers:

> They worked competently with graphics and visual effects, and used editing tools to intersperse film of Foley with video of rolling news footage. While Bigley and Berg's videos were produced in Arabic, Foley's was in English with subtitles.[3]

This is an important point, as change had occurred not only through the higher production values, but also the perception of the intended audience in the East and West alike, with the videos doubling as both recruitment strategy and terror propaganda. The reticence of the early IS videos in the depiction of the actual beheadings was attributed to IS wanting to make the videos more amenable to coverage in the mainstream Western media; perhaps ironically creating a macabre iconoclast in the form of the ubiquitous and verbose (presumed) executioner Jihadi John, who the *Sun* likened to the parodic character Ali G because of his South London accent.[4] It soon transpired that they were far from squeamish, creating horror spectacles such as the synchronized beheading of twenty-one Coptic Christians on a moodily depicted Mediterranean beach (Figure 8.1) and, in their most high concept offering to date, a captured Jordanian air pilot is immolated

---

[2]Ian Johnston, "The Rise of ISIS," *The Independent*, September 3, 2014, accessed March 17, 2015, http://www.independent.co.uk/news/world/middle-east/the-rise-of-isis-terror-group-now-controls-an-area-the-size-of-britain-expert-claims-9710198.html.

[3]Guy Adam, "Five Minutes of Savagery and a Video as Slick as it is Sickening," *The Daily Mail*, August 21, 2014, 4–5

[4]Before the success of the movies *Borat* (Larry Charles, 2006), *Brüno* (Larry Charles, 2009), and *The Dictator* (Larry Charles, 2012), actor and comedian Sacha Baron Cohen had a degree of success on British television portraying Ali G, a character designed to satirically reflect trends in British urban youth culture. James Beal and Peter Sampson, "The Ali G Jihdi," *The Sun*, August 21, 2014, 4–5.

FIGURE 8.1 Blood on the sand. Egyptian Coptic Christians are led to their death.

in a cage replete with CGI-enhanced flames and distorted screaming.[5] At the end of the video, a bulldozer crushes the cage and the remains of the pilot into the dust, closing with a shot of a charred hand poking through the debris. In these videos, the signifying bodies on display operate can be read on two levels, either as cultural artifacts or as spectacular attractions. New technology has radically affected how the transgressive representations of the body in death media have been produced, represented, distributed, and consumed.

In this context, "spectacular attraction" refers to visual renditions of the body in distress, a perverse form of "entertainment" in itself. Attention is focused upon the body affected by violent events, the fetishized, ruined form functioning as the primary source of fascination, the context of the representation becoming largely irrelevant. In contrast, in discussing the body as "cultural artefact," context is everything.[6] When referring to the body in death media as "cultural artefact," it is to denote the visual representation of the ruined body as a cultural signifier or reference point. For example, consider the execution video of the journalist Daniel Pearl (Figure 8.2); sensation-seeking viewers approached the recording purely for the explicit scenes of mutilation, but the body horror aspect of the film is secondary to its status as ideological propaganda. Pearl's religion and

---

[5]J. Malsin, "Christians Mourn Their Relatives Beheaded by Isis," *Time*, February 23, 2015, accessed March 17, 2015, http://time.com/3718470/isis-copts-egypt/.

[6]David A. Grindstaff and Kevin M. DeLuca, "The Corpus of Daniel Pearl," *Critical Studies in Media Communications* 21, no. 4 (2004): 308–12.

FIGURE 8.2 The body as cultural artifact. Screenshot from the Daniel Pearl execution video.

nationhood (Jewish American) is repeatedly stated and obliquely commented upon before his actual (or re-enacted) execution. Here, the body possesses a totemic value borne out by the myriad discourses generated by the video's dissemination.[7] The distinction between the body being either site of spectacle or cultural artifact provides an organizing duality: meaning (the body as cultural artifact) and spectacle (the body as spectacular attraction). Of course, the status of the media body, in an age when digital technology allows the construction of highly convincing simulations and where wars are fought out in the media as much as on the battleground, is sometimes fiercely contested, and there is an underlying tension between (and a desire for) the simulated and the real underpinning postmodern culture, one in which there is a radical contingency of meaning.

In its traditional cinematic form, the snuff myth drew primarily from the notion that it represented the filmed killing of a human being, containing a strong element of erotic sadism, supposedly circulated among an underground clientele

---

[7]Susan Sontag, *Regarding the Pain of Others* (London: Hamish Hamilton): 62.

for entertainment purposes and economic gain.[8] In its fictional contexts, snuff was a hidden product, a covert object of desire, available only to a supremely depraved elite with the money or determination to secure access to it: an unholy grail of celluloid decadence and moral bankruptcy. The contemporary reality of snuff is that it has become an open product for which the perpetrators desire maximum coverage and exposure. In recent years, the visual rendition of human sacrifice has become all too real, but rather than appealing to morbidly prurient impulses, the principal motive has been that of utilizing shock imagery for ideological capital of debatable worth. Furthermore, it could be argued that snuff has now gone mainstream, with videos depicting the beheading of individuals embroiled within the world of criminal Mexican drugs cartels going viral on Facebook in 2013, alerting moral guardians among traditional western media sources to a new strain of freely available imagery of murder and mutilation.[9]

When the first consistent stream of snuff videos emerged from Iraq in 2004, they were initially restricted to Internet shock sites such as Ogrish and Consumption Junction, but they are now circulated on major social networking sites, engendering a self-reflexivity in spectators that disingenuously offers a mordant commentary on the medium itself. While remaining strict in its policing of the uploading of the actual videos themselves, YouTube hosts a proliferation of reaction videos, which include narcissistic depictions of the often melodramatic or tasteless responses of spectators to murder videos such as *Three Guys, One Hammer*.[10] There is a sense of shiftless and bathetic horror that permeates *Three Guys, One Hammer*, a video of two men who (in partnership with a third accomplice) had carried out a series of sadistic murders and earned themselves the sobriquet "The Dnepropetrovsk Maniacs," mutilating and killing a man with a hammer and screwdriver. Leaked onto the Internet in December 2008, it was just one of a number of videos recovered from the killers' mobile phones and shown during their subsequent murder trial. The video's reputation helped to establish a new extreme in violent representations, and sympathy for the victim, whose demise was reduced to a ghoulish attraction, meant its notoriety engendered numerous reaction videos.[11] Here, you can watch people watching snuff, allowing for a reflection upon whether

---

[8]See Julian Petley, "'Snuffed Out': Nightmares in a Trading Standards Officer's Brain," in *Unruly Pleasures: The Cult Film and Its Critics*, edited by Xavier Mendik and Graeme Harper. (Guildford: FAB Press, 2000).

[9]Will Grant, "Facebook Beheading Video: Who was Mexico's Jane Doe?," *BBC News*, November 4, 2013, accessed September 16, 2014, http://www.bbc.co.uk/news/magazine-24772724.

[10]Cara Van Olson, "The Dnepropetrovsk Maniacs," *Crime Library*, November 26, 2012, accessed September 1, 2014, http://www.crimelibrary.com/blog/2012/11/26/serial-killer-spotlight-the-dnepropetrovsk-maniacs/index.html.

[11]Sam Anderson, "Watching People Watching People Watching," *New York Times*, November 25, 2011, accessed October 1, 2014, http://www.nytimes.com/2011/11/27/magazine/reaction-videos.html?pagewanted=all&_r=0.

it is a contemporary manifestation of sheer exhibitionism or somehow redolent of a collective need for moral correction.

Such phenomena indicate how the snuff viewer is now positioned in respect to reality death media, the perception of which has radically altered as means of production and distribution have changed. The ongoing evolution of film, video, and Internet technology has been instrumental in developing the mythology of snuff, providing necessary tools for a process which has culminated in the execution video that has become a paradoxically grim but banal feature of online resources that openly betray their prurient intentions through self-administered names such as Bestgore.com. Such sites have accommodated a disquieting confluence of death, sex, and technology, representing a kind of popular cultural endgame that has bled gradually into the mainstream as now defined by social media.

The Internet marked a radical step in the evolution of snuff. Rather than the modest, and highly selective distribution of mondo and death film (which are discussed elsewhere in this book) on VHS and DVD, which was limited in many countries such as the UK due to stringent censorship laws, death footage (including genuine images of premeditated murder) became instantly accessible to millions. Indeed, the shock sites that proliferated on the Internet offered a continuation of the mondo and death film through a fundamentally different medium. Ogrish, the most notable and influential of the early shock sites, became prominent because of its willingness to showcase ideologically motivated snuff videos, and was accused of working in an unwitting symbiosis with radicalized enemies of the west, with the site guaranteeing a previously unattainable global audience. However, before returning to look at Ogrish, it is useful to look first at the influence of new media on the emergence of contemporary snuff and its roots in stern religious and political ideology.

As handheld video cameras became cheaper and more readily available from the late 1980s onward, Islamic extremist and terrorist networks quickly realized the potential of their utility. Within a decade or so, Islamist propaganda mutated from the firebrand declarations of radical clerics and last testaments of suicide bombers to color-coordinated executions with an almost kitsch mise-en-scene, allowing the jihadists access to a large Muslim and Arab audience online.[12] Western journalists remarked on the development, but it was the murder of Daniel Pearl that brought the public's attention to a new form of extremist Islamist propaganda video and he became the first prominent westerner to join the iconography of a nascent, quasi-documentary subgenre: the beheading video.

The actual body spectacle in the Pearl video is, though shocking, mercifully elliptical. A montage of images of wounded Palestinian children and explosions cuts to video footage of Pearl naked from the waist up with his executioner sawing

---

[12]Jason Burke, "Theatre of Terror," *The Observer*, November 21, 2004, 13.

at his throat. There is a cut which effects a transition to the sight of Pearl's head almost completely removed, before a final cut to a still of Pearl in a bloodied shirt, head lolling back, and throat slit. It is obvious that this image is actually from before the decapitation, so the images shown are not in continuous sequence, and the entire slaying lasts only a few seconds. The denouement is a shot of the executioner in a white t-shirt raising Pearl's severed head into the air, a particularly disquieting image in that the killer's face is concealed by Pearl's. Testimony from the trial of those involved in the killing revealed that a technical error actually prevented the initial throat slit from being captured, with one accomplice having neglected to remove the lens cap. Indeed, retrospective knowledge of this "behind the scenes" incident lends the whole exercise a level of gruesome farce.[13] For the final ninety seconds, Pearl's raised head is superimposed against a black background down which scroll a list of demands by the National Movement for the Restoration of Pakistani Sovereignty,[14] the militant group which abducted him. This climax is marked finally by a conventional visual flourish, fading to black and hinting at the rudimentary cine-literacy of the perpetrators.

Therefore, in terms of actual content, the visual detail of dismemberment in the video is by any standards extreme, but still relatively chaste in comparison to those that would emerge later. The "snuff" aspect of the video also lacks the harrowing audio element that the majority of subsequent beheading videos contain. In this sense, the video is very much a "new media product," with fragmented snippets of news used to contextualize its centerpiece killing as part of an ongoing historical struggle against a perceived Western imperialism. However, the video established some stylistic methods that would be adopted by Al Qaeda in Iraq, and subsequently refined by IS. Death in these videos is contextualized within an ideologically skewed documentary narrative, delivering both a message and a defiant gesture of aggressive, ruthless resistance, with the identity and cultural standing of the victim carefully articulated, as they are visibly coerced into offering apologies for their varied affiliations. In addition, news footage and graphics are used as expositional tools and provide visual reinforcement of the spoken message. The death of the captive is presented in almost sacrificial terms, with their cultural, political, and religious identity accentuated before the explicit death pay off that combines meaning and spectacle, ideology, and entertainment.

The Daniel Pearl killing had been regarded as a horrific anomaly until the release of a video in May 2004 depicting the beheading of an American contractor, Nick Berg (Figure 8.3), who was looking for work in Iraq in the wake of the 2003

---

[13]Mike Mount, "Khalid Sheikh Mohammed: I beheaded American reporter," *CNN.com/International*, March 15, 2007, accessed August 26, 2014, http://edition.cnn.com/2007/US/03/15/guantanamo. mohammed/.
[14]Ibid.

FIGURE 8.3 The beheading aesthetic. Screenshot from the Nick Berg execution video.

invasion and subsequent occupation by US-Coalition forces. Posted on an Islamic website and bearing the title "Abu Musab al-Zarqawi shown slaughtering an American," was a video that defined snuff as a consequence of war.[15] In grainy imagery captured on a digital video (DV) camera, Berg is seen sitting in a medium long shot, wearing an orange Guantanamo Bay style orange jumpsuit in front of five armed hooded men. One of the men behind Berg reads a statement that refers to the "Satanic degradation" of Iraqi prisoners, and promises the mothers and wives of American soldiers that coffins will be arriving to them one by one. After identifying himself to the camera, Berg is wrestled to the ground and decapitated with a large knife by an assailant, all of which is captured in a sustained take without recourse to cutaways.

This represented a turning point in the war of images that accompanied the occupation of Iraq, with the clip coming to the attention of CNN and Fox News after a tip off. After the news channels had downloaded the clip, it disappeared from the jihadist site, only to be picked up by Ogrish who billed it as the big

---

[15]Mark Oliver, "The Life and Death of Nick Berg," *Guardian*, May 12, 2004,7.

cyber-event of the day.[16] Thanks to the new technologies of digital media and their ability to capture images and transmit them globally, Berg's death, despite its rigorously concealed and intimate spatial and temporal setting, had become a globally broadcast public execution. As Kellner has noted, digitization had transformed culture, producing new modes of spectacle and domains of technoculture, and the Berg murder video, grainy, crudely edited, and pixilated, represented the spectacle of the "real" in the extreme.[17] Pictures of Berg's headless jumpsuited body hanging from a Baghdad highway overpass soon also found their way onto the net. New media technology, it seemed, had effectively eliminated the private sphere and everything was now visible, from the mundane to the macabre. For the mainstream media, the death of Berg resurrected and accentuated the dialogs that circulated following the surfacing of the Pearl murder video. In the context of the increasingly fractious Iraq occupation and the Abu Ghraib prisoner abuse imagery that had filtered out to the mass media, the Berg case confirmed that the Internet was now seen by the public as an alternative to mainstream print and television news organizations. It was estimated that nearly one quarter of American Internet users went online to view some of the more graphic war images that were deemed too gruesome or horrific for mainstream newspapers and television to display, yet those who actively sought out explicit representations of the conflict testified to being uneasy about their availability.[18] Mainstream American outlets used restraint in distribution of the footage, showing Berg sitting in front of his captors but cutting away before the execution.[19] It was the second time in just under a fortnight that graphic images had appeared with the potential to alter the perceptions and attitudes of a mass audience of all cultural and political affiliations and degrees of engagement. Berg's last moments appeared on a day when CNN reported that the U.S. government possessed photos of Abu Ghraib prisoners being sodomized with chemical glow sticks, presenting news editors, or at least those with aspirations to journalistic rigor, with extremely difficult editorial calls to make.[20]

However, it was soon apparent that anyone wishing to view the uncensored execution (not unedited: the shock sites often played bowdlerized versions of

---

[16]David Talbot, "Terrorist's Increasingly Turn to the Internet," *Technology Review Online*, accessed May 12, 2014, http://www.technologyreview.com/Infotech/14150/page5/.

[17]Douglas Kellner, *From 9-11 to Terror War: The Dangers of the Bush Legacy*, (Lanham, MD: Rowan and Littlefield):15.

[18]Deborah Fallows and Lee Rainie, "The Internet as a Unique News Source," *Pew Internet & American Life Project*, accessed June 22, 2014, http://www.pewinternet.org/2004/07/08/internet-as-unique-news-source/.

[19]Peter Johnson, "A Death Caught on Tape: Should it Run or Not?," *USA Today*, 2005, accessed July 25, 2014, http://usatoday30.usatoday.com/life/columnist/mediamix/2004-05-11-media-mix_x.htm.

[20]Randy Dotinga, "Press Wrestles with Grim Clips," *The Christian Science Monitor*, accessed June 12, 2015, http://www.csmonitor.com/2004/0526/p02s01-usgn.htm.

executions that cut more or less straight to the violence) or the Abu Ghraib tableaux merely needed Internet access. Berg's killing precipitated a number of hostage execution videos being released, the majority being issued by Abu Musab al-Zarqawi's Tawhid and Jihad group and another insurgent group, the Army of Ansar Alsunnah.[21] Usually, the group issued an initial video showing the hostage in captivity pleading for their life or reading political statements from a script, followed by the second video release depicting the beheading of the captive. The hostage was characterized as a cultural artifact, with attendant signifiers like the Guantanamo Bay style orange jumpsuits, prior to the spectacle of their physical annihilation. It was soon apparent that the beheadings had become Internet events, and when a hostage or hostages had been executed, users would visit sites like Ogrish repeatedly until the footage they were seeking was posted. Indeed, such was the number of execution tapes released that Ogrish actually offered a menu where you could choose to download and watch the murder of your choice. It was estimated that the number of visitors to Ogrish rose on average from 150,000 to 750,000 when the beheadings of Nick Berg and Ken Bigley (at this stage, it has to be noted that the beheading video still possessed a certain ghoulish novelty) were premiered.[22] The archival (for which read "database") nature of websites allowed death sites like Ogrish to create subgenres that fetishized different forms of real-life body horror and death media, and by October 2005, Ogrish had over forty beheading videos available. The individuals in control of such shock sites were hardly circumspect about how the beheading videos bolstered the appeal of his site.

According to Dan Klinker, webmaster of a leading online gore site, *Ogrish*.com, consumption of such material is brisk. Klinker, who says he operates from offices in Western and Eastern Europe and New York City, says his aim is to "open people's eyes and make them aware of reality." It is clear that many eyes have taken in these images thanks to sites like his. Each beheading video has been downloaded from Klinker's site several million times, he says, and the Berg video tops the list at 15 million. "During certain events (beheadings, etc.) the servers can barely handle the insane bandwidths—sometimes 50,000 to 60,000 visitors an hour," Klinker says.[23]

Despite the unease expressed in the mainstream about the existence of such sites, Ogrish avoided censorship until August 2005, when a network provider in Germany denied access to the site.[24] Ogrish effectively had a year's grace in terms

---

[21]Robert Fisk, "Terror by Video," *The Independent*, July 26, 2004, 18.

[22]Brad Stone, "Inside the Dark Corners of the Net," *Newsweek*, May 18, 2014, http://www.newsweek.com/plain-text-inside-dark-corners-net-127109.

[23]Talbot, "Terrorist's Increasingly Turn to the Internet."

[24]Tom Sanders, "Network Provider Censors Gory Website," *The Citizen Lab*, 2005, accessed July 1, 2014, http://www.vnunet.com/vnunet/news/2141588/provider-censors-web-content.

of freedom to disseminate images over the net in the West before it came under increasing pressure due to its facilitation of jihadist and insurgency propaganda. Photography and film have always been integral to propaganda in both its modern and postmodern variants, but as James Harkin suggests, what differentiated the new breed of jihadist extremism is that the terror spectacles are composed with online distribution firmly in mind:

> While it would be facile to say that Ogrish and the Jihadis are in league with one another, both are canny and nimble new operators in the subterranean world of online media and adept at feeding the appetites of its omnivorous consumers. And just as Ogrish cannot be understood as a traditional media outlet, al-Qaeda is not a traditional anti-colonialist group trying to liberate territory from an imperial oppressor. If a globally coherent organization called al-Qaeda can be said to exist at all. Its members do not have geography or a national history. They are spread thinly around the globe, and form less of an organization than a loose network and a franchise whose existence appears to be kept alive largely through media.[25]

In Harkin's prognosis, while there is nothing new about the use of photography and film to promote terrorist causes, there is an aspect of the relationship enjoyed between the jihadist groups and Ogrish that is genuinely without precedent and that is the outcome of two different sets of sophisticated groups adapting quickly to the new digital media landscape and nurturing a relationship that was beneficial to both parties. The jihadists have a distribution outlet and guaranteed audience at Ogrish while the clips themselves, of such a range and volume they are subgeneric, drew a sizeable number of visitors to the site. Grindstaff and DeLuca[26] surmise that the relationship of mass media to terrorism can be interrogated in two vital ways: does mass media coverage inherently legitimize terrorism or, conversely, does terrorism as a mass media phenomenon ultimately trivialize or undermine political aims? In the first instance, it could be seen that terrorist utilization of means of image distribution like Ogrish represents a victory in itself, while in an alternative reading, it is merely playing into the oppressive representational systems it aims to usurp.

In the case of Daniel Pearl, the fact the lens cap was on did not deter his captors from conveying the moment of death, as they merely re-enacted the event. However, for those with the fortitude to closely read the images, it was obvious that they were witnessing an act of mutilation rather than murder.

---

[25]James Harkin, "Shock and Gore," *FT.com/Arts and Weekend*, 2006, accessed May 8, 2014, http://www.ft.com/cms/s/0/1373c930-8325-11da-ac1f-0000779e2340.html#axzz3VFIlHKj.

[26]Grindstaff and DeLuca, "The Corpus of Daniel Pearl," 318.

Similarly, after the Nick Berg execution footage was posted on the Internet, its veracity was questioned. What is interesting about the Nick Berg episode is that the conspiracy theories surrounding his death were discussed seriously in the mainstream press, focusing upon supposedly unresolved anomalies regarding Berg's disappearance and the content of the tape itself. The ability of digital media to provide compelling simulacra meant Berg's death was potentially just another propaganda manipulation. Even the admittedly oblique death sequence (where the camera goes in close on the decapitation and becomes pixilated in the manner of a found footage horror film) was not considered sufficient proof of his death. For those who accepted it was Berg's corporeal form being decapitated, it was the identity of his killers that was disputed and whether or not the video showed murder or mutilation:

> Iraq in flames, Washington an object of disgust. What to do? At this pivotal moment, CNN and Fox News are tipped off to a clip of an American citizen being beheaded. The victim is a 26-year-old idealist from Pennsylvania, Nick Berg. Despite the perpetrators being masked, the vile deed is deemed the work of al-Qaeda. The timing of the video was brilliant for the West. Media pundits judged the crime a deeper evil than the systemic torture of innocent Iraqis. But some people sensed a rat. But if it was not al-Qaeda, who? Surely not Uncle Sam. That's too dark, even for the CIA. While this video shows a human body having its head chopped off, it does not necessarily portray an act of murder.[27]

Therefore, in an apt formulation in a world of post 9/11 conspiracy theories, it was speculated here that digital media *may* have been used to create the impression of the slaughter of an American citizen that did not happen in actuality. Nevertheless, the death of Berg heralded a spate of beheading videos featuring western citizens who had been kidnapped by the Zarqawi group. In these, human beings are reduced to the status of stage props. Often, the executioner pauses from his task, so the camera can refocus upon the spectacle of the victim attempting to breathe through a severed windpipe. The audio track is often integral to the visceral power of the execution videos, with the body manipulated to create as distressing a spectacle as possible, and the cries of the victim are upsetting not just because they testify to the endurance of pain but the way they signify the limits of language itself.

Ogrish was a well-organized site, both in terms of design layout and providing easy access to stills and video clip archives while possessing a distinct anticensorship editorial voice. It developed peer-to-peer networks to accrue material and also

---

[27]Richard Neville, "Who Killed Nick Berg?," *Sydney Morning Herald Online*, May 28, 2004, accessed August 7, 2014, http://www.smh.com.au/articles/2004/05/28/1085641717320.html.

pioneered the use of web filtering software to cull newsworthy clips for the site.[28] The site originated in the Netherlands in 2000 and its archives of transgressive visual material were open till 2006 when the domain name redirected to LiveLeak, which was billed as a YouTube-inspired successor to Ogrish. During that time, Dutchman Dan Klinker was the closest it came to having a public face, and as head of the site from 2002, he occasionally made guarded pronouncements to the press. Klinker refused to be interviewed in person during this period, preferring to conduct interviews with reporters via e-mail. The site was candid about how it came to amass its archive of material:

Q.   Where do you guys get all these images and videos?

A.   During the years Ogrish.com has been around, we have been able to establish a content network. This network consists of more than 50 people from all over the world working in a variety of professions—including law enforcement and medical personnel. In addition to this content network, we also receive submissions on a daily basis from people who happen to come across certain scenes and capture it on camera. Ogrish owns the copyrights to much of the content that is displayed on the website. We often buy this content and have to make sure we are not breaking any privacy laws and that we have permission from the people who captured the images and/or featured in certain images.[29]

From the outset, Ogrish attracted criticism for the pop-ups and links the site carried to hardcore pornographic websites that belonged to the more extreme part of the spectrum, a feature which served ironically to reinforce the old mythology regarding snuff and its purported links to the outer fringes of the sex industry. Ogrish's content was contentious enough to begin with, and the close proximity to sadistic porn was strongly suggestive of a form of exploitation far removed from the already tenuous claims that the atrocity footage may have claimed to being a form of alternative reportage. However, the accusation that the porn advertisements cheapened the site's attempts at "respectability" was met with the defense that the adult-orientated advertisements were vital to cover the site's costs as regards to bandwidth, content acquisition, technical services, and legal fees accrued from defending itself from censorship and suppression.[30] Before its abrupt disappearance in early 2006, Ogrish changed its design from a dark and graphic intensive layout to a faster loading, cleaner layout, in what was widely construed as a rather self-conscious repositioning of the website. Instead of the

---

[28]Harkin, "Shock and Gore."
[29]Dan Klinker, "Ogrish FAQ," 2006, accessed January 17, 2006, http://www.ogrish.com/faq.html.
[30]Ibid.

portentous "Can You Handle Life" tagline, the new logo was "Uncover Reality," with an editorial insistence that the site was an "uncensored news" website as opposed to a repository for "gore" or "shock" footage. The "incorporation" of Ogrish into LiveLeak in October 2008 was effectively its shutdown, though the Ogrish forums endured. As is common with fan response to a perceived external intervention in exclusive or limited special interest communities, LiveLeak was initially unpopular with the Ogrish fan base, being regarded as an anemic version of its predecessor that lacked visual identity and an authorial voice, and, perhaps most importantly, was not sufficiently gory or unpleasant.[31]

LiveLeak has prevailed, gaining in popularity and attracting media opprobrium in January 2007 after it hosted the execution video of Saddam Hussein, an event captured on a mobile phone camera.[32] Under the banner "redefining the media," LiveLeak repositioned itself as a news site with an emphasis on reality footage of often violent events taken by citizen journalists in Iraq and Afghanistan, and serving as a fecund source of amateur reportage. In the absence of the original identity established by Ogrish, the most compelling candidate for succession is Bestgore.com, an unashamed and unrepentant gore and death site whose home page banner offers "Incredibly Graphic Video, Image and Movie Galleries of Blood." This is now the go-to-site for the latest high-profile snuff footage, having showcased contentious death media such as *1 Lunatic, 1 Ice Pick* and *Three Guys, One Hammer*.[33] The former title is an eleven-minute long graphic video, which partly conforms to the classical archetype of snuff as a sadistic mixture of sex and death. As New Order's *True Faith* plays in the background, a naked man tethered to a bed frame is stabbed and dismembered. The man is dissected and pieces of him fed to a dog. It was established that the killer was a part-time porn model Luca Magnotta and his victim Lin Jun. Magnotta conducted a knowing flirtation with the media through a series of videos, a cyberspace version of the Jack the Ripper epistles of the nineteenth century.[34] The video itself was an embodiment of "pure" porno snuff, showcasing one room, one camera setup, sexual sadism, mutilation, and death. It was posted on a website that attracted millions of hits and achieved a form of commercially viability through the accompaniment of

[31]"Why is LiveLeak Censored?," 2007, accessed May 3, 2007, http://www.Ogrishforum.com/showthread.php?t=141876&highlight=LiveLeak+censorship.

[32]Ned Parker and Ali Hamdani, "How One Mobile Phone Made Saddam's Hanging a Very Public Execution," *The Times*, January 1, 2007, 1.

[33]Simon Houpt, "Bestgore and Its Ilk: Frontline Journalism or Goad to Further Violence?," *The Globe and Mail*, June 8, 2012, accessed October 27, 2014, http://www.theglobeandmail.com/arts/bestgore-and-its-ilk-frontline-journalism-or-goad-to-further-violence/article4242980/

[34]Christine Blatchford, "The web can enable freedom in dictatorships, but it can also embolden psychopaths," *National Post*, May 30, 2012, accessed October 7, 2014, http://fullcomment.nationalpost.com/2012/05/30/luka-rocco-magnotta-1-lunatic-1-ice-pick/.

advertisements and pop ups for hardcore pornography. It seems that the evolution of snuff was now encapsulated in the technological transformation from analog into the digital realm, from the mythical cinematic 8-mm loop to the real death mpeg. It had gone from a fictional idea of snuff as a closed, hidden, clandestine activity to one that in reality was openly distributed and easily accessible, clickbait for the lulz.

Bestgore fulfils the same function Ogrish did in its most influential period as a repository for death footage and, in its willingness to host and disseminate Islamic State terror videos, has courted similar opprobrium as its forebear. Deliberately provocative editorial comment accompany the news articles, photos, and videos on the site, along with a queasy mix of extreme right wing politics, including holocaust revisionism, and advertisements for, and links to hardcore pornography. The 2015 posting of Moaz Al Kasebeh, a Jordanian air force pilot, being burned alive in a cage was accompanied by a brief factual outline of the event before offering concluding comments that mirrored the revenge narrative of the video and detoured into bizarre antisemitism:

The Islamic State granted Lt. Kasaesbeh the type of death he had been dealing to the defenseless children throughout Iraq, Syria, and possibly elsewhere. What went around, came around for him. Trapped in a confined space, he painfully burned to death. Mainstream press is now in overdrive, calling the pilot's death martyrdom, saying he paid with his life for freedom for us all, and glorifying war he helped to perpetuate. David "my values are Jewish values" Cameron paid tribute to the pilot and called his death the "sickening murder by ISIL's barbaric terrorists." None of them gives a poop about all the children he had burned to a crisp alive.[35]

A screenshot of the pilot in flames accompanies the video and text, with the body utilized once more as cultural artifact (Lt. Kasaesbeh's nationhood and his role as a fighter pilot) and spectacular attraction (his body consumed and blackened by flames). The comments section muses upon its veracity ("These pukes don't need to fake this shit"), pours vitriol on IS, offers numerous Zionist conspiracy theories and reaches a consensus that the video offers an effective spectacle if one is seeking an experience that sates prurient appetites ("This is the worst video LOL"). Just to add to this potent mix of textual and visual signifiers, at the time of writing, the page carries graphic mpeg advertisements and links to sites such as Punishtube.com, which proclaims it offers "the most extreme porn." The site's mission statement proclaims that it is an anticensorship enterprise, devoted in

---

[35]Ate, "Burned to Death in Cage," *Bestgore*, accessed March 16, 2015, http://www.bestgore.com/execution/jordan-pilot-execution-video-burned-to-death-in-cage-isis/.

communicating uncensored information and exposing the "truth," a quest that has led to legal difficulties and incarceration for the site owner Mark Marek.[36] Like Ogrish, the site has been accused of fostering more violence behind the cloak of anarchic-free journalism, perhaps a symptom of an online culture in which modes of transmission and reception are transforming at an astounding rate. Indeed, it is no longer necessary to visit shock sites to stream or download specific videos when snuff can be sent directly to a targeted spectator through a Twitter feed. IS has proved adept at using social media to not only distribute gruesome imagery and rhetoric for propaganda purposes, but also to surreptitiously arrange media set pieces.[37]

Web 2.0 has allowed for a more fluid and interactive means of creating and generating user content, a situation accommodated by the increasing development and influence of smartphone and social media technology. Consequently, as the dissemination and consumption of real death imagery has grown exponentially with the sophistication, portability, and accessibility of new moving image devices, the latest stage of snuff is located securely in the public realm, allowing IS to distribute material directly by hijacking popular hashtags to showcase images of extreme brutality. Recent execution videos created and distributed by IS are cinematic and HD ready, exemplified by a 2014 clip depicting the beheading of sixteen Syrian captives and a postmortem shot of the American Hostage Peter Kassig. The video offers a multilayered narrative including a brief history of the group itself and spectacular footage of their "successes." It ends in a mass beheading of the Syrian captives, embellished with evocative shots of the desert and the intercutting between the grimly determined faces of the murderers and the fearful and unbelieving expressions of their captives. The decapitations provide a coda for a revenge story, where IS members are avenging "innocents" killed by Syrian troops through the ritual execution of kidnapped victims, all of whom are alleged former Syrian air pilots responsible for lethal airstrikes. In 2004, widespread revulsion and speculation in the Muslim world on the counter-productive effect of murder videos emerging from Iraq meant that the insurgent groups operating there curbed their production.[38] However, for IS, the media revulsion appears to have a galvanizing effect with no immediate end in sight for its production of increasingly elaborate snuff scenarios.

When it finally arrived as an instantly accessible spectacle for public consumption, "real" snuff was a tool of ideological exchange rather than the

---

[36]Houpt, "Bestgore and Its Ilk."

[37]Con Coughlin, "How Social Media is Helping Islamic State to Spread Its Poison," *The Telegraph*, November 5, 2014, accessed November 12, 2014, http://www.telegraph.co.uk/news/uknews/defence/11208796/How-social-media-is-helping-Islamic-State-to-spread-its-poison.html.

[38]Frederic Jameson, *Signatures of the Visible* (London and New York: Routledge, 1992): 1.

manifestation of a (still never-proven) profit-driven, extreme form of pornography. Despite this evolution of snuff into a propaganda tool, what has remained is the notion that to watch real images of premeditated murder is ethically wrong, liable to corrupt the spectator on a psychological and emotional level, while cheapening, degrading, and dehumanizing the victim. The reactive gaze, intensified through the medium of the hand-held camera, invites our collusion, adhering to the idea that transgressive representations are inherently pornographic in nature and that they hold the spectator in rapt, mindless fascination, what Fredric Jameson has referred to as the "film as Medusa," where the visual exerts a hypnotically pointless spell.[39]

The distinction between technology and media content has become increasingly less secure, with the digital camera or smartphone becoming increasingly affordable and easy to handle, and with excellent, user-friendly distribution networks becoming available to allow the circulation of imagery. In effect, it has become one more effective weapon of modern ideological conflict, with actual body horror imagery becoming a recurrent and familiar characteristic of radical Islamist propaganda. In the varied twenty-first century beheading videos of western hostages in Iraq and Syria, we can discern clearly the representational act preceding and bringing about the violent act: the camera elicits the ratification of violence, granting genuine snuff a profoundly performative aspect. There now exists a symbiotic relationship between consumers and producers of real death media. Speculation in the Western press had it that a Twitter campaign influenced the manner of Moaz Al Kasebeh's death, with IS using a hashtag to glean inspiration from its supporters. It was suggested that, before the final choice of death by immolation had been decided, demise by chainsaw or hungry crocodile had also been mooted as possible alternatives.[40]

If it is conceded that all cultural representations are to some extent performative, the urge to capture transgressive images of the human body in distress through new media (and here the overriding impulse is to reduce the body to the status of cultural artifact) can be seen to have tangible material consequences. In an act of supreme self-reflexivity, IS shot a video capturing the enthusiastic reaction of a crowd watching the burning of the pilot on large screens around Raqqa.[41] In

---

[39]Ibid., 1.

[40]Duncan Gardham and John Hall, "Was Jordanian Pilot Burned Alive after Sick Twitter Campaign among ISIS Supporters to Name His Method of Death?," *Mail Online*, February 4, 2015, accessed March 13, 2015, http://www.dailymail.co.uk/news/article-2939196/Was-Jordanian-pilot-burned-alive-sick-Twitter-campaign-ISIS-supporters-method-death.html.

[41]Gianluca Mezzofiore, "Isis Set Up Giant Screens in Raqqa Showing Jordanian Pilot Burning to Death Cheered on by Crowds," *International Business Times*, February 4, 2015, accessed March 15, 2015, http://www.ibtimes.co.uk/isis-set-giant-screens-raqqa-showing-jordanian-pilot-burning-death-cheered-by-crowds-1486614.

the global age of new media, "lived" culture (that is, the day to day experience of people and communities which were once recorded by outside witnesses, be they film-maker, news photographer, or television crew) is now documented by the participants themselves in socio-cultural theaters. One of the subsidiary effects of this is an increase in performativity within lived cultures and a compulsion to capture everything on camera. Yet, while the death media discussed in this chapter is now a very "open" product, the traditional cinematic notion of snuff as a product distributed among hidden and arcane networks was resurrected through the concept of "the dark net;"[42] a term used to describe the transgressive online subcultures that have proliferated on the deep web, the disreputable underbelly of the Internet. Accessible only through a deep web browser like Tor, which also grants the user anonymity (a claim that is being increasingly contended), the dark net has flourished as a marketplace for drugs, organized crime, and the sex industry, with goods and services paid for by the virtual bitcoin currency.[43]

It has been rumored that manifestations of "traditional" porn snuff exist in a secret encrypted corner of the dark net, yet nothing tangible has surfaced yet, despite sites like hurt2thecore and Violent Desires setting outer limits for criminal and depraved imagery.[44] That said, it is not beyond plausibility that beneath the convoluted access routes and layers of digital obfuscation, real death porn is only a click away.

While new media has facilitated a change in how the body *in extremis* is represented, it is not because of technological determinism, but rather how technological innovations are utilized by historical agents influenced by complex socio-cultural, religious and political movements. At the risk of being crudely reductionist, it is reasonable to assert that if Iraq had not been invaded in 2003, there would be markedly less genuine snuff videos available for consumption, for the simple fact that there would be a striking diminution in the volume of combat or beheading videos created in Iraq during that period. Radical Islamist groups, of course, would still have been available to kidnap and murder Western hostages for propaganda purposes, but the freedom afforded jihadist groups to stage beheadings by the relative anarchy in postinvasion Iraq would have been denied to them. In genuine snuff, we encounter a materiality/performativity of the image that has concrete and mortal consequences. As Bianca O'Blivion says of the torture porn TV channel in *Videodrome* (David Cronenberg, 1983), "it bites."

---

[42]M.F. Jones, "The Ultimate Guide to the Deep Web," *Sick Chirpse*, 2014, accessed February 12, 2015, http://www.sickchirpse.com/deep-web-guide/2/.
[43]Ibid.
[44]Patrick O'Neill, "Internet's Worst Pedophile Abruptly Shuts Down His "Pedo Empire," *The Daily Dot*, June 24, 2014, accessed March 4, 2015, http://www.dailydot.com/crime/lux-pedoempire-child-porn-shut-down/.

PART TWO

"SNUFF" ACROSS FILM AND TELEVISION

9 UNFOUND FOOTAGE AND UNFOUNDED RUMORS: THE MANSON FAMILY MURDERS AND THE PERSISTENCE OF SNUFF

Mark Jones and Gerry Carlin

t is accepted that the earliest appearance of the phrase "snuff movie" is in Ed Sanders' 1971 book, *The Family: The Story of Charles Manson's Dune Buggy Attack Battalion*. According to Sanders, an anonymous associate of Manson's group claimed that he had seen films of ritualized human sacrifices made by the Family, providing details of a short movie depicting a female victim murdered on a beach. When asked how much he knew of such cinematic activity, his reply was rambled but chilling:

> I knew, I know, I only know about one snuff movie. I, uh, you know ... I just know like a young chick maybe about twenty-seven, short hair ... yeah ... and chopped her head off, that was ... [1]

This alleged, but unprovable murder is one of many attributed to the Manson Family, dubbed "The Love and Terror Cult" by *Life* magazine,[2] as they brought the 1960s hippy dream to a bloody conclusion. After spending more than half of

---

[1] Ed Sanders, *The Family: The Story of Charles Manson's Dune Buggy Attack Battalion* (London: Rupert Hart-Davis, 1972): 232. Ellipses in original.
[2] *Life* 67, no. 25 (December 19, 1969).

his life in prison and reform school for various petty crimes, Charles Manson had found his way to San Francisco in the midst of 1967's Summer of Love, rapidly acquiring a coterie of chiefly young female acolytes who would follow him to Los Angeles a year later. Living communally on the Spahn Ranch and in Death Valley, they prepared for an imminent racial apocalypse, prophesized by Manson through his interpretations of such diverse sources as the Book of Revelations and The Beatles' "White Album." During the brutal Tate/LaBianca murders of August 1969—supposedly intended to hasten the war—the perpetrators daubed "Healter Skelter" and other Beatles-related phrases in blood on the walls of the victims' homes. In addition to nine proven homicides, chief prosecutor Vincent Bugliosi estimated that the group may have been responsible for up to thirty-five killings,[3] but whether any of these murders were filmed is unclear. Evidence of such visual mementoes is sourced chiefly in the unverifiable testimony reported by Sanders,[4] who has himself been reticent about the extent of his knowledge, stating "I can't go into it. I can't even talk about it. I do not possess any of those movies, so all those people who are paranoid about it can rest at ease. I do not know where any of them are."[5] Sanders' denial seems like an implicit confirmation, the slippage between absence and actuality generating the possibility of the films' existence, securing their place as snuff's mythological *ur-texts*. Subsequent cultural allusions have consolidated the myth, and Mansonian traces in cinematic snuff are still apparent in the twenty-first century.

Despite uncertainty and ambiguity over the "snuff movies," there is abundant evidence of the Family's involvement in other film-related activities. The earliest footage was shot in 1968, including some at Beach Boy Dennis Wilson's house,[6] although these films have vanished.[7] Also missing is explicit material allegedly made by notorious pornographer, Marvin Miller, in March 1969.[8] Terry Melcher's proposed documentary on the Family was never made,[9] but the documentary *Manson* (Robert Hendrickson and Laurence Merrick, 1973) was released after the trial. In a letter to gossip tabloid *Hollywood Star* in 1976,[10] Manson himself hinted at involvement in a lucrative international porn trade, while Family associate

---

[3]Vincent Bugliosi with Curt Gentry, *Helter Skelter: The True Story of the Manson Murders* (New York: W. W. Norton, 1994): 640.

[4]Adam Gorightly, *The Shadow Over Santa Susana: Black Magic, Mind Control and the "Manson Family"Mythos* (San Jose, CA: Writers Club Press, 2001): 263–64.

[5]Ed Sanders, "The Family" [interview], *IT* 127, April 6,1972: 45.

[6]Sanders, *The Family* (1972): 51, 114.

[7]Ed Sanders, *The Family: The Manson Group and Its Aftermath* (New York: Signet, 1990):403–05.

[8]Sanders, *The Family* (1972): 31, 159. It should be noted that both of these references are removed in later editions of Sanders' book.

[9]David Felton and David Dalton, "The Book of Manson," *Rolling Stone* 61 (June 25, 1970): 32–33.

[10]Manson quoted in *The Manson File*, edited by Nikolas Schreck (New York: Amok Press, 1988): 171.

Bobby Beausoleil appeared in Kenneth Anger's *Invocation of My Demon Brother* (1969) and *Lucifer Rising* (1972), to which he would also contribute music, and exploitation western *The Ramrodder* (Van Guylder and Ed Forsyth, 1969), which was actually shot at the Spahn Ranch. Manson also served briefly as a technical advisor for a proposed Universal Studios film about the second coming of Christ.[11] Indeed, the tarnished aura of Hollywood informs the Family's story, from its early days driving a Volkswagen bus with "Hollywood Productions" lettered on its side,[12] to occupancy of the Spahn Ranch, used in numerous classic westerns, B-movies, television series, and advertisements. Inhabiting a film set imbued the Family with a performative gestalt, in which role-play and ritual supplanted mundane reality,[13] and Sanders reports several instances in which the Family stole film and video equipment which they used to record their activities.[14] These supposedly included at least one orgy,[15] but as with the other instances these films now occupy a space between myth and hearsay.

Similarly elusive are the pornographic and sadistic home movies allegedly made by the Family's victims. While explicit films featuring Sharon Tate and her husband, Roman Polanski, are well documented,[16] more contentious are numerous accounts of pornography featuring other show business figures.[17] Most infamously, footage depicting the beating and sexual assault of a drug dealer who had allegedly swindled some of the subsequent victims was supposedly made at the Polanski/Tate residence only a few days before the murders.[18] Again, these rumors of celebrity porn vary between the vaguely speculative and the obsessively detailed, its intangibility encouraging prurience and voyeurism, its absence upholding the *possibility* of existence while consolidating its mythic status.

Several months passed after the Tate/LaBianca murders without any arrests or credible leads, giving rise to frenzied media speculation which often alluded to the personal and creative lives of the victims and their associates.[19] Typically,

---

[11]Felton and Dalton, "The Book of Manson," 32.
[12]Jeff Guinn, *Manson: The Life and Times of Charles Manson* (New York: Simon & Schuster, 2013): 109. According to Sanders the sign read "Holywood Productions." See *The Family* (1972): 42.
[13]Bugliosi, *Helter Skelter*, 628.
[14]Sanders, *The Family* (1972): 201, 211, 227.
[15]Jerry LeBlanc and Ivor Davis, *5 to Die* (Los Angeles, CA: Holloway House Publishing, 1970): 142–43.
[16]Bugliosi, *Helter Skelter*, 47.
[17]Sanders, *The Family* (1990): 404–05; but see Greg King, *Sharon Tate and the Manson Murders* (Edinburgh: Mainstream Publishing, 2000): 170.
[18]King, *Sharon Tate*, 169.
[19]J.D. Russell, *The Beautiful People: The Pacesetters of the New Morality* (New York: Apollo Books, 1970): 94.

commentators found parallels to the murders in movies by Polanski and Tate. Chief prosecutor Vincent Bugliosi stated:

> These seven incredible murders were perhaps the most savage, bizarre, nightmarish murders in the recorded annals of crime…Roman Polanski, could not himself have conceived of a more monstrous, macabre scene of human terror and massacre than that which took place at his own residence in the early morning hours of August 9th 1969.[20]

Repulsion (1965), *Cul-de-Sac* (1966), and *Rosemary's Baby* (1968) were repeatedly cited in the media as examples of Polanski's cinematic perversity, while Tate's short credit list was similarly mined for its kinky quotient, encompassing ritual sacrifice in *Eye of the Devil* (J. Lee Thompson, 1966), glossy sex and sadism in *Valley of the Dolls* (Mark Robson, 1967), and *12+1* (Nicolas Gessner, 1969) and vampirism in Polanski's own *The Fearless Vampire Killers* (1967). As the private lives of victims were mined for information, many suggested that this was, in the words of one neighbor, a case of "Live freaky, die freaky,"[21] weirdo-celebrity lifestyles exacting a horrible price.

These repeated references to *outré* work and lifestyle choices caused the murders to move rapidly from the category of the bizarrely inexplicable to the tragically inevitable. The excessively performative aspect of the slayings seemed to lack rational or even perverse motives, and could be understood only in terms of narrative causality. Writing after the murders, but before the apprehension of the killers, Jean Baudrillard noted the

> murder of idols exemplary because, by a kind of fanatical irony, it lent material form, in the very details of the murder and its staging, to some of the characteristics of the films which had won fame and success for the victims…. Mindless, unreflected murders and yet *"reflected" in advance* (here, astonishingly, to the point of precise imitation) *by mass-media models*…. This alone defines them: their spectacular connotation as news items, such that they are conceived from the outset as film scenarios or as reportage, and their desperate attempt in pushing back the limits of violence to be "irrecuperable," to transgress and smash that mass-media order, to which they are in fact party even in their asocial vehemence.[22]

---

[20]*Manson*, directed by Robert Hendrickson and Laurence Merrick (1973).
[21]LeBlanc and Davis, *5 to Die*, 223.
[22]Jean Baudrillard, *The Consumer Society: Myths and Structures*, translated by Chris Turner (London: Sage, 1998): 179.

It is the extreme brutality of the murders which paradoxically locates them within the cinematic order they are attempting to explode. Whether intentionally or not, they were theatrical events, performed for their spectacular consumability. In their combination of savagery and salaciousness, they duplicate the climactic frenzy of extreme cinema. When the perpetrators were finally identified as a hippie cult, even more bizarre than the most outlandish speculation had anticipated, this gruesome horror tale had its cast of characters, and rumors persisted that there were cinematic records of the crimes.[23] Inverting Baudrillard's argument, that in attempting to escape the mass media order the murders are thereby recuperated by it, the only truly irrecuperable act would have been to film the murders. It is within this paradox of irreproducible representation—it can be recorded but not legitimately consumed—that we find the conceptual origin of the modern snuff movie and the moral panics surrounding it.

It would take several years for snuff to become a fully fledged urban myth. While it was rumored in the porn industry from the early 1970s,[24] its complete absence from the 1970 *Report of the Commission on Obscenity and Pornography* suggests a general lack of substantiation. Nevertheless, the theatrical release of *Snuff* in 1976 capitalized upon the growing mythology, some of which had apparently been orchestrated as a publicity gimmick.[25] Shot in Argentina in 1971 and based loosely on the Manson case, *Snuff* began life as an unmarketable exercise in hippie-cult exploitation entitled *The Slaughter*. This was transformed by the distributor into *Snuff* through the removal of all of the credits and the addition of a final scene in which the sexualized murder of a female cast member is presented as real.

Although inspired by Manson, *The Slaughter* can be identified as part of a cycle of counter-cultural movies which predate the murders. Throughout the 1960s, biker films became increasingly unrestrained in their hedonistic displays, moving from studio productions such as *The Wild One* (LászlóBenedek, 1953), through independent films like *The Wild Angels* (Roger Corman, 1966) and low-end exploitation productions like *The Bride and the Beasts* (John Donne, 1969). *The Slaughter*, whose extended opening sequence depicts two female bikers, adopts certain generic traits, but departs from them in its deployment of specifically Mansonian details, including a charismatic male guru named Satán and his female assassins, their wealthy, glamorous victims and ill-defined

[23]Stephen Milligen, "*The Bloodiest Thing that Ever Happened in Front of a Camera*": *Conservative Politics, "Porno Chic" and* Snuff (London: Headpress, 2014): 11.

[24]Laura Lederer, "Then and Now: An Interview with a Former Pornography Model," in *Take Back the Night: Women on Pornography*, edited by Laura Lederer (New York: Bantam Books, 1982): 57–58.

[25]David Kerekes and David Slater, *Killing for Culture: An Illustrated History of Death Film from Mondo to Snuff* (London: Creation Books, 1994):18–20.

revolutionary politics.[26] In the climax of *The Slaughter*, the previously scattered Mansonian references become focused, as one of the female assassins taunts and stabs a pregnant blonde actress, the film seemingly ending on her echoing scream. It is on this allusion to the Sharon Tate murder that *Snuff* supervenes, the fictional frame apparently broken as a young female member of the film crew is sexually molested, mutilated, and finally eviscerated. The previous victim remains supine but invisible in the bed, the abrupt switch from inept exploitation aesthetics to a supposedly *vérité* scene signaled by "behind the scenes" footage of *The Slaughter*'s crew filming the "snuff" murder. As the camera supposedly runs out of film, the screen goes white while anxious voices are heard muttering "did you get it all?" and "let's get out of here." This attempt at a seamless transition between scenes is marked by some duplicated set dressing, and the hurried ushering away of a woman resembling the murderer of the pregnant actress. However, the onscreen appearance of the filmmakers, at least one other camera, some conventional reverse-angle editing and occasional point of view shots belie *Snuff*'s attempted aura of cheap veracity.[27] The "murder" itself is presented dispassionately, and despite being the ostensible climax of "the picture they said could NEVER be shown,"[28] is markedly lacking in overt sadism or pornographic spectacle. Only in the culmination with a ritual gesture, when the killer holds aloft the victim's entrails and emits an orgiastic scream, is any possible motivation beyond mere scopophilic excitement suggested. The echo effect distorting the killer's scream duplicates that utilized when the pregnant actress dies at the end of *The Slaughter*, this double climax becoming an explicit audio-visual reference to the Manson murders.

While generating fascination and outrage, the film ultimately failed in its attempts to confirm the rumors of South American snuff porn, suggesting that it possesses other qualities which allowed for it to become a focus for the debate. It has been proposed that *The Slaughter*'s very ineptitude contributes to this reading, a film so truly bereft of any signifiers of "quality" that the only means of recuperating investment was to turn it into a supposedly irrecuperable object.[29] However, what actually legitimizes the promotion of *The Slaughter* as *Snuff* is its hesitant, but palpable utilization of Mansonian details at multiple levels. The appended climax is less obviously connected to the Manson murders, although the black-garbed female accomplice perhaps evokes the Family's similarly clad

---

[26]Eithne Johnson and Eric Schaefer spend some time locating *Slaughter*'s generic identity: it is, they determine, probably a roughie/kinky. Eithne Johnson and Eric Schaefer, "Soft Core/Hard Gore: *Snuff* as a Crisis in Meaning," *Journal of Film and Video* 45, nos. 2–3 (Summer/Fall 1993): 48.

[27]Alexandra Heller-Nicholas, "Snuff Boxing: Revisiting the *Snuff* Coda," *Cinephile* 5, no. 2 (Summer 2009): 10–15.

[28]Johnson and Schaefer, "Soft Core/Hard Gore," 44.

[29]Kerekes and Slater, *Killing for Culture*, 18.

murderous young women. Despite their fractured production, *The Slaughter* and *Snuff* both partake of the Family aura, with the latter film's extra-textual reference to the origin of the "snuff" myth ultimately permitting further speculation on the existence of the snuff movie.

Snuff itself—or, more specifically, its climactic sequence—is something of a stylistic anomaly in the historical trajectory of the phenomenon. Until camcorder aesthetics recently took hold in the horror genre, only a handful of films presented fictional found footage diegetically, unfiltered through on-screen viewers. 1970s "snuff movies" after *Snuff* would all appear intradiegetically, as fake intertextual items within standard narrative films. Even the notoriously convincing *Cannibal Holocaust* (Ruggero Deodato, 1980) frames its atrocity sequences within a narrative where a surrogate audience anticipates horrified theatrical audience responses. Similarly, the pornographic death footage in *Emanuelle in America* (Joe D'Amato, 1977) is offset by an appalled, yet fascinated intradiegetic response by the eponymous character. Featuring gang rapes, extreme torture and murder, and shot on grainy Super 8 in jungle locations with paramilitary perpetrators and elaborate torture chambers,[30] the films uncovered by Emanuelle's investigations into private sex clubs are presented as the extreme accoutrements of rich degenerates with jaded sexual palates. Once more invoking the aura of rumored South American origins, the films feature a highly convincing facsimile of the mythical snuff porn described by antipornography campaigners. However, it is this very faithfulness to the imagined object which amplifies their artifice, with wealthy, decadent clients consuming debauched materials under the protection of powerful political and media interests. This perverse underground elite is again rooted in Ed Sanders' book,[31] and the film at least partly mounts a critique of capitalism's commodification of cruelty, militarism, and political corruption. *Snuff*'s position within a wider but still covert network of exploitation would be later alleged by Maury Terry, who located the Manson Family as a link in a Satanic chain headed by a man he named Manson II.[32] Even in Terry's tale of ritual abuse, child pornography and multiple murder, snuff films are talismanic but elusive objects. In *Emanuelle in America*, even when we witness Emanuelle present at the production of the films, the audience is shown not her point of view of the torture and murder, but the resultant degraded footage. The film seems to suggest that the sole irrecuperable aspect of such terrible abuse is its mediation and replication as snuff.

---

[30]In *Joe D'Amato, Totally Uncut* (Roger A. Fratter, 1999), the director reveals that the snuff films were shot on 35mm and "purposefully scratched" to resemble the lower definition medium.
[31]Sanders, *The Family* (1972): 228 and (1990): 404.
[32]Maury Terry, *The Ultimate Evil: An Investigation into a Dangerous Satanic Cult* (London: Grafton, 1988).

The association of snuff with South America was always tenacious and speculative, its "real" roots more firmly planted in Mansonian and US porn culture mythology. Shortly after *Snuff* and *Emanuelle in America* implicated unspecified South American nations, the Brazilian *cinema da Boca* production *Vítimas do Prazer: "Snuff"* (Cláudio Cunha, 1977) featured two American producers who, having already filmed a brutal attempted rape and murder (seen behind the opening credits), embark upon a new production in which the lead actress will be shot dead on camera in a supposed accident. The framing narrative is an overwrought satire on US attitudes to the low value of life in South America, and in case the audience has missed the commentary upon American hegemony, the film ends bathetically with Doris Day singing "Que Sera, Sera (Whatever Will Be, Will Be)" over the closing credits. The plot of the snuff movie is obscure, but it includes an orgiastic ritual involving nudity, fire, and an axe wielded dangerously near to a writhing actress. The climactic shooting is oddly mundane, though the hippie rituals are highly reminiscent of the Manson Family "pretend-to-hack" movies reported by Ed Sanders.[33] Similarly bleak is *The Evolution of Snuff* (Andrzej Kostenko and Karl Martine, 1978), a highly fabricated "documentary" about German sex films, the supposed suicide of a featured female performer giving dubious credence to its argument that pornography causes the "death of the soul." Despite its title, there is no snuff or pseudo-snuff in the film; the supposed genuine footage is appended to the film's ending, in which a man disguised with a bag on his head presents gruesome outtakes from *The Last House on the Left* (Wes Craven, 1972) as if they were authentic. Prior to this, snuff is only signaled at the film's opening, displaying a similarly fake *Daily Mirror* headline announcing "Girl Slaughtered For Snuff Film." Among the interviewees is Roman Polanski, who states that "after all sexual taboos on screen were broken … the next step is to kill someone for real." In this meta-snuff film, it is not the referencing of Mansonian details which legitimizes the theme, but the direct link to the Family's victims through Polanski's several brief but talismanic appearances.

As the snuff phenomenon became globalized, Hollywood productions would continue to make the short journey over the border in search of snuff. In Paul Schrader's *Hardcore* (1979), the snuff producer Ratan has just returned from Tijuana, Mexico, and within this post-*Deep Throat* culture, it is implied that extreme and illegal pornography is now too dangerous to film on American soil. In *Hardcore*, the US is deeply divided between small town piety and urban degeneracy, following Jake Van Dorn (George C. Scott) from his prosperous Calvinist environment in Michigan, to the fleshpots of California in search of Kristen (Ilah Davis), his fourteen-year-old runaway daughter. He hires a private

---

[33]Sanders, *The Family* (1972): 227–28.

investigator, Andy Mast (Peter Boyle), who discovers a pornographic loop featuring a passive, apparently naïve, Kristen being stripped and groped by two men. Posing as a pornographer, Van Dorn ultimately views a short black and white film in which a standard sadomasochistic set up is suddenly interrupted by Ratan entering and abruptly murdering first the male torturer, and then the bound woman. Operating amid a shadowy porn underworld, Van Dorn's quest establishes snuff's connections with the straight porn industry, and the shared signifiers (a bedroom, two men, one passive woman) in the only two films we witness seemingly confirm the fears of 1970s antipornography campaigners in proposing a continuum between erotica and necro-porn.[34]

Hardcore takes inspiration from the investigations of Sharon Tate's father, who followed up rumors of drug connections and went undercover as a hippie in an attempt to track down his daughter's murderers.[35] California's seedy underbelly serves as a stark embodiment of the transformation of the 1960s free love ethos into a culture of commodified, commercialized sex, and in her adolescent flight from bourgeois respectability and repression, Kristen resembles the middle-class runaways who made up most of the Manson Family. But where in Manson lore snuff occurred under the demented direction of a counter-cultural guru (carrying some bizarre transcendental significance), in *Hardcore*, it is presented as the outer limit of porn's moral degeneracy and crass commercialism. Despite this, Kristen expresses preference for her new life, her protestation that "I didn't fit into your goddamned world" effectively an echo of the Manson Family's statements of alienation. However, she capitulates and reaches out to her weeping father in affirmation of family values. Ratan is gunned down in the street by Mast, who tells Van Dorn "Go home pilgrim. There's nothing you can do. You don't belong here." This sense of moral impotence, along with the rising crane shot which closes *Hardcore*, is an uncanny echo of the closing moments of Polanski's *Chinatown* (1974), whose themes of unpunished corruption, incest, and murder contrast sharply with *Hardcore*'s familial redemption, though both acknowledge the persistence of worlds beyond salvation.

Hardcore's splicing of elements from the Tate family's investigations and the Family's social disaffection is an indication of the Mansonian origins and aura of the snuff movie. 1970s snuff narratives drew repeatedly from Manson lore to validate the concept, but the closest the decade came to the replication of snuff was in *The Last House on Dead End Street* (1977),[36] whose writer/director Roger

---

[34]See Carolyn Bronstein, *Battling Pornography: The American Feminist Anti-Pornography Movement, 1976–1986* (New York: Cambridge University Press, 2011): 83–126.

[35]Simon Wells, *Charles Manson: Coming Down Fast* (London: Hodder & Stoughton, 2009): 301.

[36]According to a contribution the director made to an online forum it was apparently shown as *The Cuckoo Clocks of Hell* in 1974. See Jackson's contribution to this volume, *n*25.

Watkins was heavily influenced by Sanders' book.[37] Terry Hawkins (played by Watkins himself), a jailbird with male and female acolytes, lures four jaded swingers to a rambling deserted building where they are ritually tortured and killed on film. Parallels with the Family and the Tate murders abound, including sadistic orgies, home-made pornography, ghastly mutilations performed upon decadent socialites, and a garbled philosophy of ego-annihilation and death. Motivated partly by revenge for stolen film ideas (reflecting Manson's anger with record producer Terry Melcher, previous inhabitant of the Tate murder house), Terry's snuff films are generated by a demand, expressed by the film distributer/victim, for "something different." The film repeatedly emphasizes the mediation and recording of these murders, with the repeated presence on screen of the camera operator and frequent direct address' shots of him advancing menacingly toward the spectator.

The film sometimes resembles the media stereotype of the snuff movie, though this is largely because of low production values and degenerated print quality. Only one brief sequence is unambiguously presented as part of the actual snuff movie being made, signaled by camera shake, a running projector sound effect, and the absence of diegetic noise. The tortures and murders are presented much more theatrically, the *grand guignol* setting underscored by an uncomfortable combination of the carnivalesque and surgical cruelty. Terry's hieratic mask and gnomic intonations conflate Greek tragedy, sacred ritual, and the bearded Manson, while the murder of the pornographer's wife (seen earlier at the orgy being brutally whipped in blackface make-up by a hunchback) sets the template for subsequent cultural expectations of what snuff might actually look like. Tied to a table, surrounded by tools with the murderers acting out a dark satire of a medical procedure, her face is cut and her legs removed, before she is revived from unconsciousness to witness her final mutilation and disembowelment. It is much more prolonged and sadistic than the conclusion of *Snuff*, whose appended climax was filmed later but widely distributed earlier, three years after *The Last House on Dead End Street* was made but almost certainly before it was screened. Ironically then, the birth pangs of post-Manson fictional snuff is nearly as obscure as that of the actual object, engendering its own separate mythologies of production and reception. *The Last House on Dead End Street*, unlike *Snuff*, does not attempt to masquerade as an actual murder movie. It resembles *The Slaughter* in its indebtedness to Manson, but avoids generic exploitation tropes in its utilization of the rumors that surrounded the Manson Family. Ultimately, it achieves a somewhat tacit agreement with *Emanuelle in America* and *Hardcore* regarding the irrecuperable nature of snuff, something all the more disquieting

---

[37]David Kerekes and Mikita Brottman, "The Cuckoo Clocks of Hell—An Interview with Roger Watkins," *Headpress* 23 (June 2002): 104–06.

given the film's refusal to form any moral judgment in its adoption of the protagonist's delirious subjective state.

As Manson's notoriety was refashioned by early 1980s postpunk subcultural groups, his status shifted from the irrecuperable to the radical.[38] Indeed, it became possible to recast Mansonian analogs with straightforward and purportedly realistic representations of the Family's activities, with two notable re-enactments appearing in the 1980s: *Manson Family Movies* (John Aes-Nihil, 1984) and *Judgement Day Theater: The Book of Manson* (Raymond Pettibon, 1989). Neither film depicts snuff activity, but both adopt stylistic modes evoking home movies as if in consolation for the notoriously absent Family films. *Manson Family Movies* has no diegetic sound, featuring instead audio recordings of Manson, Family members and some apposite songs and orchestral pieces. A note at the end of the film claims that footage was shot at authentic locations, and well-informed viewers will recognize virtually all the footage as sourced in published accounts. Filmed on home video with very low production values, it resembles a dress rehearsal by an amateur dramatic company obsessed with Manson. This amateurish aesthetic allows it to represent the murders through slapdash, vérité methods, but the use of intertitles, close-ups of labeled objects, and melodramatic over-performance expose narrational aspects akin to silent cinema. *The Book of Manson*, though also unremittingly unprofessional to the point where it could indeed be found footage, is unconcerned with authentic period representation, exhibiting a greater concern with Manson's philosophy than with details of the slayings. Obviously shot in modern suburban houses and gardens, no attempt is made at authentic set dressing or costume design, although the period is evoked through anachronistic t-shirts featuring 1960s icons. The Tate murder sequence reproduces some infamous details, including one of the murderers licking Sharon Tate's blood from her knife, and although almost every other aspect of this sequence is markedly inaccurate, its self-reflexivity and camcorder aesthetic purposefully evokes the aura of snuff. Evincing socio-political intent, as well as a revisionist erasure of Manson's extreme racism, one extended scene depicts Manson expounding elements of his philosophy while jamming with Jimi Hendrix as the Tate murder is occurring. Exhibiting the peculiar obsession with Manson as a symbol of nihilistic extremes, both of these low-budget, self-consciously cultish productions rely for their rationale on the absence of the lost Manson Family footage, the continuing mythology generating an ironically inauthentic simulacra in which snuff is defined as a complementary aesthetic.

Although the Family persisted as the occasional model for exploitation films featuring wayward counter-cultural groups throughout the 1970s and 1980s,

---

[38]Gerry Carlin and Mark Jones, "'Helter Skelter' and Sixties Revisionism," in *Countercultures and Popular Music*, edited by Sheila Whiteley and Jedediah Sklower (Farnham: Ashgate, 2014): 105–06.

including *Thou Shalt Not Kill... Except* (Josh Becker, 1985) and *555* (Wally Koz, 1988), their connection to snuff was obscured, both by an increasing distance from events of the late 1960s and the arrival of a new iconography. In succeeding years, films such as *Henry, Portrait of a Serial Killer* (John McNaughton, 1989) and *Man Bites Dog* (Benoît Poelvoorde, RémyBelvaux and André Bonzel, 1992) showed snuff being produced by and for the psychopathic serial killer, tending toward a pseudo-documentary style and engendering analyses of voyeurism and moral responsibility. Retaining its status as signifier of irrecuperability, snuff also gained prominence as a theme and plot device in mainstream thrillers like *Mute Witness* (Anthony Waller, 1994) and *8mm* (Joel Schumacher, 1999), in which it is overdetermined as the ultimate taboo. With the spread of inexpensive, accessible video technology, the likelihood of snuff's actual existence increased, further diluting its connection with Manson lore.

Snuff's theoretical affinities to the material and representational properties of film is, however, evident in the very form and style of Jim VanBebber's *The Manson Family* (2003).[39] It is a painstaking attempt to synthesize the popular constituents of Manson mythology, making extensive use of a complex, intricate array of faked but visibly granulated source or archive footage, black and white news clips, pristine dramatic reconstructions, and dramatized interviews. Some material reproduces scenes from the 1973 *Manson* documentary, replicating certain formal properties and endowing it further with the caché of authenticity. A framing narrative, dated 1996, depicts a television presenter researching and assembling material for a Manson documentary. Some scenes, particularly fictional contemporaneous interviews with members of the Family, might have been produced for this documentary and are signaled by horizontal lines simulating the properties of video tape playback. The film constantly gestures toward the "real" and its documented representation, the varied montage function maintaining this realism, providing multiple and often contradictory viewpoints of the same narrative events.

The distinct formal properties of these formats are edited together relatively seamlessly, the visual register of particular images serving as an index of their chronology within the nonlinear narrative. However, there is occasional blurring of such features. For example, during Manson's faux crucifixion and an orgy involving the ritual sacrifice of a dog,[40] only occasionally does the image texture display grains. Here, the reference to authentic footage might be legitimized by

---

[39] *The Manson Family* apparently began production in 1988, but was only completed and released in 2003. Van Bebber has directed various industrial music videos, and the production of *The Manson Family* was supported by bands such as Skinny Puppy and Pantera (Chas Balun, DVD booklet *The Manson Family*, Anchor Bay Entertainment, 2005).
[40] Both events are reported in Ed Sanders, *The Family* (Boston, MA: Da Capo Press, 2002): 76, 166.

occasional glimpses of a figure with a movie camera, alluding to the legendary lost Manson snuff films of ritualized murder. However, the utilization of similar techniques in the Tate murder sequence, where filming was unlikely, unsettles such readings. In its modes of veracity, *The Manson Family* merely *alludes* to snuff film-making, avoiding direct presentation and retaining its intangibility even in the most faithful reconstructions. In 2004, the television film *Helter Skelter* (John Gray) was unable to even allude to snuff, despite a focus on the Family's inner dynamics (rather than the investigation and trial centralized in the similarly titled 1976 TV movie), reconstructions of group ceremonies, visual confirmation of the ownership of a film camera, and a comment that life at the Spahn Ranch is "like being in a movie." Although snuff movies have been the subject of television crime dramas since 1976,[41] they are typically ensconced safely within a fictional framework and subjected to police investigation and prosecution, a dramatic safeguard inapplicable to the elusive Manson snuff movies.

The early twenty-first century saw a mini-boom in Manson-inspired material. *Snuff-Movie* (Bernard Rose, 2005) revived the Manson analog narrative, elaborating upon the connection to snuff as its protagonist, horror film maker Boris Arkadin (Jeroen Krabbé), promises over the film's opening credits that "all the violence, all the suffering, the horror, all of it, will be real. I give you my word." The first section of the film imitates the gothic trappings of Hammer horror, soon revealed as an extended sequence from Arkadin's most recent film, and is reminiscent of Polanski's own Hammer pastiche, *Dance of the Vampires* (1967). It is being watched at a party at the film-maker's house, which is itself being filmed by a documentary crew producing the footage we are now watching. Significantly, the music is a recognizable pastiche of The Beatles' "Helter Skelter" and the low quality documentary film is gradually spliced with shots from another homemade movie, featuring a trio of hippie chicks who crash the party and bloodily murder the guests. Arkadin survives, having been called away (echoing Polanski's absence from home during the Manson murders), but his wife (heavily pregnant like Sharon Tate), who is also the star of the film we have been viewing, is one of the victims. The murder footage is without sound, accompanied only by the familiar aural signifier of a running projector. The cameraman then retrieves the documentary filmmaker's equipment and, in a verbal allusion to the Tate-LaBianca murder scene blood graffiti, tells one of the other killers to "snuff this piggy." The film then cuts to archive news footage, used within a contemporary commentary by (real) documentary maker Nick Broomfield, reflecting upon the

---

[41]Milligen, *The Bloodiest Thing*, 223–24; Julian Petley, " 'Snuffed Out': Nightmares in a Trading Standards Officer's Brain," in *Unruly Pleasures: The Cult Film and Its Critics*, edited by Xavier Mendik and Graeme Harper (Guildford: FAB Press, 2000): 209.

Arkadin murder case (which apparently occurred in 1975 in Highgate) and the potential effects of screen violence.

The main narrative gets underway when Arkadin apparently begins to make a semi-improvisational film based on the murders, using hidden cameras at the location of the original killings. These scenes are spliced with supposedly found footage derived from various sources (closed circuit television, spy cams, hacked webcams etc.), and it is revealed that the putative fictional film is to be real, an "unstoppable, uncensorable" online snuff movie. This section of the film climaxes unexpectedly with the crucifixion of the actress playing Arkadin's wife, surrounded by a crowd who have apparently just appeared. A rationale for the bloody ritual is offered here, when Arkadin calls upon God to intervene or for Satan to appear, either of which would provide some kind of supernatural meaning and justice. The next morning, in a still bloodied bedroom, Arkadin is murdered on camera by his disabled son at the behest of a hooded man, whose voice indicates he may have been the cameraman in the earlier snuff killing. Alternatively, he may be the devil Arkadin previously invoked. The film's final narrative twist sees Arkadin and his wife actually alive, well and in preproduction on a snuff themed horror film. After a diegetic "thank you" to an actor in response to a compliment, Arkadin/Krabbé turns to the camera and, with a theatrical flourish, says to the viewer "thank you very much."

Arkadin's planned production may, of course, be the film we have just watched. If, as the film initially suggests, he was the survivor of a Mansonian massacre, he differs somewhat from Polanski, whose early 1970s films, particularly *Macbeth* (1971), only gestured toward such representations.[42] The film's conflicting realities, scrupulously maintained by various representational means, eventually collapse in upon themselves. The film's very structure, in which each layer is revealed as a fiction created by an apparent outer "reality," and wherein death movies are produced at every level, testifies to the ever-receding nature of snuff. The parallels to the Tate murders are extensive and detailed, and after returning us to the origins of the snuff myth, the film provides a series of snuff's cinematic iconography, through sleazy exploitation ruses, blood drenched horror iconography, *vérité* documentary form, and closed-circuit surveillance footage. All of these are equally convincing and equally unreal, as is the mysterious hooded character who materializes at the end of the film as a *deus ex machina*, instructing Arkadin's son in murder and making gnomic utterances about God and destiny, endowing *Snuff-Movie*'s analysis of snuff with a Mansonian validation. In this incessantly postmodernist movie, the ritual crucifixion and the satanic guru are the only truly ineluctable elements.

---

[42]Mikita Brottman, " 'Strange Images of Death': Manson, Polanski, *Macbeth*," in *Hollywood Hex: Death and Destiny in the Dream Factory* (London: Creation Books, 1999): 57–87.

Snuff remains a potent theme for meta-textual cinema, and its origin in the lost Manson Family movies, largely ignored in contemporary mainstream representation, retains currency in both art and exploitation cinema. This is apparent in *Resurrecting The Street Walker* (Özgür Uyanık, 2009). Here, *The Street Walker* alluded to is an unfinished 1980s film embedded within at least two strata of mockumentary footage, with Ed Sanders' *The Family* cited in the authoritative outer layer as the origin of the term "snuff movie." However, a supposed quotation from Charles Manson which provides the film's epigraph, although resembling a testified remark by Manson, is unsourced in any of the documents on the case. The Manson murders do not in any way resemble the accidental killing which, if it occurred, would make *The Street Walker* a snuff movie. Much more pertinent, though lacking any explicit reference to Manson, is *The Life and Death of a Porno Gang* (Mladen Djordjevic, 2009), in which a band of itinerant actors, artists, and drug addicts tour the Serbian countryside in a painted van, performing porno theater and cavorting nude in nature, much like the Family as depicted in Hendrickson and Merrick's *Manson* documentary. This erotic cabaret goes awry after they are commissioned by a German intermediary to make snuff films for wealthy international collectors. These partial parallels and inauthentic citations attest to Manson's abiding if tenuous presence in cult cinema.

Since the emergence of the myth of snuff in the early 1970s, it has attained a symbolic identity that remains restricted largely to fiction. In the absence of a real snuff film, its only material presence is *in* film. In its replicability and iconicity, snuff both confirms and challenges Baudrillard's definition of the real as "that of which it is possible to give an equivalent reproduction."[43] Snuff has been continually reproduced and represented but never found. In a mediatized reality, it is the ultimate absent referent, and the multifarious need for it to exist locates it just out of reach of the endless movements of perverse and political desire. Its continuing nonexistence accelerates and consolidates its mythic possibility, and in a field in which rumor and anecdote prevail over evidence, the legendary Manson Family snuff movies—perhaps buried somewhere in Death Valley, or in a New York brownstone apartment safe—continue to promise the most realistic opportunity for the emergence of a genuine object.

---

[43]Jean Baudrillard, *Simulations*, translated by Paul Foss, Paul Patton, and Philip Beitchman (New York: Semiotext[e], 1983): 146.

10 WILD EYES, DEAD LADIES: THE SNUFF FILMMAKER IN REALIST HORROR

Neil Jackson

The fictional snuff filmmaker has become an important constituent of the "realist" branch of the horror genre,[1] allowing for reflection upon the exponential development of the snuff phenomenon in the 1970s. Within this decade, the snuff filmmaker emerged as an infrequent but potent entity within realist horror without recourse to a tangible social referent, with the unproven rumors of a snuff subculture proving ample ground for speculation upon what kind of individual (or collective) would create such a cinematic artifact. This led to several striking interpretations of the human monster figure, as much a response to an emerging urban mythology as it was to an existing element within a generic framework.

Although representations of the snuff-filmmaker have often been steeped in socio-sexual aberration, he (and it is almost always *he*) is shown to be as much, and in many ways exclusively, a cinematic phenomenon as a proven social entity. Although not necessarily ubiquitous within popular narratives (like, for example, the literary and cinematic serial killer), the image of the snuff filmmaker resonates in several (often overlooked or marginalized) films, both exemplifying and mediating assumptions about the realist horror paradigm. In achieving

---

[1] For insight and elaboration upon the use of this generic term, see Cynthia Freeland, "Realist Horror," in *Philosophy and Film*, edited by Cynthia Freeland and Thomas Wartenberg (New York/London: Routledge, 1995).

this, several snuff-themed narratives demonstrate how a monstrous strain of masculinity accommodates the phallocentric dictates of the camera eye, finding a conduit in the figure of the snuff filmmaker himself.

The fictional snuff filmmaker became defined partly through his deluded, perverse aspirations to creative expression, and the ensuing analyses observe ideas regarding male-ordained assumptions about sexuality, social power and the limits of patriarchal authority, arguing that the snuff filmmaker is not a fixed icon, but malleable and fluid regardless of his particular social manifestation. For the purposes of historical specificity, the discussion is limited to a point in the late 1980s, by which time his role as a cultural bogeyman engendered a distinct set of critical, theoretical and technological considerations. Indeed, the emphasis upon the creators of *celluloid* (as opposed to video or digital) atrocities within a specific epoch allows for a discussion of the dynamic that has developed between the snuff filmmaker and the construction and dissemination of the mechanical death image itself.[2] To varying degrees of success and distinction, these themes are centralized in films such as *The Last House on Dead End Street* (Roger Watkins, 1977), *The Evolution of Snuff* (Andrzej Kostenko and Karl Martine, 1978), *Effects* (Dusty Nelson, 1980), *Special Effects* (Larry Cohen, 1984) and an episode of the US TV crime drama *Miami Vice* (entitled *Death and the Lady* [Colin Bucksey, 1988]). All of these examples engage directly with the rumors of a snuff underground in the 1970s, a phenomenon compounded by the release of films from the independent exploitation sector, such as *Snuff* (Michael and Roberta Findlay, 1976), and, from the Hollywood mainstream, *Hardcore* (Paul Schrader, 1979). These titles presented versions of the snuff-filmmaker either as a figure mired in an artless, debased and perverted porno underworld, or as a flamboyant auteur whose deviant cinematic vision is an expression of his contempt for, and dislocation from, any form of moral or social consequence. This places special emphasis upon the snuff-filmmaker not only as architect and bearer of the assumed patriarchal cinematic gaze, but also as an emblem of broader concerns regarding class and economic exploitation. This sets the discussion apart from films which presented snuff as merely one aspect of the varied *modus operandi* of a selection of rapists, torturers, serial killers or shadowy corporate entities.[3]

The notion of the snuff-filmmaker as perverse artist has its generic corollary in the common convention of the "creative" ingenuity of the serial killer.[4]

---

[2]See the chapters by Julian Petley and Mark Astley in this volume, which elaborate upon the meanings generated by nonfictional death videos in the digital age.

[3]See *Emanuelle in America* (Joe D'Mato, 1976), *Videodrome* (David Cronenberg, 1983), *Henry Portrait of a Serial Killer* (John McNaughton, 1990) and *Man Bites Dog* (Rémy Belvaux, André Bonzel and Benoît Poelvoorde, 1992).

[4]See, for example, *Silence of the Lambs* (Jonathan Demme, 1991), *Se7en* (David Fincher, 1995), *Copycat* (Jon Amiel, 1995).

However, many snuff-themed narratives have contained, whether consciously or not, a self-reflexive foregrounding of cinematic technology, making processes of objectification, humiliation and annihilation visible as primary signifiers of patriarchal control, often enhancing our understanding of the very processes that are being enacted onscreen. Some films emerged from the independent exploitation production sector, seemingly cheap, vulgar and noticeably removed from mainstream dictates of classical construction, "taste" and visual propriety, frequently underscored by a chaotic, even apocalyptic inversion of generic structures. However, closer inspection of their formal and thematic strategies—however crude—reveals a sustained engagement with concurrent modes of exploitation and exploration through appropriation of the emergent conventions of snuff-fiction.

None of this is to suggest that these films were all consciously negotiating the radical infiltrations of second wave feminism and its subsequent impact upon cultural theory.[5] Nevertheless, it is striking upon close inspection how these titles are cognizant of the aesthetic, economic, and ideological frameworks upon which the fictional snuff subgenre has been formed, evincing formal strategies that make visible a series of tensions and ruptures that threaten to dismantle the patriarchal dominion actively pursued by the snuff filmmaker. The very presence of a human monster, wielding a movie camera and engaged in the act of creating images that climax in the violent death of the victim, allow these films to reveal an often impotent, hysterical drive toward personal affirmation, exposing the limits to which men can truly control the images and narratives they strive to produce as emblems of social and interpersonal power.

In this sense, any attempt to deal with the representation of the snuff filmmaker is immediately confronted with the ubiquity of the male, human monster. Cynthia Freeland has argued convincingly that:

> much realist horror involves male violence against women, but there may also be issues about violence in general as it relates to social class, race and urban alienation.[6]

Freeland's contextual foci, steeped in questions of how the terror of the real repeatedly invokes "leftist" (if not always explicitly Marxist) preoccupations, provides a useful, concise framework for the cultural parameters within which

---

[5]Notable examples from this period would include Molly Haskell's *From Reverence To Rape*, first published in 1974 and revised in 1987, Laura Mulvey's 1975 essay "Visual Pleasure and Narrative Cinema" (widely anthologized, but originally published in the British journal *Screen*) and E Ann Kaplan's 1983 study, *Women and Film: Both Sides of the Camera*.
[6]Freeland, "Realist Horror," 135.

the realist horror canon has developed. The snuff filmmaker has often embodied not only sadistic drives latent within the cinematic gaze, but also functioned as a conduit for questions of the economic and artistic exploitation of particular social groupings.

The 1970s mythology of the porno-snuff movie developed more or less concurrently with the development of feminist film theory, and it is tempting to read the snuff filmmaker as a perverse response to a radical intellectual challenge. Laura Mulvey's idea of the masculinized "erotic contemplation"[7] of the objectified female form has been both exercised and overwhelmed when the sadistic gaze of the snuff filmmaker has been portrayed on the film. Her argument emphasized the dynamic of the scopophilic, narcissistic and sadistic pleasures enabled by the objectification of idealized female images, and was founded in an analysis of the tendencies of classical Hollywood film. However, the exploitation film has been much more overt in its objectification of the female body, and the proliferation of sexually violent (as well as hardcore pornographic) titles in the 1970s[8] provides a succinct, tangible reference point for this cine-cultural journey toward a proliferation of explicit visual representation.

This historical trajectory was founded partly in a process identified by Mulvey, which invariably demanded a form of punishment or narrative containment to allay the castrating threat embodied by female characters. If we accept Mulvey's argument that the audience is constructed and positioned as a masculine entity, the visual emphasis in snuff-themed narratives, with their primary onscreen bearer of the look intent upon enacting and recording sexual assault and dismemberment, transplants the sense of women's "to-be-looked-at-ness"[9] into considerations of "to-be-violated-ness" or "to-be-murderously-exploited-ness." Consequently, any conciliatory visual pleasure experienced through idealized images of beauty is supplanted by a distinct form of *un-pleasure* bound by the limits of spectatorial tolerance for extreme images of violent death. This might lead to reasonable assumptions that these snuff themed narratives merely enact Mulvey's argument *in extremis*, with female punishment embellished with any number of obscene physical details, the voyeuristic gratification of narrative cinema supplanted by a drive toward pure sadism. However, the films under discussion actively engage and dramatize a transfer of "voyeuristic and fetishistic mechanisms"[10] into the literalized expression of perversion, and the recurrent presence of a series of self-reflexive strategies also allows for a contemplative

---

[7]Laura Mulvey, "Visual Pleasure and Narrative Cinema," in *Movies and Methods Volume II*, edited by Bill Nicholls (Berkeley: University of California Press, 1985): 309.
[8]See the introduction to this volume.
[9]Mulvey, "Visual Pleasure," 309.
[10]Ibid.

discourse that runs concurrently with the hysterical expression of deviant male desire which often reaches beyond the realm of the sexual.

I argued at length in an article on *Cannibal Holocaust* (Ruggero Deodato, 1980)[11] regarding the dual discourses of self-reflexivity and immersion in the film's graphic and explicit images of violent death. This allowed the film to at once wallow in, and offer a critique of a skillfully orchestrated series of mock-documentary sequences depicting sexual torture, rape, dismemberment and, most contentiously of all, the real onscreen killing of a variety of animals. I.Q. Hunter has since argued that a set of elitist prejudices has traditionally insisted upon a "class based assumption that 'low' genres cannot do self-reflexivity and that the audience stands in need of correction,"[12] a tendency exemplified by titles such as Michael Haneke's *Benny's Video* (1992)and *Funny Games* (1997).

However, a distinct level of critical introspection within the subgenre harks back to the proto-snuff filmmaker text, *Peeping Tom* (1960), whose litany of self-reflexive devices, very consciously orchestrated by director Michael Powell, almost obliges its cinematic progeny to assume an at least marginally objective position regarding the ethical obligations of a subgenre partly rooted in images of abject female terror. N.A. Morris sees *Peeping Tom* as a film concerned with the seemingly contradictory manner in which both Romanticism and an objectively "scientific" reflexivity might be embodied in the individual artist, achieving this through the use of devices which repeatedly evoke the cinematic apparatus. Morris argues that the film's obsessive rendition of the deviant drives of its central character, Mark (Carl Boehm)

> offered these observations long before film theory began seriously examining the relationship between mainstream cinematic pleasure and unconscious libidinal drives … [Mark] meets his horror show death, to the accompaniment of his own recorded screams, in the ultimate "snuff" movie in which subject and filmmaker, producer and consumer, victim and exploiter, voyeur and exhibitionist, self and image, finally collapse.[13]

Therefore, a retrospective account of *Peeping Tom* (with its male monster, furtive English porn industry milieu, "creative" murders, embodied infamously by Mark's improvised mirror and spiked tripod devices, and emphasis upon sado-sexual dynamics in the exchange of looks between object and subject) allows for the notion that snuff actually existed as a theoretical concept prior to its entry into the lexicon of urban mythology. The contemporary critical rejection

---

[11]Neil Jackson, "*Cannibal Holocaust*: Realist Horror and Reflexivity," *Postscript* 21, no. 3 (2002): 32–45.
[12]I.Q. Hunter, *British Trash Cinema* (London: British Film Institute, 2013): 162.
[13]N.M. Morris, "Reflections on Peeping Tom," *Movie* 34–35 (1990):96.

of the film in the UK[14] was not only a reflection of its affront to the cultural establishment's taste dictates, but also testament to its brilliant awareness of the complex relationship between a morally contentious film and its audience. This is itself reflective of the conceptual disturbance evoked by the very idea of snuff, and the film suggests that the pleasures and gratifications embedded in the experience of entertainment consumption are rooted in psychological drives that are inherently oppressive and domineering (embodied in the oedipal slant of Mark's neurosis and the tension between voyeur and subject, both within the text [Mark and his victims] and beyond it [the audience and its position determined through Mark's narrative status as both victim and monster]). Such is the emphasis placed upon Mark's determination to capture the singular moment where terror intersects with mortality; Ian Christie argues that *Peeping Tom* may actually suggest that "the perfect film might be a snuff film... the ultimate unfilmmable moment."[15]

Peeping Tom, with its gleeful blurring of the perceived demarcation of art and exploitation, displayed a complexity and sophistication that subsequent snuff-fictions have struggled to negotiate ever since. Powell's film existed in advance not only of the critical and theoretical tools that came to accommodate its cultural rehabilitation, but also of the urban mythology of snuff itself. It utilized the properties of film language (and more importantly, its eponymous figure's deranged cinematic sensibility) to evoke male sexual neurosis, a strategy which English critics derided in the most stereotypically repressive and haughty manner imaginable. While the film is locked into a specifically English ambience of socio-sexual melancholy, the other chief snuff-filmmaker narrative of the decade, *The Wild Eye* (Paolo Cavara, 1967), is very much concerned with the relationship between the Italian mondo school of documentary filmmaking[16] and the global, often undeveloped cultures its central character, Paolo (Philippe Leroy), is seen to exploit. Italian in origin and given scant global distribution in an English

---

[14]Critic John Patterson summarizes the reaction of the UK critical establishment thus: "'beastly' (Financial Times), 'dreadful' (Sunday Dispatch), 'corrupt and empty' (Evening Standard), 'perverted nonsense' (Daily Worker)... Observer critic CA Lejeune, who grabbed her handbag, said loudly, 'I'm sickened!' and flounced out. She never thought to mention this walk-out in her own review (during which she wrote, 'I don't propose to name the players in this beastly film')." John Patterson, *"Peeping Tom* may have been nasty but it didn't deserve critics' cold shoulder," *The Guardian*, November 13, 2010, accessed June 8, 2015, http://www.theguardian.com/film/2010/nov/13/peeping-tom-john-patterson.

[15]Ian Christie, interviewed as part of *Peeping Tom*, UK Blu Ray/DVD special features, (Optimum Releasing).

[16]For comprehensive overviews and insights into the mondo film, see David Kerekes and David Slater, *Killing for Culture: An Illustrated History of Death Film from Mondo to Snuff* (London: Creation Books, 1995) and Mark Goodall, *Sweet and Savage: The World Through the Shockumentary Film Lens* (Manchester: Headpress, 2006).

language version, it represents the great missing link in the development of the snuff filmmaker as a genre icon. Respectively, it consolidates and anticipates the self-reflexive modes of *Peeping Tom* and *Cannibal Holocaust*, mounting an explicit critique of the methods of mondo through its portrayal of a filmmaker whose obsessive global pursuit of human frailty and cruelty allows for the exploitation of opium addicts and the attempted bribery of Buddhist monks. Moreover, his misanthropy drives him to manipulate events during the Vietnam war, physically rearranging the execution of a Vietcong suspect for compositional and lighting effect. Finally, following a tip-off regarding the imminent bombing of a café-bar filled with locals and US servicemen alike, Paolo does nothing to warn them, endangering himself, his camera crew, and the unwitting objects of his lens. Unlike *Peeping Tom*, the film *responds* to an existing popular subgenre rather than anticipating a milieu and set of attitudes, and is also part of a loosely related group of films (encompassing not only the snuff-themed *Effects* and *Special Effects*, but titles as diverse as *The Stunt Man* [Richard Rush, 1980] and *Shadow of the Vampire* [E. Elias Merhige, 2000]) which assess the relationship between the dangerous creative and intellectual vanities of the film director and the very nature of the medium itself. Despite emerging from very diverse contexts, *Peeping Tom* and *The Wild Eye* established a prehistorical foundation for the snuff filmmaker in the ensuing decades.

This is very much in evidence in Eithne Johnson and Eric Schaefer's establishment of a theoretical link between *Peeping Tom* and *Snuff*. Although radically different in cultural value (indeed, the films are diametrically opposed in everything from conception to execution) Johnson and Schaefer emphasize shared "connection[s] between male sadism and photography insofar as the director 'overpowers' the actress explicitly so that this action will be caught on film."[17] However, while *Peeping Tom* plays very consciously with this concept of power and image construction, discussion of such tropes in relation to *Snuff* is bound by a set of *received* rather than *contained* significances, its shoddily appended climactic murder sequence severed from any internal dynamics and its critical interest bound by extra-textual dynamics of marketing and scandal mongering. *Snuff*'s climax was merely the lackluster punchline to an elaborate practical joke, a marketing scam that sought to convince the public that a genuine murder had been committed on film. Nevertheless, the delirious, penultimate image of a deranged film director brandishing the innards of his female victim and addressing the camera directly with an orgasmic roar, exemplifies the perceived cultural drive toward a murderous patriarchal gaze. The film's sudden, final cut to black (following a brief burst of light phenomena in which the image of the

---

[17]Eithne Johnson and Eric Schaefer, "Soft Core/Hard Gore: Snuff as a Crisis in Meaning," *The Journal of Film and Video* 45, nos 2–3 (1993): 40–59.

filmmaker is subsumed) functions as a sly (possibly unintentional) joke, the murderous triumph of the perpetrator undercut when he is suddenly informed by his cohorts behind the camera that they've run out of film. No sooner has the snuff filmmaker ritually expressed and captured his self-perceived triumph, than he is forced to make haste and flee the scene, defeated by the practical reality of insufficient film stock and reminded of the abject "reality" of his deed.

This interplay between a fictional world and snuff pornography's descent further into the mire is a constant refrain of the ensuing subgenre. In its attempts to pass off a series of staged incidents as a cautionary documentary on the moral, economic and creative travails of the German sex film industry, *The Evolution of Snuff*[18] is founded upon an elaborate complex of distortions and manipulations far in excess of those presented in the climax to *Snuff*. Like that film, it has been subjected to postproduction modifications instigated by its distributor, Atlas Films, seeking to capitalize upon a contemporaneous cultural controversy. Indeed, the film seems to have used *Snuff* partly as a structural and economic template through its attempt to exploit and capitalize upon an existing film via the addition of only the most tangentially related violent material.

Most of the film focuses upon the attempts of German director Robert Furch[19] to cast and shoot an updated version of Aristophanes Greek comedy of sexual mores, *Lysistrata*. It foregrounds an assortment of conventional porn industry scenarios in which aspirant male and female performers are cast, arranged and photographed by Furch, intercut with talking-head interviews, behind the scenes footage, and short film extracts. Although much of this is patently faked or heavily contrived (a sense given further weight in the awkward English language dub, another feature which provides immediate qualification to its fragile claims to authenticity), the film is given further shape by a voiceover which seeks to contextualize Furch's career within an assortment of industrial and socio-political contexts. However, one detail of the film's production is distorted and subsequently exploited for maximum sensational effect: during Furch's attempts to complete production on *Lysistrata* in 1975, his star Claudia Fielers committed

---

[18]The film circulates most commonly under the somewhat cumbersome title *The Evolution of Snuff: Confessions of a Blue Movie Star* and, oddly enough, both titles appear onscreen and several minutes apart in the version under review. The film's credited director is the almost definitely pseudonymous "Karl Martine" with the Polish director Andrzej Kostenko credited with the role of "Artistic Supervision." Kostenko himself appears onscreen as an interviewee in the first of the bookend sequences which open and close the film. In light of this, it seems reasonable to surmise that he was responsible for at least some of this footage.

[19]Furch was an actual German film and TV industry veteran, whose directorial credits *Teenager Report—Die ganzjungen Madchen* (1973) and *Geheimtechniken der Sexualitat* (1973) were attempts to cash in on the international popularity of the softcore *Schulmadchen Report* films emerging from Germany in the early 1970s.

suicide through poisoning,[20] an event which the director seized upon to lend tenuous credence to the structural framework which propagates the porno snuff myth which the film is all too willing to embellish.

Of course, this strategy also forced the original project to pursue a significantly different direction. As the title suggests, snuff is posited as a teleological inevitability, the outer limits of an industry in which its participants, to quote from the voiceover, suffer "a wearing down process that leads to the death of the soul…the end result is a turbulent amalgam of cogwheels, flesh, celluloid and human anguish…a slice of death!"

Like *The Wild Eye* and its relationship to the mondo movie, but without any kind of sustained and consistent critical objectivity, the film offers opprobrium toward moral malpractice in the sex film industry. Its focus upon standard pornography illuminates Furch's frustrations at the interlocked systems of market demand, economic necessity and his own creative limitations. However, the film's strategies for linking snuff to the standard processes of the pornographic film industry are especially superficial, with Furch's attempts to justify his methods on grounds of pragmatism and necessity having little in common with the representation of snuff filmmaking appended to the opening and closing sequences. In fact, an initial viewing of the film primes the spectator for some form of connection between Furch and the snuff underworld, but this never actually transpires, a symptom of the utter disconnection between the film's midsection and its brief, snuff-themed bookends. Evidently, the film has little genuine faith in its stated project of charting the inevitability of snuff as a natural extension of the banal, depressing world essayed for the vast majority of its running time.

In a familiar shock-horror headline fashion, the film opens with images of German and English newspapers which proclaim "Unsuspecting Porno Girl Butchered in Front of Camera" and "Girl Slaughtered For Snuff Films," which appear to define snuff as a manifestation of sexual exploitation and debased pornographic tastes. However, this position begins to unravel immediately when a frame analysis of the image of the English newspaper (the *Daily Mirror*, itself, along with the *Observer*, the subject of a wry joke in *Peeping Tom*) reveals it to be a mere fabrication: the story underneath the headline is actually a report on the fraught position of the British car industry. From the outset then, crude, barely concealed fakery is fundamental to the film's sensationalist aspirations. For all of its self-proclaimed status as a "political warning against debasement" (a sentiment voiced onscreen by German novelist, Carl Amery), the film's desperate recourse to a crudely doctored tabloid newspaper article places it in the realms of the

---

[20]See (the wryly pseudonymously authored) Onan, "Now That Masturbation isn't a Dirty Word, what's Wrong with Pornography?," *Video Viewer*, September 1982, 56.

exploitation tactics deployed in the attempt to pass off *Snuff* as a *bona fide* document of real sexual murder. The adoption of a stern, condemnatory moral tone is frequently at odds with the film's excitable recourse to images that trade in the economy of sexual exploitation. In its clumsy imposition of the opening and closing snuff-themed segments, the whole film can quite easily be read as a self-righteous and palpably dishonest diatribe against the whole of the sex film industry.

Like *Snuff*, therefore, *The Evolution of Snuff* is far more interesting when appreciated as a cinematic hoax, whose self-reflexive properties are as much an accidental function of its erratic construction as they are of any artful or intelligent interrogation of the material. The film's cognizance of historical and mythological dimensions of snuff is evident in the opening sequence, in which Roman Polanski is interviewed briefly about its alleged existence. Polanski's presence, evoking the murder of his wife, Sharon Tate, by the Manson family in 1969, subtextually introduces the spectre of snuff's underground origins.[21] As one of a series of interviewees articulating the inevitability of snuff, his comment on the "dangerous" potential of the movie camera aligns his own position as an esteemed, critically acclaimed filmmaker, with both Furch and the figure of the supposed snuff filmmaker presented at the climax.

Preceded by a solemn verbal warning and an extended female scream on the soundtrack, what is striking about the final sequence is not only its rigorously contrived and artificial construction, but also its conflation of anecdotal evidence and hearsay, incorporating rumors of South-American snuff-rings, the filmed records of the death of John F. Kennedy and Jack Ruby and the ethical strategies deployed by the Italian mondo subgenre. The latter example is marked by the interviewee's description of filmmakers manipulating African military forces[22] to accommodate the visualization of summary executions (as well as blithely filming the consumption of humans by lions), indicating that the controversies of the mondo cycle were already circulating within a discursive space apt to conjoin it with the distinct generic boundaries of snuff.

---

[21] See Ed Sanders, *The Family* (Boston, MA: De Capo Press, 2002). Rumors of the Manson Family's alleged snuff movies, allegedly depicting a variety of ritualistic human and animal slayings, are documented in this book. Indeed, Sanders' book is widely credited as the original source of the term "snuff movie."

[22] The film appears to be referencing *Africa Addio* (1966) here. Directed by mondo movie veterans Gualtiero Jacopetti and Franco Prosperi, they faced growing criticism for their alleged complicity in the execution of a Simba rebel fighter in the Democratic Republic of the Congo. However, neither was found guilty of the charges and they denied staging any activity for the sole purposes of the film. This is also documented in the film *The Godfathers of Mondo* (David Gregory, 2003), where the newspaper headlines from the time are used in conjunction with testimony offered by Jacopetti. This film was released as a special supplemental DVD as part of Blue Underground's *Mondo Cane Collection* (2003).

FIGURE 10.1 The anonymous, self-proclaimed snuff filmmaker from *The Evolution of Snuff*, dirs Andrzej Kostenko and Karl Martine (Monopol Film, 1978).

Using a fixed, static camera, the alleged snuff filmmaker is interviewed in medium shot (see Figure 10.1), his disguise of a plain paper grocery bag over his head lending the sequence a particularly farcical tone, but sufficiently evocative of the hooded sex criminal or serial-killer that had already infiltrated popular consciousness.[23] Speaking into a microphone, and surrounded by the varied accoutrements of a slovenly lifestyle (including a whisky glass), the interviewee is also notable for other aspects of his attire, which have surface connotations of the outlaw biker subculture, placing him beyond the strictures of conventional social groups. When probed about the "cold blooded" nature of his alleged snuff enterprise, the interviewee merely implicates the public in its equally cold blooded desire to *see* such films, a crude encapsulation of the arguments articulated in both *Peeping Tom* and *The Wild Eye*. However, in its appropriation of a varied range of death-film signifiers, the sequence is effectively severed from much of the

---

[23]For example, in the USA, the so-called Zodiac Killer, who terrorized San Francisco from the late 1960s through the 1970s, was described by eyewitnesses as wearing some form of hood during his attacks. In the UK, the use of a leather mask was a significant element in the attacks perpetrated by Peter Cook, the Cambridge Rapist, who committed a series of attacks in the mid-1970s.

preceding eighty minutes through its identification of snuff as a product of varied global cinematic practices, and not just the logical extension of pornographic sensation. Its desperate claims to authenticity are finally undermined when it inter-cuts the interview with outtakes from *The Last House on the Left* (Wes Craven, 1972) as supposed fragments from the snuff film the interviewee claims to have made, a strategy which might have been more effective had Wes Craven's film not become so widely seen on a global scale.[24] Therefore, although founded upon a totally fraudulent proposition, *The Evolution of Snuff* is notable for its elaboration of the snuff filmmaker as a cultural terrorist, the visual convention of the hooded perpetrator projecting forward to far more resonant twenty-first century images of Islamic jihadists brandishing the heads of executed captives for the purposes of political and ideological capital. Nevertheless, the absurdity of the interviewee's physical appearance and the crude, opportunistic appropriation of fictional footage from an infamous exploitation film, reduce the film's supposedly revelatory, apocalyptic climax (an ambition underlined by the final inscription "The End … and the end of all humanity") to little more than a bad taste prank, much like that which motivated the minds behind *Snuff* before it.

The crude flippancy of *The Evolution of Snuff* is largely a symptom of its bastardized form. However, in *The Last House on Dead End Street* a distinct level of authorial engagement infuses the snuff filmmaker with a tangible social malevolence. This is a marked contrast to the contrived demeanor of the interviewee in *The Evolution of Snuff*, as the film's cynicism and sense of impotent rage is engendered by a genuine creative impulse, channeled directly through an onscreen surrogate. This is especially instructive in light of the onscreen presence of Roger Watkins (under the pseudonym Steven Morrison) as the film's hate-fueled protagonist, Terry Hawkins, and his multiple roles as writer, producer and director (as "Victor Janos") of a project that characterizes the snuff filmmaker as an expression of both sexual and socio-economic dysfunction. Terry's proclamation that "nobody's interested in sex anymore" positions snuff as the endgame of pornographic representation and is part of his process of personal corruption that incorporates drug dealing and pimping, activities which denote the iniquities of a criminal underclass and for which he has already served prison time when the film commences. The subsequent orchestration and realization of his peculiarly ritualized snuff films becomes linked directly to his hysterical drive toward artistic and inter-personal control. Furthermore, in anticipation of a strategy that would later be deployed extensively in *Cannibal Holocaust*, the film also incorporates

---

[24]The presence of these outtakes seems to have been the result of *The Evolution of Snuff* being distributed by Atlas Films, the same company that handled *The Last House on the Left* in several European territories. Interestingly, the footage has never been included in any release version of Craven's film, but has since surfaced as supplementary material on DVD releases. See David A. Szulkin, *Wes Craven's Last House on the Left: The Making of a Cult Classic* (Guildford: FAB Press, 1997):154.

imagery of genuine cattle slaughter in its early section, a direct evocation of genuine death which foreshadows, and in some way authenticates the simulation of violent murder and mutilation which takes up much of the latter sections of the narrative.

Shot throughout 1972 and 1973, but not released until 1977,[25] *The Last House on Dead End Street* anticipates the assumed link between a sleazy porn subculture and the production of snuff films, while also very obviously drawing from the already mythologized activities of Charles Manson, with Terry's unisexual gang of miscreants and dropouts evoking the outsider community of The Family (Figure 10.2). Furthermore, the notion of a socially alienated snuff gang, under the

FIGURE 10.2 Terry Hawkins (Roger Watkins) and his gang of miscreants in *The Last House on Dead End Street* dir. Roger Watkins (Production Concepts Ltd./ Today Productions Inc., 1977).

---

[25]The film was shot under the title *The Cuckoo Clocks of Hell*, culminating in a rough cut approaching three hours in length. This was trimmed to 115 minutes to attract potential distributors, but following a lengthy period of litigation initiated by a cast member, the film was eventually released in its current seventy-seven-minute version, a running time unapproved by Watkins himself and very much the product of extensive restructuring by its initial distributor, Warmflash Productions. Nevertheless, the film remains an expression of an authorial sensibility that is consistent across several films (see note 26 below). This has appeared theatrically in various territories, and on video/DVD as *The Funhouse* and *Last House on Dead End Street*, the latter of which was an obvious attempt to cash in on the success of *The Last House on the Left* (1972). For a comprehensive, authoritative overview of the film's conception, production and distribution history, see *Headpress* 23(June 2002): 67–143.

direction and manipulation of a singularly obsessed figurehead, inverts the idea of snuff as a function of top to bottom class exploitation. Indeed, Terry's stated resentments for "hot to trot rich bastards" defines his actions as a form of class revenge, a communal activity channeling his frustrated ambitions as a filmmaker against the economic group that has financed his films. This is a pithy, satirical encapsulation of the time-honored antipathy of creative artists and their financiers, and in one of a series of grimly humorous gestures throughout the film, it is suggested that snuff is the latest variation upon an American economic sensibility "built upon innovation." This is given further ironic force when Terry orchestrates the grotesque murder of his paymasters, literally destroying the economic wellspring of his work. Here, "innovation" is seen to serve nothing but the interests of jaded, morally eroded sensation seekers, and the gang's prolonged bouts of psychological and physical tortures descend further into total social anarchy as they are enacted upon a series of greedy landlords, venal pornographers and criminal capitalists.

Although the film's porno underworld is rendered as a squalid urban landscape of seedy apartments and derelict industrial spaces, much of the snuff activity is not defined exclusively in sexual terms. Instead, this is supplanted by an emphasis upon ritualistic activity, in which both male and female victims are subjected to a series of filmed torments before their ultimate execution. Furthermore, assumed porno-snuff conventions are problematized as male *and* female characters both indulge and endure physical torture and sexual humiliation. The most pronounced inversion of this is the climactic moment where, in a radical reversal of the subject-object dynamic of pornography, Steve (Alex Kregar aka Steve Randall), a career pornographer, is forced to fellate a goat's hoof protruding from a female gang member's zip-fly, before his eyeball is pierced by a power drill brandished by Terry in the same gleeful manner in which he previously wielded an 8mm camera. This oscillation of conventional gender roles through extreme, sexualized power-play defines men and women alike as bearers of the phallus in this deranged expression of class war.

The use of masks and robes by all of the gang imbues these sequences with a level of theatricality and flamboyance seemingly at odds with the degraded visual textures of the film overall, but this emphasis defines the very process of orchestrated death as a performative action, and is a detail significant in relation to later examples of the artistic embellishments of the snuff auteur. Besides his role as director of the snuff films, an authorial position that he invokes repeatedly and dementedly ("I'm directing this fucking movie!") as the film draws toward its final moments, Terry actively participates in front of the camera, his histrionics another manifestation of his hysteria, the total auteur to the point where his personality develops and disintegrates in reflection of the formal chaos of the film itself. His obsessive desire to dominate and control other minds and bodies to the point of termination is also a self-reflexive gesture toward the limits of masculine dominance, with the final rituals of humiliation, torture and dismemberment serving nothing other than an artistic will that has become inextricably tangled with the burdens of social, sexual and economic despair. The visibility of Watkins onscreen as the articulator of his own creative frustrations and resentments elaborates upon the presence of Michael Powell in the home movie sequences of *Peeping Tom*, as the father of Mark. Indeed, the much more direct identification of Watkins with his own protagonist is testament to his career as a director of idiosyncratic porn features,[26] a job taken up by Watkins as his attempts at a more conventional and relatively mainstream career were denied.

This patriarchal, yet gender inclusive use of snuff as a tool of socio-economic rebellion (the film is replete with images of women wielding the camera as well as being subjected to excruciating psychological and physical torture) is given further resonance by the film's own poverty stricken status.[27] Yet, this proved no hindrance to an often highly inventive and stylized play with lighting effects, sound (including the extensive use of library sourced ambient drones and electronically treated choral vocals) and a disregard for classical conventions of spatial and temporal continuity, all of which compound the film's nihilistic project and general ambience of decay and claustrophobia. Frequent images of the snuff gang peering directly into the camera at the spectator, often backlit by their own equipment, situate the film firmly within the self-reflexive tendencies of other snuff themed narratives, the direct return of the gaze underscoring the film's defiant and despairing world view in which social outcasts are manipulated by a wayward patriarch. In one final allusive gesture, Steve is forced to observe his own humiliation and murder as a mirror is placed in his field of vision, a fusion of the subjective and objective confrontation of mortality which *Peeping Tom* had instigated over a decade previously, and which persists in snuff fictions to this day. The gang's final retreat into darkness in the closing image—literally disappearing into the grain of the celluloid—affirms artful chaos as a guiding principle, not only for the film's socially maladjusted milieu, but for cinema itself.[28]

---

[26]Particularly worthy of attention in this regard are *Her Name Was Lisa* (1980), *Corruption* (1983), and *Midnight Heat* (1983), films which transcend the common structural and formal limitations of feature film pornography to evince a creative personality seemingly at war with the film culture in which he found himself working. Bill Landis argues that *Last House on Dead End Street* is "motivated by a hate of pornography and the swingers who create it ... almost a scream against having to make a living as a pornographer." See Bill Landis, *Sleazoid Express* (New York: Fireside, 2002), 148–49.

[27]According to Landis, the film was made possible through "a $1,500 loan from [Watkins'] father that basically paid his rent, kept him high on metamphetamine and a dash of heroin, and put him to sleep with booze every night throughout the shoot ... Dad [who worked at a film developing lab] also contributed and developed all the film he needed." Landis, *Sleazoid Express*, 151.

[28]The effectiveness of this final shot is diminished somewhat by the imposition of a brief narration informing us that Terry and his gang were incarcerated for their crimes, a cursory nod toward moral equilibrium that recalls the narrative dictates of the Hays Code that collapsed only a decade previously. This narration was a product of the aforementioned distributor alterations for the final release version of the film.

Because of its overwhelming negativity, the use of snuff as a tool of class rage in *The Last House on Dead End Street* has no real revolutionary charge. Instead, it becomes the futile emblem of psychotic rage. In that sense, it is both a generic forebear and counter-balance to a sequence of titles in which murderous auteur figures utilize their position as an expression of their presumed social and cultural class superiority, extending the familiar notion of the masculinized gaze as a symptom of gender objectification and control. As the subgenre moved into the 1980s, snuff filmmaker narratives became ever more replete with reflection upon the boundaries of cinematic truth and the sense of dominion inherent in the actions of their respective male monster figures. They also establish further links between male power and perverse artistry, defining their protagonists as arch manipulators of both cinematic experience and the lives of colleagues and acquaintances involved in their work. Moreover, these are filmmakers who operate beyond a furtive porno underground, producing independent art film experiments, or even mainstream entertainment. Snuff filmmakers move into the public sphere in pursuit of sensation hungry mainstream audiences, adopting multiple layers of irony in establishing a pattern of unwitting complicity.

In *Effects*, Lacey Bickel (John Harrison) is an independently wealthy filmmaker who produces and directs an experimental film in which he manipulates and murders members of his cast and crew. His status as the offspring of a ruling economic elite (he may even have engineered the death of his parents in a plane crash) reinforces a moral and social estrangement, whose perversions range from sado-sex themed snuff films (which may or may not be faked) to elaborate, self-funded experiments. This allows the film to envision a contrast between grubby hardcore aesthetics and the polished veneer of the film (entitled "Something's Wrong") that Lacey appears to be shooting. The participation of actors and technicians unaware of their director's intentions (he shoots their private moments through the use of hidden cameras, before orchestrating the pursuit and murder of the film's special make up effects technician[29] from a remote position in the production headquarters) allows him to construct his snuff project as a parallel production to the one that is actually scripted. When Lacey screens a supposedly genuine snuff film to some of his crew members, its base artlessness is conveyed through the static camera, the awkward performance of the onscreen victim and

---

[29]The film's frequent emphasis upon the physical mechanics of cinematic illusion is given a further self-reflexive layer through the presence of real-life make-up artist and pioneer of "splatter" effects, Tom Savini, in an acting role. Retrospectively, this is compounded by the fact that the film's make-up effects artist is played by Joseph Pilato, who would later be the subject of one on Tom Savini's most infamous effects in George A. Romero's *Day of the Dead* (1985).

its focus upon an S & M dynamic of sadistic coercion, all played out in silent black and white. Lacey teases initially that this was originally produced in England, before suggesting that he may have actually shot the film himself as a student and that nobody was hurt for real. However, the project on which Lacey is now embarking is very much an experimental exercise in the limits of verisimilitude, something that will be eventually sold to the public as a film called "Duped: The Snuff Movie." The presentation of this title on a movie theater marquee in the film's final image seems to suggest that Lacey's cynical contempt has met with some form of public approval, exhibited to paying audiences as a meditation on distinctions between reality and artifice.

Such themes are also centralized in *Special Effects*. Chris Neville (Eric Bogosian) is a director who, after being dismissed from his duties in charge of a $30 million Hollywood sci-fi fantasy, strangles to death an aspiring young actress (having filmed the whole event) and weaves the footage into an independent project telling her life story using the doppelganger of his victim in the lead role. His recent public humiliation is leavened by his claims that his latest project is a return to his artistic roots as an independent figure, but his New York apartment bears all the hallmarks of a personal decadence, exemplified by the hidden camera which he uses to record all of his personal sexual exploits. He is first heard in the title sequence name-checking Abraham Zapruder as his greatest filmmaking inspiration, before he is later introduced examining the footage of the shooting of Lee Harvey Oswald, linking him explicitly to the idea of filmed death as a cornerstone of the experiential aspect of national trauma. This is underlined throughout the film, not only through Chris' snuff production, but also through his other murderous activities, including strangulation of a suspicious colleague by a strip of celluloid.

Unlike Lacey in *Effects*, the film ultimately essays the failure of Chris to assert his will, his own attempts at waving reality and fiction into a cinematic narrative becoming thwarted by a collection of other insecure patriarchs (the victim's estranged husband, a lawyer determined to see his life turned into a film and a police detective serving as technical advisor on Chris' snuff project), all of whom become somehow complicit in the snuff murder. Tony Williams has provided an exemplary account of *Special Effects* and its battery of self-reflexive modes, aligning the economically constrained practices of such an independent exploitation film with avant-garde underground practices. These are seen to have particular weight when they are overseen from the radically minded authorial position of the film's director, Larry Cohen. Williams argues:

> *Special Effects* … is particularly instructive in showing how a low budget underground film using a narrative structure can interrogate the negative

effects of the male gaze and, at the same time, deliver a form of visual pleasure that is not compromised by the dominant ideology.[30]

Williams stresses Cohen's use of nonclassical modes to disrupt ideological assumptions, but this is not to suggest that all exploitation films achieve the same level of rigorous, critical self-reflexivity. Nevertheless, the self-reflexive awareness of other titles referenced earlier locates Cohen's film within a lineage, making definite links between the oppressive, objectifying practices of the mainstream Hollywood filmmaker and the murderous activities of a snuff underground. It even goes so far to imply that the former is merely a precursor and culturally entrenched form of the latter in its exploitation and victimization of the desperate wannabe, what Chris calls the "glorification of the nobody…Dorothy Stratten, Frances Farmer…murder, madness. That's what stars are made of." The film is certainly a key bridging text in its elaboration upon the conceptual possibilities of the snuff filmmaker, incorporating his celebrity and artistic manipulations as further elements which, through Cohen's authorial control, ultimately signal his artistic and social impotence.

In this context, "Death and the Lady," an episode from the fourth season of *Miami Vice*, contains a summation of the examples of the snuff filmmaker cited thus far, incorporating all of those elements of artistic ambition, pornographic objectification, economic-class exploitation and crass hucksterism evident in previous incarnations (Figure 10.3). Milton Glantz (Paul Guilfoyle) is an internationally renowned artist who has cynically chosen to work in the field of pornography to, in the words of his publicity blurb "bridge fine arts and popular media, redeeming images of suffering with technical precision" (a description met by the series' lead hero character, Detective Crockett [Don Johnson], with the riposte "I call that stuff dirty movies"). He is arrogantly brazen in his conceit, presenting snuff as a hedonistic public spectacle for a large audience, and in the public space of an erotic film festival. Moreover, he is shown receiving an award for his efforts (a statuette depicting a disembodied female foot clad in high heels and fishnet stockings) indicating that both the art world and porn industry has openly embraced the sensational possibilities of snuff, thrusting the filmmaker further into the realms of media celebrity. Glantz film is replete with slick 1980s postmusic video impact aesthetics, encompassing stylized lighting, rapid continuity cutting, reverse angles, fetishistic close-ups (lips, knives, eyes) and an ambience of erotic fantasy, all scored to music by English goth-rock band, Fields Of The Nephilim. Rather than adopting a realist, long-take approach that preserves the

---

[30]Tony Williams, "*Special Effects* in the Cutting Room," in *Underground USA: Filmmaking Beyond the Hollywood Canon*, edited by Xavier Mendikand Steven Jay Schneider (London and New York: Wallflower Press, 2002): 54.

FIGURE 10.3 Milton Glantz (Paul Guilfoyle) in *Miami Vice: Death and the Lady*, dir. Colin Bucksey (Michael Mann Productions/Universal Television, 1987).

temporal unity of the moment of death, Glantz snuff film is an attempt at stylistic concealment like that in *Special Effects*, this time preserving the possibility of the real through extra-textual tease and sensation.

This is put into play by an onstage announcement prefiguring the snuff sequence—"the very next moment of this film will change your mind forever about art and pornography!"—that conflates these seemingly polarized visual cultures. However, the sudden interruption by a cast member hysterically claiming to the gathered audience that the murder was not faked locates that narrative amid the familiar theme of the moral limits of transgressive artistic expression. This guides the rest of the episode, with Crockett remaining contemptuous of Glantz' work while gradually unraveling the circumstances behind the creation of his film. Indeed, Glantz' cinematic venture is shown to be part of a wider artistic exploration of human mortality, his elaborate private studio apartment playing host to exploitable models and homeless vagrants alike, and his public persona is projected through flamboyant media appearances and lavish poolside parties. Furthermore, as it is revealed that Glantz hired two identical actresses for his film (recalling the double motif explored more rigorously in *Special Effects*), it is suggested (but never absolutely confirmed, despite an eyewitness and much circumstantial evidence) that one of them, a drug addicted, terminal cancer patient, was paid in advance to perform in genuine "murder inserts," at once an act of euthanasia and homicide which the victim uses to provide economic aid to her own sick father.[31] This provides another layer to the process of economic exchange and artistic exploitation outlined in the earlier examples, Glantz' wealth facilitating his perversions while providing temporary fiscal respite to the family of his victim.

Crockett's climactic confrontation with Glantz is founded upon their oppositional claims to masculine dominance, a theme set up in an early exchange when the latter's suggestion that, as detective and artist, they are similarly in pursuit of "truth" is summarily rejected by the former. Crockett's professional failure to prove Glantz' execution of the "perfect murder, all in the name of art," results in a final act of inter-personal violence, this time enacted *upon* the filmmaker. The verbal and physical interaction of the pair is striking, with Crockett articulating his rage ("You think violence is attractive? You think violence is chic and artistic?") before an attack upon Glantz that is reminiscent of a male-on-female domestic assault. Glantz' former verbosity and arrogance is supplanted by an almost speechless passivity, succumbing to Crockett's assault as if in masochistic acceptance of the charges brought against him. Crockett's final contemptuous act of dumping Glantz' best film award in the lap of a drunken hobo is the final expression of both his and the show's sense of moral righteousness. Nevertheless, the episode never absolutely affirms Glantz' guilt, his blank acceptance of physical punishment and private humiliation serving as the scant justice for his apparent deeds. While seemingly forthright in its critique and judgment of Glantz, the episode is also cognizant of a certain institutional powerlessness in the face of the unproven status of snuff pornography, preserving a degree of ambiguity sufficient to preserve the mythology.

The foregoing analyses have identified the snuff filmmaker variously as pornographer, prankster, sadistic voyeur, hysterical narcissist, perverse artist, pop cultural terrorist, class avenger, class exploiter, and art-film experimentalist. Collectively, this has enabled the sense of a moral anarchist operating at polarized extremes of the social scale, meeting niche cultural demands while gratifying a varied range of social and sexual perversions. Earlier emphasis upon links between the snuff filmmaker and the porn industry placed him at the nadir of an already disreputable cultural form, with the notion of a debased ideologue developing

---

[31]This narrative convention of the sick, dying victim assumes the status of "twist in the tale" in the 2002 episode of *CSI* entitled "Snuff." The episode includes the seemingly irrelevant detail of the suspected snuff filmmaker, a veteran of the porn industry, dealing with a persistent fever. However, when his guilt is proven by the climax of the episode, his punishment is exacerbated by a certain poetic justice— unbeknownst to the filmmaker, his victim was HIV positive and the spray of arterial blood from her wounds has also infected him.

out of representations of institutionalized misogyny. While the victimization of women ran as a constant focal element, this branched out into a more diverse set of thematic concerns, with the snuff filmmaker visiting his monstrous acts upon a wider milieu and establishing a profile that manifested amid criminal subcultures and social elites alike. The presence of the snuff filmmaker in films emergent from art, exploitation and mainstream sensibilities consolidated his status as a key genre icon into the twenty-first century, serving as the progenitor of figures such as Dino Velvet in *8mm* (Joel Schumacher, 1999), Boris Arkadin in *Snuff Movie* (Bernard Rose, 2005), James Parker in *Resurrecting the Streetwalker* (Özgür Uyanık, 2009) and Vukmir in *A Serbian Film* (Srđan Spasojević, 2010). All of these titles are indicative of a global phenomenon, charting the latest stages in an evolutionary generic process accommodating the snuff filmmaker's transition into the digital age. *A Serbian Film* in particular represents the outer extremities of the snuff filmmaker's current iconic potential, marking the point in which he might be read, many feel unconvincingly,[32] as an allegorical surrogate for atrocities committed at the level of murderous, ethnopolitical oppression. The snuff filmmaker's traditional spaces of psycho-sexual and socio-economic dysfunction have expanded into areas redolent of an even broader ideological imperative, making him a monster finely attuned to the shifting possibilities of modern horror narratives and their ever more immediate infiltration of the real.

---

[32]Journalist David Cox has commented that "this claim has been derided as a pathetic attempt to accord respectability to a straightforward exercise in sensationalist depravity ... You can just about see why [director] Srdjan Spasojevic found a resemblance between [the film's explicitly rendered] experiences and those of his country's citizenry during the last quarter of a century. Yet if you saw the film without having been tipped off, it's inconceivable that you'd make the connection yourself. If you've been briefed in advance, what strikes you is how utterly the action being depicted fails to illuminate its supposedly parallel political equivalent ... An allegory could certainly be inferred. *A Serbian Film* might well be telling us that only someone a bit daft would try to make an allegorical film." David Cox, "*A Serbian Film*: When Allegory Gets Nasty," *The Guardian*, December 13, 2010, accessed June 8, 2015, http://www.theguardian.com/film/filmblog/2010/dec/13/a-serbian-film-allegorical-political.

11 THE MEDIATION OF DEATH IN FICTIONAL SNUFF: REFLEXIVITY, VIEWER INTERPELLATION, AND ETHICAL IMPLICATION

Xavier Aldana Reyes

The iconic opening sequence of Michael Powell's *Peeping Tom* (1960) laid down the aesthetic and stylistic grounds for fictional snuff. In it, an initial extreme close-up of an eye opening suddenly, as if awakened brusquely during sleep, is quickly aligned with the point of view (POV) of the viewfinder of a 16-mm camera being held at waist height. An establishing shot showing a poorly lit street where a woman is smoking is presented in traditional objective cinematic fashion. As the silhouette of a man in a trench coat approaches her, a cut to the three-lens camera signals he is the person holding the home-movie hardware. The next shot, a zoom-in so extreme that the image blurs, is significant, for it indicates the film's temporary entry into the world of the intradiegetic camera; this transition is also marked by the whirring sound of its rolling. From here on in, the scene is portrayed through a partitioned lens (vertical and horizontal lines split the frame into four squares), which serves as a further reminder that the scene is mediated; it is a result of the film's momentary incursion into the line of vision of a man who is the conscious taping agent. This moment, therefore, is also impossibly direct. The action appears more immediate because the woman, who we discover is a prostitute, speaks and looks at the camera, seemingly questioning the viewer, who stands in the place of a mute cameraman. The use of a subjective POV, which would be later exploited by the slasher cycle of the late 1970s and early 1980s, creates an illusion of spectatorial involvement that is accentuated when it becomes increasingly clear that a visual record of murder, and not sex, is the man's obvious intention.[1]

Although we should distinguish the resulting product—a black and white reel which cameraman and killer Mark (Carl Boehm/Karlheinz Böhm) is himself watching—from the initial color, lens-filtered images, Powell's film demonstrates a clear desire to collapse recording agent and viewer. The rest of *Peeping Tom* is mostly concerned with Mark's warped psychology as well as with making his "snuff" project understandable: the rationale for his condemnable behavior is made explicit when he attempts to explain to a terrified girlfriend (Anna Massey) that his experiment seeks to capture the reactions of his victims as they helplessly watch their impending deaths. In a sense, *Peeping Tom* is an example of fictional snuff and Mark's films are snuff films *avant la lettre*, exploring the limitations of filmed murder more than fifteen years before the *Snuff* (Michael and Roberta Findlay [uncredited], 1976) scandal suddenly brought awareness to this supposed underground cinematic practice and made its possible detrimental effects on the audience a matter of public concern.[2] At the same time, because *Peeping Tom* places a strong emphasis on its antihero and his damaged personality, it manages to also act as a reflection on the process of watching death on film. If the film cannot, to maintain suspension of disbelief, remind the viewer about the constructed nature of its images—nobody *actually* dies in the film—it still engages with the nature of simulated murder.

The tension between a simulacral drive that will convince the viewer that what is happening on screen is real, as well as the self-aware nature of the fabrication of the filmic experience, is intrinsic to fictional snuff-themed films, as other examples such as *Last House on Dead End Street* (Roger Watkins, 1977) or *Cannibal Holocaust* (Ruggero Deodato, 1980) show. In fact, it is possible that early fictional snuff's reflexivity may be directly responsible for the accentuated self-awareness of more modern entries in the genre. Whether a result of influence or of broader shifts in contemporary horror—the emphasis on reflexivity and immediacy championed by the rise of "found footage horror"[3] —fictional snuff seems, since the turn of the

---

[1]This is not to suggest the film does not actively show that the sensual thrills of sex are pathologically connected with death in the mind of this individual. See Parveen Adams, "Father, Can't You See I'm Filming?," in *Supposing the Subject*, edited by Joan Copjec (London: Verso, 1994): 185–200, and Carol J. Clover, *Men, Women and Chain Saws: Gender in Modern Horror Film* (Princeton, NJ: Princeton University Press, 1993): 166–81.

[2]See David Kerekes and David Slater, *Killing for Culture: An Illustrated History of Death Film from Mondo to Snuff* (London: Creation, 1993): 302–05; Julian Petley, " 'Snuffed Out': Nightmares in a Trading Standards Officer's Brain," in *Unruly Pleasures: The Cult Film and Its Critics*, edited by Xavier Mendik and Graeme Harper (Guildford: FAB Press, 2000): 205–07.

[3]See Alexandra Heller-Nicholas, *Found Footage Horror Films: Fear and the Appearance of Reality* (Jefferson, NC: McFarland, 2014).

millennium, to be especially preoccupied with deconstructing the human morbid compulsion to consume images of death.[4] The highly contrived manner in which this is achieved can even exceed the more straightforward exploitation aesthetics that fictional snuff has come to be recognized for.[5] In other words, fictional snuff is becoming openly self-reflexive, if not necessarily "reflectionist," and this is having an effect on films' own construction of their audiences.[6] My contention is that these developments in fictional snuff are offering viewers a more participatory and active metanarrative role that is, in itself, exploitative. Their direct implication via interpellation and accusation means viewers are directly informed in the viewing process and encouraged to judge their own ethical stance in relation to fictional snuff, its consumption (and that, more generally, of real death) and the drive to engage with it in the first instance. As I will show, rather than rely on this recriminatory strategy to deflect responsibility, fictional snuff is using ethical involvement to its own affective advantage.

Types of fictional snuff and their respective reflexive dimensions

Fictional snuff may be divided into four categories, or subgenres, according to framing style: films about snuff, faux snuff, the snuff mockumentary, and the serial killer video diary.[7] It is important to note that, while I do not intend to be exhaustive in my taxonomy, framing techniques inflect fictional snuff, and its exponents follow certain stylistic and narrative patterns according to the effect they intend to achieve. Narrative and stylistic decisions are strongly connected to the degree of self-reflection the films allow for and are in symbiotic relation with them: the framing narrative is often determined by the desired effect, and the desired effect is motivated and shaped by the framing narrative. For example, fictional snuff presented as found footage is automatically bound by certain space,

---

[4] I am using the term "fictional snuff" throughout to distinguish it from the "real" thing, that is, actual recordings of murders sold for profit.

[5] The epitome of deconstructive fictional snuff is *Snuff-Movie* (Bernard Rose, 2005). See Xavier Aldana Reyes, *Consuming Mutilation: Affectivity and Corporeal Transgression on Stage and Screen* (PhD thesis, Lancaster University, 2013): 225–37.

[6] This term was coined by Matt Hills to refer to critical approaches that read horror films in relation to their social context in "Cutting into Concepts of 'Reflectionist' Cinema? The *Saw* Franchise and Puzzles of Post-9/11 Horror," in *Horror After 9/11: World of Fear, Cinema of Terror*, edited by Aviva Briefel and Sam J. Miller (Austin, TX: University of Texas, 2011): 107–23. My use of the term "reflexive" thus indicates the more internal textual awareness of role and purpose that has become an increasingly important part of contemporary exploitation films.

[7] There are films that do not fall easily into any of these categories, such as *Exhibit A* (Dom Rotheroe, 2007), a found footage film where the killer does not set out to tape the murders.

time and coherence rules prescribed by the internal logic of this specific framing, such as the need to legitimize a recording agent or the presence of the camera in certain sequences.[8] Although fictional snuff continues to be preoccupied with the capacity of cinema to simulate reality, it has also become increasingly meta-textual, exploring the genre's own contrivances.

The first of the fictional snuff categories, the film about snuff, is the most standard and mainstream. It follows classical Hollywood narrative conventions, and tends to mix the thriller format with splashes of horror and graphic violence. This film, although specifically targeted at the adult market, may be intended for a general audience and therefore excludes strong graphic scenes. Snuff scenes appear intradiegetically by having the main character/s watch a film or tape, which can be presented partially or, as in the case of *Cannibal Holocaust*, encompass a significant part of the action.[9] The goal for the main characters varies: to investigate someone's abduction or murder, as in *Hardcore* (Paul Schrader, 1979), *Mute Witness* (Anthony Waller, 1994) and *8MM* (Joel Schumacher, 1999), or to research the snuff myth, as in *Tesis* (Alejandro Amenábar, 1996) or *Snuff 102* (Mariano Peralta, 2007). Extreme versions of this type of narrative exist, for example, *The Bunny Game* (Adam Rehmeier, 2010), where plot is sacrificed in lieu of realistic violence, or *A Serbian Film* (Srđan Spasojević, 2010). However, the gory aspects of these films are often strong enough to guarantee them other appellatives, such as torture porn.[10] The degree to which these films explore the mediation of death differs, as do their messages. More mainstream films, such as *8MM* and *Hardcore*, position snuff and their makers as clear villains and the investigators as moral crusaders. Others, such as *Tesis* or *Snuff 102*, seem more interested in the pleasures involved in the viewing and taping of the material, which is conflated, in both instances, with misogyny. The extent to which films about snuff explore the effects of watching snuff fluctuates: those that look into the myth itself question its existence at a human level ("why would anyone watch this?"); explicit films such as

---

[8]For more on the possibilities and constraints afforded by found footage framing, see my forthcoming "The *[•REC]* Quartet: Affective Possibilities and Stylistic Limitations of Found Footage Horror," in *Digital Horror: Haunted Technologies, Network Panic and the Found Footage Phenomenon*, edited by Linnie Blake and Xavier Aldana Reyes (London and New York: I. B. Tauris, 2015), pp. 149–60, and "Reel Evil: A Critical Reassessment of the Found Footage Phenomenon," *Gothic Studies* 17, no. 2 (2015, forthcoming).

[9]*Cannibal Holocaust* famously relies on a Chinese box structure: the tape showing the deaths of a film crew is discovered by a later expedition while exploring the same territory. Footage from both tapes is included in the film.

[10]See Pete Cashmore, "Will This New Movie Kill off Torture Porn for Good?," *The Guardian*, August 28, 2010, accessed October 16, 2014. http://www.theguardian.com/film/2010/aug/28/torture-porn-frightfest-quiz; Erik Piepenburg, "Testing Horror's Threshold for Pain: Rodleen Getsic in the Horror Film *The Bunny Game*," *The New York Times*, September 14, 2012, accessed October 16, 2014, http://www.nytimes.com/2012/09/16/movies/rodleen-getsic-in-the-horror-film-the-bunny-game.html?pagewanted=all&_r=0.

A Serbian Film are more complex and necessitate individual studies that can trace case-by-case critical and ethical engagements.[11] Even though the intradiegetic snuff in them may be manipulated to look like "found footage," films about snuff are not invested in passing for the real thing and introduce their framing narratives as clearly fictional. For example, they include a cast of characters or use objective POVs to shoot the action taking place in the film's time.

Quite the opposite, faux snuff is constituted by films that attempt to look entirely like a found snuff document.[12] To this end, they rely on recordings allegedly extracted from handheld cameras or webcams, and thus have an amateur finish (grainy, unfocused images or muffled sounds). Although real snuff remains, for the moment, a myth, these films have obviously taken their cues from death videos, particularly of online executions, and have, in time, been influenced by the aesthetics of previous entries in the fictional snuff canon.[13] Generally speaking, faux snuff intends to shock and disturb as simulacra of real death tapes that may have been discovered by accident and whose contents tend to serve little or no real narrative purpose. It is, therefore, the subgenre which is the least interested in questioning the logic and ethics of violent representation. Although such a task may be undertaken at a compositional level or through specific comments made by the intradiegetic characters (almost exclusively the killers themselves), this is not the main purpose of the films. Instead, because the films strive for mimesis, the focus remains the generation of shock, outrage, fear, and gross out. In this respect, one could argue that texts belonging in this category are more traditionally and straightforwardly exploitative, as they do not hold any ethical pretenses or seek to disturb the process of gullibility inherent to their consumption. Quite the opposite, faux snuff explicitly avoids signaling its own artificial nature so that it can position itself as a limit-experience or filmic challenge.[14] The most important exponents of this fictional snuff strand are the *August Underground* series, comprising *August Underground* (Fred Vogel, 2001), *August Underground's Mordum* (Fred Vogel, Christie Whiles and Michael Todd

---

[11]See, for example, Shaun Kimber, "Transgressive Edge Play and *Srpsky Film/A Serbian Film*," *Horror Studies* 5, no. 1 (2014): 107–25.

[12]The label "faux snuff" was coined by Steve Jones, "Dying to Be Seen: Snuff-Fiction's Problematic Fantasies of 'Reality,'" *Scope: An Online Journal of Film and Television Studies* 19 (2011): 1–22, accessed December 10, 2011, http://www.scope.nottingham.ac.uk/February%202011/Jones.pdf.

[13]The main distinction between a death video—for example, the infamous "two men, one hammer" murder video—and snuff is that snuff is sold on the black market for commercial gain. See *The Dark Side of Porn: Does 'Snuff' Exist?* (Evy Barry, 2006).

[14]The term "limit-experience" was coined by Michel Foucault in a 1978 interview. I am using it here to refer to a type of action that prods the edge of (human) life, whether it be through its intensity, extremity or impossibility. See Michel Foucault, *The Essential Works of Foucault 1954–1984: Power*, vol. 3, edited by James D. Faubion, trans. by Robert Hurley et al. (New York: New Press, 2000): 239–97.

Schneider, 2003), and *August Underground's Penance* (Fred Vogel, 2007), and Shane Ryan's *Amateur Porn Star Killer* trilogy (2006, 2008, and 2009).[15]

The third category, the snuff mockumentary (a twist on documentaries about real serial killer cases, such as those of Ed Gein or Ted Bundy), follows televisual conventions.[16] Like other mockumentaries, these films center on the narration of a case or series of them, often presented as historical or real, with B-roll and talking heads discussing them and their relevance. Facts are provided alongside either "real" snuff footage recovered from fictional archives and personal records, or else staged re-enactions of key moments in the case.[17] What is distinctive about the snuff mockumentary is that it is not usually parodic but rather grounds itself firmly within the horrific. Additionally, the mockumentary may appear to be charting a series of murders, at least superficially, but these are almost ineluctably portrayed as having an immediate impact on the present: the serial killer is still on the loose and might therefore be an actual "real" threat to the viewer. At the same time, the format of the mockumentary allows for a more overt challenging of the ethical implication of the viewer than that of faux snuff. Most notably, in *The Poughkeepsie Tapes* (John Erick Dowdle, 2007), the act of viewing is implicitly defied through a confrontation with Cheryl (Stacy Chbosky), the only survivor of the Poughkeepsie killings and who ends up developing Stockholm syndrome. At this point, the viewer has already seen an earlier version of Cheryl being abused and degraded by the killer, and her interview—prying and excessive—can therefore be read as either a voyeuristic exercise in the recording and consumption of psychological trauma or as an ambiguous exploration of that experience. The viewer may be addressed, by extension, through questions asked by the various interviewees or may be put in the difficult position of feeling they should not be watching this material at all. Other films that attain similar results include *S&Man* (J. T. Petty, 2006) and *Resurrecting the Streetwalker* (Özgür Uyanık, 2009).[18]

The serial killer video diary is related to the snuff mockumentary but is closer stylistically to faux snuff's prevalent found footage look. Unlike the snuff documentary, there is no filtering of events by subjects external to the intradiegetic

---

[15]On the *Amateur Porn Star Killer* series, see Steve Jones' contribution to this volume.

[16]The snuff documentary should not be confused with the real documentary about snuff films, such as the aforementioned *The Dark Side of Porn* or *Snuff: A Documentary about Killing on Camera* (2008, USA, dir. Paul von Stoetzel). The latter are not fictional and generally examine the (in)existence of real snuff films.

[17]For a more general account of the history and traits of the mockumentary, see Craig Hight, *Television Mockumentary: Reflexivity, Satire and a Call to Play* (Manchester: Manchester University Press, 2010).

[18]In the case of the latter, this snuff subgenre can be heavily dependent on the serial killer video diary. Interviews with relatives and friends may be interspersed with a substantial number of videos that chronicle the protagonist's descent into murder, generally as a result of obsessive compulsions. Their overall reliance on the documentary as the main working framework blends into the type of psychological case study more typical of the serial killer video diary.

action: the selection of scenes, where it exists, is carried out by the killers themselves. They may delete or tape over scenes they do not find relevant or in order to achieve specific effects. In these films, the serial killer often reaches out to potential viewers, making them complicit in the act of murder by virtue of their curiosity. Since, like the mockumentary, the video diary is invested in analyzing the psychology of the killer, namely, why they murdered and why they felt the need to record events, the result is a more overt analysis of scopophilia. While faux snuff puts the emphasis on the spectacle of violence itself and on counterfeit death, the serial killer video diary does not, on the whole, purport to look fictional and is, instead, heavily concerned with its own morbid nature. As Ernest Mathijs has argued, the "layered (though seemingly) direct mode of representation [...] invites considerations of reflexivity from the start."[19] The resulting products are ostensibly hypocritical films that take advantage of the shocking value of its death sequences while admonishing the voyeurism of the potential audience. Because the killer passes as the maker of the film, this means authorship may also be deflected onto a second, fictional character, and with it, the film's own ethical responsibility. Films that fall into this category include *Zero Day* (Ben Coccio, 2003), *The Last Horror Movie* (Julian Richards, 2003) and *Man Bites Dog/C'est arrive près de chez vous* (Rémy Belvaux, André Bonzel and Benoît Poelvoorde, 1992), although the latter is shot by a film crew following the exploits of a serial killer.

It could be argued that, as a filmic genre, fictional snuff may simply be following the natural self-referential phase that all genres undergo. As critics Thomas Schatz and Paul Schrader have suggested, "[t]ypically, films produced later in a genre's development tend to challenge the tidy and seemingly naïve resolutions of earlier genre films," and they are "painfully self-aware" of their position within a given tradition.[20] This should not necessarily lead to a waning of affect, as realism is compatible with a reflexive and deconstructive style.[21] In fact, in its postmillennial incarnations, fictional snuff consciously aligns with the representational tradition of the death film in order to generate a form of affective surplus on viewers. In other words, no longer an obscure concept, fictional snuff uses and exploits its own mechanics and myths. The questioning of ethical grounds on the part of viewers serves both to immerse them within the action and to create a sense of voyeuristic debt: viewers are somehow responsible for the actions on screen, since they have voluntarily decided to watch them. Although fictional snuff does not

---

[19]Ernest Mathijs, "*Man Bites Dog* and the Critical Reception of Belgian Horror (in) Cinema," in *Horror International*, edited by Steven Jay Schneider and Tony Williams (Detroit, MI: Wayne State University Press, 2005): 325.
[20]Thomas Schatz, *Hollywood Genres: Formulas, Filmmaking and the Studio System* (New York: McGraw Hill, 1981): 33; Paul Schrader, "Notes on Film Noir," *Film Comment* 8, no. 1 (1972): 12.
[21]See Neil Jackson, "*Cannibal Holocaust*, Realist Horror, and Reflexivity," *Postscript* 21, no. 3 (2002): 32–45.

presume enjoyment of the violence, it is premised on a certain morbid curiosity. Rather than manipulating the viewer for sadistic copycat purposes, fictional snuff appropriates the very rhetoric historically used against it to ensnare her/him into its promise of the limit-experience of death through visual images.

For the remainder of this chapter, I turn to *The Last Horror Movie*, a hugely contrived serial killer video diary. This case study allows me to illustrate some of the techniques used by one particular film to implicate viewers in the snuff exchange.

Interpellation, implication, and affective surplus in *The Last Horror Movie*

As I have pointed out, fictional snuff concerned with the recording of horrific events is especially playful in its exploitative self-awareness, and acts as a reflection on the leisurely consumption of mutilation. It is precisely this exacerbated reflexivity that makes it a potentially uncomfortable cinematic experience. As an extreme example of a film that very actively engages its viewer in the visual game it proposes, *The Last Horror Movie* holds an uncomfortable mirror to its audience as a means of examining the representational limits of violence and the concomitant ethical engagement of its watching. Through the video killer diary format, the film merges various conventions established by faux snuff, the slasher cycle and films about snuff—especially *Henry: Portrait of a Serial Killer* (John McNaughton, 1986), which it actively referenced in posters, covers and general promotion materials. Its direct attack on its target audience is thus specific to the film itself and, although it also speaks to the dangers of the contemporary cult of the serial killer, it most importantly serves as a comment on the uneasy complicity at the heart of reflexive fictional snuff.[22] In *The Last Horror Movie*, the recordings of the killer's acts are only part of a wider film that contextualizes and legitimizes the violence it exploits, yet simultaneously condemns its consumption.

As James Rose has noted, the first five minutes of *The Last Horror Movie* are a clear homage to the slasher tradition, with their recreation of a derivative and recognizable murder scenario.[23] A voiceover during the opening credits sequence informs us that a serial killer convicted for the murder of six teenagers in a

---

[22]I am, more specifically, referring to both the attraction of the vigilante serial killer in the style of HBO's *Dexter* (2006–2013) and the Jigsaw killer in the *Saw* franchise (2004–2010, USA, James Wan et al.), and the cult of "murderabilia." On the latter, see Ian Conrich, "Mass Media/Mass Murder: Serial Killer Cinema and the Modern Violated Body," in *Criminal Visions: Media Representations of Crime and Justice*, edited by Paul Mason (Cullompton: Willan Publishing, 2003): 156–71.
[23]James Rose, *Beyond Hammer: British Horror Cinema since 1970* (Leighton Buzzard: Auteur Publishing, 2009): 113–14.

summer camp has recently escaped from a maximum security facility in Illinois. The film then cuts to a neon American diner, *Starvin' Marvin's*, in Michigan and to a young working mother (Lisa Renée) cleaning and closing up. After speaking to son Michael and asking him to wait for her to get back, the lights go out and a loud bang is heard. Cue suspense music follows and an abandoned Halloween mask appears on the floor. As the waitress bends down to pick it up, the frame reveals the figure of the killer (Christopher Adamson), knife in hand, who stands up and stabs. But as the weapon strikes, the image changes to static; this is only the first of many anticlimaxes in *The Last Horror Movie*, where the gory shot is either occluded or omitted altogether. The setting changes to what could be an ordinary room in an ordinary house, and to a middle-aged, professional-looking man (Kevin Howarth) who quickly introduces himself as Max and begins to explain that the film we are watching is a video we hired from a rental store. He has recorded over it and viewers are about to watch a documentary about the crimes he has committed. A quick sneak peek sequence relocates the action to a public toilet, where Max is bashing a man's head in with a hammer, the image partially occluded by a urinal. The scene returns to Max, who promises everything will make sense in the end. The killer's use of *The Last Horror Movie* VHS tape as the basis for his experiment is significant. He summarizes the characterization of the original film as "two-dimensional," with the dialog deemed "frankly embarrassing," and proceeds to suggest that what he has to offer will be "much more interesting." Max goes on to compare his recording experiment with horror films and expresses the opinion that both are scary. This is important: the original *The Last Horror Movie* is a horror film, presumably a late 1970s or early 1980s slasher, and Max's video, the documentary embedded within the film, a supernumerary or über-text that replaces it. Ultimately, since both films serve the same purpose, namely, to entertain through extreme violence and fear, they are interchangeable, especially since Max never renames his video diary.

The body of Max's film is composed of a series of murder set pieces, with often laborious build-ups and asides to the camera, and includes substantial footage of Max going about his professional life as a wedding cameraman. Assisted by homeless Ben (Joe Hurley), who has been hired to hold the camera, *The Last Horror Movie* documents some of the over fifty killings Max claims to have committed. Up to this point, the film does not appear to be particularly challenging or original, but Max is quick to introduce himself as an atypical serial killer. He is not misogynistic, he mixes his murders so no profile can be built, killing is not all he does, he is fond of his family and ex-girlfriend Petra (Antonia Beasmith) and he makes a point of explaining that he does not kill because he watched too many horror films or because he is mad. Rather, his filming of death is a "personal project" about "something [he] [is] trying to understand," one that is intrinsically linked to the problematic lack of exposure that serial killers face. Similarly, the film subverts expectations. In one telling scene that starts with a predatory POV shot reminiscent of *Halloween* (John Carpenter, 1978), Max approaches a boy waiting to be picked up from school and asks him if he wants a lift home. The assumption that viewers might be witnessing the beginning of what will turn out to be a shocking case of child murder is frustrated, as it quickly becomes apparent that the boy is the son of his sister Sam (Christabel Muir). On another occasion, what begins as an attack on an old lady quickly transforms into a visit to grandma. For all its promise of violence, the film defers its revealing, with the camera often cutting away during or prior to the killings. In the first official murder scene, Tim (Paul Conway), an assistant manager strapped to a chair, kicks the camera out of the way before he receives the first blow of Max's hammer. The camera falls off, Tim is left out of the frame and only two drops of blood stain the camera lens to signal the fact he is being attacked. Similarly, the gun aimed at alcoholic Bill (Jim Bywater) is never fired, despite a slow build-up that seems to frame the inevitability of his death. Max's preferred methods of attack do not involve heavy wounding, at least during the first half of the film. Bricks, hammers and saucepans knock the victims out and, if anything, leave a faint trail of blood. In one of the most shocking scenes, the effect is not obtained through special effects but, rather, through a match cut that connects a blow to the head with the tenderizing of a steak. As we can see, expectations based on previous horror and fictional snuff are overturned as *The Last Horror Movie* takes pains to show its preference of concept over aesthetics.

The film also plays with the idea of feigning death, offering a direct reflection on the limitations of its filming. One key scene that shows ex-fiancée Petra being strangled by Max is soon revealed to be a rehearsal for the play *The Duchess of Malfi*. Petra's immediate reaction, to ask if she was convincing, seems to neatly summarise the main concern of the film: what is the appeal of watching "taped" death? Is the allure even the idea of watching death, or is it the performance and quality of mimicry that interests audiences? In other words, perhaps fictional snuff should be celebrated for its contrivance. As the film seems to establish connections with revenge tragedy—not incidentally often referred to as blood tragedy—and the staging of violence, Max cannot help but exclaim that real death is less stressful. "You may be wondering if this is a joke. Not a very tasteful joke, but a joke nonetheless. Well, it is! Isn't it?" he asks the camera and, by extension, the viewer. The answer is not at all obvious. On the one hand, it is all a joke. The real viewer knows they are watching a film called *The Last Horror Movie*, which happens to have been hijacked by a fictitious voyeuristic killer. They also know that all the violence in it is fake, because the film features a director and purports to be a VHS tape, a form of video technology that is no longer widely available. The obvious question should not therefore be whether *The Last Horror Movie* manages to suspend disbelief successfully. This might vary depending on the viewer and their previous experiences of watching horror and, more specifically, fictional snuff of the serial killer video diary variety. It might also depend on context: whether they have chosen to view this film of their own accord, or they have accidentally encountered a clip online. But if anyone is to watch Max's project to the end, they must, at least, play along as the gullible audience and accept his proposition. A desire to know what happens might be the main driving force here: why does Max keep repeating that he has it all under control? How will the film end?

The third act is premised precisely on the expectation that the narrative will create the need to carry on watching, and sees Max turning the tables and attacking the audience for its morbid curiosity. Suspecting that one natural outcome of enduring his tape is that viewers might want to report him to the police, Max concludes that they have become dangerous to him. Threatening with an imminent break into their living rooms, he explains:

> You think this is some art-house film that's meant to look like a home movie. You don't think this is the only copy of this film. You don't think I was waiting while you hired it from the video store or that I followed you home. I wonder where you are now. Are you standing by a window? Maybe I'm looking at you right now.

The film obviously flounders here. It loses the original compulsion to show, and descends into a piece of unconvincing criticism of its hypocritical audience that left a number of journalists and film critics unsatisfied.[24] However, whether we believe this gimmick to be effective or not, the jab at the audience's uneasy complicity with the spectacle, the insidious "why are you still watching?" mantra, seems to stem from an inherent need to make viewer and victim understand their roles within the process of the consumption of recorded death. In one of the final scenes, Max returns to his derisive comments to explain the reasoning behind his project:

> If I could get people to watch it like it was an ordinary film [...] they'd have a chance to draw some conclusions. Then we could have a meaningful discussion. [...] See, I do believe the ones who saw the film managed to get at least a sense of what I was trying to achieve. Once they were able to see their own experience as part of the whole project, which is, I think, something of a success, really. The problem is I haven't been able to get anyone to respond in an interesting way. [...] What about you? Do you have something to say?

---

[24]See, for example, Peter Whittle, "*The Last Horror Movie* Review," *The Sunday Times*, May 15, 2005, 15; Peter Bradshaw, "*The Last Horror Movie* Review," *The Guardian*, May 13, 2005, accessed November 1, 2012, http://www.theguardian.com/theguardian/2005/may/13/8. I should point out, however, that these responses are not necessarily representative of the overall critical reception of the film.

The prospect that this idea should be considered at the level of real interaction is untenable and, I would argue, should not be entertained. To begin with, the chances that potential American viewers, who are part of the market for this film, would be renting a tape from a local English video store are very low. The likelihood of Max waiting twenty-four hours a day outside this site, particularly when he would seem to have a day job, is similarly implausible.

What is at stake here, then, is not the film's intention to actually scare the viewer into believing they *really* are in danger. As I have shown, there is very little evidence of a solid attempt at realism beyond the obvious video diary framing style. Instead, *The Last Horror Movie* seems compelled to force viewers into reflecting about the process of consumption they have chosen to engage with, thus recriminating the same voyeurism that was fostered by Max at the beginning of the film. For example, a scene towards the end showing a male victim/viewer before his execution irreverently challenges any claims to veracity by positing itself as artificial. Viewers are meant to recognize that the victim is watching the same tape they are, but the man's TV screen shows footage from a scene that was deleted from the final cut. To attack *The Last Horror Movie*, or any other fictional snuff film, for its lack of verisimilitude would be to miss the point. Instead, the fact that the film chooses to ground its "you watch, you die" premise on the rerecording of VHS tapes would seem to profess, as Johnny Walker has argued, an allegiance to the video nasties scandal and show reverence for horror classics such as *The Texas Chain Saw Massacre* (Tobe Hooper, 1974), which the director cited as an important influence.[25] The confrontational nature of fictional snuff is filtered in *The Last Horror Movie* through a voyeuristic lens that owes more to reflexive spectacles like those of *Peeping Tom* or *Henry*. Instead of assessing its capacity to pass for the real thing, *The Last Horror Movie* should be evaluated for its gradual conflation of viewer and victim, which spells out the potential masochistic pleasure of fictional snuff. This technique rests on viewer interpellation, that is, the (semi) direct address of the audience and its artificial condemnation.

Breaking the fourth wall is an old motif that had already preoccupied playwrights such as Brecht in the first half of the twentieth century.[26] Cinematically, addressing the viewer is perhaps even more taboo because, as has been suggested, film works on the premise that such interactions are detrimental to viewer immersion. As Nick Browne explains, there is an unwritten

---

[25]Johnny Walker, "Nasty Visions: Violent Spectacle in Contemporary British Horror Cinema," *Horror Studies* 2, no. 1 (2011): 123–24. The title of the film also cites David Winters' *The Last Horror Film* (1982), which was also associated with the video nasty scandal and contains self-reflexive, film-in-film elements. See Francis Brewster, Harvey Fenton, and Marc Morris, *Shock! Horror!: Astounding Artwork from the Video Nasty Era* (London: FAB Press, 2005): 221.
[26]See Berthold Brecht, *Brecht on Theatre: The Development of an Aesthetic*, trans. John Willett (London: Methuen, 1964).

prohibition against the "meeting," though no such act is literally possible, of actor's and spectator's glances, a prohibition that is an integral feature of the sequence as a "specular text." In its effect on the spectator, the prohibition defines the different spaces he [sic] simultaneously inhabits before the screen. By denying this presence in one sense, the prohibition establishes a boundary at the screen that underscores the fact that the spectator can have no actual physical exchange with the depicted world, that he [sic] can do nothing relevant to change the course of the action. It places him [sic] outside the action.[27]

The Last Horror Movie depends on extreme viewer engagement to create affective surplus, a surplus that relies, not on the capacity for viewers to believe they are in danger but, rather, to question their rightful enjoyment of the snuff film they are watching. For Max's film to make sense, the viewer *must be made* to want to watch, but this forms the basis for later recriminations that legitimate the supposed murder of the viewer. The film thus brings viewers into the representational chain of taped death at a fictional level while potentially forcing them to reflect about their experience and its ethical dimensions. When, at one point, Max tells the camera, "it's important that you participate fully in this project," it would appear that he is addressing assistant Ben, but I would argue that the viewer is also being interpellated. The expendability of the cameraman is, in fact, emphasized later, when Ben is killed and replaced by another, equally disposable, recording subject.

What *The Last Horror Movie* foregrounds, like most reflexive fictional snuff, is the complicity of the viewer, who becomes an indirect cameraman and participant, if only at the affective and ethical levels. This realization is at the core of the film, particularly given Max's need to distinguish himself from the viewer, who he understands as someone with feelings of superiority and who cannot possibly condone his actions. Max thus legitimizes his role as moral educator. Before killing a man, a tape viewer that acts as the audience's surrogate, Max's question to him carries the import of four decades of fictional snuff: "[w]hy did you watch that film to the end? Did you think it was real? [...] Supposing it wasn't a joke, do you think there would be something wrong with you for watching until the end?" *The Last Horror Movie* serves to illustrate how fictional snuff has explicitly placed reflexivity at the center of the cinematic experience, welcoming viewers to watch first, only to then punish them for their morbid interest. As such, it could hardly be a better study of the history and critical reception of fictional snuff through the latter half of the twentieth century or, indeed, of the controversies it continues to generate.

---

[27]Nick Browne, "The Spectator-in-the-Text: The Rhetoric of *Stagecoach*," *Film Quarterly* 29, no. 2 (1975–1976): 36.

12 "WHY WOULD YOU FILM IT?" SNUFF, *SINISTER*, AND CONTEMPORARY US HORROR CINEMA

Shaun Kimber

W hen considering the representation of snuff within fictional films, *Sinister* (Scott Derrickson, 2012) may not immediately spring to mind. Indeed, as is evident from the range of contributions to this volume, we might more readily associate its range of connotations with anything from the Hollywood mainstream to varied horror, "cult" or exploitation films from a range of international production contexts. Alternatively, we may also envisage nonfiction films including death films, mondo movies, and shockumentaries, or incidents of real death captured, remediated, disseminated, and consumed online in the form of atrocity footage, execution videos, combat footage, torture material, or surveillance recordings. Allied to this, we may contemplate viewers producing and circulating their own reaction videos and commentaries linked to these recordings through a range of transmedial platforms, such as Internet shock sites, forums, and discussion boards. Alternatively, we may even contemplate the still and moving images that, in recent UK legal, political and cultural discourses have been labeled "extreme pornography."

Sinister was directed by Scott Derrickson and co-written with C. Robert Cargill.[1] The film was independently produced by Blumhouse Productions,

---

[1] As a writer and director, Scott Derrickson is also known for *The Exorcism of Emily Rose* (2005) and *Deliver Us from Evil* (2014). C. Robert Cargill, a film critic, novelist, and writer, is known for both *Sinister* and its sequel, *Sinister 2* (Ciaran Foy, 2015).

Automatik, Summit Entertainment, Alliance Films (UK), IM Global, and then sold to Summit. Blumhouse Productions are also involved in the production of the successful *Paranormal Activity, Insidious*, and *Purge* film franchises. The film is a wholly fictional, commercial feature film whose main cultural work has been to reconstruct the *idea* of snuff away from the niche cult, independent, and ultra-low budget shadows, in the full glare of popular culture. Like *Hardcore* (Paul Schrader, 1979), *8mm* (Joel Schumacher, 1999), and *Vacancy* (Nimrod Antal, 2007) before it, *Sinister* has taken the idea of the snuff movie into the mainstream, building upon, reworking and reimagining the frameworks, strategies, and themes developed in earlier films to simultaneously appropriate, manipulate, and, especially, *contain* the transgressive excesses, affects, and boundary testing linked to the snuff movie phenomena. *Sinister* keeps the idea of the possibility of real murder captured on film within transnational popular imaginations and contemporary transcultural nightmares through its engagement with, and reworking of various historical discourses underpinning the mythologies of snuff. It is contended that, without looking at the most commercially successful fictional iterations of simulated snuff, it is difficult to achieve one of the aims of this collection: to understand the place of snuff within contemporary global cultures.

Sinister constitutes one very particular utterance within the ongoing cultural dialog linked to the mythologies of snuff. Its particular intervention and contribution to this debate is its presentation of a low-risk fictional mediation which is carefully crafted generically, narratively, and formally to deliver maximum sensation and thrills without foregrounding the ethical reflexivity and unsettling complicity, ontological and epistemological instabilities, and troubling affects and assaultive elements of this erstwhile, controversial cultural phenomenon. This strategy makes *Sinister* more audience, reviewer, and regulator friendly, affording clearer opportunities for visual, aural, and narrative pleasure, despite its repeated and sustained focus upon cinematic representations of "real" death. As Scott Tobias states,

> It's all done in questionable taste, mucking around in the nasty terrain of snuff films and children in constant peril, but *Sinister* is smart and well-crafted, and it scarcely gives the audience a moment to breathe.[2]

The British Board of film Classification (BBFC), which classified *Sinister* "15" in theaters and on DVD/Blu-ray commented,

---

[2]See "Sinister," Scott Tobias, *A.V. Club*, accessed May 16, 2015, http://www.avclub.com/review/sinister-86511.

The film contains sight of various families being murdered... However, the scenes in question are presented using grainy old film footage and are fairly undetailed... The BBFC's Guidelines at "15" state "Violence may be strong but should not dwell on the infliction of pain or injury"... The scenes of strong horror are permissible at "15" where the Guidelines state "Strong threat and menace are permitted unless sadistic or sexualised."[3]

In other words, while offering fabricated illusions characterized by immediacy and realism, Sinister plays down the more visceral, sadistic, and sexualized aspects of the idea of snuff found in many snuff-themed fictional films, helping it to circumvent censure, moral outcry, and controversy. This strategy was deliberately reversed in the case of *A Serbian Film* (Srdjan Spasojevic, 2010). In the UK, extensive cuts were required to simulated scenes involving either the intradiegetic recording of snuff sequences or the viewing of previously filmed snuff sequences, for the film to be granted an eighteen certificate by the BBFC.[4]

Sinister plays on fears of the unknown operating within everyday life, foregrounding a supernatural entity that haunts the domestic arena and, as the narrative progresses, it relies less on cause and effect logic and more on imaginative leaps and narrative gaps. It is within this context that the realist horror trope of found snuff footage is blended with the idea that the analog and digital images of snuff are themselves possessed by the ancient pagan figure of Bughuul.[5] Locating the film within a wider production context illustrates how, through its generic hybridizing of supernatural and realist horror paradigms and its deployment of a marketable horror monster (the film was sequelized in 2015), it has been able to insulate itself from some of the resistance to realist and ultra-realist enactments of snuff within other less-commercial mainstream horror films. This is because, as Steve Jones suggests when discussing *Paranormal Activity* (Oren Peli, 2007), the absorption of supernatural elements within realist horror films helps to not just blur, trouble, and play with the subgeneric boundaries between them, it also helps to temper the immediacy and authenticity of the representation of death.[6]

While there is some variance in the reported box office figures, *Sinister* is by far the most commercially successful snuff-themed horror film to be produced in the twenty-first century. It was produced on a budget of $3 million and took

---

[3]"Sinister," *British Board of Film Classification*, accessed May 5, 2015, http://www.bbfc.co.uk/releases/sinister-2.

[4]See Shaun Kimber, "Transgressive Edge Play and *A Srpski Film/A Serbian Film*," *Horror Studies* 5, no. 1 (2014): 107–25.

[5]See Cynthia A. Freeland, "Realist Horror," in *Philosophy and Film*, edited by Cynthia A. Freeland and Thomas E. Wartenberg (London: Routledge, 1995): 126–42.

[6]Steve Jones, "Dying to Be Seen: Snuff-Fiction's Problematic Fantasises of 'Reality,'" *Scope*, 19 (2011): 1–22.

$87,727,803 at the global box office ($48,086,904 in the US and $39,640,904 internationally).[7] During 2013, it earned a further $12,539,179 in DVD and Blu-ray sales in the US alone.[8] According to Box Office Mojo, its worldwide box office takings in 2012 were $77.7 million ($17.75 million in its opening weekend and domestically grossing $48.1 million, screening in 2,625 theaters) making it the seventieth most successful film in terms of box office in the US in 2012.[9] In the rest of the world, the film took $29.6 million.[10] In the UK, it earned $10.6 million and screened in 370 theaters, making it the forty-fifth most popular film in cinemas, beating all other horror films that year except *The Woman in Black* (James Watkins, 2012), which ranked fourteenth.[11] As with many contemporary horror films, the majority of *Sinister's* revenue will be generated from what Labato & Ryan characterizes as horror's long-tail ancillary markets, such as DVD, Blu-ray, and online streaming and download services.[12]

Comparing *Sinister* against other fictional snuff-themed films underscores its commercial success. *15 Minutes* (John Herzfeld, 2001) made on a budget of $52 million took $24,375,436 in the US and $31,956,428 internationally, making a worldwide box office total of $56,331,864.[13] *Untraceable* (Gregory Hoblit, 2008) made on a budget of $35 million took $28,687,835 in the US and $23,971,759 worldwide, making a total of $52,659,594.[14] Produced on a budget of $19 million, *Vacancy* took $35.3 million at the worldwide box office, taking $19.4 million in the US and $15.9 elsewhere,[15] while *My Little Eye* (Marc Evans, 2002) produced for an estimated $2 million took £2,566,742 at the UK box office and a further €1,235,150 in Italy and Spain.[16] In the US, *V/H/S* (Adam Wingard et al., 2012), a

[7]"Sinister," *The Numbers*, accessed May 5, 2015, http://www.the-numbers.com/movie/Sinister#tab=summary.

[8]Ibid.

[9]"Sinister," *Box Office Mojo*, accessed May 5, 2015, http://www.boxofficemojo.com/movies/?id=sinister.htm.

[10]"Sinister," *Box Office Mojo—Foreign*, accessed May 5, 2015 http://www.boxofficemojo.com/movies/?page=intl&id=sinister.htm.

[11]"Sinister," *Box Office Mojo—Foreign—UK*, accessed May 5, 2015, http://www.boxofficemojo.com/movies/?page=intl&country=UK&id=sinister.htm.

[12]Ramon Lobato and Mark David Ryan, "Rethinking Genre Studies Through Distribution Analysis: Issues in International Horror Movie Circuits," *New Review of Film and Television Studies* 9, no. 2 (2011): 188–203.

[13]"15 Minutes," *The Numbers*, accessed May 5, 2015, http://www.the-numbers.com/movie/15-Minutes#tab=summary.

[14]"Untraceable," *Box Office Mojo*, accessed May 5, 2015, http://www.boxofficemojo.com/movies/?id=untraceable.htm.

[15]"Vacancy," *Box Office Mojo*, accessed May 5, 2015, http://www.boxofficemojo.com/movies/?id=vacancy.htm.

[16]"My Little Eye," *Internet Movie Data Base—Box Office*, accessed May 5, 2015, http://www.imdb.com/title/tt0280969/business?ref_=tt_dt_bus.

fictional, found footage snuff-themed franchise launched in the same year, only took $100,345 (screening in just nineteen theaters),[17] *V/H/S 2* (Simon Barrett et al., 2013) earned $21,833[18] (and around $800,000 globally)[19] and *V/H/S Viral* (Marcel Sarmiento, 2014) grossed just $2,756[20] and a further $34,629 in domestic video sales.[21] If we compare the commercial success of *Sinister* to other snuff-themed fictional films released since 2000, we see a similar pattern. *A Serbian Film* earned €6,975 in Serbia[22] and $1,541 in Brazil,[23] whereas *Afterschool* (Antonio Campos, 2008) earned $3,911 at the US box office.[24] Due to limited theatrical releases and straight to DVD distribution, box office figures and DVD sales figures were not available for a range of other postmillennial fictional films that engage with the mythology of snuff including *Snuff 102* (Mariano Peralta, 2007), *The Poughkeepsie Tapes* (John Etick Dowdle, 2007), *Megan is Missing* (Michael Goi, 2011), and *The Cohasset Snuff Film* (Edward Payson, 2012). Even when you look back to *8mm*, although it took $96.6 million at the worldwide box office ($36.9 million in the US and $60.0 million in the rest of the world), it was produced on a budget of $40 million, making it, at least in terms of cost-to-profit ratio, less commercially successful than *Sinister*.[25]

Sinister belongs to a long tradition of snuff-themed fictions that, as Julian Petley suggests, deliberately make "cinematic play" with "snuff-like" elements[26] within their narratives. This might include "apparently 'documentary' episodes" of simulated real-life murders "inserted into the fictional story,"[27] something Joel Black echoes when he suggests that "a number of commercial filmmakers have

---

[17]"V/H/S," *Box Office Mojo*, accessed May 5, 2015, http://www.boxofficemojo.com/movies/?id=vhs. htm.

[18]"V/H/S 2," *Box Office Mojo*, accessed May 5, 2015, http://www.boxofficemojo.com/movies/?id=vhs2. htm.

[19]"V/H/S 2," *Box Office Mojo—Foreign*, accessed May 5, 2015, http://www.boxofficemojo.com/movies/? page=intl&id=vhs2.htm.

[20]"V/H/S: Viral," *Box Office Mojo*, accessed May 5, 2015, http://www.boxofficemojo.com/movies/? id=vhsviral.htm.

[21]"V/H/S: Viral," *The Numbers*, accessed May 5, 2015, http://www.the-numbers.com/movie/V-H-S-Viral#tab=summary.

[22]"A Serbian Film," *Internet Movie Data Base—Box Office*, accessed May 5, 2015, http://www.imdb.com/title/tt1273235/business.

[23]"A Serbian Film," *Box Office Mojo—By Country*, accessed May 5, 2015, http://www.boxofficemojo. com/movies/intl/?page=&country=BR&id=_fASERBIANFILM01.

[24]"Afterschool," *The Numbers*, accessed May 5, 2015,http://www.the-numbers.com/movie/Afterschool# tab=summary.

[25]"8mm," *Box Office Mojo*, accessed May 5, 2015, http://www.boxofficemojo.com/movies/?id=8mm. htm.

[26]Julian Petley, "'Snuffed Out': Nightmares in a Trading Standards Officers Brain," in *Unruly Pleasures: The Cult Film and Its Critics*, edited by Xavier Mendik and Graeme Harper (Guildford: FAB Press, 2002): 207.

[27]Ibid.

adopted the strategy of incorporating what seems to be authentic death-film footage within their cinematic fictions" in an attempt to "push the envelope" of realist horror.[28] Linda Badley characterizes *Sinister* as the most recent example of what she calls "meta-snuff," in which "the making and viewing of a snuff film is a plot device and theme."[29] Taking this point a little further, Xavier Aldana Reyes divides fictional snuff into four subcategories that are differentiated according to an individual film's framing style, degree of self-reflexivity, and affective charge: "films about snuff"; "faux snuff"; "the snuff mockumentary"; and "the serial killer video diary."[30] Reyes suggests that "the film about snuff" is the most common and mainstream form, almost always following the conventions of classical narrative, with the tension between simulations of the real and awareness of their fabrication balanced in favor of the latter.[31] *Sinister* can be seen as constituting a very particular iteration of "the film about snuff," through its blending of the mystery thriller format with both realist and supernatural horror. The snuff-like elements appear intradiegetically in the form of a flawed main character watching Super 8mm home movies where the film-within-a-film found footage is manufactured.[32] This particular strategy has become a recurring visual and thematic motif within several mainstream snuff-themed narratives, such as *Hardcore* and *8mm*, where a lone male protagonist watches celluloid snuff projected onto a screen and has a tangibly uncomfortable physical response to the experience, and then struggles in his attempts to assert his masculine authority amid the surrounding moral breakdown that the encounter with snuff has engendered. What makes *Sinister* a fascinating object of study is how its particular rendition of "meta-snuff" or "the film about snuff" has enabled it to become such a mainstream success.

Sinister can therefore be clearly distinguished from other films that have been more direct, controversial, or self-reflexive in negotiating the visual and thematic terrain of snuff. For example, Jones refers to "faux snuff," a film that tries to pass itself off as an actual snuff movie through an immediate and authentic representation, with few markers of its constructed nature, such as *August Underground* (Fred Vogel, 2001).[33] Similarly, Badley identifies "pseudo snuff," a category within which fictional texts, such as *Cannibal Holocaust* (Ruggero Deodato, 1980), pretend

---

[28]Joel Black, "Real(ist) Horror: From Execution Videos to Snuff Films," in *Underground USA: Filmmaking Beyond the Hollywood Canon*, edited by Xavier Mendik and Steven Jay Schneider (London: Wallflower Press, 2002): 66.

[29]See Linda Badley's contribution to this volume.

[30]See Xavier Aldana Reyes's contribution to this is volume.

[31]Ibid.

[32]During *Sinister*, multiple references are made to 8mm film and the fact that the fake snuff home movies were shot on 8mm film. However, the films were actually captured on Super 8mm stock. See *Sinister*, Director's Commentary, Blu-Ray, Scott Derrickson, and *Sinister* Writers Commentary, Blu-Ray, Scott Derrickson, and C. Robert Cargill (both Momentum Pictures, UK, 2012).

[33]Jones, "Dying to Be Seen: Snuff-Fiction's Problematic Fantasises of 'Reality.'"

to be a snuff movie or incorporate footage in which real people or animals die onscreen.[34] As noted earlier, Reyes makes reference to the "snuff mockumentary," a twist on the real serial killer documentary such as *The Poughkeepsie Tapes* (John Erick Dowdle, 2007), and the "serial killer video diary" which is linked narratively to the "snuff mockumentary" and stylistically to "faux snuff," but which focuses on the first person filming of the serial killer, such as *The Last Horror Movie* (Julian Richards, 2003).[35] Finally, Joel Black identifies snuff-themed fictions in which supposedly real deaths captured on film are passed off as fictional within the wider framing narrative.[36] Here, fictional filmmakers take purportedly real footage and try to make it look fabricated enough to pass as fiction, a narrative conceit featured in *Effects* (Dusty Nelson, 1980), *Special Effects* (Larry Cohen, 1984), and, more recently, *Smash Cut* (Lee Demarbre, 2009).

Sinister produces its own expression of the snuff myth, but it also perpetuates the notion of snuff's presence within transnational popular cultures. Alexandra Hellier-Nicholas has suggested that "the power inherent in the word 'snuff' is dependent upon its vagueness; its enigmatic force stems directly from its elusiveness as a concept."[37] As such, the idea of snuff lacks a precise definition or history and is informed by a range of textual, extratextual, and intertextual variables which tend to offer more misdirection and misinformation than a clear-cut understanding of this phenomena.[38] According to Petley, "Of all the myths generated by controversies about horror films ... that of the snuff movie is the most persistent and hard to dispel."[39] He argues that although there is no proof of the existence of snuff movies, several fictional films have given a form to the myth. This is a point developed by Black:

> Not only do fictional horror films in the tradition of *Snuff* ... incorporate staged snuff sequences to make themselves appear shockingly real, but these fictional films also *give reality* to snuff films. In making use of snuff sequences to arouse terror in viewers and to produce the horror effect, horror films and thrillers also play on people's suspicions that an underground subculture exists in which snuff films are made and marketed.[40]

---

[34]See Badley, in this volume.

[35]See Reyes, in this volume.

[36]See Black, "Real(ist) Horror."

[37]Alexandra Hellier-Nicholas, *Found Footage Horror Film: Fear and the Appearance of Reality* (Jefferson, NC: McFarland, 2014): 58.

[38]For elaboration, see Neil Jackson's introduction to this volume.

[39]See Petley, " 'Snuffed Out,' " 205. See also Julian Petley, "Cannibal Holocaust and the Pornography of Death," in *The Spectacle of the Real: From Hollywood to Reality TV and Beyond*, edited by Geoff King (Bristol: Intellect, 2005): 173–86.

[40]Black, "Real(ist) Horror," 68.

Therefore, the idea of snuff is simultaneously absent as sociocultural or legal artifact, but very much present within popular discourse and culture. As Kerekes and Slater suggest, "snuff... is a fascinating, but illogical concept... a malleable and terrifying supposition. Snuff is something unseen—on our very doorstep—but unseen."[41] For Mark Jones and Gerry Carlin, snuff's physical absence has not disproved its existence; instead, its unavailability is what sustains its mythic possibility.[42] It is within this environment, where the mythologies of snuff have thrived, transformed, intertwined, and mutated, that *Sinister's* particular enactment of the mythology has materialized.

Somewhat paradoxically, *Sinister's* engagement with the idea of snuff can be seen to be, on the one hand, direct and conscious, while, on the other hand, being indirect and unconscious, engaging, conflating, and reworking historical discourses associated with the mythology of snuff. Petley asserts that various groups and commentators have discussed snuff films as if it is "an established fact of modern life," and often in pursuit of ideological causes. This has promoted an urban legend which has in turn engendered a range of powerful discourses, folk devils and, from time to time, moral panics,[43] becoming persuasive, imaginative frameworks that filmmakers draw upon when devising their snuff-themed fictions.

Sinister's framing narrative and simulation of snuff has been influenced not only by other snuff-themed fictions—which have themselves been shaped by and help perpetuate wider snuff-related discourses—but also by discussions linked to the suggested presence of snuff films within true crime fiction.[44] The film focuses on Ellison Oswalt (Ethan Hawke), a struggling true crime writer who moves his unwitting wife, Tracy (Juliet Rylance), and children, Trevor (Michael Hall D'Addario) and Ashely (Clare Foley), into the house where previous occupants, the Stevenson family, were murdered. Ellison's primary motivation is to kick-start his career, which has been flagging since the success of his earlier true crime book, *Kentucky Blood*, by investigating the murders and solving the mystery of the disappearance of Stephanie (Victoria Leigh), one of the Stevenson children. Eventually, Ellison begrudgingly takes up the offer of help from a local Deputy (James Ransone) when it becomes clear to him that he has happened upon a series of related murders and disappearances.[45] It is while

---

[41]David Kerekes and David Slater, *Killing for Culture: An Illustrated History of Death Film from Mondo to Snuff* (London: Creation Books, 1993), 310.

[42]See Mark Jones and Gerry Carlin's contribution to this volume.

[43]See Petley, "'Snuffed Out,'" 209.

[44]See Ed Sanders, *The Family: The Story of Charles Manson's Dune Buggy Attack Battalion* (St Albans: Panther Book Limited, 1973).

[45]The Deputy helps to discover the connection between the murders and disappearances and is the only character to survive and return in *Sinister 2*.

investigating strange noises emanating from the attic that Ellison discovers a box containing five Super 8mm home movies and a projector, which become the focus of his investigations. Therefore, a key way in which *Sinister* is able to temper its engagement with the idea of snuff is through its use of simulated snuff as a narrative device with which to thematically explore the fame hungry selfishness and bad decision-making of Ellison. In doing so, the film self-reflexively plays upon the idea of snuff to do its cultural work, rather than exploiting it to pose ethical questions, highlight ontological and epistemological uncertainties, or foreground the more assaultive aspects of the mythologies of snuff.

Taking this a little further, *Sinister* is very careful to avoid any direct engagement with sex–murder associations found in some feminist, journalistic, and religious discourses that have sought to link the idea of snuff to murder within hardcore pornography and/or recorded violent and sexual child abuse.[46] Although links can be made between *Sinister*'s simulation of snuff films and 8mm pornography through their amateur production values and grainy aesthetic styling, this, as Gill suggests, simply reflects a "perverse form of nostalgia" one that as Lehman argues "displaces current anxieties onto doubly outmoded porn technology."[47] Additionally, the film's main evil force Bughuul/Mr Boogie (Nicholas King), a pagan deity associated with the occult, does not physically kill any children or make the recordings of the murders himself. Rather, he influences the children under his supernatural spell to kill their parents and siblings while recording the murders on cine cameras. In doing so, Bughuul lures his child victims away from the physical world, trapping them in his netherworld where he consumes their souls over time. In this way, *Sinister* is very careful that any actual or implied cruelty or ritualized abuse acted upon the children under Bughuul's paranormal control takes place offscreen and outside of the simulated snuff sequences. Thus, another significant factor within *Sinister*'s fictional versioning of the idea of snuff is its undercutting of the more transgressive aspects of the sex–murder, satanic, or sexual child abuse discourses surrounding its mythology through their disavowal, displacement, and reworking.

Sinister contains six fictional Super 8mm home snuff movies that are woven into the film's narrative, and the simulated found footage movies involve six killer children who, under the influence of Bughuul, document the murder of their families. The films-within-the-film, all clearly labeled on the spool canisters discovered by Ellison, start with *Family Hanging Out* (2011), which appears before the title sequence, and is followed by *BBQ* (1979), *Pool Party* (1986), *Sleepy Time*

---

[46]See Petley, " 'Snuffed Out'."

[47]See Peter Lehman, "*8mm* will the Real Machine Please Stand Up?," *Jump Cut: A Review of Contemporary Media* 43 (July 2000): 16–20; and Pat Gill, "Taking It Personally: Male Suffering in *8mm*," *Camera Obscura* 18, no. 1 (2003): 176.

(1998), and *Lawn Work* (1986). *Sinister* ends with the filming of *House Painting* (2012) where Ashley murders Ellison and the rest of her family. At the heart of these Super 8mm films is a carefully measured aesthetic and affective balancing act between their amplification of amateur "caught-on-tape" realism[48] and their ameliorating "hyper aestheticisation strategies."[49] The simulated snuff home movies offer the illusion of an authentic mediation of actuality while blending into this caught-on-camera footage suspense, surprise, and spectacle, in an attempt to increase its affective impact upon audiences.[50] The outcome is the simultaneous playing down of fictional snuff's troubling qualities, while playing up its status as entertaining horror spectacle. In other words, the D.I.Y. caught-on-film aesthetic offers the requisite horrific chills, while the film remains very careful to position its snuff footage as not real or realistic.

Sinister, like many snuff-themed fictions before it, employs a mixture of production techniques, analog technologies, and low-tech realism to add a degree of authenticity, directness, and immediacy to its simulated snuff movies. The fake murder scenes were shot on location on Super 8mm film ahead of principle photography, with the express purpose of keeping it quick, real, and in camera, with all of the signatures and imperfections this brings.[51] This strategy directly and deliberately drew upon the discursive connotations of Super 8mm as a nonexpensive, nonprofessional, domestic technology. This is what Geoff King has referred to as a "hierarchy of degrees of implied authenticity" associated with Super 8mm's amateur, authentic, and unpredictable representation of the real.[52] As a direct result, the fictional found footage scenes deliberately replicate the formal devices and representational codes and conventions associated with amateur and documentary filmmaking. This includes decontextualized footage, low-grade film stock, shaky, hand-held camera work, subjective POV, improvised composition and framing, poor quality, grainy images lacking in tonal contrast and textural detail, over and under exposed images, muffled and distorted sound, and actors who do not feature in the rest of the film.[53] The combination of this mode of production with what West refers to as the "context of production" helps to increase *Sinister*'s reality effect.[54] The fake snuff films were not only shot on Super 8mm equipment, but the narrative impulse behind

---

[48] See Amy West, "Caugth on Tape: A Legacy of Low-Tech Reality," in *The Spectacle of the Real: From Hollywood to Reality TV and Beyond*, edited by Geoff King (Bristol: Intellect, 2005): 83–98.

[49] See Black, "Real(ist) Horror," 66.

[50] See Ibid. and West, "Caught on Tape."

[51] See Derrickson's "Directors Commentary" and Scott Derrickson and C. Robert Cargill's "Writers Commentary."

[52] See Geoff King, *American Independent Cinema* (London: I. B. Tauris, 2005): 114.

[53] See Petley, "*Cannibal Holocaust* and the Pornography of Death," 178; and West, "Caught on Tape," 84.

[54] See West, "Caught on Tape," 85.

their filming by the fictional snuff filmmakers who physically, if not spiritually, controlled the filming process was to document their murderous actions, thus capturing their homicidal impulses and amplifying the realist qualities of the short films.

However, *Sinister* also draws upon a number of formal devices and layered postproduction framing strategies to help it ameliorate some of the directness and immediacy implied by the realism of the Super 8mm films. The film's fictional home snuff movies are constructed to heighten their potential as thrilling spectacles by employing a range of aesthetic and aural flourishes that help to dampen their more confrontational aspects. While many other snuff-themed films, including *A Serbian Film*,[55] *8mm*, and *Vacancy*, have employed similar strategies, it is particularly marked in *Sinister*. The editing of *Sinister*'s snuff films temporally follows a conventional logic of short, quick shots rapidly edited to increase pace, tension, and drama. For example, *BBQ* involves a number of jump cuts between an assortment of brief shots that draws direct attention to the fact it has been carefully put together as a result of postproduction (rather than in-camera) techniques. This is in clear opposition to the home invasion scene in *Henry: Portrait of a Serial Killer* (John McNaughton, 1986), which was shot in one continuous take, increasing its manufactured impression of authenticity.[56]

In *Sinister*, the intradiegetic camera's positioning and movement within the simulated Super 8mm snuff sequences also provides clearly marked clues to the killers' identity. In *Lawn Work*, when the interdiegetic camera is fixed and static, the killer is coded as being within the scene, sitting in the family lounge distanced from her mother, father, and sister. However, when the camera is handheld and the image more immediate and improvised, the killer is behind the camera and missing from the shots of her family. Such formal and narrative strategies help to heighten the suspense and drama of this footage, simultaneously muting its impression of authenticity as viewers are encouraged to scan the screen for clues to the mystery and the invisible forces operating within the frame as much as any markers of realism. The fictional snuff sequences are also presented through a range of devices which enhance the sense of their status as cinematic constructs, including shots of surfaces upon which the images are projected, the outer edges of the Super 8mm film and the screens of digital devices. Furthermore, it is significant that the arrangement of fake Super 8 snuff sequences was reordered in postproduction. *Lawn Work*, which is often seen as the most memorable and affective due to its artfully

---

[55]See Kimber, "Transgressive Edge Play," 111–14.
[56]See Shaun Kimber, *Controversies: Henry: Portrait of a Serial Killer* (Basingstoke: Palgrave MacMillan, 2011): 105. The home invasion scene in *Henry: Portrait of a Serial Killer* was cut in the UK from 1991 to 2003.

constructed and well-timed jump scare, was moved to be the penultimate film-within-a-film to manage its impact on audiences.[57]

The tempering of the unreal snuff sequences can also be observed in the soundtrack, interlacing nondiegetic score and sound design to emphasize emotive sounds. In *Pool Party*, this is achieved by using the dark ambient track *"A Body of Water,"* [58] as well as heightened sound effects such as the noise of Super 8mm film running through the sprockets of a projector, over dialog and atmospherics. The aim of this auditory strategy is to encourage audiences to *feel* something about the fictional snuff scene rather than *believing* what they are seeing is real.[59]

Another factor that helps to contain the directness and immediacy of the fake snuff films is the integration of the increasingly supernatural elements within them. For example, in *Pool Party*, the third of the found footage films to be viewed, there is the first glimpse of the green, luminescent liquid that is used by the children to drug their families, which is then followed by the first sighting of Bughuul. It is from this point that Bughuul starts to actively inhabit the Super 8mm films and the digital copies Ellison makes of them. In this way, the supernatural presence of Bughuul increasingly lives within and possesses the analog and digital snuff images as they become the gateway into his realm.

A number of narrative framing devices linked to the representation of film violence also work in tandem with *Sinister's* generic blending and aesthetic balancing act, modulating the film's potential to test audience boundaries and thresholds.[60] As King suggests, in most films "a balance is usually found between intense orchestrations of violence and legitimating frameworks that make it more palatable for both audiences and regulators."[61] The precise figuration of fictional violence within *Sinister's* Super 8mm snuff films offers an interesting example of the interplay between what David E. Morrison calls "depicted violence" and what Marsha Kinder refers to as "narrative orchestration of violent attractions."[62] For Morrison, depicted violence can assault audience sensibilities both through

---

[57]See Scott Derrickson and C. Robert Cargill, "Writers Commentary."

[58] See *"A Body of Water"*, Atheistic God (Music Track, online download) Pref. Judgehydrogen, Rising Oculus Recordings, USA, 7 mins 31 secs, accessed May 15 2015. https://itunes.apple.com/us/album/atheistic-god/id259614065

[59]See Stephen Deutsch, "Editorial," *The New Soundtrack* 1, no. 1 (2011): 3–13.

[60]See Annette Hill, *Shocking Entertainment: Viewer Responses to Violence Movies* (Luton: University of Luton Press, 1997): 51–74.

[61]Geoff King, " 'Killingly Funny': Mixing Modalities in New Hollywood's Comedy-With-Violence," in *New Hollywood Violence*, edited by Steven Jay Schneider (Manchester: Manchester University Press, 2004): 129.

[62]David E. Morrison et al., *Defining Violence: The Search for Meaning* (Luton: Luton University Press, 1999): 1–7; and Marsha Kinder, "Violence American Style: The Narrative Orchestration of Violent Attractions," in *Violence and American Cinema*, edited by David J. Slocum (London: Routledge, 2012): 63–100.

its positioning within everyday moral frameworks of appropriateness, fairness, and justification, and through its amplification through the graphic realism of its representation.[63] According to Kinder, fictional violence can be employed within a film to structure its design stylistically and narratively, consequently positioning audiences' emotional responses.[64]

Speaking at the UK premier of *Sinister* at the London Frightfest in 2012, C. Robert Cargill discussed the way he and Scott Derrickson had carefully constructed the film, so that the shocks and scares were fully integrated into the narrative and carefully designed to heighten their effects as the story progressed. The express intention was to encourage audiences to experience the indefensible idea of violent murder caught on Super 8mm film, but not exploitative images of its graphic detail, thus encouraging them to fill the gaps with their imaginations. Key to this strategy was the choice to play up the ethereal scares while looking away from the grim realism of killer children murdering their drugged and helpless parents and siblings, while recording their atrocities on cine cameras. In other words, the filmmakers made the deliberate choice to frustrate the spectator's gaze by having the fictional film violence take place off screen or be heard but not seen, a considered strategy designed to unsettle and unnerve audiences rather than disturb or disgust them with the gory particulars. For example, the viewing of *Sinister's* simulated snuff films is regularly punctuated at carefully chosen moments with shots of the running projector and/or Ellison's horrified reactions as a deliberate mechanism to fragment the presentation of the films, thus avoiding stark, confrontational renditions of the violence. In *BBQ* and *Sleepy Time*, sections of the fake snuff films are observed from behind Ellison as he watches, and stronger moments of violence are viewed as obscured and unfocused reflections upon his reading glasses. Taking this idea a little further, the clearly oblique and obfuscated images of throats being slit by big knives in *Sleepy Time* also help to distance the fake snuff footage from too direct an association with death videos that foreground similar methods and have become an increasingly ubiquitous feature of the twenty-first century online culture. A particularly clear example of the fictional violence taking place off screen can be found in *Lawn Work* where, after an excruciatingly long build up to the imminent event of a family member being run over by a lawnmower, a bound body comes into shot prompting a sudden cut to Ellison's flailing reaction.

Finally, *Sinister* manages to contain the power of the simulated snuff sequences through not only the suffering of Ellison but also his implied complicity in the murder of his family and abduction of his daughter by Bughuul. As in *Hardcore, 8mm, Vacancy*, and *A Serbian Film, Sinister* positions its intradiegetic spectator as not taking any pleasure in the snuff films. Rather, the film documents the shock,

---

[63]See Morrison et al., *Defining Violence*, 1–7.
[64]See Kinder, "Violence American Style," 63–100.

torment, and psychological decline of Ellison as he becomes increasingly obsessed with investigating the truth of the films. During Ellison's first screening of *Family Hanging Out*, the template for his reception of, and response to the films is firmly established through a combination of frequent intradiegetic reaction shots of him looking visibly shocked and appalled by what he is witnessing, his use of alcohol assisting his fortitude while concurrently underscoring his emotional and physical frailties. This strategy of male "self-punishment" and "moral masochism" is well established in snuff-themed fictions, as Gill describes in relation to *8mm*:

> Allowing viewers only brief glimpses of the snuff film, *8mm* concentrates instead on the reaction shots of Welles's afflicted looks, letting his fitful starts and winces and his involuntary cries convey the horror of the screen narrative.[65]

Sinister therefore positions Ellison's interest in the Stevenson murders and his increasing preoccupation with the found Super 8mm snuff films as problematic and increasingly dangerous. For example, Ellison's choice not to phone the authorities after his discovery and viewing of films renders him complicit with the evil represented by Bughuul and, by extension, the Super 8mm films. After watching *BBQ*, Ellison picks up his mobile phone to call police but after looking at copies of *Kentucky Blood*, he hangs up. Once this decision is made, the die is cast and Bughuul appears to Ellison from within the Super 8mm films, drawing out of him characteristics linked his selfish and narcissistic obsession with regaining his fame and fortune. This ultimately leads to his and his family's violent deaths, captured in the last simulated snuff movie *House Painting*. Taking this idea a little further, Caetlin Benson-Allott has suggested that within found and faux footage horror films:

> the (fictional) primary filmmaker may be recording footage about a supernatural event, but the secondary filmmakers can use it to make another point about cinema, especially the role of the spectator in contemporary movie culture.[66]

In *Sinister*, the deep fears evoked by the secondary, extradiegetic filmmakers (middle class, neo-liberal male dread of losing money and control, and the measures he will take to regain it) augment and reframe the surface fears invoked by the primary diegetic filmmakers (killer children, supernatural monsters, and

---

[65]See Gill, "Taking It Personally," 166.
[66]Caetlin Benson-Allott, *Killer Tapes and Shattered Screens: Video Spectatorship from VHS to File Sharing* (Berkeley: California University Press, 2013): 193.

found footage snuff movies). Viewed in this way, the fears engaged and mobilized in *Sinister*, associated with the dire consequences of watching the wrong kinds of films, can be seen to self-reflexively engage with wider social and regulatory concerns linked to watching horror films in general, and the mythologies of snuff in particular.

What is being suggested here is that *Sinister* has employed rather than exploited the idea of snuff, enabling it to be much more commercially successful and audience, critic, and censor friendly. It has been contended that *Sinister* has produced its own performance of the idea of snuff and its associated mythologies, through its engagement with, and reworking of historical discourses which in turn give form to and perpetuate the myth of snuff within mainstream popular culture. It has also been argued that *Sinister* has been carefully crafted generically, narratively, and formally to deliver maximum thrills without foregrounding the ethical, reflective, and affective elements accompanying many other representations of snuff. Lastly, it was put forward that by employing the idea of snuff, *Sinister* has knowingly engaged with a range of cultural fears linked to the perceived dangers associated with watching the wrong type of films by constructing a horror narrative around a man watching films in which the murders are "real."

13 CINEMA *AS* SNUFF: FROM PRECINEMA TO *SHADOW OF THE VAMPIRE*

Linda Badley

A theatrical audience gives me life … this … thing only takes it from me.
GRETA SCHROEDER, *SHADOW OF THE VAMPIRE*

Under scrutiny, "snuff"—in the sense of a film that whether for profit or for art's sake, depicts real death[1]—tends to self-destruct. Or, as Joel Black observes, its mystique is amplified by the lack of proof of its existence, making it uniquely paradoxical. On the one hand, in that graphic evidence of murder is rigorously impounded by the police and the courts, snuff films lead "an elusive, phantom existence that cannot be verified; on the other hand, supposing that they do exist, they depict a reality so horrific that it cannot be shown except in cinematic simulations." Snuff therefore presents us with "a glimpse of ultimate reality shorn of any and all special effects, and yet a subgenre whose own elusiveness makes it seem the stuff of myth—the ultimate special effect." Not surprisingly, Black concludes, this paradox has inspired underground and mainstream filmmakers alike to embed "simulated snuff scenes … to produce the illusion of reality."[2]

In consequence, "snuff" and associated phenomena tend to fall into one or more of three categories, pseudo-, faux-, and metasnuff. Pseudosnuff films are elaborately framed hoaxes; they pretend to contain footage in which real people

---

[1]Although snuff is often noncommercial and lacking in aesthetic aims, as in footage caught coincidentally on cell phones or shot and disseminated by jihadists, this chapter focuses on commercial snuff and "snuff art."

[2]Joel Black, "Real(ist) Horror: From Execution Videos to Snuff Films," *Underground U.S.A.: Filmmaking Beyond the Hollywood Canon*, edited Xavier Mendik and Steven Jay Schneider (London: Wallflower Press, 2002): 71.

and/or animals die onscreen (*Snuff* [Michael and Roberta Findlay, 1976], *Cannibal Holocaust* [Ruggero Deodato, 1980], *Mondo Cane* [Gualtiero Jacopetti, Franco Prosperi and Paolo Cavara, 1962], *Faces of Death* [John Alan Schwartz, 1978], *The Last Broadcast* [Lance Weiler and Stefan Avalos, 1998]). Fauxsnuff, an effect of today's climate of "reality culture" as Steve Jones suggests, attempts to "pass [itself] off as authentic from the outset" and, unlike pseudosnuff, lacks a fictional frame, as in the *August Underground* trilogy (Various, 2001–2007).[3] More common than either, however, is a subcategory of metacinema that incorporates a snuff "trope" about the making and viewing of a snuff film as a plot device and theme (*Peeping Tom* [Michael Powell, 1960], *Hardcore* [Paul Scharder, 1979], *Videodrome* [David Cronenberg, 1982], *Manhunter* [Michael Mann, 1986], *Henry, Portrait of a Serial Killer* [John McNaughton, 1986], *Mute Witness* [Anthony Waller, 1995], *Strange Days* [Kathryn Bigelow, 1995], *Tesis* [Alejandro Amenábar, 1996], *8mm* [Joel Schumacher, 1999], *15 Minutes* [John Herzfeld, 2001], *My Little Eye* [Marc Evans, 2002], *Snuff 102* [Mariano Peralta, 2007], and *Sinister* [Scott Derrickson, 2012]). At their most sophisticated, pseudo- and metasnuff films explore the ramifications—aesthetic, epistemological, and ethical—of capturing and/or watching onscreen violence and death, often incriminating the audience, as in a popular metavariation on the serial killer film.

This begins with widely understood associations of early photography, pre-, and early cinema, the German Expressionist aesthetic, and the postclassical Hollywood style with death, with an understanding of the image as a kind of death and the gaze as murderous—of cinema *as* snuff. Finally, I explore this theme as it is thought to have been implicit in F.W. Murnau's *Nosferatu: eine Symphonie des Grauens* (*Nosferatu: A Symphony of Horror*, 1922) and as explored in E. Elias Merhige's *Shadow of the Vampire* (2000), a "making of" film that takes literally the "snuff" mythology surrounding Friedrich Wilhelm Murnau's German Expressionist masterpiece.

"I see dead people": The spectral nature of pre- and early cinema

The association of cinema with death and violence seems inherent in the visual media, returning to cinema's origins in photography. At its emergence, and as an indexical representation of time, cinema seemed capable of capturing and infinitely representing "the contingent, of providing the ephemeral with an endurable record," Mary Ann Doane suggests; death functioned "as a kind

---

[3]Steve Jones, "Dying to be Seen: Snuff-Fiction's Problematic Fantasies of 'Reality.'" *Scope* 19 (2011): 1–22. http://nrl.northumbria.ac.uk/5145/.

of Ur-event," as "pure contingency,"[4] and still does, as in cell phone videos that accidentally record a suicide, or as suggested in the popularity of reality television. From another perspective, however, early cinema must have been experienced as uncanny in several of the senses that Freud (1919) explored.[5] The Expressionists and Surrealists were fascinated with cinema's power to bring the unconscious to light, and Freud's understanding of the uncanny, as the effect of encountering a surmounted belief or an image or fragment as something forgotten or repressed, has informed psychoanalytic film theory. The double is intrinsically uncanny; invented (as in the case of the soul) as protection/defense against mortality; it has since become a harbinger of death. The movies produce doubles of living people and things that, because like automatons, dolls, and other things that appear to be alive when they are not, are especially uncanny.

Early cinema no doubt signified immortality of a technologically induced sort with a price of *Death 24x a Second*, as articulated by Laura Mulvey's evocative title of her 2006 work.[6] The movies bring everlasting life while turning living people and experiences into consumable images that become ghosts or phantasms—eternally, surreally repeating lifelike gestures in the limbo of the simulacrum. Thus, Tom Gunning describes the movies' "quality not just of a representation but of a zone between reality and representation, which is exactly what ghosts are. Images of people long dead."[7] Like the stars of classical Hollywood, the analog cinema of the past one hundred plus years has been superseded by video, DVD, and new digital and Internet media technologies, turning "cinema" in the traditional sense into an archaic encounter with the living dead.[8] Paradoxically, digital technology has exposed the tension between the still frame and the moving image, making us newly aware of movies' uncanny ability to capture "life" and preserve it after death, thus acutely conscious of its relation to time and mortality.

Foreshadowing cinema in this respect, still photography according to Roland Barthes has long been associated with death, most expressly in the tradition of memorial portraiture of the dead posed as if alive.[9] For the Victorians, for whom the first photographs must have seemed inherently uncanny, the technology of fairy and spirit photography exploited and enhanced this effect—through superimposition, blurring, overexposure, and other tricks—in which the photographic image freezes

---

[4]Mary Ann Doane, *The Emergence of Cinematic Time: Modernity, Contingency, the Archive* (Cambridge, MA: Harvard University Press, 2000): 144.

[5]Sigmund Freud, "The 'Uncanny'," in *The Standard Edition of the Complete Psychological Works of Sigmund Freud*, edited by James Strachey, 17 (London: Hogarth, 1919): 219–52.

[6]Laura Mulvey, *Death 24 x a Second: Stillness and the Moving Image* (London: Reaktion, 2006).

[7]*The American Nightmare*, DVD, directed by Adam Simon (United States: IFC Originals, Independent Film Channel, 2000).

[8]Mulvey, *Death 24 x a Second*, 36–37.

[9]Roland Barthes, *Camera Lucida*, trans. Richard Howard (New York: Hill and Wang, 1982).

a moment living in the present and renders it into stilled, past, dead moments. Moving to telegraphy, television, and computers, Jeffrey Sconce's *Haunted Media* (2000) traces the electronic media's association with death and the paranormal throughout popular culture, and Cætlin Benson-Allott's *Killer Tapes and Shattered Screens* (2013) is a contemporary take on the subject.[10]

In "To Scan a Ghost: The Ontology of Mediated Vision," Tom Gunning traces the conceptual history of the mediated image as liminal "phantasm"— "an image that wavers between the material and immaterial and was used by premodern philosophy and science to explain the workings of both sight and consciousness ... ."[11] The eighteenth-century science of optics sought to "explain away the ghost as a visual illusion created intentionally by means of an optical apparatus." Soon, "phantasmagoria shows," magic lantern exhibitions were staged in the late eighteenth and nineteenth centuries by projecting "phantasms of the dead"—spectral drawings and photographs that appeared, moved, and vanished— to paying audiences.[12] While showmen like Etienne Gaspard Robertson claimed their purpose as demystification—to expose the devices of mediums—the spectacle often convinced audiences of the opposite, producing the epistemological and ontological uncertainty of Todorov's "fantastic."[13] Either way, these shows constituted evidence of the "haunted" nature and soul-consuming power of the visual media, or a culture of the uncanny developed out of their ability to conjure death on screen.

The earliest films that followed were largely what Gunning calls a "cinema of attraction": a pre- or nonnarrative cinema of spectacle—of "pure visual stimulation," affect, and carnival-style entertainment.[14] One of these was arguably the first snuff film: Edison Studios' three-minute *Electrocuting an Elephant* (1903) depicted the execution of Topsy, a circus elephant, who after decades of abuse, had killed one trainer and injured another. Overseen by Thomas Edison himself, the 6,600-volt electrocution demonstrated the deadly power of alternating current (advocated by his competitor Westinghouse, in contrast to Edison's purportedly safer direct current)—associating it with the new medium of cinema and Edison Studios.[15] At the other end of the spectrum was Edison's 1910 adaptation of Mary Shelley's 1818 novel *Frankenstein* (directed by J. Searle Dawley). Complementing his elephant "snuff film" by producing a form of undead/deadly life, Edison's *Frankenstein*

[10]Cætlin Benson-Allott, *Killer Tapes and Shattered Screens: Video Spectatorship from VHS to File Sharing* (Berkeley: University of California Press, 2013).
[11]Tom Gunning, "To Scan a Ghost: The Ontology of Mediated Vision," *Grey Room* 26 (Winter 2007): 96.
[12]Ibid., 108.
[13]Tzvetan Todorov, *The Fantastic: A Structural Approach to a Literary Genre* (New York: Cornell University Press, 1975).
[14]Tom Gunning, "The Cinema of Attraction: Early Film, Its Spectator, and the Avant-Garde," in *Early Cinema: Space Frame Narrative*, edited by Thomas Elsaesser (London: BFI, 1990): 60.
[15]Sherryl Vint, *Science Fiction: A Guide for the Perplexed* (London: Bloomsbury, 2014): 19.

also betrays its investment in the cinema of attractions. Three of the film's twelve minutes are devoted to the spectacle in which the eponymous scientist flings open the doors of an immense cabinet containing a seething cauldron from which the undead monster incrementally takes shape and definition. Already, in Edison's hands, cinema and related technology had snuffed the world's largest land animal and given birth to an immortal monster in films that associated both events with the destructive power of the medium.

The German Expressionist films of the 1920s similarly betrayed cinema's origins in spectacle, if in far more sophisticated and dangerous ways. Drawing in part from a Gothic Romanticism in which sublime art is produced not through beauty and harmony but through dissonance, hazard, terror, and pain, Expressionism challenged the naturalistic norms of the current cinema. As J.P. Telotte has suggested, Expressionism was intrinsically self-reflexive, often thematizing the deceptive nature and seductive power of the medium by featuring scenes in which a showman, an insane doctor or scientist, hypnotist, or magician masterminded a crime, staged an exhibition, or created an uncanny replica, double, or automaton, as in *The Cabinet of Dr Caligari* (Robert Weiner, 1920), *The Student of Prague* (Paul Wegener, Stellan Rye and Hanns Heinz Ewers, 1913; Hanns Heinz Ewers, 1926), *Der Golem* (Paul Wegener and Carl Boese, 1920), *Waxworks* (Paul Leni, 1924), *Faust* (F. W. Murnau, 1926), as well as in Fritz Lang's *Metropolis* (1927) and his Dr. Mabuse films.[16] The carnivalesque distortions of the film's surface often projected the vision of a tyrannical and murderous madman, blurring distinctions between a key stage-managing character (Caligari, Mephisto, Rotwang, Mabuse, or Hans Beckert in Fritz Lang's *M* [1931]) and the director himself, so that the medium itself seemed murderous. Sealing this association between medium and message, Siegfried Kracauer's controversial if highly influential *From Caligari to Hitler: A Psychological History of the German Film* (1947) argued that the German Expressionist protagonist/villains, embodying the people's unconscious fear of chaos and a desire for totalitarian authority figures, "were prototypes of the madmen, charlatans and tyrants" of the Third Reich, "who took Germany, Europe, and finally of the rest of the world, into another disastrous war."[17] Similarly, Lotte Eisner's *The Haunted Screen* from 1969, working like Kracauer, from the subjective, Freudian, and ambivalent hindsight of a German Jewish exile, traced links between German Romanticism, Expressionism, and the Nazi aesthetic and mentality—hence to "snuff" in an especially horrifying sense.[18]

---

[16]J.P. Telotte, "German Expressionism: A Cinematic/Cultural Problem," in *Traditions in World Cinema*, edited by Linda Badley, Barton Palmer, and Steven Jay Schneider (Edinburgh: Edinburgh University Press, 2006): 15–28.

[17]Thomas Elsaesser, *Weimar Cinema and After: Germany's Historical Imaginary* (New York and London: Routledge, 2000): 20–21.

[18]See Ibid., 18–27.

The murderous gaze: The filmmaker as snuff artist

The notion of the filmmaker as a potential snuff artist may also be traced back to the postclassical Hollywood notion of the auteur (a point also examined in Neil Jackson's contribution to the present collection). In light of its pop-Freudian assumptions, through which art is reduced to symptom and sublimation (of trauma and neurosis) and art to a kind of psychodrama, the auteur theory is a horror story of sorts, as I have argued in an earlier essay.[19] It begins with the *Cahiers du cinema* critics, whose shared affinity for dark American genre pictures reduced postclassical cinema to a nondiscursive, inherently masculine "art of action"[20] and made Hitchcock into the "quintessential" auteur.[21] Thanks to the seminal documents of American auteurism (François Truffaut's *Hitchcock* [1967] and Andrew Sarris's *American Cinema* [1968]), which explained the auteur's "signature" in psychoanalytical terms, Hitchcock's "murderous"—obsessive, excessively controlling, death-obsessed—gaze has become synonymous with that of the visionary auteur. Horror, noir, and related genres have been redefined and refined under the aegis of Hitchcockian "suspense" until they were assimilated by the New Hollywood auteurs of the late 1960s and 1970s such as Arthur Penn, Sam Peckinpah, Brian DePalma, and Martin Scorsese, who made aestheticized violence their signature.[22] Psychoanalytic theory next inspired Laura Mulvey, who argued in 1975 that the cinematic gaze, being male, modulated between fetishistic scopophilia and sadistic voyeurism, and was deadly for women, negating female subjectivity.[23]

It is perhaps no wonder then that the auteur, envisioned as a megalomaniac genius prepared to sacrifice crew and cast members for the sake of the film, is a stereotype. Auteur biopic/"making of" films including documentaries about Werner Herzog and Francis Ford Coppola, Les Blank's *Burden of Dreams* (1982), Fax Bahr and George Hickenlooper's (and Eleanor Coppola's) *Hearts of Darkness: A Filmmaker's Apocalypse* (1991), respectively, and Clint Eastwood's fact-based

---

[19]See Linda Badley, "The Darker Side of Genius: The (Horror) Auteur Meet's Freud's Theory," in *The Horror Film and Psychoanalysis: Freud's Worst Nightmare*, edited by Steven Jay Schneider (Cambridge: Cambridge University Press, 2004): 225–28.
[20]Jim Hillier, "Introduction," "Part II: American Cinema," in *Cahiers du Cinema: The 1950s: Neo-Realism, Hollywood, New Wave*, edited by Jim Hillier (Cambridge, MA: Harvard University Press, 1985): 74.
[21]Donald Spoto, *The Dark Side of Genius: The Life of Alfred Hitchcock* (New York: De Capo Press, 1999): 495; Robert E. Kapsis, *Hitchcock: The Making of a Reputation* (Chicago, IL: Chicago University Press, 1992).
[22]Badley, "Darker Side," 225.
[23]Laura Mulvey, "Visual Pleasure and Narrative Cinema," *Screen* 16, no. 3 (1975): 6–18.

White Hunter, Black Heart (1990), about John Huston, interrogate "the pathology of the director's psyche" and confirm Werner Herzog's infamous "vision of reality" (as stated in *Burden of Dreams*) as an act of "overwhelming and collective murder."[24]

Perhaps the first direct connection between the auteur and the snuff filmmaker was made, however, by a meta-serial killer film. Michael Powell's infamous *Peeping Tom* (1960), one of the first films after Lang's *M* about a psychopathic sex murderer, anticipated the darker implications of Mulvey's "male gaze" by fifteen years, literalizing the fetishistic scopophilia and voyeuristic sadism she would find inherent in cinema in the compulsions of Mark Lewis, a focus puller who moonlights as a porn photographer/serial killer. Obsessed with the camera's power, Mark converts it into an ingeniously self-reflexive murder weapon through a tripod leg with a retractable spear and a mirror that distorts the victim's face, so that she dies transfixed in horror at the grotesquerie of her own death. Mark's aim is to make his victims comprehend in some totalizing sense their own deaths as they occur, achieving a perfect fusion of his medium (cinema as death-in-art) with life, epitomized in "woman"—the range of prostitutes, pin-up girls, fashion models, understudy actresses, and dancers he films and photographs.

Together with Hitchcock's *Psycho*, based on the case of Wisconsin serial killer Ed Gein, Powell's film explored the association between murder, cinema technology, the visual arts, and the mass media now taken for granted. And central to the serial killer mystique is the overlapping of actual cases with mass-mediated fictions, beginning with Jack the Ripper. Viewing the serial killer as a product of late capitalist media/celebrity culture, Mark Seltzer (1998) comments on the "empty circularity" of his identity; lacking a "self" outside of such social constructs, he identifies with the "type of person" projected by the media and in turn feeds into that stereotype, replenishing it.[25] This notion has increasingly written itself into the popular "profile" of the serial killer as an artist whose medium is live flesh enhanced by publicity—celebrity status and an audience being essential to his art's realization. Through a mass-mediatized "gothicization" of murder,[26] the killer's arcane rituals, signatures, and trophies constitute a kind of "snuff art," for example in the brilliantly self-reflexive *Henry, Portrait of a Serial Killer*, based loosely on the real Henry Lee Lucas, and notorious for its embedded home invasion sequence videotaped and watched by the killers that implicitly incriminates the film's audience. More often, serial murder is represented as culminating in a work of art that is part of the killer's process of self-fashioning, a process explicitly or implicitly

---

[24]Badley, "Darker Side," 224.

[25]Mark Seltzer, *Serial Killers: Death and Life in America's Wound Culture* (New York and London: Routledge, 1998): 105–25.

[26]Mark Seltzer in *Murder by Numbers*, DVD, directed by Mike Hodges (USA: Independent Film Channel, 2004).

completed in a film or a mass-mediated image. Taking this theme to a baroque extreme, the eponymous psychiatrist/serial killer of the cult television series *Hannibal* (2013–) creates an evolving work of art whose signature is testimony to his brilliance and whose insanity expressionistically informs the series' aesthetic. This understanding of murder as art and art as murder, and of the serial murderer as a technician-artist and vice versa,[27] thoroughly informs *Shadow of the Vampire*'s exploration of the mythology surrounding the making of Murnau's *Nosferatu*, to which I now turn.

The cult of *Nosferatu*: Expressionism as snuff

Although less obviously self-referential than several other seminal Expressionist films, *Nosferatu* was one of the first to reflect on the potential for innovation within the new medium, as Tom Gunning observes. Exploring "an uncanny dialectic of the visible and the invisible,"[28] of "reflections and shadow, on- and off-screen space," the film shows Murnau examining cinema's "relation to its own history and to other media"—especially scientific discourse.[29] An example is the lecture hall sequence featuring Professor Bulwer, the film's truncated version of Stoker's vampire hunter Van Helsing. Bulwer is restricted to the role of scientific authority and witness, and primarily to this one extended scene that shows him lecturing to a group of students, with the camera cutting from close-ups of a venus fly-trap closing on its victim, a spider approaching a trapped insect on its web, and a shot taken through a microscope of "a polyp with tentacles" devouring its prey. Constituting "snuff" at the microorganism level, this documentary footage radiates outward to the food chain represented in the natural world of the film—to the film's "malevolent genealogy" of bats, hyenas, horses, and even the kitten Ellen is shown playing with in the first frames.[30] The polyp is quintessentially predatory, its tentacles complementing Orlok's elongated fingers so strikingly depicted in shadows. But Bulwer dwells on its transparency; "ethereal," "a phantom almost," it uncannily lends credence to what was once thought supernatural, much as ghosts were "revealed" through nineteenth-century photographic technology, and reminds us of the phantom-like (and ultimately vampiric) nature of the medium itself. Presented without a transition, slipping imperceptibly between camera and

---

[27]Steven Jay Schneider, "Murder as Art/The Art of Murder: Aestheticising Violence in Modern Cinematic Horror," *Intensities: The Journal of Cult Media* 2, no. 1 (2003), http://intensitiescultmedia. files.wordpress.com/2012/12/schneider-murder-as-art.pdf.

[28]Gunning, "To Scan," 98.

[29]Ibid., 97

[30]Elsaesser, *Weimar Cinema and After*, 236–37.

microscope, the footage is "oddly abstracted from any specified means of seeing it, a product of cinema not wholly absorbed … a self-reflective moment that seems to float" on the screen.[31] Thus, it aligns Murnau's gaze with the implement's scientific mastery, blurring distinctions between the scientist/naturalist and the filmmaker in a subtext that surfaces in *Shadow of the Vampire*.

In its reference to visual technologies, this sequence highlights (and possibly thematizes) Murnau's "scientific" adaptation of Expressionism to naturalism, influenced by the emotionally evocative Swedish naturalism of Victor Sjöström.[32] Gilberto Perez, among others, emphasizes the film's singularity among the German Expressionists for enacting "its tale of horror … largely in natural setting rendered with emphasis."[33] Filming on location in the Slovakian mountains and Vrátna Valley at Orava Castle (including in the final shot of the ruined castle of Starhrad in Slovakia), several German municipalities including Wismar and Lubeck, and the Baltic Sea, Murnau exploited the capacity for buildings, landscapes, and natural phenomena to express extreme human emotion.

The location shooting, together with a narrator, a city scribe in the tradition of Defoe's *Journal of the Plague Year* (1722), documentary style intertitles, "authoritative" texts such as *The Book of Vampyres*, and "scientific" perspectives/ figures like Bulwer, who stand both inside and outside the narrative, lend the film the pseudoauthority of a historical record and, for its time, documentary-style realism. Through a similar logic, the vampire Count Orlok (Max Schreck) is less a symbol than a literalization of death; both ratlike and skeletal, with the bones of his skull showing through his skin, his talons growing longer throughout the film (as the fingernails of corpses, exposed by the receding flesh, are thought to grow after death), he literalizes the plague/death he embodies. Both "the agent and the icon of death," Perez notes, the vampire is "the natural cause and the supernatural symbol, metonymy combined with metaphor, at once elemental and unearthly,"[34] as when his image fades in and out through superimposition, manipulations of the negative, tinting, and "fast motion," allowing him to move at supernatural speed.

The film's "authenticity" in contrast to more recent vampire films including its immediate successor, Tod Browning's *Dracula* (1931), is legendary. For Roger Ebert, to watch *Nosferatu* is "to see the vampire movie before it had really seen itself … before it was buried alive in clichés, jokes, TV skits, cartoons and more than thirty other films. The film is in awe of its material. It seems to really believe

---

[31]Gunning, "To Scan," 98.

[32]Lotte H. Eisner, *Murnau* (Berkeley: University of California Press, 1973): 52–53, 96; Elsaesser, *Weimar Cinema and After*, 228–30.

[33]Gilberto Perez, *The Material Ghost: Films and Their Medium* (Baltimore: Johns Hopkins University Press, 1998): 123.

[34]Ibid., 125.

in vampires."[35] Apparently, for Katz and Merhige, the film achieved something like the ultimate special effect sought by the cinema of attraction: the "real" thing captured or conjured on screen—in this instance, embodied death. Death dominates the space of the frame, as in the legendary shot from the ship's hold in which Nosferatu's image glides around the perimeters of the frame to suggest that "The death ship had a new captain." Elsewhere, his superimposed image or shadow blights and transforms the natural surroundings. Thus, the shadow of the vampire's hand, at once an image of death and an effect produced by cinema technology, reaches out and grasps her heart, snuffing it as Ellen twitches and slumps. For Perez, the fusion of Expressionism with "documentary" style naturalism evokes the existential experience as never before on film. In the end, it is not simply that Ellen's sacrifice for love conquers the Black Death or even that Death itself dies, eradicated by the light of the sun. From the beginning, as Ellen anticipates and then confronts death in fear, loathing, and anguish, the film captures the experience of what Heidegger called "being toward death."[36]

For these and other, more sensational reasons, *Nosferatu* became one of the earliest cult films, and, as one blog speculates, "its cult following was the one thing that saved it."[37] Although the filmmakers changed the locations, character names, and much of the plot, Grau took the story of an Eastern European vampire's colonization of the West from Bram Stoker's *Dracula* (1897) without requesting rights to the material. When Stoker's widow sued Prana for copyright infringement and ordered all prints destroyed, the fledgling company filed for bankruptcy. Thanks to the film's (and Prana's) sanctioned "execution," all but nonexistent, *Nosferatu* acquired a mystique with parallels to that of snuff itself.

By the 1960s through the 1980s, with the influx of European arthouse cinema followed by the videotape era, the film was rediscovered through surviving prints, and sold, in muddy, fragmentary versions, in paracinema mail order catalogs alongside exploitation films like *Jail Bait* (Ed Wood, 1954),[38] with Image Entertainment and Kino International producing reconstructed and remastered DVD versions in the 1990s and 2000s. Notably, the era that mainstreamed exploitation film and helped generate the snuff phenomenon was the same one in which *Nosferatu* rose to its currently elevated status as an art film masterpiece.

The film's "lost" status, lack of information about the actor who played the vampire, and his name, Max Schreck, meaning "fright" or "terror" in German,

---

[35]Roger Ebert, "*Nosferatu,*" *Roger Ebert.com*, 1997, http://rogerebert.suntimes.com/apps/pbcs.dll/article?AID=/19970928/REVIEWS08/401010345/1023.

[36]Perez, *The Material Ghost*, 128–29.

[37]"Nosferatu," *Cult Indie Art House "B" Movies with Subtitles*, 2014, http://cultindiebmovies.wordpress.com/2014/04/28/nosferatu-a-symphony-of-horror-1922/.

[38]Joan Hawkins, "Sleaze Mania, Euro-Trash, and High Art," *Horror: The Film Reader*, edited by Mark Jancovich (London and New York: Routledge, 2002): 125–34.

contributed to rumors that he was (a) a method actor, (b) not quite human, and/ or (c) had mysteriously disappeared with the film, perhaps "snuffed" in its final frames.[39] An aura of admiration and mystery had similarly arisen around Murnau in part because, as Lotte Eisner stresses, so much was unknown: nearly half his films had been destroyed or mutilated, especially between 1919 and 1924, and, dying suddenly in his prime (in 1931, at 42), Murnau and his films virtually vanished during the sound era until well after World War II.[40] Born Wilhem Friedrich Plumpe to a family of wealthy textile manufacturers, he took the name Murnau from an artists' colony in the Bavarian Alps and jealously guarded his identity, bisexuality, and privacy.[41] Like his chief rival Lang, Murnau allowed UFA publicity to portray him as "a dandy, an aristocrat of the spirit" addressed as "Herr Docktor" (because of his university studies), setting off his natural aloofness and perfectionism.[42] His shoots were ambitious, experimental, and arduous, as Eisner states; work was "a kind of intoxication: he was fascinated and gripped by the actual processes, carried away in spite of himself, like a scientist performing an experiment in a laboratory or a surgeon during a complicated operation."[43]

In Hollywood after 1926, "Docktor Murnau" sustained this reputation of being "difficult and a recluse" immersed in astrology, Eastern philosophy, and the occult.[44] This was exacerbated by his association with producer and production designer Albin Grau, whose fascination with the occult resulted in the hermetic and alchemical symbols of the real estate contract, Orlok's naturalistically emaciated look, and probably the film's title, from a Serbian word for *undead*, included in Grau's article on "Vampires" in *Buhne and Film*, published in 1922 as publicity for the upcoming film. This included an old Serbian peasant's account of his own father who, having died without sacraments, preyed on the people of his village and was exhumed in 1884. The peasant produced an official document that said the body was undecomposed and teeth were long, sharp, and protruding.[45]

Rumors that Schreck was Murnau's vampire double were enhanced by (and confused with) those surrounding the volatile Werner Herzog/Klaus Kinski collaboration. As *Mein liebster Feind* (1999), Herzog's cinematic biography of Kinski, suggests, the collaboration resulted in an oeuvre resembling psychodrama, with a chillingly realistic, often rabid Kinski performing as the monomaniacal

---

[39]Actually, Schreck had been a performer with Max Rheinhardt's theater company, known for its naturalistic style, and after *Nosferatu* became a popular character actor in German films—none of which were released overseas. ("Nosferatu at 90: Who Was Max Schreck?," *The Vault of Horror Blogspot.com* 2012, http://thevaultof/horror.blogspot.com/2012/05/nosferatu-at-90-who-was-max-schreck.html.)
[40]Eisner, *Murnau*, 5–6.
[41]Elsaesser, *Weimar Cinema and After*, 225.
[42]Ibid., 225.
[43]Eisner, *Murnau*, 70.
[44]Elsaesser, *Weimar Cinema and After*, 226.
[45]Eisner, *Murnau*, 108–09.

Herzog's id or shadow—perhaps most notably in Herzog's stunning remake/homage of 1979, *Nosferatu: Phantom der Nacht*, with Kinski as the vampire.[46]

Cinema as snuff: Shadow of the vampire

A "deconstruction of the mythology surrounding [Murnau] and the making of *Nosferatu*" detailed above,[47] *Shadow of the Vampire* suggests the various senses, reverent and irreverent, in which the first vampire film and one of cinema's first masterpieces may have been a product of the "murderous gaze" and art as murder—thus a "snuff" film par excellence. At the time, cinema was considered "a fringe art form … second to theater … [and/or] sorcery … black magic."[48] Yet the idea for the film originated in screenwriter Stephen Katz's infatuation with *Nosferatu*'s uncanny naturalism, describing the film as "incredibly realistic to the point that you almost think you are watching an old documentary about a vampire."[49] An archival photograph of the filmmakers in lab coats and goggles further supplied the idea of Murnau approaching the film "as a scientific project"[50] and triggered the theme of cinema as modern science meeting the ancient world already implicit in Stoker's novel and the original film. Although Murnau incorporated real footage of microorganismic "vampirism," Merhige seamlessly embedded footage from the original film in iconic sequences.

Penetrating the labial center of an Art-Deco frieze, the opening credit sequence suggests with insidious elegance the voyeurism of the camera's gaze. Surveying art styles from the turn of the century to the 1920s—from art nouveau to futurism, fauvism, and cubism—the machine culture underlying many of these movements becomes increasing to the fore as a reminder of cinema as a potentially lethal technology. A succession of battle scenes from the Greeks to the historical Dracula's armies to the twentieth century follows. Thus, technology, Modernist art, and war are linked narratively and aesthetically to represent the march of change,[51] modernization colonizing the natural world and ancient cultures.

---

[46]Linda Badley, "The Shadow and the Auteur: Herzog's Kinski, Kinski's Nosferatu, and Myths of Authorship," in *Caligari's Heirs: The German Cinema of Fear after 1945*, edited by Steffen Hantke, (Lanham, MD: Scarecrow Press, 2007): 57–78.

[47]Merhige, quoted in "Interview with E. Elias Merhige," *Shadow of the Vampire*, DVD, (Saturn/Lion's Gate/Universal, 2000).

[48]Merhige, quoted in Anthony Kaufmann, "Interview: The Vampiric Arts of Merhige and Dafoe in 'Shadow,'" *Indiewire* 2000, accessed May 11, 2014, http://www.indiewire.com/people/int_Merhige_E.Elias_01010155.html.

[49]"Production Notes," *Shadow of the Vampire*, DVD (Saturn/Lion's Gate/Universal, 2000).

[50]Ibid.

[51]"Feature Commentary with E. Elias Merhige," *Shadow of the Vampire*, DVD (2000, Saturn/Lion's Gate, Universal, 2000).

The opening shot—an extreme close-up of a lens that cuts to Murnau's (John Malkovich's) eye—suggests a "cinematic territorialism" that links to this motif.[52] The next shots depict the filmmakers on a platform high above the actors and alternates between extremely low and high angles to produce anxiety in the expressionist style. Merhige explains that he intended to suggest a new "pantheon," with the filmmaker the new god or Promethean "maker" of the new century. Like the real Murnau, Malkovich dictates the actors' lines, "imposing his [auteur's] vision on the proceedings."[53]

The mystique of Murnau's technological mastery is repeatedly indicated—the air of "dandified" aristocracy complemented by the filmmakers' lab coats (accented by goggles, which protected them from the acidic dust given off by the arc lamps) and the requisite "Herr Docktor," incorporated into Malkovich's performance as a Caligari-esque/Frankensteinian mad scientist. *Shadow* thus prefigures (through hindsight) the real Murnau's *Faust*, the technological ambition and achievement of whose special effects, alongside those of *Metropolis*, would be unsurpassed until the 1960s, as Malkovich's Murnau is a type of Faust who has made a pact with the Mephistophelean Orlok. The film explores the sinister implications of Murnau's experimentalism and perfectionism, which turned the "pestilence of World War I … into an effigy"[54] and may have predicted what followed. In the penultimate sequence, in which a drugged and raving Malkovich confesses his pact with Schreck, occult symbols and swastikas are scrawled on the walls of his bedroom to predict the birth of Hitler's Nazi iconography.

Per German Expressionism, war, cinema, and snuff are linked throughout the film. In a motif that recalls Murnau's real collaboration with photographer Fritz Arno Wagner, Cary Elwes as the latter, characterized as a daredevil fighter pilot who shoots off guns to startle extras into authentic terror and refers to a particular camera as his "weapon of choice," alludes to the real Murnau's war experience. In Jim Shepard biographical novel *Nosferatu* (1998), Murnau discovers his calling as a virtuoso World War I fighter pilot who supernaturally walks away from downed airplanes and conceives of the gun sight as a camera that simultaneously aims, fires, and distances him from carnage: "I am an icy scientist, and for me their war is a laboratory experiment."[55] Sighting targets while flying gives him a "new manner of perception" that suggests the moving camera with which Murnau came to be associated: "What sort of image could the photographer record with such an advantage? What sort of image could the *motion picture* record?"[56] This notion of

---

[52]Badley, "Darker Side," 227.
[53]"Feature Commentary."
[54]Merhige, quoted in "Interview."
[55]Shepard, *Nosferatu*, 65.
[56]Ibid., 62.

the camera as lethal weapon becomes sinisterly funny at the end of the film when Malkovich and Elwes, intense and focused, work as a unit to drug Greta and shoot her snuff scene.

With Herzog's role of auteur/adventurer/conquistador *a la Fitzcarraldo/ Burden of Dreams* as another precedent, Malkovich sees himself forging a route into territory untouched by civilization. Murnau's Expressionistic naturalism becomes the techno-pioneer's conquest of nature associated with the locomotive (ominously named "Charon") that takes the company to their locations deep in the wilderness of Czechoslovakia, with the film as their guarantee of the immortality insured by such risk. Over the train, Murnau's proclaims in stentorious voiceover that "we are scientists in search of memory … that will neither blur nor fade … ," predicting that "our" art "will have a context as certain as the grave." He coerces indigenous peasants into working as extras—much as he has contracted "Schreck" (Willem Dafoe) an ancient creature he claims to have stumbled upon in a cave, to perform as himself.

Schreck's anachronistic reputation as a "method" actor, elaborated through allusions to the fraught Herzog–Kinski relationship in which "they both want each other dead, but … can't live without each other,"[57] provides the central conflict. Like the real Kinski, Dafoe's Schreck discovers his own auteurist instincts and competes with Murnau for control of the shoot. He demands makeup and relocations, views dailies, consumes "disposable" crew members and, when Ellen's death scene approaches, takes over the set, threatening "I want her now!" The question becomes who or what is *more* vampiric, Schreck or Murnau—or the cinematic apparatus itself? As in the serial killer subgenre, especially *Hannibal*, protagonist and antagonist become artful doubles. Ultimately, Schreck and Murnau reverse roles, with Murnau increasingly intent on the capture and consumption of his prey and the vampire discovering the instincts and technologies of the filmmaker. In the film's final twist, cinema technology, having possessed both Schreck and Murnau (and Wagner), trumps them all.

Apropos of *Nosferatu*'s Faustian "infernal contract" narrative, leading lady Greta Schroeder's (Catherine McCormack) lifeblood is promised to Schreck in exchange for his "live" performance. Greta's fate is sealed in the first scene when she complains about leaving Berlin's theater scene to make a mere movie. "A theatrical audience gives me life," she quips; "this … *thing* [camera] only takes it from me." "[This] is the role that will make you great as an actress," Malkovich reassures. "Consider it a sacrifice for your art." Greta thus takes on Ellen's role as Woman, lover, mother, object, and origin of the oral/aggressive drive inherent in Schreck/Nosferatu's thirst, "She came to me in the night and then she went away,"

---

[57]Merhige quoted in Kaufman.

and he has attempted to capture her in fetish images ever since, he explains—in drawing, marble, and memory.[58]

The film's "snuff" conclusion refers backward (and forward) to the venerated tradition that comes to the fore in *Psycho*, *Peeping Tom*, and the slasher and serial killer genres in which the woman-as-abject dies in a protracted scene, with Katz and Merhige departing from Murnau in making the leading lady complicit in her fate. Where *Nosferatu*'s Ellen is intelligent, strongly ethical, and selfless, McCormick's Greta is a stereotypical diva—vain, demanding, and drug-addled—prized solely for her role as woman/actress/fetish, cinema's and the vampire's natural prey. We thus feel more disturbed when the filmmakers render her helpless and fatally compliant, injecting her with morphine to prepare her for her (real) death scene, a caricature of a caricature of woman-as-victim. "In this scene you make the ultimate sacrifice," Malkovich repeats to her dilated stare.

As a crowning achievement, however, this snuff film demands nothing less than the vampire's real destruction on screen, signifying the triumph of art over mortality and even Schreck's brand of undead immortality. "If it's not in frame, it doesn't exist!" an exasperated Murnau screams at Schreck when his frantic final antics (as he snaps Wagner's neck) fall out of the camera's range. Returning to his mark, having satiated himself on the dying Greta (with Malkovich fixedly cranking Murnau's actual camera, the sound enhanced to suggest a World War I Gatling gun[59]), the vampire rises in stupefaction, dazzled by the in-pouring light, as his image merges with an image of celluloid incinerating under the heat/light of the camera's lamp. The apparatus upstages and consumes him, its lens glowing preternaturally, in a literalization of snuff that refers to the film's original title, "Burned to Light," meaning the photographic process by which images are "burned" to a celluloid print. "Now … moon chaser, monkey, vase of prehistory, finally to earth, and finally born," Murnau intones. "This will be our very own cave painting on our very own wall. Time will no longer be a dark spot on our lung."

Much earlier, in the film's most poignant scene, as Schreck tinkers with the projector late at night, he discovers the new, undead world of cinema technology for himself.[60] Extending and retracting his talons in the light, he watches with childlike fascination the shadow of his hand and gazes with preternatural arousal at a flickering image of the sunrise, which Murnau's dailies allow him to see for the first time in centuries. The image is repeated in the chilling final sequence when the shadow of the vampire's hand snuffs out Greta's beating heart. In this gesture, which duplicates the real Murnau's signature, Merhige alludes to the visionary power of the historical Murnau, Malkovich's caricature of the Pantheon auteur

---

[58]Badley, "Darker Side," 229.
[59]"Feature Commentary."
[60]See Badley, "Darker Side," 129–30.

as snuff artist, his own metacinematic feat, and a century-long heritage of horror, noir, serial killer, and exploitation film. The final image of the burning light in the lens refers back to the very first shot of Malkovich's eye sighting his target.

A metafilm about the long-dead era of silent cinema, *Shadow of the Vampire* is equally cognizant of its arrival at "the end of cinema." Released in the millennial year 2000, three years after the first marketing of film in a digital format,[61] it commemorated the birth of analog cinema and prefigured its imminent death. Finally, it represented the "end" of cinema in another sense—as postmodern metacinema, as even favorable reviews often mentioned: that the film was a postmillennial gesture for a small effete audience of critics and film buffs, an academic exercise rather than a "real" film (however, much this was Merhige's point). In representing Murnau's pioneer work as cinema just beginning to realize its creative potential, and even as it celebrates *Nosferatu*'s "documentary" naturalism, *Shadow* presents itself as a movie in the death throes of Baudrillardian hyperreality. In this way as well, its double is Dafoe's vampire, who compares himself to Tithonus, revealing that immortality without youth is a curse and that he can no longer make other vampires (or possibly never could). Representing cinema's essential association with death—cinema *as* snuff—*Shadow of the Vampire* simultaneously stands for cinema (analog, classical, and postclassical Hollywood) snuffed. Today, amid the stark brutality of the digital online snuff disseminated by drug lords and jihadists, this millennial film marks how far we have descended from the elegantly stylized "documentary" resonance of Murnau's work.

---

[61]Mulvey, *Death 24 x a Second*, 18.

14 AFFECT AND THE ETHICS OF SNUFF IN EXTREME ART CINEMA

Tina Kendall

This chapter considers the cultural mythology of the snuff film in relation to the paradigm of the "new extremism" in global art cinema. It will locate the trope of snuff —defined here as a fictional narrative device that features an ostensibly "real" act of killing captured on camera—as a key source of fascination for this group of films, known as much for their art house sensibilities and cultural credibility as they are for their willful violation of boundaries between reality and fiction, and their courting of controversy through graphic depictions of sex and violence.[1] The term new extremism has been used to describe a tendency in art cinema since around the 1990s, toward an explicit and willfully confrontational style of filmmaking embodied by the likes of Gaspar Noé, Lars von Trier, Michael Haneke, Lukas Moodysson, and others. Thematically, the extremity of these films is amply exhibited through their presentation of a range of taboo subject matter, including rape, necrophilia, incest, self-mutilation, auto-cannibalism, and so on. Aesthetically, these films deploy a range of generic conventions typically associated with exploitation or body genres, including gore, pornography, and realist horror, in order to amplify the visceral and transgressive charge of what they show. But at the same time, they incorporate these genre codes within an art house formula that also privileges a high degree of formal reflexivity, referencing a range of culturally distinct philosophical and artistic traditions. While this mixing of exploitation and art cinema codes has made for a particularly volatile reception history, the formal experimentalism of these auteur-driven films, and

---

[1]Tanya Horeck and Tina Kendall, eds, *The New Extremism in Cinema: From France to Europe* (Edinburgh: Edinburgh University Press, 2011).

their appearance in culturally reputable film festival circuits—including Cannes, Venice and Berlin—has helped to shore up their status as art.[2] Indeed, as Laura Hubner notes, "it is around the question of artistic truth and the films' projection of 'authentic' thematic concerns that the cinema of the new extremism has tended to be judged."[3] The art house credentials of these films lends cultural legitimacy to, and opens transnational channels of dissemination for, their sensational subject matter, and while the new extremism often explores similar thematic terrain to other snuff-themed films explored in this collection, it uses different strategies of containment, and is marketed to a different type of spectator.

This chapter explores what happens when the trope of snuff—with its cultural associations with cheap sensationalism, sexual exploitation, and moral degradation—is brought into dialog with the art film's connotations of quality, self-reflexivity, and criticality. Drawing on a range of films, including *Benny's Video* (Michael Haneke, 1992), *Afterschool* (Antonio Campos, 2008), *The Life and Death of a Porno Gang* (Mladen Djordjević, 2009), and *A Serbian Film* (Srdjan Spasojević, 2010), it will consider how these films rework some of the key aesthetic and extratextual features of snuff-themed movies. I will argue that the snuff device works to foreground questions about spectatorial response and responsibility that are given renewed urgency in a global digital network culture. While self-reflexivity is at least an implicit feature of most snuff-themed films, as David Kerekes and David Slater have noted of the Italian "mondo" and "cannibal" cycle, or as Johnny Walker and Alexandra Heller-Nicholas have suggested of "found footage" horror, when a snuff element is imported into extreme art cinema, it tends to amplify questions of spectatorial complicity, making ethical reflexivity a strong component of the intensely affective and problematic experience of watching.[4] Drawing from work by Vivian Sobchack,[5] Sue Tait,[6] and Michele Aaron,[7] the chapter argues that the

[2]See Jonathan Romney, "Le Sex and Violence," *The Independent*, September 12, 2004, accessed July 17, 2014. http://www.independent.co.uk/arts-entertainment/films/features/le-sex-and-violence-6161908. html, and Hampus Hagman, "Every Cannes Needs Its Scandal: Between Art and Exploitation in Contemporary French Film," *Film International* 29 (2007): 32–41.

[3]Laura Hubner, "A Vogue for Flesh and Blood? Shifting Classifications of Contemporary European Cinema," in *Valuing Films: Shifting Perceptions of Worth*, edited by Laura Hubner (London: Palgrave Macmillan, 2011): 198.

[4]David Kerekes and David Slater, *Killing for Culture: An Illustrated History of Death from Mondo to Snuff* (London: Headpress, 1995); Johnny Walker, "Nasty Visions: Violent Spectacle in Contemporary British Horror Cinema," *Horror Studies* 2, no. 1 (2011): 115–30; Alexandra Heller-Nicholas, *Found Footage Horror Films: Fear and the Appearance of Reality* (Jefferson, NC: McFarland, 2014).

[5]Vivan Sobchack, *Carnal Thoughts: Embodiment and Moving Image Culture* (Berkeley and Los Angeles: University of California Press, 2004).

[6]Sue Tait, "Visualising Technologies and the Ethics and Aesthetics of Screening Death," *Science as Culture* 18, no. 3 (2009): 333–53.

[7]Michele Aaron, *Death and the Moving Image: Ideology, Iconography, I* (Edinburgh: Edinburgh University Press, 2014).

snuff movie conceit in new extreme cinema telescopes a range of anxieties about complicit witnessing and the affective and ethical dimensions of spectatorship in a global digital network culture. In doing so, the figure of snuff works to reframe and revivify our mediated relationship with real death, conferring affective intensity to the experience of viewing the suffering and demise of others.

The aesthetics and ethics of snuff

Work to date on the cultural mythology of snuff has highlighted the way that key aesthetic and extratextual features of putative snuff films work to violate carefully sanctioned distinctions between factual and fictional modes of representation, creating a strong impression of reality in their depiction of killing on camera, which spills over onto the cultural reception of these films. The "aura of snuff" that these movies generate is, as Julian Petley notes, stubbornly persistent, with press reports feeding the mythology through periodic alleged discoveries of "the real thing."[8] The controversies around snuff movies betray deep cultural anxieties around a range of issues, including "mercenary media voyeurism and sensationalism,"[9] the "misogyny of pornography,"[10] as well as profound uncertainties around the role of images as guarantors of reality.[11] Indeed, a prime focus of existing scholarship on snuff movie mythology concerns the crisis in representation that these films stage for viewers, seeming to "testify to the verisimilitude of what is being shown on screen" while operating "self-reflexively, drawing attention to the process of filmic representation itself and demonstrating that even the most 'realist'-seeming text is in fact an artificial construct."[12]

According to Vivian Sobchack, such moments of uncertainty surrounding the status of killing on camera derive a powerful affective charge from the way they challenge cultural understandings of death as that which confounds and exceeds representation. In her discussion of Jean Renoir's *Rules of the Game* (1939), Sobchack notes a distinction between the fictional death of a human character, and the real death of a rabbit, arguing that while the man's death is "merely represented," and hence safely contained within the narrative, the rabbit's actual death exceeds narrative codes, to point to what she calls "an extratextual

---

[8]Julian Petley, "*Cannibal Holocaust* and the Pornography of Death," in *The Spectacle of the Real: From Hollywood to Reality TV and Beyond*, edited by Geoff King (Bristol: Intellect, 2005): 173.

[9]Ibid., 177.

[10]LaBelle quoted in Linda Williams, "Power, Pleasure and Perversion: Sadomasochistic Film Pornography," *Representations* 27 (1989): 39.

[11]Dolores Tierney, "The Appeal of the Real in Snuff: Alejandro Amenábar's *Tesis* (Thesis)," Spectator 22, no. 2 (2002): 45–55.

[12]Petley, "*Cannibal Holocaust* and the Pornography of Death," 179.

and animate referent, executed not only *by* but also *for* the representation."[13] This distinction relies on the spectator's "extracinematic knowledge," which works to contextualize and transform its affective function: knowing that the rabbit's death is real confers the experience of watching it with a transgressive, affective charge, because as Sobchack suggests, the sight of death "puts us in the role of someone who violates a taboo."[14] And as Sobchack goes on to note, the "titillating ambiguity" of the alleged snuff film derives precisely from its supposedly undecidable "ontological status": in these films, death is staged for the camera as if it were real, whereas our common sense tells us it couldn't possibly be.[15] What the controversy surrounding the potential existence of snuff films foregrounds above all is the "shaky extracinematic grounds" on which our experience of watching films is founded.[16]

It is precisely this uncertain, shaky ground that many of the films of the new extremism attempt to key into through their presentation of real sex, their use of real subjects in real locations, and through the slaughter of real animals. Indeed, many of these films draw their confrontational power to shock from the complex ways in which they seek to mobilize the affective, visceral force of the real within representation.[17] For instance, films such as *Anatomy of Hell* (Catherine Breillat, 2004), *Baise-moi* (Virginie Despentes and Coralie Trinh Thi, 2000), *Twentynine Palms* (Bruno Dumont, 2003), and *Ma mère* (Christophe Honoré, 2004) register this force of the real through the inclusion of explicit nonsimulated sex, the use of nonprofessional actors, and found locations that include unwitting members of the public within the fictional frame. More problematically, in *The Idiots* (1998), director Lars von Trier includes nonprofessional actors with Down Syndrome, who serve as a foil for the fictional idiots' attempts to pass off their fake "spassing" as the real deal, while Ulrich Seidl films actual dementia patients in an actual care home to serve as a kind of authentic hinterland against which the drama of fictional characters is played out in *Import/Export* (2007).

These films draw their power to shock from the same ontological instability between reality and representation that is at the heart of the mythology surrounding the snuff film. Indeed, there may be something of this ontological confusion at work in many of the controversies that the films of the new extremism have generated, as in frequent news reports detailing mass walkouts, or spectators passing out or vomiting in the aisles.[18] While these stories affirm the controversial nature of the work, they also testify to the porous, unstable boundaries between

---

[13]Sobchack, *Carnal Thoughts*, 247.
[14]Ibid., 241.
[15]Ibid., 247.
[16]Ibid.
[17]Horeck and Kendall, *The New Extremism in Cinema*.
[18]Hagman, "Every Cannes Needs Its Scandal."

reality and representation, in the sense that the fictional representation produces (or is imagined to produce) *real* effects on *real* bodies in *real* life. So regardless of whether we "know" that the spectacles of death unfolding in front of us are "only" fictional, what new extreme cinema shares with controversies surrounding the snuff film is a powerful ability to make us participate both affectively and viscerally with the spectacle of seemingly real death that is in any case *for* our enjoyment, evaluation, or discernment. As Misha Kavka notes in her essay in this volume, it is the "affective reality" that is above all privileged through the device of snuff. What new extreme cinema stages for us through this ontological instability is not so much a crisis of knowledge—is this death real or not?—as a crisis of response— how are we intended to *respond* to it?

This question of response is key for Sobchack's discussion of ethics in *Carnal Thoughts*. A prime concern for Sobchack is how we can secure an ethical responsiveness to the world through our embodied engagement with moving image culture, including a response to the images of death—both documentary and fictional—that circulate through the media. For Sobchack, it is precisely the "charge of the real" within representation that carries ethical salience. She argues: "The charge of the real always is also [...] an *ethical charge*: one that calls forth not only response but responsibility—not only aesthetic valuation but ethical judgement. It engages our awareness not only of the existential consequences *of* representation but also of our own ethical implication *in* representation."[19]

Snuff in extreme art cinema

Taking my cue from Vivian Sobchack, I want to investigate the ethical questions that arise from the filmic treatment of death as a spectacle that is offered up to our vision, and *for* our vision. However, as I'll argue, snuff mythology as it is deployed within contemporary extreme art cinema problematizes Sobchack's phenomenological and existential model of ethics, and calls for a reappraisal of some of her claims. First, I think we need to question her location of ethics as always unambiguously aligned with documentary space. For her, documentary space is charged with ethical salience because of its grounding in the filmmaker's embodied, existential relationship with profilmic reality; the spectator participates in the "ethical relationship" constituted between the "morally framed" vision of the filmmaker and his or her own.[20] But as we have already seen, these distinctions between documentary and fiction are nowhere near as stable as Sobchack assumes them to be, especially where both snuff and new extreme cinema are

[19]Sobchack, *Carnal Thoughts*, 284.
[20]Ibid., 243.

concerned. I would agree with Lisa Downing and Libby Saxton's claim in *Film and Ethics: Foreclosed Encounters* that "images of real and fictional suffering" are not opposed, but "belong, rather, to the same ethical continuum" and provide "critical perspectives on each other."[21] Secondly, I argue that we need to think about the complex ways in which new media technologies have reframed and renegotiated our cultural relationship with death, such that the sight of death is no longer subject to a shared moral vision in the way Sobchack describes. More radically, death captured on camera today no longer necessarily corresponds to an embodied, existential human vision in the same sense at all. The ubiquity of digital technologies for the generation, transmission, and consumption of images—including images of atrocity and suffering from combat videos and footage of executions, to surveillance footage of mortal accidents, and numerous other forms of body horror—have made the sight of real death more than mere mythology, and have removed it further from the moral and ethical frames that previously worked to bind it. As Sue Tait notes, the glut of such material that is available on video-sharing sites such as YouTube, LiveLeak, and others reflects "that online the normative ethical space around imagery of death is being reconfigured, and in some senses evacuated," such that screening footage of death is no longer tethered to "a sense of 'duty'," but is "treated as a source of pleasure."[22] Indeed, what I want to explore in this chapter is how the loosening of normative ethical frames and taboos surrounding death opens a valuable space of ambiguity between the spectator and moving image culture, in which one's own relationship and implication with death may be explored, revitalized, and revivified through the snuff device. More important than parsing distinctions between fiction and reality, or pleasure and unpleasure for this ethical evaluation of snuff is the task of thinking about the affective modes of response that films perform and make available to us in asking us to think about our relationship with images of death. In the films that I will discuss, renewed ethical reflexivity is made possible through an appeal to affect and the spectator's implication in what they see. As Michele Aaron suggests in *Death and the Moving Image*, the ethical potential of screening death resides precisely in the shared affective encounter between film and spectator, conceived as a "zone of raw contact between the self and others where cinema affords individuals an unscripted sense of their place in the world and in relation to the rest of humanity."[23]

In what follows, I want to think about how some of the films of the new extremism play on the conceit of the snuff film, and on the lure of death as

---

[21]Lisa Downing and Libby Saxton, *Film and Ethics: Foreclosed Encounters* (Abingdon: Routledge, 2009): 68.
[22]Sue Tait, "Visualising Technologies and the Ethics and Aesthetics of Screening Death," 346.
[23]Aaron, *Death and the Moving Image*, 117.

something that might be captured as a spectacle for our entertainment. The films I analyze here pose ethical questions, and solicit affective responses through their deployment of very different aesthetic and affective styles. These contrasting styles may be viewed in relation to Martine Beugnet and Elizabeth Ezra's distinction between an "aesthetic of expenditure" versus an "aesthetic of restraint."[24] While *The Life & Death of a Porno Gang* and *A Serbian Film* deal directly with the snuff movie conceit, and work within a showy, over-the-top, hyperbolic aesthetic and affective "mode of expenditure," *Benny's Video* and *Afterschool* address the conceit of snuff more obliquely, placing the spectacle of death within a much more subdued "aesthetic of restraint." This mode of restraint establishes a tone of banality that draws on the spectator's extracinematic and experiential knowledge, but ultimately does so to puncture this safe familiarity with the eruption of death within that frame. However, while the "aesthetic of expenditure" puts this spectacle of death on full display, the "aesthetic of restraint" more typically withholds or interrupts our access to the moment of death, to focus instead on the act of witnessing and responding to it. While "the aesthetic of expenditure" is characterized by a mood of hysteria and excess, which it uses as a form of affective contagion to implicate the spectator, the "aesthetic of restraint" produces a mood of disturbing indifference, which indicts the spectator and demands an affective response that is lacking. What is foregrounded and performed through each affective style are ethical questions about how we should respond to the images of death that these films put so sensationally and disturbingly on display for us. Ultimately, I will argue that both aesthetic and affective styles are valuable in helping us to think through, sense, and experience our problematic relationship to the spectacle of death that is insistently circulated in a global digital culture.

An aesthetic of restraint

Benny's Video and *Afterschool* reference the snuff movie trope through their respective plotlines, which feature acts of killing/death that are captured on video or digital camera, and coded as real within the diegesis. Formally, these films reference a wide variety of moving image media, drawing on the spectator's extracinematic knowledge and creating clear associations between diegetic and extradiegetic modes of capturing and responding to spectacles of violence and death in a contemporary network culture. These films operate in thematic terrain that is similar to David Cronenberg's *Videodrome* (1983, Canada) or Alejandro Amenábar's *Tesis* (1996, Spain), in which the threat of snuff is directly related to

---

[24]Martine Beugnet and Elizabeth Ezra, "Traces of the Modern: An Alternative History of French Cinema," *Studies in French Cinema* 10, no. 1 (2010): 11–38.

a context of media proliferation and overstimulation. Speaking of the film *Tesis*, Dolores Tierney notes that the role of snuff in this context works to mobilize "a fascination with (and a desire for) the real" and to "crystallize diffuse postmodern anxieties as to whether the real can be accessed at all through media/ted images."[25] While both films certainly tap into similar anxieties about the location of the real, they also dramatize and problematize the notion of affective response and the responsibility of the spectator in relation to what is seen. One of the most striking aspects of both of these films is the contrast that is established between the horrific deaths that are shown or suggested, and the tone of calm, detached, or glibly ironic distance that is established through their "aesthetic of restraint." Furthermore, both *Benny's Video* and *Afterschool* feature central characters who respond with cool detachment and indifference to deaths that they witness. As I will argue, when it is used in conjunction with the snuff device, the mode of restraint helps to articulate a crisis of response, which foregrounds questions of ethical responsibility in a media-saturated environment.

Michael Haneke's *Benny's Video* famously begins with a home video picturing the slaughter of a real pig, which Benny compulsively watches, pauses, rewinds, and rewatches, scanning the image for signs that would reveal the truth of death, and offer up the shock of the real. Meanwhile, Benny is surrounded by multiple television screens and video monitors that reflect back endless images of violence, suffering, and death: from the television news reports telling of death and political violence in Bosnia, to schlocky exploitation videos that he hires at the local video shop, to his own home videos, Benny's existential reality is made up of media images. In Brigitte Peucker's view, the film thus gestures toward the ways in which media images have "anaesthetized our capacity to respond to scenes of suffering."[26] Under the cover of objectivity, she notes, television coverage offers a cold, detached, and "sanitized version of the real precisely where the spectator has come to feel that she has access to immediacy."[27] The problem, as staged by *Benny's Video*, is not so much that Benny is intellectually incapable of telling the difference between "real" death and death that is staged for our information (as in the news media) or for our entertainment (as in the schlocky horror films he watches). Rather, the film suggests that in the face of so many endlessly repeating images of death, the normative ethical frames that once bound and differentiated such images are being eroded. The crisis that is staged at the outset is hence not a crisis of ontology—how we might discern what is real from what is not—but a crisis of response. Benny's role in the film is to foreground questions about the role

---

[25]Tierney, "The Appeal of the Real in Snuff," 45.
[26]Brigitte Peucker, *The Material Image: Art and the Real in Film* (Stanford, CA: Stanford University Press, 2007): 136.
[27]Ibid.

of the spectator in relation to images of suffering and death, and to problematize the very notion of an appropriate affective response, which would mitigate the violent intensity of images.

This is the backdrop against which the snuff device is played out in *Benny's Video*, as Benny invites a young girl who he meets at a local video shop home with him. Once in his room, Benny shows the girl his video of the slaughtered pig, shows her the weapon used to kill it, and then—after a childlike exchange of dares—Benny ends up shooting the girl with the same stun gun used to kill the pig. As she falls, we see that this scene has been captured on one of Benny's ubiquitous cameras, and as she writhes and screams partially out of frame, Benny frenetically reloads his gun and shoots her several more times until she finally dies. The next sequence shows Benny calmly pouring himself a glass of water, then opening and eating a pot of yoghurt (Figure 14.1).

Part of the visceral intensity of this scene lies in the way that the conditions surrounding this girl's death—in particular the sound of her screams—mimic and evoke those of the real slaughtered pig that we see in the opening sequence, the real lending an existential weight to the fiction, as Sobchack would have it. However, more significant than parsing such distinctions between reality and fiction in this scene is the stark contrast between the weighty ethical and existential stakes of what is shown, and the aesthetic and affective frame that contains it. What is most striking about Haneke's blocking of this sequence is the way that both cameras—Haneke's and Benny's—remain in the position of static, unmoved observers. Indeed, the fact that we can't quite see the girl's death, but have access to it only through Benny's

FIGURE 14.1 *Benny's Video*, dir. Michael Haneke (Bernard Lang/Langfilm/Wega Film, 1992).

monitor, is significant. Like the nonhuman, fixed stare of Benny's video camera, Haneke's aesthetic of restraint is diffident and impassive, refusing to respond to the death that it registers. If the problem, as Haneke sees it, is the cool indifference to death that is propagated through media spectatorship, it is curious that Haneke should choose a style that so closely emulates that detachment. However, as many critics have suggested, the aim of Haneke's "aesthetic of glaciation" is to confront spectators with the image of their own indifference so as to provoke them—or in Haneke's own words, to "rape the spectator into autonomy."[28]

What has been less frequently commented on is the way that in doing so, *Benny's Video* explicitly references snuff movie mythology to place images of suffering— real and imagined—on a single continuum. Rather than attempt to separate out "bad" exploitation from "good" art, or reality from fiction, it suggests that we recognize what Eugenie Brinkema calls "the force of the violence of all images."[29] In doing so, it attempts to renew our ability to respond to images of death and suffering that abound across these multiple networks of images, not by modeling a normative ethical response that would keep violence at bay, but by encouraging us to recognize our complicity in the spectacles of death that are produced for us to witness and enjoy. This involves a shift from a normative conception of ethics, to an intersubjective one, which is opened up as a dialog between moving image and spectator.

Antonio Campos's 2009 film *Afterschool* picks up where *Benny's Video* leaves off, extending Haneke's critique of televisual and cinematic violence to the context of new media—Lisa Mullen's essay for the UK DVD sleeve notes refer to it, on page four, as "an inquiry into the YouTube generation." It tells the story of Rob, who is "addicted to fuzzy cameraphone footage," which "has the thrill of pornography" because in contrast to the rest of the world around him, these images seem real. Campos's indebtedness to Haneke is painstakingly clear, as the film develops a plot similar to that of *Benny's Video*, in which Rob accidentally films the violent and bloody death of two girls while setting up an establishing shot in the hallway of his school. Rather than call for help, Rob moves into the frame and sits with one of the girls, listening to her screams as she slowly dies. Later, he learns that the event was captured by a security camera, and also by a third, unseen mobile phone camera, and that the footage has been uploaded anonymously onto the Internet. Aesthetically, Campos's film emulates the tone of indifference generated by *Benny's Video*, but what interests me here is the way that it locates this indifference in the forms of spectatorship that are opened up by new media platforms such as YouTube.

---

[28]Catherine Wheatley, *Michael Haneke's Cinema: The Ethic of the Image* (New York: Berghan Books, 2009): 78.

[29]Eugenie Brinkema, "How to Do Things with Violences," in *A Companion to Michael Haneke*, edited by Roy Grundmann (Oxford: Wiley-Blackwell, 2010): 368.

Afterschool explicitly addresses the framing of death in a digital network culture through an opening montage sequence, which cuts together popular Internet memes, including footage of a baby laughing as it opens a package, teenagers fighting in a car park, a boy crashing while attempting a stunt on a bike, footage of the death by hanging of Saddam Hussein, a cat playing piano, combat footage of wounded and dead soldiers, and hard-core pornography (Figures 14.2–14.5). If, as Peter Bradshaw notes in his review of the film, YouTube is a "lawless world of unauthored, unpoliced material,"[30] one of the things *Afterschool* examines through the snuff motif is the way that these changes to our media landscape impact on our modes of response and responsibility. Indeed, this film explicitly uses the snuff narrative to acknowledge the way in which video-sharing sites now cater to the desire to see real death outside of the officially sanctioned ethical frames provided by mainstream media formats. *Afterschool* draws our attention to one of the consequences of the proliferation of surveillance and digital mobile phone cameras, and online-viewing platforms: namely, that death is always already a potential spectacle for others to view.

[30]Peter Bradshaw, "Afterschool," *The Guardian*, August 20, 2009, accessed April 30, 2014. http://www.theguardian.com/film/2009/aug/20/afterschool-review.

FIGURES 14.2–14.5 *Afterschool*, dir. Antonio Campos (Borderline Films/Hidden St. Productions, 2008).

It suggests that everything that we experience, including our deaths, is now capturable, uploadable onto video-sharing networks, where it may be endlessly screened, commented on, shared, liked on Facebook, and so on.

While this opening sequence acknowledges the way that YouTube might be seen to cater to appetites for media voyeurism, it also aims to implicate spectators, by playing up the dissonance between individual images, and the effect of their collocation. Indeed, the juxtaposition of these images works to create a leveling effect that the film suggests is an integral part of new media formats such as YouTube. Unlike the kind of weighty existential salience that the sight of documentary death has for Sobchack, YouTube appears to mingle life and death, laughter and horror indiscriminately; in this sequence, laughing babies and cats playing pianos rub jowls with dead dictators and hard-core pornography. And this is only partially a result of editing in this sequence, which gestures toward the underlying computational processes that are a fundamental part of new media technologies. Indeed, on a material level, this indifferentiation between disparate image contexts is, in D.N. Rodowick's terms, a fundamental aspect of digital modes of image capture, which rely on the algorithmic translation of representation into computation and information. One result, he notes, is that digital media remain "agnostic" or indifferent to what they show, and "insensitive to the qualities of things and thoughts."[31] *Afterschool* suggests that digital media's indifference to different image contexts constitutes an ethical challenge for us as spectators. By modeling this disturbing indifference through an aesthetic of restraint, *Afterschool* solicits an affective response that would compensate for digital media's insensitivity. In doing so, it dramatizes the spectator's complicity in what he or she watches, aligning us affectively and ethically against the potential for indifference in digital media.

In both of these films, what is felt as truly shocking is not the seeming reality of the deaths they offer for our entertainment, but the affective mood of cold indifference that these films display toward their material, foreclosing a moralistic, emotional response in favor of detached, unflinching criticality. I would argue that the ethical potential of both films lies in the way that they ask spectators to navigate this affective dissonance between content and form, and to consider our own embeddedness within the structures of exploitation that reverberate across our digital image ecology.

An aesthetic of expenditure

In sharp contrast to the aesthetic indifference cultivated by *Benny's Video* and *Afterschool*, *The Life & Death of a Porno Gang* and *A Serbian Film* are hyperbolic and over-the-top, featuring dramatically explicit and gory set pieces in which death and other unspeakable acts are framed as "artistic" spectacles for paying customers. Both films deal directly with the snuff movie conceit through plots involving a porn film director and a porn film star, who—despite starting out with more artistically and politically motivated intentions—are drawn in to the seedy underworld of the snuff movie industry. Both films are highly self-reflexive, referencing a wide range of filmic traditions, from contemporary torture porn to Yugoslav Black Wave cinema. Mladen Djordjević has noted the influence of a range of "art movie," "b-horror," and contemporary "Japanese horror film" antecedents on *The Life and Death of a Porno Gang*, including Paul Morrissey, John Waters, Alejandro Jodorowsky, and Takashi Miike.[32] Similarly, Srdjan Spasojević says that he was "most influenced by American auteurs of the 70s like Friedkin, Peckinpah, Cronenberg, Carpenter, Walter Hill and others" in making

---

[31]D.N. Rodowick, *The Virtual Life of Film* (Cambridge, MA: Harvard University Press, 2007): 130.
[32]Mladen Djordević, "Mladen Djordević—Interview for Splatting Image," *Filmske-Radosti*, January 19, 2010, accessed July 23, 2014, http://www.filmske-radosti.com/content/mladen-%C4%91or%C4% 91evi%C4%87-interview-forsplatting-image.

A Serbian Film.[33] However, what sets both *The Life and Death of a Porno Gang* and *A Serbian Film* apart from those cinematic precursors is the extremity of their thematic content and aesthetic approach. Indeed, both films have been critiqued for their "grimly nihilistic"[34] depictions of "pornography and ultra-violence," while *A Serbian Film*, in particular, has gained notoriety as perhaps "the nastiest film ever made."[35] By highlighting this disparate range of high- and subcultural influences and courting controversy through their depictions of taboo subjects, both films arguably tap into the pre-existing global market that has been created for new extreme cinema through international festival circuits.

At the same time, however, both films are framed as deeply personal political statements about life in contemporary Serbia. And indeed, both directors have insisted that the extremity of their films is motivated by, and should be understood within, this social and political context. For instance, Mladen Djordjević has claimed that *The Life and Death of a Porno Gang* is "socially and politically engaged in [the] context of contemporary Serbia," noting that his film is clearly a direct reflection of "consequences of the wars" and "growing up in an era when seeing uncensored shots of war atrocities on TV was a normal thing."[36] Similarly, Spasojević has regularly defended the extreme imagery in *A Serbian Film* by saying that the film "is an honest expression of the deepest feelings that we have about our region," which has, for the last few decades "been dominated by war and political and moral nightmares."[37] Moreover, in the UK DVD booklet for *A Serbian Film*, Spasojević notes that his aim is to "put complex issues" of Serbian national identity "on show for the whole world to judge."

It is significant, however, that although they are "Serbian" films—made by Serbians about life in Serbia—both *Life and Death of a Porno Gang* and *A Serbian Film* are made for, and addressed to, non-Serbian audiences. As I will argue, this positioning of audiences as more than just distant onlookers is a crucial aspect of the way that each film reworks the snuff device as a means of addressing a political context that may be *about* Serbia, but which primarily implicates and indicts Western spectators. While both films engage with the social and political context of Serbia, and explore questions of national identity, they do so by mediating the image of Serbia through a distinctly Anglo-American/Western European

---

[33]Virginie Sélavy, "A Serbian Film: Interview with Srdjan Spasojevic," *Electric Sheep Magazine*, December 5, 2010, accessed August 6, 2014, http://www.electricsheepmagazine.co.uk/features/2010/12/05/a-serbian-film-interview-with-srdjan-spasojevic/.

[34]Budd Wilkins, "The Life and Death of a Porno Gang," *Slant Magazine*, September 10, 2012, accessed August 6, 2014, http://www.slantmagazine.com/dvd/review/the-life-and-death-of-a-porno-gang.

[35]Geoffrey McNab, "*A Serbian Film*: Is This the Nastiest Film Ever Made?," *The Independent*, November 19, 2010, accessed August 6, 2014, http://www.independent.co.uk/arts-entertainment/films/features/a-serbian-film-is-this-the-nastiest-film-ever-made-2137781.html.

[36]Djordjević, "Mladen Djordjević—Interview for Splatting Image."

[37]Sélavy, "A Serbian Film: Interview with Srdjan Spasojevic."

perspective. Both films recycle Western clichés of Eastern European primitivism and otherness, imagining the Balkans as a backward geographical zone synonymous with pornography, violence, and snuff, in ways that echo the exploitative ethos of the mondo film, and which are amply on display in torture porn franchises such as *Saw* (Various, 2004–2010) or *Hostel* (Eli Roth, Scott Spiegel 2005–2011). As Spasojević suggests, although they may be statements about political life in contemporary Serbia, these films are staged explicitly *for* the West's consumption, and indeed, for our entertainment. Like other new extreme films such as *Import/Export* and *La Vie nouvelle* (Philippe Grandrieux, 2002), both films are involved in tracing relations between East and West, and confronting the West with its own violent imaginary about what happens "over there." In this way, they implicate spectators within the uneven relations of economic and political power between the two contexts, making ethical reflexivity a significant—if highly problematic—dimension of the act of looking on. As I will argue, both films' extreme, nasty, and over-the-top "aesthetic of expenditure" plays an important role within this task of implicating spectators as more than just remote or voyeuristic onlookers.

The snuff device is an explicit part of this critique. In Mladen Djordjević's *The Life and Death of a Porno Gang*, a group of ex-porn stars found a live "porno theatre" with the intention of producing challenging avant-garde art, but are eventually drawn into a snuff conspiracy through Franz, a former war reporter who discovers a "foreign market" for footage of Bosnian war atrocities. As part of his plan to supply fresh material for this black market, Franz convinces the troupe to become "the first snuff artists in the world." The troupe initially resists, but because of their desperate circumstances, they are eventually forced into this new line of work. They begin to recruit marginalized Serbian civilians—those without hope or future prospects—who consent to having their actual deaths choreographed, performed, and filmed as part of the troupe's sketches. As we are told explicitly, the market for such films is European and American. In keeping with its "aesthetics of expenditure," *The Life and Death of a Porno Gang* puts these snuff-performances confrontationally on show, through a series of gory and explicit set pieces. These set pieces frame death as a voyeuristic spectacle, as much for the troupe's fictional "European and American" clients as for their real-world counterparts beyond the frame. But at the same time, the film also mediates our illicit and voyeuristic vision of these deaths through the implicated and empathetic gazes of the porno troupe members (Figure 14.6). In these snuff-performances, the victim, the camera, and the rest of the performance troupe—including the camera operators and those not directly involved in the performed killings—remain visible throughout. While the diegetic inclusion of the camera helps to confer its illicit images with an aura of authenticity, the insistence on the implicated and empathetic gazes of the camera operators and the rest of the performance troupe intervenes to undermine and question the scene's construction as a source of voyeuristic titillation. Part of

FIGURE 14.6 *The Life and Death of a Porno Gang*, dir. Mladen Djordjevic (Film House Bas Celik, 2009).

what makes these scenes so brutal to watch is that we can't help watching from the distinctly Serbian gaze of both performers and victims, at the same time as we are made aware of our position as both external to and responsible for these performances. The grim realism of these sequences serves to remind spectators of the dire economic and social realities that have forced both performer and victim into the snuff video arena in the first place, and of the spectator's place within this economy. As the doubling of the diegetic with extradiegetic spectators makes clear, it is ultimately the Western appetite for violent spectacle, and the uneven economic conditions between East and West, which are to blame for the deaths.

This strategy of confronting the West with its responsibility for, and implication in, Eastern degradation is also amply demonstrated in the director's statement that directly precedes the feature film on the Revolver Entertainment DVD release of *A Serbian Film*. In this roughly four-minute long segment, Spasojević appears against the familiar mise-en-scène of the publicity interview, delivering a highly self-reflexive direct to camera statement that contextualizes the film for audiences in the United Kingdom. Acknowledging claims about the "politically very incorrect" aspects of *A Serbian Film*, Spasojević notes that the original intention of the film was not to shock, but to "face the beasts of its own time" and to "express our honest personal sentiments about our region, the last two decades of war" and the "moral and political nightmare" that Serbia has been facing in the wake of that turbulent history. However, he also says that they wanted to put those issues into a "universally comprehensible context, so that everyone outside our environment could relate to it." As he goes on to note, "the reason for showing the almost unshowable scenes in such unrestrained and direct manner is that the violation, humiliation and ultimate degradation of being must be felt and experienced by every viewer so that it cannot be ignored." In other words, the political effectivity of the film relies, in Spasojević's view, on a spectator who is forced to feel—rather than simply intellectually grasp—the "horrors of history."[38]

This understanding of *A Serbian Film* as constituting a necessarily grueling physical ordeal for spectators has been playfully acknowledged in its reception history. At its premier during the South by Southwest festival, for example, the film was preceded by an invitation to audience members to collectively "[snort] lines of salt, [squeeze] lime juice into their eyes, and [take] shots of tequila" in order to "understand what the Serbs have been through."[39] This stunt acknowledges the film's framing as political allegory, which seeks to translate the horrors of Serbian history into a visceral ordeal that spectators must endure, in order to understand the legacies of Milošević and Kosovo and what Spasojević calls the "everyday pornography" of economic and social degradation in contemporary Serbia. The film's unremitting extremity is thus situated as an appropriate means of confronting spectators with—and punishing them for—their complicity in the wider economic and visual economy that the film addresses. Indeed, although publicity stunts such as these attempt to playfully recuperate the film's viciousness as a form of masochistic pleasure, *A Serbian Film*'s apocalyptic intensity makes it clear that its violence is not just *for* us, but also explicitly *about* us as well. The film's "aesthetic of expenditure" aims to push past boundaries of what can be tolerated, to contaminate pleasure with disgust and horror, and to thus transform a desire for voyeuristic spectacle into a hesitant—if uncertain—mode of introspection and ethical questioning. The snuff device, I would argue, plays a vital role here: as in all of the films discussed in this chapter, the importance of the snuff motif resides in its explicit acknowledgment of the role of the spectator, and the crisis of response that it articulates within this context.

As with the "aesthetic of restraint," the aim of the "aesthetic of expenditure" is thus to expose our position as complicit, confronting us with the consequences of our desire to look on voyeuristically from a position of superiority and privilege, while disavowing our participation within that same context. But while *Benny's Video* and *Afterschool* rely on a mood of disturbing indifference in order to do so, *Life and Death of a Porno Gang* and *A Serbian Film* rely on excess, bringing the full force of cinematic spectacle to the task of implicating us affectively and ethically with the sight of death. And yet, as modes of ethical engagement,

---

[38]Adam Lowenstein, *Shocking Representation: Historical Trauma, National Cinema, and the Modern Horror Film* (New York: Columbia University Press, 2005).

[39]Eric Kohn, "'A Serbian Film' Shocks Midnight Audiences at SXSW," *Wall Street Journal*, March 15, 2010, accessed August 5, 2014, http://blogs.wsj.com/speakeasy/2010/03/15/a-serbian-film-shocks-midnight-audiences-at-sxsw/.

both of these aesthetic approaches also have their limits. While the "aesthetic of restraint" deploys a mood of indifference to prompt an affective critical response from spectators, it runs the risk of coming across as pedantic and "disdainfully moralistic"—and hence of alienating spectators altogether.[40] On the other hand, an "aesthetics of expenditure" relies on a spectator who is willing to grasp his or her dual role as both viewing subject and target of extreme cinema's virulence, and capable of reflecting on their involvement in what is being shown. Extremity as an ethical strategy thus risks catering to the very desires that it would purport— at least in extratextual statements and interviews—to critique. As Shaun Kimber notes, while a film such as *A Serbian Film* may engage in a "transgressive edge play," it also affords viewers the opportunity to "distance themselves from its content" and to "find pleasure in both its formal styling and thematic motivations."[41]

Nonetheless, I believe that both of these aesthetic poles are valuable to the extent that they help to articulate a crisis in response and responsibility in relation to contemporary moving images. In doing so, they open up a potentially productive space for spectators to consider their profound involvement in this broader context of networked viewing in a global context. The snuff device does not *demand* ethical reflexivity, but foregrounds it as an important—and yet highly problematic— aspect of the disturbing and complex experience of watching others die for our enjoyment. In foregrounding questions of affect and ethical implication, rather than parsing distinctions between reality and fiction, or art and entertainment, these films can help us to think through the terms of our relationship to the spectacle of death that is relentlessly circulated in a global digital culture.

---

[40]Romney quoted in Wheatley, *Michael Haneke's Cinema*, 77.
[41]Shaun Kimber, "Transgressive Edge Play and *Srpski Film/A Serbian Film*," *Horror Studies* 5, no. 1 (2014): 114.

15 A VIEW TO A KILL: PERSPECTIVES ON FAUX-SNUFF AND SELF

Steve Jones

To date, scholarly debate about the content of snuff-themed fiction has predominantly focused on two cojoining issues: realism and affect.[1] That emphasis is unsurprising given snuff's ontological foundations. Unlike other horror subgenres—such as the werewolf film, the zombie movie, the slasher flick, and torture porn—simulated snuff is not principally defined by its content, but rather by its realist form.[2] Although pertinent then, the attention devoted to realism in scholarly writing about snuff has resulted in undertheorization of feigned snuff narratives' symbolic meanings.

This chapter seeks to offer one alternative interpretation of snuff-fiction's narrative content, examining what the simulated snuff form reveals about self. Although largely disparaged as cultural trash, fabricated snuff films give voice to complex social ideas. Numerous deep-seated fears that underpin both interpersonal interactions and self-conception are routinely reified as horror in these films. Moreover, snuff-fiction's particular articulation of self encapsulates concerns about selfhood that are similar to those expressed in concurrent philosophy. That is not to suggest that the horror filmmakers in question have been directly influenced by recent movements in self-philosophy, but rather that

---

[1]See, for example, Joel Black, "Real(ist) Horror: From Execution Videos to Snuff Films," in *Underground USA: Filmmaking Beyond the Hollywood Canon*, edited by Xavier Mendik and Steven Jay Schneider (New York: Columbia University Press, 2012); Isabel Cristina Pinedo, *Recreational Terror: Women and the Pleasures of Horror Film Viewing* (Albany: University of New York Press, 1997): 64.

[2]It is noted that snuff-themed films do share broad thematic, situational, and character tropes. However, simulated snuff films are foremost recognizable as faux-snuff by their realist aesthetics.

the films and philosophy in question are products of the same climate of ideas. Fake snuff movies and philosophy occupy different cultural spheres and certainly utilize very different languages, yet their contiguity becomes apparent via their correlating visions of self.

Here, I will address a particular form of snuff-fiction that has grown in popularity since the fin-de-siècle: faux-snuff. Rather than embedding snuff sequences in a broader narrative framework—a technique employed in *Hardcore* (Paul Schrader, 1979), *Cannibal Holocaust* (Ruggero Deodato, 1980), and *8mm* (Joel Schumacher, 1999), for example—faux-snuff films such as *Tumbling Doll of Flesh* (Tamakichi Anaru, 1998) and *August Underground* (Fred Vogel, 2001) are fictional simulations: attempts to mimic what real snuff might look like.[3] Faux-snuff is not only the antecedent of snuff-themed "classics" such as *Cannibal Holocaust,* but also of the "found footage" boom that followed in the wake of *The Blair Witch Project*'s box-office success. The latter has been notably succeeded by numerous fantastical, camcorder-shot pseudo-reality horror films such as *Paranormal Activity* (Oren Peli, 2007) and *Grave Encounters* (The Vicious Brothers, 2011). However, many indie horror filmmakers have equally latched onto the same techniques to create realistic visions of filmed murder, resulting in faux-snuff films such as *The Great American Snuff Film* (Sean Tretta, 2003) and *Thumb'N'It* (Paul T. T. Easter, 2012), for example.

One particular case study will provide a focal point for this chapter: Shane Ryan's *Amateur Porn Star Killer* series (2007–2009). Ryan's trilogy concerns a homicidal male—known as "Brandon"—who records, charms, has sex with, and then murders young women. The three films repeat the same cycle of events. The series epitomizes the faux-snuff methodology, being mainly constituted by real-time, camcorder-shot footage, while encapsulating characteristic shifts in recent self-philosophy, which will be delineated in the next section. The paradigm drawn upon below is aligned with Farmer and Tsakiris's proposal that self is comprised of three elements: "Bodily Social Self," "Narrative Self," and "Phenomenological Self."[4] Their unified, tripartite model summates numerous key trends within contemporary self-philosophy. Once established, I will delineate how this paradigm manifests in *Amateur Porn Star Killer,* exploring some of the complications that arise from balancing these three elements of selfhood. Finally, faux-snuff's

---

[3]It is acknowledged that no genuine snuff movie has ever been found, and thus faux-snuff is a fiction based on a myth; see Julian Petley, "Cannibal Holocaust and the Pornography of Death," in *The Spectacle of the Real: From Hollywood to Reality TV and Beyond,* edited by Geoff King (Bristol: Intellect, 2005): 173. For a detailed discussion of the differences between faux-snuff and conventional narrative films that contain snuff sequences, see Steve Jones, "Dying to Be Seen: Snuff-Fiction's Problematic Fantasises of 'Reality,'" *Scope* 19 (2011).

[4]Harry Farmer and Manos Tsakiris, "The Bodily Social Self: A Link between Phenomenal and Narrative Selfhood," *Review of Philosophy and Psychology* 3, no. 1 (2012): 125–44.

contribution to debates about selfhood will be expounded, paying particular attention to the collapse of various ostensibly dichotomous relationships.

Theory/self

Traditionally, approaches to selfhood have been divisive. Arguably, the most notable divergence has been between philosophical-theoretical approaches to self on one hand and scientific/empirical approaches on the other. The "explanatory gap" debate is indicative of that opposition, being founded on the premise that "third-person scientific theories" fail to capture the "qualitative first-person experience of mental states."[5] Although some thinkers, such as Martin, remain skeptical about the possibility that "the self" can become a "unitary explanatory postulate" while disciplines lack a shared theoretical framework,[6] there have been significant advances toward developing such unification in recent years. Butler is among the theorists who have sought to broach the gap by championing the legitimacy of "first-person descriptions of experience" alongside "third-person scientific descriptions."[7] Dullstein presents theory of mind itself as "an interdisciplinary debate," involving "not only philosophers of different backgrounds, but also psychologists and neuroscientists."[8] Moreover, Thomson's belief in a future of "promiscuous miscegenation" between all "philosophical traditions and styles" is founded on perceiving the self as a bridging point between various schools of thought.[9]

Key to such bridging has been an emphasis on the body. Corporeality unifies various branches of neuroscience, social/cognitive/developmental psychology, phenomenology and philosophy of mind, bringing empirical study and theoretical discussion of self into a continuum.[10] More specifically, the body has become

---

[5]M. Pauen, "Materialism, Metaphysics, and the Intuition of Distinctness," *Journal of Consciousness Studies* 18, nos. 7–8 (2011): 71; see also Declan Smithies, "The Significance of Cognitive Phenomenology," *Philosophy Compass* 8, no. 8 (2013): 734–37.

[6]Robert Hanna, Gerald Izenberg, Raymond Martin, Norbert Wiley, and Jerrold Seigel, "Me, Myself, and I: The Rise of the Modern Self," *Annals of the New York Academy of Sciences* 1234, no. 10 (2011): 118.

[7]Jesse Butler, "Introspective Knowledge of Experience and Its Role in Consciousness Studies," *Journal of Consciousness Studies* 18, no. 2 (2011): 143.

[8]Monika Dullstein, "The Second Person in the Theory of Mind Debate," *Review of Philosophy and Psychology* 3, no. 2 (2012): 233. See also D.I. Dubrovskii, "Subjective Reality and the Brain: An Essay on a Theoretical Solution to the Problem," *Herald of the Russian Academy of Sciences* 83, no. 1 (2013): 59–60.

[9]Iain Thomson, "In the Future Philosophy Will Be Neither Continental nor Analytic but Synthetic: Toward a Promiscuous Miscegenation of (All) Philosophical Traditions and Styles," *The Southern Journal of Philosophy* 50, no. 2 (2012): 191.

[10]See Adrian Alsmith, John Tetteh, and Frédérique de Vignemont, "Embodying the Mind and Representing the Body," *Review of Philosophy and Psychology* 3, no. 1 (2012): 2; Beate M. Herbert and Olga Pollatos, "The Body in the Mind: On the Relationship between Interoception and Embodiment," *Topics in Cognitive Science* 4, no. 4 (2012): 693; J.C. Berendzen, "Coping without Foundations: On Dreyfus's Use of Merleau-Ponty," *International Journal of Philosophical Studies* 18, no. 5 (2010): 637.

a conduit for discussing the self as belonging in the world, divesting self of its modernist, solipsistic connotations. In contemporary debate then, a Merleau-Pontian emphasis on embodiment such as Zahavi's[11] is typically favored over Cartesian-influenced accounts of independently existent minds. *Pace* Descartes, in contemporary debate it is frequently taken for granted that embodiment is a prerequisite for selfhood, and that selves are intersubjective.[12] Farmer and Tsakiris's term "Bodily Social Self" neatly encapsulates that belief. The body situates the self in the world, and enables interaction with other embodied beings. Furthermore, socio-embodiment shapes self-conception: "Bodily Social Self is based on the recognition that one's own body can be the object of other's perceptions and thus that the bodies of others are like one's own."[13]

Movement away from a Cartesian position in twentieth-century philosophy has facilitated a rendition of consciousness studies that evades the pitfalls of egoism.[14] As Berendzen posits,[15] the emphasis on embodiment has divested the conventional mind-body hierarchy of legitimacy. One result is clearer integration between materialist science and phenomenology. Thus Farmer and Tsakiris refer to a second strand—the Phenomenological Self—as operating alongside the Bodily Social Self.[16] Indeed, recent discussions regarding internal mental states are informed by the dual roles embodiment and phenomenology play in understanding others,[17] demonstrating that the Bodily Social Self cannot be reduced to behaviorism. Again, such discussion elucidates connections between analytical and empirical study of the self.[18]

The third stand Farmer and Tsakiris identify is Narrative Self. Following the propositions of thinkers such as Ricoeur, MacIntyre, and Dennett, the Narrative Self is the element that allows one to apprehend their continued existence over time. Phenomenological experiences, memories, and aspirations for the future

---

[11]Dan Zahavi, *Subjectivity and Selfhood: Investigating the First-Person Perspective* (London: MIT Press, 2005): 159.

[12]See A.A. Johnstone, "The Basic Self and Its Doubles," *Journal of Consciousness Studies* 18, nos. 7–8 (2011): 176–77; V. Gallese and C. Sinigaglia, "How the Body in Action Shapes the Self," *Journal of Consciousness Studies* 18, nos. 7–8 (2011): 135; Alvin I. Goldman, "A Moderate Approach to Embodied Cognitive Science," *Review of Philosophy and Psychology* 3, no. 1 (2012): 71.

[13]Farmer and Tsakiris, "The Bodily Social Self," 128.

[14]See Zahavi, *Subjectivity and Selfhood*, 100.

[15]Berendzen, "Coping without Foundations," 629.

[16]Farmer and Tsakiris, "The Bodily Social Self," 126.

[17]See Herbert and Pollatos, "The Body in the Mind," 696; W.E.S. McNeill, "Embodiment and the Perceptual Hypothesis," *The Philosophical Quarterly* 62, no. 248 (2012): 573; Jaime A. Pineda, "Sensorimotor Cortex as a Critical Component of an 'Extended' Mirror Neuron System: Does It Solve the Development, Correspondence, and Control Problems in Mirroring?," *Behavioral and Brain Functions* 4, no. 47 (2008): 47.

[18]See Zahavi, *Subjectivity and Selfhood*, 177; Pauen, "Materialism, Metaphysics, and the Intuition of Distinctness," 85.

are gathered together to provide the self with temporal and ontological stability. Again, this facet of self has been utilized across various disciplines. For example, Gallagher has made a case for Narrative Self's relevance to a variety of empirical disciplines including neuroscience and psychiatry.[19] Unsurprisingly, Narrative Self has also been adopted within much developmental psychology, where language acquisition is a key issue in theorization about self-formation.[20]

Alone, the Narrative Self is clearly flawed. One's self-narrative begins before language acquisition occurs. Moreover, since the "author" is not present in the instance of their own demise, the narrative can never be complete.[21] As such, the Narrative Self cannot offer a comprehensive account of personal identity. A more satisfying paradigm is offered by joining Narrative Self with Bodily Social Self and Phenomenological Self. Indeed, Narrative Self enables the subject to order and reflect upon their phenomenological experiences. Strawson's complaint that the "stream of consciousness" metaphor does not match actual experiences of being conscious[22]—of interrupted, fragmented, memory-laden thought processes—can be usefully revised once Phenomenological Self and Narrative Self are combined. Narrative Self brings the experiences of the Phenomenological Self into temporal continuity.[23] As Farmer and Tsakiris have it, the Narrative Self is "constituted through the stories that we and others tell about ourselves."[24] Pace Zahavi's insistence that "the decisive paradigm shift…from a philosophy of subjectivity to a philosophy of language" has more recently "been replaced by a return to consciousness,"[25] it would be more accurate to suggest that narrative theory has been combined with phenomenology to compensate for weaknesses in both.

Narrative Self and Bodily Social Self are also symbiotic. One's self-narrative is shaped by external sociocultural factors. Although Schechtman rightly observes that autobiographical accounts are biased by one's first-person perspective,[26]

---

[19]Shaun Gallagher, "Philosophical Conceptions of the Self: Implications for Cognitive Science," *Trends in Cognitive Science* 4, no. 1 (2000): 14–21. See also Sally Prebble, Donna Addis, and Lynette Tippett, "Autobiographical Memory and Sense of Self," *Psychological Bulletin* 139, no. 4 (2013): 815–40; Butler, "Introspective Knowledge of Experience and Its Role in Consciousness Studies," 138.

[20]See Kenneth J. Gergen, "The Self as Social Construction," *Psychological Studies* 56, no. 1 (2011): 111.

[21]See David Lumsden, "Whole Life Narratives and the Self," *Philosophy, Psychiatry, & Psychology* 20, no. 1 (2013): 1–10.

[22]Galen Strawson, *Selves: An Essay in Revisionary Metaphysics* (Oxford: Oxford University Press, 2009): 139.

[23]For an interesting variation on this approach see John Devlin Smith, "Self-Concept: Autopoiesis as the Basis for a Conceptual Framework," *Systems Research and Behavioral Science* 31, no. 1 (2014): 32–46.

[24]Farmer and Tsakiris, "The Bodily Social Self," 125.

[25]Zahavi, *Subjectivity and Selfhood*, 147–48.

[26]Marya Schechtman, "Memory and Identity," *Philosophical Studies* 153, no. 1 (2011): 70.

Narrative Self is intimately intertwined with processes of intersubjective communication.[27] Self-narration is a "social process" because we "coconstruct" our narratives.[28] Narrative Self also compensates for weaknesses in the Bodily Social Self model. Since the body provides continuity for one's sense of self over time, it could be suggested that the self is simply material. Self-narration bridges between continuity and self-conception without reducing the self to corporeality alone.

Although different terms may be utilized to express their ideas, Farmer and Tsakiris's unified self paradigm is shared by various theorists.[29] For some theorists, unified models are either the product of, or are facilitating multidisciplinary engagements with self.[30] This disciplinary fusion crucially parallels the tripartite paradigm's main strength: amalgamating separate elements into a more coherent, integrated structure. Just as the "specifically modern conception of the self" as "fragmented" is largely rejected in contemporary debate,[31] the interdisciplinary field of self-studies is itself becoming less fissured.

Over the last decade, that field—encompassing philosophy, psychology, and the sciences—has been gradually finding a shared language. Scholarly discourses are not the only means of articulating these ideas, however. Issues of self are also reified in culture, as the following dissection of *Amateur Porn Star Killer* will demonstrate. One aim of analyzing cultural representations via the language of selfhood scholarship is to bridge another disciplinary gap. By nature of their story-telling devices, fictional narratives are particularly apposite as a route into understanding Narrative Self. Fiction is communicative, and thus social. Film's various elements—scripting, performance, editing, image composition, lighting, sound, and so forth—are forms of communication that operate in a different way to the language-based conventions of academic work. Thus, a second objective of this approach is to evince how cultural representations *contribute* to theoretical discussion of self.

---

[27]See Marjorie Jolles, "Between Embodied Subjects and Objects: Narrative Somaesthetics," *Hypatia* 27, no. 2 (2012): 309–11; Gallagher, "Philosophical Conceptions of the Self."

[28]Dullstein, "The Second Person in the Theory of Mind Debate," 246–47; see also Erife Tekin, "How Does the Self Adjudicate Narratives?," *Philosophy, Psychiatry, & Psychology* 20, no. 1 (2013): 27; Zahavi, *Subjectivity and Selfhood*, 108–09.

[29]Including Johnstone, "The Basic Self and Its Doubles," 182; Butler, "Introspective Knowledge of Experience and Its Role in Consciousness Studies," 132; Jennifer H. Pfeifer and Shannon J. Peake, "Self-Development: Integrating Cognitive, Socioemotional, and Neuroimaging Perspectives," *Developmental Cognitive Neuroscience* 2, no. 1 (2012): 55.

[30]See Hanna et al., "Me, Myself, and I," 119; Thompson in Krista Tippett, Thomas Metzinger, Evan Thompson, and Pim van Lommel, "To Be or Not to Be: The Self as Illusion," *Annals of the New York Academy of Sciences* 1234, no. 1 (2011): 8.

[31]Hanna et al., "Me, Myself, and I," 114.

Trilogy/self

In order to explain how self is rendered in *Amateur Porn Star Killer*, I return to Farmer and Tsakiris's three aspects of self, beginning with Phenomenological Self. Faux-snuff is principally invested in killers' first-person perspectives, and *Amateur Porn Star Killer* epitomizes that trope. The trilogy is constituted by footage captured via Brandon's camcorder (killer-cam). Resultantly, the narrative events are mainly (although not exclusively) shot from Brandon's point-of-view. At this basic level, much of the series' duration is spent replicating a singular perspective on the world. This is a characteristic trope of the faux-snuff film. In this way, faux-snuff evokes the foundational problem that self-philosophy has sought to address since Descartes: that embodiment restricts one's perceptual frame. We each experience the world from a limited, singular position.

Despite the widespread rejection of Descartes' dualistic approach, self-theorists remain fundamentally interested in the kinds of access introspective subjectivity provides to one's self, and the various ways we apprehend others' states. Phenomenology's continued prominence in the field evinces theorists' sustained fascination with inner-perspectives on lived experience. Indeed "first-personal access to one's own experiential life" is presupposed in any claim to selfhood.[32] The same lexis ("first-person") is employed in film studies to refer to the hand-held shooting technique employed in faux-snuff. Although complicated by various other factors (as I will demonstrate),[33] this mode of camerawork provides a natural bridge between film and philosophy that is a useful starting point for comparison.

However, some caveats are immediately necessary. First, it is inadequate to suggest plainly that first-person camera provides identificatory access to Brandon by placing the audience "in" his position. Like Cartesian dualism, psychoanalytically infused models—such as Braddock's, which leaps between viewing positions, empathy, and identification[34]—tend to be treated skeptically in the current intellectual climate. The identificatory paradigm has long been contested in reference to uses of first-person camerawork in horror film (particularly the slasher film),[35] so those ideas will not be dwelt upon here

---

[32]Zahavi, *Subjectivity and Selfhood*, 12–14; see also Farmer and Tsakiris, "The Bodily Social Self," 129.

[33]There are budgetary advantages to shooting in an "amateur" style and utilizing widely available home-video cameras, especially for independent filmmakers. For example, Shane Ryan claims that the budget for *Amateur Porn Star Killer* was $45 in total. For a detailed discussion of microbudget faux-snuff and its "underground," antimainstream connotations, see Steve Jones, *Torture Porn: Popular Horror After Saw* (Basingstoke: Palgrave-Macmillan, 2013): 171–78.

[34]Louise Braddock, "Psychological Identification, Imagination and Psychoanalysis," *Philosophical Psychology* 24, no. 5 (2011): 3.

[35]For example, see Gregory Currie, *Image and Mind: Film, Philosophy and Cognitive Science* (Cambridge: Cambridge University Press, 1995): 174–75; Peter Hutchings, *The Horror Film* (Harlow: Pearson, 2004): 195–96.

other than to support rejection of the identification premise. Secondly, it is worth noting that *Amateur Porn Star Killer*'s first-person camerawork does not capture Brandon's full phenomenological experience. Rather, only an audiovisual representation of Brandon's viewpoint is conveyed. Without access to his other sensations, and associated qualia—his experiences—the film's rendition of his Phenomenological Self is incomplete. That said, the faux-snuff form offers an additional compensatory gesture. Faux-snuff's realist mode is partially a tactic to draw the viewer into an affective engagement.[36] As with other faux-snuff films such as the *August Underground* series, *Amateur Porn Star Killer* blends graphic sexual depictions with explicit violence. Drawing on the conventions established within body genres, faux-snuff films frequently provoke visceral reactions from viewers, including fear, anger, and disgust. That is, the narrative's mechanisms do not prompt identification with Brandon or the victims, but instead offers ways into interacting with the text that remain attuned to the viewer's own embodied perspective. The gambit may not be successful for all individual viewers, but where efficacious, faux-snuff's realist body-horror expedites sensational experience in compensation for Brandon's phenomenologically evacuated first-person perspective.

These provisos are necessary insofar as Phenomenological Self alone is inadequate as an explanatory framework. The second strand—Narrative Self—fortifies and enriches the picture of selfhood. Being presented almost entirely from Brandon's perspective, the *Amateur Porn Star Killer* movies are explicitly coded as Brandon's story. Brandon provides the trilogy's continuity, unlike the victims who are present (and are killed) within single films. Additionally, the films stand-in for Brandon's self-narrative: the footage is explicitly referred to as such within the series. In *Amateur Porn Star Killer 2*, Brandon directly explains that he uses the camcorder to document his life: "[i]n 20 years I'm not going to remember everything, but I'm going to have it on camera … it's nice to sit back and enjoy [your own life] like a movie." Accordingly, the footage captured constitutes Brandon's memories of his experiences.

Narrativization permits the subject to organize their phenomenological experiences into continuity over time. The Narrative Self thereby does more than allowing the subject to access and reflect on sensations relative to previous and consequent happenings. Much like Brandon's footage, Narrative Self provides temporal coherence, allowing the subject to envisage his or her experiences as unified across time. Just as the three films provide an increasingly detailed picture of Brandon as they develop, the Narrative Self enables the subject to

---

[36] See Jones, "Dying to Be Seen."

better evaluate the significance of their actions, rather than perceiving every incident in isolation. The "movie" version[37] of *Amateur Porn Star Killer 2* is especially pertinent in this regard, since its overarching narrative is interpolated with Brandon's (auto)biography: his development as a murderer. Incidents from Brandon's past are also represented via camcorder footage and are thus part of his self-narrativization schema. The camcorder offers a frame of significance, both capturing and *preserving* various occurrences. Delineating his homicidal history as part of *Amateur Porn Star Killer 2* denotes that Brandon's Narrative Self is comprised of memories in which he victimizes others.

The Phenomenological Self's stream of consciousness is not entirely overcome by its Narrative Self organization, however. *Amateur Porn Star Killer 2* is still driven by a largely real-time depiction of seduction and murder. Segments of Brandon's past are distinctly memory-like, interrupting the chronological flow at tangentially relevant moments. For example, after entering Brandon's apartment, Brandon exhibits his sexual motivation by groping "Victim #12" (as the character is credited). She is unaware of the threat posed, and tells him to "be patient" while she changes outfits in his bathroom. As she dresses, Brandon waits, rubbing his crotch. At this point, one of his memory-footage segments intersects the temporal flow. The footage—labeled "Victim #2" in an onscreen caption—depicts a couple having sex in a car. The film returns to the narrative present when "Victim #12" returns from the bathroom. In this case, the interpolated memory-footage provides access to what appears to be Brandon's daydreaming as he waits. His arousal in the narrative present manifests as a sexual incident from his kill-catalog. The method encapsulates the disjointed quality of phenomenological stream of consciousness, while also evoking the Narrative Self's organizational structure.

Furthermore, since the three films are entirely constituted by Brandon's recorded footage constructed (edited) together into a time line, the films replicate the artificial, reflective nature of self-narrativization. The Narrative Self is constituted not by experiences, but by severely biased renditions of self-memory. The camcorder footage's pastness is apt because narrativized reflection on the self is likewise an *ex post facto* mode of arranging experiences. It is also apposite that the footage is skewed toward Brandon's first-person perspective,

---

[37] *Amateur Porn Star Killer* 2 was released in two formats: the "snuff" version and the "movie" version. The latter is intersected with captions outlining Brandon's history, and footage of previous kills. The film also contains an extradiegetic score and postproduction effects (such as colored filters) not present in the snuff cut (which instead pertains to faux-snuff realism). As such, the two versions offer a bridge between faux-snuff and conventional narrative films that contain snuff themes (rather than seeking to emulate snuff). All references to *Amateur Porn Star Killer 2* in this chapter will refer to the "movie" version.

since Narrative Self is biased in orientation: the narrative is shaped around events the subject considers significant in formulating who they are at any given moment.

The films are constituted almost exclusively by footage of sexualized murders. *Amateur Porn Star Killer* is not only about Brandon's actions however, but also how Brandon himself is composed via his deeds. As a reflection of Brandon's Narrative Self, the series' repeated plot indicates that his identity is constituted by those homicides. Indeed, as a caption in *Amateur Porn Star Killer 2* reveals, although he is most commonly referred to as Brandon, he also adopts the aliases Christian and John Lee. Thus, the caption identifies Brandon as "The Killer."[38] "Brandon" is a persona that belies the man's identity as murderer. "The Killer" is only meaningful as a killer. In order to author his own autonomous meaningfulness, he must eradicate others. Consequently, the victims are coauthors in Brandon's Narrative Self story:[39] both parties are necessary to affirm "The Killer" qua killer. Although slaying is contra-social, it is not asocial. Even when they are harmful, sex, homicide, and conversation—the three activities Brandon engages in during these films—are interpersonal engagements. Since those relations define Brandon's identity, *Amateur Porn Star Killer* depicts Brandon as a Bodily (contra) Social Self.

Faux-snuff evokes many of the elements found in contemporary philosophy of self then, yet the tripartite model's unity is complicated by the series' murder-based plots. Homicide is dependent on a relationship between killer and victim, but the victim is eradicated during the engagement. That is, the victims vanish in the moment they constitute "The Killer" qua killer. Brandon's identity is thus jeopardized as much as it is constituted by the engagement. Resultantly, *Amateur Porn Star Killer* centralizes not only sexual slaughter, but also Brandon's compulsive drive to repeat the same murderous actions across the trilogy. In their own brutal fashion, these films convey that the process of self-narrativization is "an on-going process,"[40] which "continually amends itself,"[41] and so is experienced as "perpetual (re)begin[ning]."[42]

---

[38]Although it is revealed that the Killer's birth name is Reid at the close of *Amateur Porn Star Killer 2*, the film's final caption subsequently refers to the Killer as Brandon, signaling that Brandon remains the primary name by which the Killer is known in the series.

[39]It is also worth noting that the actors playing lead victims in the first two films (Michiko Jiminez and Kai Lanette, respectively) are credited as cowriters and codirectors alongside Shane Ryan (who plays Brandon): that is, the victims are coauthors in a meta sense.

[40]Metzinger in Tippett et al., "To Be or Not to Be," 6.

[41]Jefferson A. Singer, Pavel Blagov, Meredith Berry, and Kathryn M. Oost, "Self-Defining Memories, Scripts, and the Life Story: Narrative Identity in Personality and Psychotherapy," *Journal of Personality* 81, no. 6 (2013): 570.

[42]Thomson, "In the Future Philosophy Will Be Neither Continental nor Analytic but Synthetic," 194.

Self/perspectives

Envisaged as a process of becoming rather than simply being, selfhood is divested of egoistic connotations. The self is neither fixed nor autoconstituting. *Amateur Porn Star Killer*'s prolonged first-person camerawork could be misconstrued as centralizing Brandon, but it more pertinently signals inadequacies with solipsistic conceptions of self. Events are depicted from one position when shot via killer-cam, but that technique also excludes all other possible perspectives. The form reifies Brandon's contra-sociality, which culminates in his willingness to eradicate others. By formally omitting other viewpoints, the killer-cam motif reflects Brandon's failure to acknowledge selfhood's interdependent nature. Every individual's subjectivity is founded on a claim to legitimacy. Brandon's willingness to murder other people unambiguously exhibits his inability to perceive his victims as equal to himself. The emphasis placed on his first-person perspective in these films hypostatizes Brandon's sociopathology via the biased camerawork, and by associating that viewpoint with destructive, criminal behavior.

The series' first-person self-narration thereby evades lapsing into the kind of autonomy prizing self-realization Gergen warns against.[43] As Gergen has it, even the most private memory is "a collectively defined action … fashioned within a complex relational history."[44] The diegetic videos point toward such interconnectedness. Despite Brandon's discussion of his camcorder footage as a personal *aide memoire*, the cassettes are not private per se. Indeed, *Amateur Porn Star Killer*'s closing captions assert that Brandon disseminated his murder videos by substituting them with tapes from more than eighty video-rental stores. As another caption in *Amateur Porn Star Killer 2* has it, this means "all of his victims were exposed to the public through [sic] VHS." His videos are expressly communal documents.

The films undercut any sense that Brandon's autodocumentation is simply to be construed as narcissistic self-bolstering by bridging to broader, collective spheres. Brandon's self-narrativization is more akin to the kind of reflexivity that transforms the subject into an object: that which is reflected upon. For Sartre, such deliberation necessitates perceiving oneself as an other,[45] and so is imbued with a third-personal, intersubjective sensibility. Since Brandon's videos are public articles—intentionally disseminated to the populace by Brandon himself—a viewer other than Brandon is implied in the very making of the tapes. His pathologized self-filming is an example of "compensatory hyperreflexivity"; voluntary "reflective

---

[43]Gergen, "The Self as Social Construction," 112.
[44]Ibid., 114.
[45]Jean-Paul Sartre, *The Transcendence of the Ego: An Existentialist Theory of Consciousness* (New York: The Noonday Press, 1957): 65.

self-monitoring in an attempt to compensate for...diminished self-presence."[46] Brandon's autodocumentation exposes flaws in his self-conception that can only be remedied by accommodating rather than eliminating other perspectives.

Although the films are principally relayed from Brandon's first-person vantage point, it is significant that other perspectives are briefly included. These distinct deviations from the series' normative mode occur at analogous junctures in each movie, taking one of three forms. The first occurs when Brandon hands the camera to his victims. For example, in *Amateur Porn Star Killer 3*, Brandon's victim-to-be (Nikki) takes the camera while Brandon searches for his car keys. Although brief and naturalistic, shifting to the target-subject's perspective draws attention to how oppressively exclusive the series' primary filming position is. Switching to an alternative outlook, however fleetingly, undercuts the legitimacy of sovereign, egoistic selfhood. In the second type of deviation, the camera perspective is similarly disconnected from Brandon's first-person viewpoint during some incidents of violence. Brandon puts the camera down to film himself harming Stacy in *Amateur Porn Star Killer*, for example. Although the footage is still "his," the vantage point is uncoupled from Brandon's point-of-view. Brandon's first-person perspective is not totalizing, and so his filmed autodocumentation does not equate to unerring, autonomous self-possession.

The third deviation is the most significant. In the final moments of each film, Brandon captures his own face on camera. In *Amateur Porn Star Killer 2* and *3*, these sequences last over a minute, representing the trilogy's most sustained engagements with Brandon. In all three films, Brandon is only shown at length after the lead victim has been dispatched. This recurring pattern has a causal flavor, connoting that Brandon's identity is indeed constituted by killing. As a process of self-narrativization, these moments allow Brandon to locate himself relative to the murders he commits. He is only captured as "complete" in the afterglow of homicide. However, it is also only at these junctures that Brandon is in need of completion. Eliminating his victim-to-be—who complements Brandon as a killer-to-be—entails divesting himself of the counterpart who brings meaning to his identity.

One reason that murder cannot provide an adequate foundation for self-construction is because the act is ephemeral. Despite Brandon's attempts to capture homicide on video, the murders remain transitory rather than constitutive. His attempts to preserve himself as killer after-the-fact are equally unsound. Homicide denotes that Brandon apprehends other subjects' claims to self as insignificant compared with his own fulfillment. However, filming himself in this manner underscores just how *equal* Brandon and his victims are. Brandon uses the same apparatus to capture both himself and his victims. Consequently, Brandon is

---

[46]Zahavi, *Subjectivity and Selfhood*, 137.

most knowable—to himself and to *Amateur Porn Star Killer*'s viewer—when he occupies the same representational field as his victims. Brandon treats his victims as subhuman objects while filming them. When he records his own visage on camera, it is also as an object rather than as a subject. As an articulation of his sociopathology, the camcorder footage—a recording, distanced from immanent events—is apposite, since the mode inherently objectifies more than it subjectifies.

In this light, it is apparent that Brandon's attempts to self-narrate via first-person filming are self-abnegating. Killer-cam may principally exclude other perspectives, but the mode also displaces Brandon. Because he operates the camcorder, Brandon remains offscreen for the majority of the series' duration. Since faux-snuff footage is explicitly located within the crime scene as the act unfolds, the form ostensibly provides more intimate access to filmed murder than other fictional forms do. However, Brandon's semipresence is a constant reminder of the viewer's profound distance both from the action and from Brandon himself.

Despite being the series' core, Brandon remains tantalizingly out of the viewer's reach. That ungraspable quality is apt, encapsulating why both faux-snuff and self are so fascinating. "Snuff" and "self" seem to indexically refer to objects, but neither snuff nor self can be pinned down as objects. The snuff myth is constituted not by any one single object, but rather a network of representations, allegations, and speculations. Faux-snuff is the closest available iteration of that myth, and its constructed falsity attests to the unattainability of real snuff. Faux-snuff cannot replicate authentic snuff because there is no genuine article: faux-snuff hypostatizes the *mythology*. Self is similarly slippery. Much like Brandon, self is an ever-present foundational core that is simultaneously ungraspable. Brandon's first-person perspective limits the viewer's ability to perceive him. The viewing frame is inadequate to capture both Brandon and his perspective in a sustained fashion. This constraint encapsulates the essential problem that self poses for philosophers: our (in)ability to understand the world begins with our limited access to others and to ourselves. Based on such intangibility, some scholars have argued that self is an illusion.[47] Much like snuff then, self could be read as a constructed mythology.

Yet, such argumentation abandons self too hastily. It is not self, but rather the *language* of self that fails: like Brandon's first-person perspective, the language of self offers a limited frame that is unable to provide a holistic picture. Like snuff, self is not a locatable object per se, but is a nexus of ideas, speculations, and discourses. It is only by apprehending the broader interconnections between various articulations of self that selfhood might be understood. This is why recent shifts toward interdisciplinary theorization are vital in moving away from the traditionally limited and limiting frameworks of selfhood studies. Precisely the same is true for our understanding of snuff.

---

[47]See Tippett et al., "To Be or Not to Be."

Self/implications

As the *Amateur Porn Star Killer* series illustrates, faux-snuff reflects various concerns that have been concurrently raised in the field of self-studies. However, this chapter has not sought to impose a paradigm on *Amateur Porn Star Killer*, to reclaim the subgenre from its maligned status, or to uncover some supposed "hidden truth" about faux-snuff narratives. The primary objective has been to demonstrate what can be gained by apprehending the already existent similarities between ideas conveyed via film and those expressed via scholarship (outside of film studies). As proposed in the early stages of this chapter, the field of contemporary self-studies is notably characterized by its dissolving disciplinary divisions. Thomson's Hegelian vision of a philosophy that "sublat[es] dichotomous oppositions" by synthesizing traditions[48] succinctly encapsulates the power of combining extant ideas: doing so requires reimagining conventionalized assumptions. One such supposition might be that neuroscience experiments and textual readings of popular culture occupy entirely separate spheres. The ideas offered within recent self-philosophy are applicable to both, and so bridge between those apparently antithetical domains of thought.

The *Amateur Porn Star Killer* films epitomize why faux-snuff is so apt as a contributor to that ethos. The trilogy routinely disturbs seemingly absolute binary oppositions, each of which are fundamental to self-conception. Despite reputedly portraying murder sprees in a manner that solely objectifies the victims and identifies with the killer, *Amateur Porn Star Killer* demonstrates that faux-snuff is principally invested in the tipping points between victim and killer. Homicide is not self-bolstering eradication of the Other in these movies. Although focused on engagements between Brandon and his victims, none of the *Amateur Porn Star Killer* films are mainly spent probing death, the victim qua victim, or the killer qua killer. Rather these films explore the build to homicide. As such, the trilogy is focused not on polarized binaries but on the infra-dichotomous states between life and death, victim and killer.

The faux-snuff form provides a natural conduit for this kind of exploration because the form playfully blurs supposed dichotomies between fantasy and reality, fiction and truth. As I have argued elsewhere,[49] faux-snuff filmmakers do not necessarily seek to trick viewers into believing realistic looking events are genuine. Ryan certainly does not try to obscure or quell skeptical reactions to the verité-style footage contained in his trilogy. Indeed, he openly provokes such incredulity from the series' outset. *Amateur Porn Star Killer* opens with captions

---

[48]Thomson, "In the Future Philosophy Will Be Neither Continental nor Analytic but Synthetic," 191.
[49]Jones, "Dying to Be Seen."

that proclaim snuff's inauthenticity. These statements include *Hardcore* director Paul Schrader's comments regarding the public's "willingness to believe" in snuff, and a declaration that snuff remains an "urban legend." All three films contain credit sequences, exposing their artifice. The second film was packaged on DVD in two edits (a "snuff" cut and a "movie" version), and the trilogy was later released in 3D.[50] These formal interventions underline that the films are contrived, edited, commercial products. Although no genuine snuff has been proven to exist, faux-snuff remains powerful because its mechanisms underscore a truth about self. The idea that individuals might film, sell, or consume murder for entertainment, profit, or sexual gratification summates the human capacity for contra-sociality. Faux-snuff is horrifying not because the footage looks realistic, but because its apparent authenticity is a reminder of how real human cruelty is. The snuff myth may have been articulated in many different forms, but it retains its impact precisely because contra-sociality is so at odds with the intersubjectivity on which selfhood is founded.

Moreover, faux-snuff's playful approach to authenticity is potent precisely because "truths" are products of intersubjectivity. Absolute truths are unattainable because humans have no access to objectivity. Our viewpoints are necessarily limited and subjective because humans are embodied. "Truths" are formed when enough individuals concur on specific points. Consequently, as Gergen observes, "knowledge of the world and self finds its origins in human relationships," because beliefs are "brought into being through historically and culturally situated social processes."[51] Cultural objects are thus part of a truth-making process. In the case of faux-snuff, several "truths" are created. First, as a representation of human interaction, faux-snuff communicates a "truth" about human relationships, probing how complex intersubjectivity is. Second, faux-snuff perpetuates a false truth that genuine snuff exists. That is, the extant idea that snuff is being manufactured is bolstered by the film, which perpetuates the notion that snuff is plausible. Indeed, "snuff" only exists as a nebulous human discourse: the myth is constituted by intersubjective truth-making alone. Third, one of the "culturally situated social processes" Gergen refers to is reified by bridging between snuff and self-studies. The two might be thought of as incompatible because the former is typically perceived as culturally inferior to the latter. Historically, scholarly proclamations have been treated as offering "truths" that are more legitimate than those offered by, for example, fiction films. When both are perceived as intersubjective agreements—communication processes—that hierarchical distinction is exposed as being somewhat arbitrary.

---

[50]Cinema Epoch released the double disc version of *Amateur Porn Star Killer* 2 in 2008. Mongolian Barbeque released the 3D trilogy DVD in 2012.
[51]Gergen, "The Self as Social Construction," 109.

Although filmmakers and philosophers may utilize significantly different languages, to ignore the similarities between the ideas and themes raised in those respective forms of communication is tantamount to willful negligence. The separation between scholarship about self and representations of selves is comparable to the Cartesian split between mind and body: scholarship and the sciences have been traditionally associated with the mind, while popular culture (and the arts more generally) have been perceived as being of the body and the audiovisual senses. That hierarchical relationship is as flawed as the dualistic premise the difference is founded on.

Faux-snuff offers numerous reasons for spanning established disciplinary and cultural divisions. The "truth" constructed around snuff is that of a base, deviant, unjustifiable mode of filmmaking: a cultural product that represents human interaction at its worst. As I have demonstrated in this chapter, such denigration is myopic. Those who wish to territorialize self-studies might consider it irreverent to bridge between the "lowest of the low" and the heights of current intellectual understanding. However, much stands to be gained from collapsing the conventional dichotomies that separate disciplines and investigating the dialectical spaces in which dialog can occur.

LIST OF CONTRIBUTORS

Xavier Aldana Reyes is a senior lecturer in English at Manchester Metropolitan University and specializes in Gothic and Horror literature and film. He is the author of *Body Gothic* (University of Wales Press, 2014) and of the forthcoming *Horror Film and Affect* (Routledge, 2016), and the coeditor of *Digital Horror* (I. B. Tauris, 2015).

Mark Astley gained his PhD from the University from Manchester and is currently an independent scholar. His research interests are transgressive cultures on the dark net, paracinema, and creepypasta.

Linda Badley, Professor at Middle Tennessee State University, has published widely in film studies and popular culture. Her most recent book is *Lars von Trier* (Illinois, 2011). She is currently coediting *Indie Reframed: Women Filmmakers and Contemporary American Cinema* (Edinburgh). With Barton Palmer, she coedits Edinburgh University Press's companion series Traditions in World Cinema and Traditions in American Cinema.

Gerry Carlin is a Senior Lecturer in English at the University of Wolverhampton. He has published on Modernism and the avant-garde, cultural theory, and the literature and culture of the 1960s.

Nicolò Gallio received a PhD in film studies from the University of Bologna. He has published articles on horror films and "mondo" movies, and widely addressed the impact of digital media on the film industry by analyzing the role of crowdsourcing and crowdfunding in contemporary audiovisual economies. He lectures at the University of Brighton in Hastings.

Simon Hobbs lectures at the University of Portsmouth. His research areas include extreme art film, exploitation film, European art cinema, and paratextual studies. He has published works on transnational extreme art cinemas, and the DVD presentations of *Cannibal Holocaust* and *Salo, Or the 120 Days of Sodom.*

Neil Jackson teaches film at the University of Lincoln and has published on popular cinema in various books and journals. He is currently preparing a critical study of Hollywood's representation of the adult film industry.

Mark Jones is a senior lecturer in English and course leader for MA Popular Culture at the University of Wolverhampton. He has published chapters and articles on diverse aspects of popular culture, including horror films, science fiction, popular music, and pornography.

Steve Jones is a senior lecturer in media at Northumbria University. His research is principally focused on representations of sex and violence, the philosophy of self, gender politics, and ethics. His recent work includes the monograph *Torture Porn:*

Popular Horror after Saw (Palgrave-Macmillan, 2013), and the edited collection *Zombies and Sexuality* (McFarland, 2014). For more information, please visit www. drstevejones.co.uk

Misha Kavka is Associate Professor of Media, Film and Television at the University of Auckland. She is the author of *Reality Television, Affect and Intimacy* (Palgrave Macmillan, 2008) and *Reality TV* (Edinburgh University Press, 2012), and has published widely on affect in relation to film, television, and media technologies.

Tina Kendall is Senior Lecturer and Course Leader for Film Studies at Anglia Ruskin University. She has published widely in the area of extreme cinema, and is coeditor of *The New Extremism in Cinema: From France to Europe* (Edinburgh University Press, 2011). Her more recent work focuses on boredom and the attention economy of contemporary media.

David Kerekes is a co-founder of the publishing house Headpress. He is coauthor of the books *Killing for Culture: An Illustrated History of Death Film from Mondo to Snuff* (Creation, 1994), revised and updated as *Killing for Culture: From Edison to ISIS* (Headpress, 2015), and *See No Evil: Banned Films and Video Controversy* (Critical Vision, 2001). He is the author of *Sex Murder Art: The Films of Jörg Buttgereit* (Critical Vision, 1994) and has written extensively on popular culture. His meditation on family and the Italian Diaspora, Mezzogiorno, was published by Headpress in 2012. www. worldheadpress.com.

Shaun Kimber is a senior lecturer in media theory at Bournemouth University. He is the author of *Controversies: Henry: Portrait of a Serial Killer* (Palgrave, 2011) and is currently working on the coauthored book, *Writing & Selling Horror Screenplays* (Kamera).

Mark McKenna is a lecturer in media, film, and photography at Glyndwr University, Wrexham, and is currently completing a PhD at the University of Sunderland on the marketing a distribution of the video nasties. He hosts an online archive of materials related to the UK video distributor VIPCO (http://vipcosvault.co.uk), and is currently editing a book about global media censorship with John Mercer and Oliver Carter.

Xavier Mendik is Director of Graduate Studies in the School of Media at Birmingham City University, from where he runs the *Cine-Excess* International Film Festival. He has written extensively on European cult and horror film traditions, and is currently completing a feature-length documentary on 1970s Italian cult film.

Julian Petley is Professor of Screen Media at Brunel University, and Visiting Professor at De Montfort University. He is one of the Principal Editors of the *Journal of British Cinema and Television*, and his works on horror include contributions to the *Blackwell Companion to the Horror Film* (Wiley-Blackwell, 2014) and *Horror Zone* (I. B. Tauris, 2010). He also coedited, with Steve Chibnall, *British Horror Cinema* (Routledge, 2002).

Clarissa Smith is Professor of Sexual Cultures at the University of Sunderland, UK. Her research focuses on media cultures and, more specifically, on sexualities, pornography, and popular culture, and her publications include *One for the Girls! The Pleasures and Practices of Reading Women's Porn* (Intellect, 2007) and *Studying Sexualities: Theories, Representations, Practices* (with Niall Richardson and Angela Werndly, Palgrave, 2013). She is currently writing *Sex, Sexualisation and the Media* for Palgrave's Key Issues in Media Series and is a founding coeditor of the Routledge journal *Porn Studies*.

Johnny Walker is a lecturer in media at Northumbria University. He is the author of *Contemporary British Horror Cinema: Industry, Genre and Society* (Edinburgh University Press, 2015), founding coeditor of the *Global Exploitation Cinemas* book series (Bloomsbury) and has contributed articles to journals such as *Horror Studies* and collections such as *Merchants of Menace: The Business of Horror Cinema* (Bloosmbury, 2014).

Thomas Joseph Watson lectures in media studies at Teesside University. His research investigates the role of film form in the depiction of violence in contemporary audio-visual media. He has published on pornography, documentary film, and experimental video-art.

SELECT BIBLIOGRAPHY

Aaron, Michele. *Death and the Moving Image: Ideology, Iconography, I.* Edinburgh: Edinburgh University Press, 2014.

Adams, Parveen. "Father, Can't You See I'm Filming?" In *Supposing the Subject*, edited by Joan Copjec, 185–200. London: Verso, 1994.

Ahmed, Sara. *Queer Phenomenology: Orientations, Objects, Others.* Durham, NC and London: Duke University Press. 2006.

Aldana Reyes, Xavier. *Consuming Mutilation: Affectivity and Corporeal Transgression on Stage and Screen.* PhD thesis. Lancaster University, 2013.

Aldana Reyes, Xavier. "The *[•REC]* Quartet: Affective Possibilities and Stylistic Limitations of Found Footage Horror." In *Digital Horror: Haunted Technologies, Network Panic and the Found Footage Phenomenon*, edited by Linnie Blake and Xavier Aldana Reyes. London and New York: I.B. Tauris, 2015.

Aldana Reyes, Xavier. "Reel Evil: A Critical Reassessment of the Found Footage Phenomenon." *Gothic Studies* 17, no. 2 (2015, forthcoming).

Alsmith, Adrian, John Tetteh, and Frédérique de Vignemont. "Embodying the Mind and Representing the Body." *Review of Philosophy and Psychology* 3, no. 1 (2012): 1–13.

Anderson, Donald L. "How the Horror Film Broke Its Promise: Hyperreal Horror and Ruggero Deodato's *Cannibal Holocaust*." *Horror Studies* 4, no.1 (2013): 109–25.

Attwood, Feona, and Clarissa Smith. "Extreme Concern: Regulating 'Dangerous Pictures' in the United Kingdom." *Journal of Law and Society* 37, no. 1 (2010): 171–88.

Attwood, Feona. "Immersion: 'Extreme' Texts, Animated Bodies and the Media." *Media, Culture & Society* 36, no. 8 (2014): 1186–95.

Barker, Martin. *A Haunt of Fears: The Strange History of the British Horror Comics Campaign.* London: Pluto, 1984.

Barker, Martin, ed. *The Video Nasties: Freedom and Censorship in the Media.* London: Pluto, 1984.

Barker, Martin, Jane Arthurs, and Ramaswami Harindranath. *The Crash Controversy: Censorship Campaigns and Film Reception.* London: Wallflower Press, 2001.

Barker, Martin, and Kate Brooks. *Knowing Audiences: Judge Dredd, Its Friends, Fans, and Foes.* Luton: University of Luton Press, 1998.

Barker, Martin, and Julian Petley, eds. *Ill Effects: The Media Violence Debate.* London: Routledge, 2002.

Barthes, Roland. *Camera Lucida.* Translated by Richard Howard. New York: Hill and Wang, 1982.

Baudrillard, Jean. *Simulations*. Translated by Paul Foss, Paul Patton, and Philip Beitchman. New York: Semiotext(e), 1983.

Baudrillard, Jean. *The Consumer Society: Myths and Structures*. Translated by Chris Turner. London: Sage, 1998. [Orig. 1970].

Beatson, Peter. "Mapping Human Animal Relations." In *Theorizing Animals: Re-thinking Humanimal Relations*, edited by Tania Signal and Nik Taylor, 21–58. Boston, MA: Brill, 2011.

Belk, Russell. *Collecting in a Consumer Society*. London: Routledge, 2001.

Bell, Martin. "TV News: How Far Should We Go?" *British Journalism Review* 8, no.1 (1997): 7–16.

Benson-Allott, Caetlin. *Killer Tapes and Shattered Screens: Video Spectatorship from VHS to File Sharing*. Berkeley: California University Press, 2013.

Berendzen, J.C. "Coping Without Foundations: On Dreyfus's Use of Merleau-Ponty." *International Journal of Philosophical Studies* 18, no. 5 (2010): 629–49.

Betz, Mark. "Art, Exploitation, Underground." In *Defining Cult Movies: The Cultural Politics of Oppositional Taste*, edited by Mark Jancovich, Antonio Reboll, Julian Stringer, and Andy Willis, 202–22. Manchester: Manchester University Press, 2003.

Beugnet, Martine and Elizabeth Ezra. "Traces of the Modern: An Alternative History of French Cinema". *Studies in French Cinema* 10, no. 1 (2010): 11–38. DOI: 10.1386/sfc.10.1.11/1.

Black, Joel. "Real(ist) Horror: From Execution Videos to Snuff Films." In *Underground USA: Filmmaking Beyond the Hollywood Canon*, edited by Xavier Mendik and Steven Jay Schneider, 63–75. London: Wallflower Press, 2002.

Bordwell, David. "Film Interpretation Revisited." *Film Criticism* 27, no. 3 (1993): 93–119.

Braddock, Louise. "Psychological Identification, Imagination and Psychoanalysis." *Philosophical Psychology* 24, no. 5 (2011): 639–57.

Brecht, Berthold. *Brecht on Theatre: The Development of an Aesthetic*. Translated by John Willett. London: Methuen, 1964.

Brewster, Francis, Harvey Fenton, and Marc Morris. *Shock! Horror!: Astounding Artwork from the Video Nasty Era*. London: FAB Press, 2005.

Brinkema, Eugenie. "How to Do Things with Violences." In *A Companion to Michael Haneke*, edited by Roy Grundmann, 354–70. Oxford: Wiley-Blackwell, 2010.

Bronfen, Elisabeth. *Over Her Dead Body: Death, Femininity and the Aesthetic*. Manchester: Manchester University Press, 1992.

Bronstein, Carolyn. *Battling Pornography: The American Feminist Anti-Pornography Movement, 1976–1986*. New York: Cambridge University Press, 2011.

Brophy, Philip. "Horrality: The Textuality of Contemporary Horror Films." *Screen* 27, no. 1 (1986): 2–13.

Brottman, Mikita. "'Strange Images of Death': Manson, Polanski, *Macbeth*." In *Hollywood Hex: Death and Destiny in the Dream Factory*, 57–87. London: Creation Books, 1999.

Brottman, Mikita. *Offensive Films*. Nashville: Vanderbilt University Press, 2005.

Brown, William. "Violence in Extreme Cinema and the Ethics of Spectatorship." *Projections* 7, no. 1 (2013): 25–42.

Browne, Nick. "The Spectator-in-the-Text: The Rhetoric of *Stagecoach*." *Film Quarterly* 29, no. 2 (1975–1976): 26–38.

Bugliosi, Vincent with Curt Gentry. *Helter Skelter: The True Story of the Manson Murders*. New York: W. W. Norton, 1994.

Butler, Jesse. "Introspective Knowledge of Experience and Its Role in Consciousness Studies." *Journal of Consciousness Studies* 18, no. 2 (2011): 128–45.

Caputi, Jane. *The Age of Sex Crime*. Bowling Green, OH: Bowling Green State University Popular Press, 1987.

Carlin, Gerry and Mark Jones. "'Helter Skelter' and Sixties Revisionism." In *Countercultures and Popular Music*, edited by Sheila Whiteley and Jedediah Sklower, 95–107. Farnham: Ashgate, 2014.

Carline, Anna. "Criminal Justice, Extreme Pornography and Prostitution: Protecting Women or Promoting Morality?" *Sexualities* 14, no. 3 (2011): 312–33.

Carrabine, Eamonn. "Crime, Culture and the Media in a Globalizing World." In *The Routledge Handbook of International Crime and Justice Studies*, edited by Bruce Arrigo and Heather Bersot, 397–419. London: Routledge, 2013.

Carroll, Noel. *The Philosophy of Horror, or Paradoxes of the Heart*. New York/London: Routledge, 1990.

Caufield, Schung. "The Plight of the Screen Animal: Animal Disappearance and Death on Film." *Film Matters* 2, no. 2 (2011): 18–22.

Chippendale, Peter. "How High Street Horror is Invading the Home." *The Sunday Times*, May 23, 1982.

Clover, Carol J. *Men, Women and Chain Saws: Gender in Modern Horror Film*. Princeton, NJ: Princeton University Press, 1993.

Cohen, Stanley. *States of Denial: Knowing about Atrocities and Suffering*. Cambridge: Polity, 2001.

Coke, Demond. *Confessions of an Incurable Collector*. London: The Whitefriars Press, Ltd., 1928.

Conrich, Ian. "Mass Media/Mass Murder: Serial Killer Cinema and the Modern Violated Body." In *Criminal Visions: Media Representations of Crime and Justice*, edited by Paul Mason, 156–71. Cullompton: Willan Publishing, 2003.

Cox, David. "*A Serbian Film*: When Allegory Gets Nasty." *The Guardian*, December 13, 2010. Accessed March 8, 2012. http://www.theguardian.com/film/filmblog/2010/dec/13/a-serbian-film-allegorical-political.

Crane, Jonathan. "Scraping Bottom: Splatter and the Herschell Gordon Lewis Oeuvre." In *The Horror Film*, edited by Stephen Prince, 150–66. New Brunswick, NJ: Rutgers University Press, 2004.

Cumberbatch, Guy. "Legislating Mythology: Video Violence and Children." *Journal of Mental Health* 3, no. 4 (1994): 485–94.

Currie, Gregory. *Image and Mind: Film, Philosophy and Cognitive Science*. Cambridge: Cambridge University Press, 1995.

Davies, Nick. *Flat Earth News*. London: Chatto and Windus, 2008.

DeVos, Andrew. "The More You Rape Their Senses, The Happier They Are: A History of Cannibal Holocaust." In *Cinema Inferno: Celluloid Explosions from the Cult Margins*, edited by Robert Weiner and John Cline, 76–100. Lanham, MD: Scarecrow press Inc., 2010.

Dickie, John. "Stereotypes of the Italian South." In *The New History of the Italian South: The Mezzogiorno Revisited*, edited by Robert Lumle and Jonathan Morris. Exeter: University of Exeter Press, 1997.

Dickinson, Kay. "Troubling Synthesis: The Horrific Sights and Incompatible Sounds of Video Nasties." In *Sleaze Artists: Cinema at the Margins of Taste, Style, and Politics, edited by Jeffrey Sconce*, 167–88. Durham, NC: Duke University Press, 2007.

Dixon, Wheeler W. *A History of Horror*. New Brunswick, NJ: Rutgers University Press, 2010.

Doane, Mary Ann. *The Emergence of Cinematic Time: Modernity, Contingency, the Archive*. Cambridge: Harvard UP, 2000.

Downing, Lisa. "Stuff and Nonsense: The Discursive Life of a Phantasmatic Archive." In *Porn Archives*, edited by Tim Dean, Steven Ruszczycky, and David Squires, 249–60. Durham, NC: Duke University Press, 2015.

Downing, Lisa and Libby Saxton. *Film and Ethics: Foreclosed Encounters*. Abingdon: Routledge, 2009.

Dubrovskii, D.I. "Subjective Reality and the Brain: An Essay on a Theoretical Solution to the Problem." *Herald of the Russian Academy of Sciences* 83, no. 1 (2013): 59–69.

Dullstein, Monika. "The Second Person in the Theory of Mind Debate." *Review of Philosophy and Psychology* 3, no. 2 (2012): 231–48.

Dworkin, Andrea. *Pornography: Men Possessing Women*. London: Women's Press, 1979/1999.

Egan, Kate. *Trash or Treasure? Censorship and the Changing Meanings of the Video Nasties*. Manchester: Manchester University Press, 2007.

Eisner, Lotte H. *Murnau*. Berkeley: University of California Press, 1973.

Ellis, John. *Visible Fictions: Cinema, Television, Video*. London: Routledge, 1992.

Elsaesser, Thomas. *Weimar Cinema and After: Germany's Historical Imaginary*. New York and London: Routledge, 2000.

Farmer, Harry and Manos Tsakiris. "The Bodily Social Self: A Link between Phenomenal and Narrative Selfhood." *Review of Philosophy and Psychology* 3, no. 1 (2012): 125–44.

Fenton, Harvey. *Cannibal Holocaust and the Savage Cinema of Ruggero Deodato*. Godalming: FAB Press, 2011, 2nd edition.

Foucault, Michel. *The Essential Works of Foucault 1954–1984: Power*, vol. 3, edited by James D. Faubion. New York: New Press, 2000.

Freeland, Cynthia A. "Realist Horror." In *Philosophy and Film*, edited by Cynthia A. Freeland and Thomas E. Wartenberg, 126–42. London: Routledge, 1995.

Freud, Sigmund. "The 'Uncanny'." In *The Standard Edition of the Complete Psychological Works of Sigmund Freud* (*Volume 17*), edited by James Strachey, 219–52. London: Hogarth, 1919.

Fuchs, Christian. *Social Media*. London: Sage, 2014.

Gallagher, Shaun. "Philosophical Conceptions of the Self: Implications for Cognitive Science." *Trends in Cognitive Science* 4, no. 1 (2000): 14–21.

Gallese, V. and C. Sinigaglia. "How the Body in Action Shapes the Self." *Journal of Consciousness Studies* 18, no. 7–8 (2011): 117–43.

Gelder, Ken. "Review of *Killing for Culture*." *Postscript* 1, no. 3 (2002): 131–33.

Genette, Gerard. *Paratexts: Thresholds of Interpretation*. Cambridge: Cambridge University Press, 1997.

Gergen, Kenneth J. "The Self as Social Construction." *Psychological Studies* 56, no. 1 (2011): 108–16.

Gill, Pat. "Taking it Personally: Male suffering in *8mm*." *Camera Obscura* 18, no. 1 (2003): 157–87.

Gladwin, Phil. "Reality Bites: Writers Get Clever." *Script Magazine*, May/June 2009, 36.

Goldman, Alvin I. "A Moderate Approach to Embodied Cognitive Science." *Review of Philosophy and Psychology* 3, no. 1 (2012): 71–88.

Goodall, Mark. "Shockumentary Evidence: The Perverse Politics of the Mondo Film." In *Remapping World Cinema: Identity, Culture and Politics in Film*, edited by Stephanie Dennison and Song Hwee Lim, 118–25. London: Wallflower Press, 2006a.

Goodall, Mark. *Sweet and Savage: The World Thorough the Shockumentary Film Lens.* London: Headpress, 2006b.

Gorightly, Adam. *The Shadow Over Santa Susana: Black Magic, Mind Control and the "Manson Family" Mythos.* San Jose, CA: Writers Club Press, 2001.

Grindstaff, David A. and Kevin M. DeLuca "The Corpus of Daniel Pearl." *Critical Studies in Media Communications* 21, no. 4 (2004): 308–12.

Guinn, Jeff. *Manson: The Life and Times of Charles Manson.* New York: Simon & Schuster, 2013.

Guins, Raiford. "Blood and Black Gloves on Shiny Discs: New Media, Old Tastes, and the Remediation of the Italian Horror Film in the United States." In *Horror International*, edited by Steven Jay Schneider and Tony Williams, 15–32. Detroit, MI: Wayne State University Press, 2005.

Gunning, Tom. "The Cinema of Attraction: Early Film, Its Spectator, and the Avant-Garde." In *Early Cinema: Space Frame Narrative*, edited by Thomas Elsaesser. London: BFI, 1990.

Gunning, Tom. "To Scan a Ghost: The Ontology of Mediated Vision." *Grey Room* 26 (2007): 94–127.

Hagin, Boaz. "Killed Because of Lousy Ratings: The Hollywood History of Snuff." *Journal of Popular Film and Television* 38, no. 1 (2010): 44–51.

Hagman, Hampus. "Every Cannes Needs Its Scandal: Between Art and Exploitation in Contemporary French Film." *Film International* 29 (2007): 32–41.

Hanna, Robert, Gerald Izenberg, Raymond Martin, Norbert Wiley, and Jerrold Seigel. "Me, Myself, and I: The Rise of the Modern Self." *Annals of the New York Academy of Sciences* 1234, no. 10 (2011): 108–20.

Haskell, Molly. *From Reverence to Rape: The Treatment of Women in the Movies.* Chicago, IL: The University of Chicago Press, 1974.

Hawkins, Joan. *Cutting Edge: Art Horror and the Horrific Avant Garde.* Minneapolis: University of Minnesota Press, 2000.

Hawkins, Joan. "Sleaze Mania, Euro-trash, and High Art." In *Horror: The Film Reader*, edited by Mark Jancovich, 125–34. London and New York: Routledge, 2002.

Heller-Nicholas, Alexandra. "Snuff Boxing: Revisiting the *Snuff* Coda." *Cinephile* 5, no. 2 (2009): 10–15.

Heller-Nicholas, Alexandra. *Found Footage Horror Films Fear and the Appearance of Reality.* Jefferson, NC: McFarland, 2014.

Herbert, Beate M. and Olga Pollatos. "The Body in the Mind: On the Relationship between Interoception and Embodiment." *Topics in Cognitive Science* 4, no. 4 (2012): 692–704.

Hight, Craig. *Television Mockumentary: Reflexivity, Satire and a Call to Play.* Manchester: Manchester University Press, 2010.

Hillier, Jim. "*Cahiers du Cinema: The 1950s: Neo-Realism, Hollywood, New Wave.* Cambridge, MA: Harvard University Press, 1985.

Hills, Matt. "Para-Paracinema: The *Friday the 13th* Films as Other to Trash and Legitimate Film Cultures." In *Sleaze Artists: Cinema at the Margins of Taste, Style, and Politics*, edited by Jeffrey Sconce, 219–39. Durham, NC: Duke University Press, 2007.

Hills, Matt. "Cutting into Concepts of 'Reflectionist' Cinema? The *Saw* Franchise and Puzzles of Post-9/11 Horror." In *Horror after 9/11: World of Fear, Cinema of Terror*, edited by Aviva Briefel and Sam J. Miller, 107–23. Austin: University of Texas, 2011.

Hobbs, Simon. "*Cannibal Holocaust:* The Paratextual (Re)construction of History." In *Popular Media Cultures*, edited by Lincoln Geraghty. Basingstoke: Palgrave Macmillan, 2015.

Horeck, Tanya and Tina Kendall, eds. *The New Extremism in Cinema: From France to Europe*. Edinburgh: University of Edinburgh Press, 2011.

Hornle, Julia. "Countering the Dangers of Online Pornography-Shrewd Regulation of Lewd Content?" *European Journal of Law and Technology* 2, no. 1 (2011): 1–26.

Hubner, Laura. "A Vogue for Flesh and Blood? Shifting Classifications of Contemporary European Cinema." In *Valuing Films: Shifting Perceptions of Worth*, edited by Laura Hubner, 198–214. London: Palgrave Macmillan, 2011.

Hunter, I.Q. *British Trash Cinema*. London: BFI/Palgrave Macmillan, 2013.

Hutchings, Peter. *The Horror Film*. Harlow: Pearson, 2004.

Irvine, Janice M. "Transient Feelings: Sex Panics and the Politics of Emotions." *GLQ: A Journal of Lesbian and Gay Studies* 14, no. 1 (2008): 1–40.

Itzin, Catherine, "Pornography and the Construction of Misogyny." *Journal of Sexual Aggression* 8, no. 3 (2002): 4–42.

Jackson, Neil. "*Cannibal Holocaust*, Realist Horror, and Reflexivity." *Post Script: Essays in Film and the Humanities* 21, no. 3 (2002): 32–45.

Jameson, Frederic. *Signatures of the Visible*. London and New York: Routledge, 1992.

Jancovich, Mark. "'A Real Shocker': Authenticity, Genre and the Struggle for Distinction." *Continuum: Journal of Media and Cultural Studies* 14, no. 1 (2000a): 25–6.

Jancovich, Mark. "Cult Fictions: Cult Movies, Subcultural Capital and the Struggle for Distinction." *Cultural Studies* 16, no. 2 (2000b): 306–22.

Jauregui, Carolina. "'Eat It Alive and Swallow It Whole!': Resavoring Cannibal Holocaust as a Mockumentary." *Invisible Culture* 7 (2004): 7.

Johnson, Eithne and Eric Schaefer. "Soft Core/Hard Gore: Snuff as a Crisis in Meaning." *Journal of Film and Video* 45, no. 2–3 (1993): 40–59.

Johnson, Paul. "Law, Morality and Disgust: The Regulation of 'Extreme Pornography' in England and Wales." *Social & Legal Studies* 19, no. 2 (2010): 147–63.

Johnson, Peter. "A Death Caught on Tape: Should It Run or not?" *USA Today*, September 5, 2004. Accessed July 25, 2014. http://usatoday30.usatoday.com/life/columnist/mediamix/2004-05-11-media-mix_x.htm.

Johnstone, A.A. "The Basic Self and Its Doubles." *Journal of Consciousness Studies* 18, no. 7–8 (2011): 169–95.

Jolles, Marjorie. "Between Embodied Subjects and Objects: Narrative Somaesthetics." *Hypatia* 27, no. 2 (2012): 301–18.

Jones, Steve. "Dying to be Seen: Snuff Fiction's Problematic Fantasies of 'Reality'". *Scope: An Online Journal of Film and Television Studies*, 19 (2011). Accessed July 10, 2014. http://nrl.northumbria.ac.uk/5145/1/Jones.pdf.

Jones, Steve. *Torture Porn: Popular Horror after Saw*. Basingstoke: Palgrave-Macmillan, 2013.

Jones, Steve and Sharif Mowlabocus. "Hard Times and Rough Rides: The Legal and Ethical Impossibilities of Researching 'Shock' Pornographies." *Sexualities* 12, no. 5 (2009): 613–26.

Kahn-Harris, Keith. *Extreme Metal: Music and Culture on the Edge*. London: Berg, 2007.

Kaplan, E. Ann. *Women and Film: Both Sides of the Camera*. New York: Routledge, 1983.

Kapsis, Robert E. *Hitchcock: The Making of a Reputation*. Chicago, IL: Chicago University Press, 1992.

Kellner, Douglas. *From 9-11 to Terror War: The Dangers of the Bush Legacy*. Lanham, MD: Rowan & Littlefield Publishers, 2003.

Kendrick, James. "A Nasty Situation: Social Panics, Transnationalism and the Video Nasty." In *Horror Film: Creating and Marketing Fear*, edited by Steffen Hantke, 153-72. Jackson: University Press of Mississippi, 2004.

Kennedy, Julia and Clarissa Smith. "His Soul Shatters at About 0: 23: Spankwire, Self-Scaring and Hyberbolic Shock." In *Controversial Images: Media Representations on the Edge*, edited by Feona Attwood, Vincent Campbell, I.Q. Hunter, and Sharon Lockyer, 239-53. Basingstoke: Palgrave Macmillan, 2013.

Kerekes, David. "Apocalypse Cultured." In *Headpress* 1, edited by David Flint, David Kerekes, and David Slater. Manchester: Headpress, 1991.

Kerekes, David. ed. "Funhouse." *Headpress* 23 (2002): 67-143.

Kerekes, David and David Slater. *Killing for Culture: An Illustrated History of Death Film from Mondo to Snuff*. London: Creation Books, 1994. Second Edition 1995.

Kerekes, David and David Slater. *See No Evil: Banned Films and Video Controversy*. Manchester: Headpress/Critical Vision, 2000.

Kimber, Shaun. *Controversies: Henry: Portrait of a Serial Killer*. Basingstoke: Palgrave MacMillan, 2011.

Kimber, Shaun. "Transgressive Edge Play and *A Srpski Film/A Serbian Film*." *Horror Studies* 5, no. 1 (2014): 107-25.

Kinder, Marsha. "Violence American Style: The Narrative Orchestration of Violent Attractions." In *Violence and American Cinema*, edited by David J. Slocum, 63-100. London: Routledge, 2012.

King, Geoff. " 'Killingly Funny': Mixing Modalities in New Hollywood's Comedy-With-Violence." In *New Hollywood Violence*, edited by Steven Jay Schneider, 126-43. Manchester: Manchester University Press, 2004.

King, Geoff. *American Independent Cinema*. London: I.B. Tauris, 2005a.

King, Geoff, ed. *The Spectacle of the Real: From Hollywood to Reality TV and Beyond*. Bristol and Portland, OR: Intellect, 2005b.

King, Greg. *Sharon Tate and the Manson Murders*. Edinburgh: Mainstream Publishing, 2000.

Kleinhans, Chuck. "Introduction: Prior Constraints." *Cinema Journal* 46, no. 4 (2007): 96-101.

Kozma, Alicia. "Ilsa and Elsa: Nazisploitation, Mainstream Film and Cinematic Transference." In *Naziploitation! The Nazi Image in Low-Brow Cinema and Culture*, edited by Daniel H. Magilow, Elizabeth Bridges, and Kristin T. Vander Lugt. London and New York: Continuum, 2012.

Lancaster, Roger N. *Sex Panic and the Punitive State*. Berkeley: University of California Press, 2011.

Landis, Bill. *Sleazoid Express*. New York: Fireside, 2002.

LeBlanc, Jerry and Ivor Davis. *5 To Die*. Los Angeles, CA: Holloway House Publishing, 1970.

Lederer, Laura. "Then and Now: An Interview with a Former Pornography Model." In *Take Back the Night: Women on Pornography*, edited by Laura Lederer, 45-59. New York: Bantam Books, 1982.

Lehman, Peter. "*8mm* will the Real Machine Please Stand Up?" *Jump Cut: A Review of Contemporary Media* 43 (2000): 16–20.

Lesberg, Sandy. *Violence in Our Time*. London: Pebbles Press, 1977.

Linda, Badley. "The Darker Side of Genius: The (Horror) Auteur Meets Freud's Theory." In *The Horror Film and Psychoanalysis: Freud's Worst Nightmare*, edited by Steven Jay Schneider, 225–28. Cambridge: Cambridge University Press, 2004.

Lindeperg, Sylvie. *Nuit et Brouillard: Un Film dans L'histoire*. Paris: Odile Jacob, 2007.

Linkman, Audrey. *Photography and Death*. London: Reaktion, 2011.

Linzey, Andrew, ed. *The Global Guide to Animal Protection*. Urbana: University of Illinois Press, 2013.

Lobato, Ramon. *Shadow Economies of Cinema: Mapping Informal Film Distribution*. London: BFI, 2012.

Lobato, Ramon and Mark David Ryan. "Rethinking Genre Studies Through Distribution Analysis: Issues in International Horror Movie Circuits." *New Review of Film and Television Studies* 9, no. 2 (2011): 188–203.

Lockwood, Dean. "All Stripped Down: The Spectacle of 'Torture Porn'." *Popular Communication* 7, no. 1 (2009): 40–48.

Lowenstein, Adam. *Shocking Representation: Historical Trauma, National Cinema, and the Modern Horror Film*. New York: Columbia University Press, 2005.

Lumsden, David. "Whole Life Narratives and the Self." *Philosophy, Psychiatry, & Psychology* 20, no. 1 (2013): 1–10.

Lutz, Deborah. "The Dead Still Among Us: Victorian Secular Relics, Hair Jewelry, and Death Culture." *Victorian Literature and Culture* 39, no. 1 (2011): 127–42.

Macbean, James. "Godard's *Weekend*, or the Self Critical Cinema of Cruelty." *Film Quarterly* 22, no. 2 (1968–1969): 35–43.

Mackinnon, Catherine. *Only Words*. Cambridge MA: Harvard Press, 1993.

Magilow, Daniel H. "Introduction: The Nazi Image in Low-Brow Cinema and Culture." *Naziploitation! The Nazi Image in Low-Brow Cinema and Culture*, edited by Daniel H. Magilow, Elizabeth Bridges, and Kristin T. Vander Lugt. London and New York: Continuum, 2012.

Malamud, Randy. "Animals on Film: The Ethics of the Human Gaze." *Spring* 83 (2010): 135–60.

Martin, John. *Seduction of the Gullible: The Truth Behind the Video Nasty Scandal*. Liskeard: Stray Cat Publishing, 2007.

Massumi, Brian. "The Future Birth of the Affective Fact: The Political Ontology of Threat". In *The Affect Theory Reader*, edited by Melissa Gregg and Gregory J. Seigworth, 52–70. Durham, NC and London: Duke University Press, 2010.

Mathijs, Ernest. "*Man Bites Dog* and the Critical Reception of Belgian Horror (in) Cinema." In *Horror International*, edited by Steven Jay Schneider and Tony Williams, 315–35. Detroit, MI: Wayne State University Press, 2005.

Mathijs, Ernest and Xavier Mendik. "Introduction: Making Sense of Extreme Confusion: European Exploitation and Underground Cinema." In *Alternative Europe: Eurotrash and Exploitation Cinema since 1945*, edited by Ernest Mathijs and Xavier Mendik, 1–18. London: Wallflower Press, 2004.

McCance, Dawne. *Critical Animal Studies: An Introduction*. Albany: State University of New York, 2013.

McColgan, Aileen. "General Defences." In *Feminist Perspectives on Criminal Law*, edited by Lois Bibbings and Donald Nicholson, 137–58. London: Cavendish, 2000.

McGlynn, Clare and Erika Rackley. "Criminalising Extreme Pornography: A Lost Opportunity." *Criminal Law Review* 4 (2009): 245–60.

McGlynn, Clare and Erika Rackley. *Why Criminalise the Possession of Rape Pornography?* Durham Law School Briefing Document. Durham University, 2014.

McNeill, W.E.S. "Embodiment and the Perceptual Hypothesis." *The Philosophical Quarterly* 62, no. 248 (2012): 569–91.

Middleton, Jason. *Documentary's Awkward Turn: Cringe Comedy and Media Spectatorship.* London: Routledge, 2014.

Milligen, Stephen. *"The Bloodiest Thing that Ever Happened in Front of a Camera": Conservative Politics, "Porno Chic" and Snuff.* London: Headpress, 2014.

Mizuta Lippit, Akira. "Death of an Animal." *Film Quarterly* 56, no. 1 (2002): 9–22.

Moore, Allison. "An Eliasian Perspective on the Intentional Actions and Unintended Consequences of the Criminalisation of 'Extreme Pornography'." *Journal of the International Network of Sexual Ethics and Politics* 1 (2013): 19–35.

Morgan, Ed. "Cannibal Holocaust: Digesting and Re-Digesting Law and Film." *S. Cal. Interdisc* 16 (2006): 555–70.

Morris, N.M. "Reflections on Peeping Tom." *Movie*, no. 96 (1990): 34–35.

Morrison, David E. et al. *Defining Violence: The Search for Meaning.* Luton: Luton University Press, 1999.

Mulvey, Laura. "Visual Pleasure and Narrative Cinema." *Screen* 16, no. 3 (1975): 6–18.

Mulvey, Laura. *Death 24 x a Second: Stillness and the Moving Image.* London: Reaktion, 2006.

Murphy, Bernice M. *The Rural Gothic in American Popular Culture: Backwoods Horror in American Popular Culture.* Basingstoke: Palgrave, 2013.

Murray, Andrew D. "The Reclassification of Extreme Pornographic Images." *The Modern Law Review* 72, no. 1 (2009): 73–90.

Neale, Steve. "Questions of Genre." In *Film Genre Reader II*, edited by Barry Keith Grant, 178–202. Austin: University of Texas Press, 1986.

Nicholls, David. "Godard's Weekend: Totem, Taboo and the Fifth Republic." *Sight and Sound* 49, no. 1 (1979): 22.

Oliver, Mark. "The Life and Death of Nick Berg." *The Guardian*, May 12, 2004.

Onan. "Now That Masturbation Isn't a Dirty Word, What's Wrong with Pornography?" *Video Viewer*, September 1982.

Ooijen, Erik Van. "Cinematic Shots and Cuts: On the Ethics and Semiotics of Real Violence in Film Fiction." *Journal of Aesthetics & Culture* 3 (2011). Accessed May 7, 2012: DOI: 10.3402/jac.v3i0.6280.

Paasonen, Susanna. *Carnal Resonance: Affect and Online Pornography.* Boston, MA: MIT Press, 2011.

Palmer, Randy. *Herschell Gordon Lewis, The Godfather of Gore: The Films.* Jefferson, NC: McFarland, 2006.

Parfrey, Adam. *Apocalypse Culture.* Washington, DC: Feral House, 1987.

Parker, Ned and Ali Hamdani. "How One Mobile Phone Made Saddam's Hanging a Very Public Execution." *The Times*, January 1, 2007.

Pauen, M. "Materialism, Metaphysics, and the Intuition of Distinctness." *Journal of Consciousness Studies* 18, no. 7–8 (2011): 71–98.

Perez, Gilberto. *The Material Ghost: Films and Their Medium.* Baltimore: Johns Hopkins University Press, 1998.

Petley, Julian. "'Snuffed Out': Nightmares in a Trading Standards Officer's Brain." In *Unruly Pleasures: The Cult Film and Its Critics*, edited by Xavier Mendik and Graeme Harper, 203–19. Guildford: FAB Press, 2000.

Petley, Julian. "Let the Atrocious Images Haunt Us". In *Tell Me Lies: Propaganda and Media Distortion in the Attack on Iraq*, edited by David Miller, 164–75. London: Pluto, 2004.

Petley, Julian "Cannibal Holocaust and the Pornography of Death." In *The Spectacle of the Real: From Hollywood to Reality TV and Beyond*, edited by Geoff King, 173–86. Bristol: Intellect, 2005.

Petley, Julian. "Nazi Horrors: History, Myth, Sexploitation." In *Horror Zone*, edited by Ian Conrich, 205–26. London: I. B. Tauris, 2009a.

Petley, Julian. "Pornography, Panopticism and the Criminal Justice and Immigration Act 2008." *Sociology Compass* 3, no. 3 (2009b): 417–32.

Petley, Julian. "Setting the Censorship Standard." *Index on Censorship* (2009c). Accessed March 21, 2014. http://www.indexoncensorship.org/2009/04/setting-the-censorship-standard/.

Petley, Julian. *Film and Video Censorship in Modern Britain*. Edinburgh: Edinburgh University Press, 2011.

Petley, Julian. "Are We Insane? The 'Video Nasty' Moral Panic." *Recherches sociologiques et anthropologiques* 43, no. 1 (2012). http://rsa.revues.org/839.

Peucker, Brigitte. *The Material Image: Art and the Real in Film*. Stanford, CA: Stanford University Press, 2007.

Pfeifer, Jennifer H. and Shannon J. Peake. "Self-Development: Integrating Cognitive, Socioemotional, and Neuroimaging Perspectives." *Developmental Cognitive Neuroscience* 2, no. 1 (2012): 55–69.

Pineda, Jaime A. "Sensorimotor Cortex as a Critical Component of an 'Extended' Mirror Neuron System: Does It Solve the Development, Correspondence, and Control Problems in Mirroring?" *Behavioral and Brain Functions* 4, no. 47 (2008).

Pinedo, Isabel Cristina. *Recreational Terror: Women and the Pleasures of Horror Film Viewing*. Albany: University of New York Press, 1997.

Plasketes, George. "Romancing the Record: The Vinyl De-Evolution and Subcultural Evolution." *Journal of Popular Culture* 26, no. 1 (1992): 109–22.

Powers, James. "Italian Picture A Sadistic Orgy." *The Hollywood Reporter*, February 20, 1963, 3.

Prebble, Sally, Donna Addis, and Lynette Tippett. "Autobiographical Memory and Sense of Self." *Psychological Bulletin* 139, no. 4 (2013): 815–40.

Pronay, Nicholas. "British Newsreels in the 1930s: Their Policies and Impacts." In *Yesterday's News: The British Cinema Newsreel Reader*, edited by Luke McKernan, London: British Universities Film & Video Council, 2002.

Rhodes, Gary D. "Mockumentaries and the Production of Realist Horror." *Post Script* 21, no. 3 (2002): 46–60.

Rodowick, D.N. *The Virtual Life of Film*. Cambridge, MA: Harvard University Press, 2007.

Rose, James. *Beyond Hammer: British Horror Cinema since 1970*. Leighton Buzzard: Auteur Publishing, 2009.

Russell, Catherine. *Narrative Mortality*. Minneapolis/London: University of Minnesota Press, 1995.

Russell, J.D. *The Beautiful People: The Pacesetters of the New Morality*. New York: Apollo Books, 1970.

Sanders, Ed. *The Family: The Story of Charles Manson's Dune Buggy Attack Battalion.* St Albans: Panther Book Limited, 1973.

Sanders, Ed. *The Family: The Manson Group and Its Aftermath.* New York: Signet, 1990.

Sanders, Ed. *The Family.* Boston, MA: Da Capo Press, 2002.

Sartre, Jean-Paul. *The Transcendence of the Ego: An Existentialist Theory of Consciousness.* New York: The Noonday Press, 1957.

Schaefer, Eric. *"Bold! Daring! Shocking! True!": A History of Exploitation Films 1919–1959.* Durham, NC: Duke University Press, 1999.

Schatz, Thomas. *Hollywood Genres: Formulas, Filmmaking and the Studio System.* New York: McGraw Hill, 1981.

Schechtman, Marya. "Memory and Identity." *Philosophical Studies* 153, no. 1 (2011): 65–79.

Schneider, Steven Jay. "Murder as Art/The Art of Murder: Aestheticising Violence in Modern Cinematic Horror." *Intensities: The Journal of Cult Media* 2, no. 1 (2003). http://intensitiescultmedia.files.wordpress.com/2012/12/schneider-murder-as-art.pdf.

Schrader, Paul. "Notes on Film Noir." *Film Comment* 8, no. 1 (1972): 8–13.

Schreck, Nikolas, ed. *The Manson File.* New York: Amok Press, 1988.

Sconce, Jeffrey. "'Trashing' the Academy: Taste, Excess and an Emerging Politics of Cinematic Style." *Screen* 36, no. 4 (1995): 371–93.

Seltzer, Mark. *Serial Killers: Death and Life in America's Wound Culture.* New York and London: Routledge, 1998.

Sheehan, Paul. "Against the Image: Herzog and the Troubling Politics of the Screen Animal." *Substance: A Review of Theory & Literary Criticism* 37, no. 3 (2008): 117–36.

Shepard, Jim. *Nosferatu,* New York: Knopf, 1998: 65.

Sherryl, Vint. *Science Fiction: A Guide for the Perplexed.* London: Bloomsbury, 2014.

Singer, Jefferson A., Pavel Blagov, Meredith Berry, and Kathryn M. Oost. "Self-Defining Memories, Scripts, and the Life Story: Narrative Identity in Personality and Psychotherapy." *Journal of Personality* 81, no. 6 (2013): 569–82.

Slade, Joseph W. "Violence in the Hardcore Pornographic Film: A Historical Survey." *Journal of Communication* 34, no. 3 (1984): 148–63.

Slater, Jay, ed. *Eaten Alive! Italian Cannibal and Zombie Movies.* London: Plexus, 2002.

Smith, Clarissa. "It's Important That You Don't Smell a Suit on It: Aesthetics of Alt Porn." In *Porn After Porn: Contemporary Alternative Pornographies*, edited by Enrico Biasin, Giovanna Maina, and Federico Zecca. Udine: Mimesis Press, 2014.

Smith, Clarissa et al. "Memorandum submitted by Dr Clarissa Smith et al (CJ&I 341)" 2006. Accessed June 8, 2015. http://www.publications.parliament.uk/pa/cm200607/cmpublic/criminal/memos/ucm34102.htm.

Smith, John Devlin. "Self-Concept: Autopoiesis as the Basis for a Conceptual Framework." *Systems Research and Behavioral Science* 31, no. 1 (2014): 32–46.

Smithies, Declan. "The Significance of Cognitive Phenomenology." *Philosophy Compass* 8, no. 8 (2013): 731–43.

Sobchack, Vivian. "Inscribing Ethical Space: Ten Propositions on Death, Representation and Documentary." *Quarterly Review of Film and Video* 9, no. 4 (1984): 283–300. DOI: 10.1080/10509208409361220.

Sobchack, Vivian. "The Charge of the Real: Embodied Knowledge and Cinematic Consciousness." In *Carnal Thoughts: Embodiment and Moving Image Culture*, 258–85. Berkeley, Los Angeles and London: University of California Press, 2004.

Sontag, Susan. *On Photography.* New York: Delta Publishing, 1973.

Sontag, Susan. *Regarding the Pain of Others*. London: Penguin, 2003.

Spoto, Donald. *The Dark Side of Genius: The Life of Alfred Hitchcock*. New York: Da Capo Press, 1999.

Spzunar, John. *Xerox Ferox: The Wild World of the Horror Film Fanzine*. Manchester: Headpress, 2012.

Squalor, Randy. "Postcard from Colonel Kurtz: RealiTV [sic] and the Death Film." In *Flesh and Blood... Compendium!* Surrey: FAB Press, 2004.

Stibbe, Arran. *Animals Erased: Discourse, Ecology, and Reconnection with the Natural World*. Middletown, CT: Wesleyan University Press, 2012.

Strawson, Galen. *Selves: An Essay in Revisionary Metaphysics*. Oxford: Oxford University Press, 2009.

Szarycz, Gregory. "The Representation of Animal Actors: Theorizing Performance and Performativity in the Animal Kingdom." In *Theorizing Animals: Re-thinking Humanimal Relations*, edited by Tania Signal and Nik Taylor. Boston, MA: Brill, 2011.

Szulkin, David A. *Wes Craven's Last House on the Left: The Making of a Cult Classic*. Guildford: FAB Press, 1997.

Tait, Sue. "Visualising Technologies and the Ethics and Aesthetics of Screening Death." *Science as Culture* 18, no. 3 (2009): 333–53.

Tekin, Erife. "How Does the Self Adjudicate Narratives?" *Philosophy, Psychiatry, & Psychology* 20, no. 1 (2013): 25–28.

Telotte, J.P. "German Expressionism: A Cinematic/Cultural Problem." In *Traditions in World Cinema*, edited by Linda Badley, Barton Palmer, and Steven Jay Schneider, 15–28. Edinburgh: Edinburgh University Press, 2006.

Terry, Maury. *The Ultimate Evil: An Investigation into a Dangerous Satanic Cult*. London: Grafton, 1988.

Thompson, Bill. *Soft Core: Moral Crusades Against Pornography in Britain and America*. London: Continuum Publishing, 1994.

Thompson, Kenneth. *Moral Panics*. London: Routledge, 1998.

Thomson, Iain. "In the Future Philosophy Will Be Neither Continental nor Analytic but Synthetic: Toward a Promiscuous Miscegenation of (All) Philosophical Traditions and Styles." *The Southern Journal of Philosophy* 50, no. 2 (2012): 191–205.

Tierney, Dolores. "The Appeal of the Real in Snuff: Alejandro Amenábar's *Tesis (Thesis)*." *Spectator* 22, no. 2 (Fall 2002): 45–55.

Tippett, Krista, Thomas Metzinger, Evan Thompson, and Pim van Lommel. "To Be or Not to Be: The Self as Illusion." *Annals of the New York Academy of Sciences* 1234, no. 1 (2011): 5–18.

Todorov, Tzvetan. *The Fantastic: A Structural Approach to a Literary Genre*. New York: Cornell UP, 1975.

Tudor, Andrew. *Monsters and Mad Scientists*. Oxford: Blackwell Ltd., 1989.

Van der Knaap, Ewout, ed. *Uncovering the Holocaust: The International Reception of Night and Fog*. London: Wallflower Press, 2006.

Vanzant, Iyanla. *Don't Give It Away!: A Workbook of Self-Awareness and Self-Affirmations for Young Women*. New York: Simon and Schuster, 1999.

Walker, Johnny. "Nasty Visions: Violent Spectacle in Contemporary British Horror Cinema." *Horror Studies* 2, no. 1 (2011): 115–30.

Watson, Thomas Joseph. "There's Something Rotten in the State of Texas: Genre, Adaptation and the Texas Vibrator Massacre." *Journal of Adaptation in Film & Performance* 6, no. 3 (2013): 387–400.

Wells, Simon. *Charles Manson: Coming Down Fast*. London: Hodder & Stoughton, 2009.

West, Amy. "Caught on Tape: A Legacy of Low-Tech Reality." In *The Spectacle of the Real: From Hollywood to Reality TV and Beyond*, edited by Geoff King, 83–98. Bristol: Intellect, 2005.

Westbrook, John. "Digesting Godard Filming Bataille: Expenditure in Week-End." *Contemporary French and Francophone Studies* 9, no. 4 (2005): 345–52.

Wheatley, Catherine. *Michael Haneke's Cinema: The Ethic of the Image*. New York: Berghan Books, 2009.

Whitehead, Peter. "Week-End." *Films and Filming* 15, no. 5 (1969): 34.

Whittle, Peter. "*The Last Horror Movie* Review." *The Sunday Times*, May 15, 2005, 15.

Wilkinson, Eleanor. "Perverting Visual Pleasure: Representing Sadomasochism." *Sexualities* 12, no. 2 (2009): 181–98.

Williams, Linda. "Power, Pleasure and Perversion: Sadomasochistic Film Pornography." *Representations* 27 (Summer 1989): 37–65.

Williams, Linda. "Film Bodies: Gender, Genre and Excess." *Film Quarterly* 44, no. 4 (1991): 2–13.

Williams, Linda. "Pornographies On/Scene, or Diff'rent Strokes for Diff'rent Folks." In *Sex exposed: Sexuality and the Pornography Debate*, edited by Lynn Segal and Mary McIntosh, 223–65. New York: Rutgers University Press, 1992.

Williams, Linda. *Hard Core: Power, Pleasure, and the "Frenzy of the Visible."* Berkeley: University of California Press, 1999.

Williams, Linda, ed. *Porn Studies*. New York: Duke University Press, 2004a.

Williams, Linda. "Second Thoughts on *Hard Core*: American Obscenity Law and the Scapegoating of Deviance." In *More Dirty Looks: Gender, Pornography and Power*, edited by Pamela Church Gibson, 165–75. London: BFI, 2004b.

Williams, Tony. "'*Special Effects*' in the Cutting Room." In *Underground USA: Filmmaking Beyond the Hollywood Canon*, edited by Xavier Mendik and Steven Jay Schneider, 51–62. London and New York: Wallflower Press, 2002.

Wingrove, Nigel and Marc Morris. *The Art of the Nasty*. Surrey: FAB Press/Salvation, 2009, 2nd edition.

Zahavi, Dan. *Subjectivity and Selfhood: Investigating the First-Person Perspective*. London: MIT Press, 2005.

INDEX